IMPERIAL LEGACY

THE OTTOMAN IMPRINT ON THE BALKANS
AND THE MIDDLE EAST

✧ IMPERIAL LEGACY ✧
THE OTTOMAN IMPRINT ON THE BALKANS
AND THE MIDDLE EAST

EDITED BY

L. CARL BROWN

NEW YORK   COLUMBIA UNIVERSITY PRESS

Columbia University Press
New York   Chichester, West Sussex
Copyright © 1996 Columbia University Press
All rights reserved

Library of Congress Cataloging-in-Publication Data
Brown, L. Carl (Leon Carl), 1928–
    Imperial Legacy The Ottoman Imprint on the Balkans and the Middle East /
    edited by L. Carl Brown.
        p.   cm.
    Includes bibliographical references (p.) and index.
    ISBN 0–231–10304–2
    1. Middle East—History—1517–   2. Africa, North
    —History—1517–1882.   I. Brown, L. Carl (Leon Carl), 1928– .
    DS62.4.B679   1995
    909'.09712561—dc20   95–15506
                                                                  CIP

Casebound Editions of Columbia University Press books are printed on permanent
and durable acid-free paper.
Printed in the United States of America
c 10 9 8 7 6 5 4 3 2 1

CONTENTS

MAPS AND ILLUSTRATIONS

ACKNOWLEDGMENTS

Generous support for the preparation of this book in all its phases has been provided by the Center of International Studies, the Department of Near Eastern Studies, and the Program in Near Eastern Studies at Princeton University and by the Institute of Turkish Studies.

I thank the following for permission to use illustrations.

The Turkish Ministry of Foreign Affairs for several of the photographs found in the excellent publication, *Ottoman Architectural Works Outside Turkey.*
The Topkapi Palace Museum for the portrait of Sultan Abdulhamid II and the lithograph of the grand vizier receiving a European diplomat.
The *Journal of Turkish Studies* and its editor, Sinasi Tekin, for photographs from *Imperial Self-Portrait: The Ottoman Empire as Revealed in the Sultan Abdul Hamid II's Photographic Albums,* edited by Carney E. S. Gavin and the Harvard Semitic Museum.
The Research Center for Islamic History, Art, and Culture, Istanbul, Turkey, for the photograph of the Gazi Husrev Mosque in Sarajevo.
The Ninth Ephoreia of Byzantine and Post-Byzantine Antiquities, Thessaloniki, for the Hamza Dey Mosque and the Alaca Imaret photographs.

Other photographs were provided by Richard B. Parker, André Raymond, and Joseph Szyliowicz.

A NOTE ON TRANSLITERATION

Transliterations of Arabic and Ottoman Turkish words are according to the following guidelines:

Standard English rather than modern Turkish orthography is used. Thus:
pasha, *instead of* paşa
Kuchuk Kaynarja, *instead of* Kuçuk Kaynarca

Arabic instead of modern Turkish transliteration is adopted for common Islamic terms. Thus;
qadi, shari'ah, ulama, *instead of* kadi, seriat, ulema

Full diacritical marks are used sparingly for Arabic transliteration. Long vowels are not indicated and not all 'ayns and 'hamzas are specified. Thus:
ulama, *and not* 'ulama.'

Full diacritical marks are, however, used in chapters 11 and 12 treating language issues.

Arabic spelling of proper names is chosen over Turkish when the individual is more associated with some part of the Arab world. Thus:
Egypt's Muhammad Ali, *not* Mehmet Ali, *but*
Sultan Abdulhamid, *not* Abd al-Hamid).

Modern Turkish proper names follow standard modern Turkish orthography. Thus:

Atatürk *and* İnönü.

The major purpose is to present familiar spellings that the general reader can more readily pronounce. Borderline cases remain, however (e.g., *medrese* vs. *madrasah, vakf* vs. *waqf*). As a fail-safe aid to the general reader, and to satisfy specialists, too, variant spellings of the more important terms and names are included in the Index.

DATES AND DURATION (NUMBER OF YEARS)
OF OTTOMAN RULE BY COUNTRY OR REGION

	DATES	DURATION
Albania	1468–1912	444
Algeria	1516–1830	314
Arabian Peninsula	(*see* al-Hasa; Hijaz; Yemen)	
Bosnia	1463–1878	396
Bulgaria	1396–1878	483
Crete	1669–1898	229
Crimea	1478–1774	296
Croatia	1526–1699	173
Cyprus	1571–1878	307
Egypt	1517–1882	365
Greece	1456–1830	374
Al-Hasa	1869–1913	44
Herzegovina	1482–1878	396
Hijaz	1517–1916	399
Hungary	1526–1699	173
Iraq	1534–1918	384
Israel/Palestine	1616–1918	402
Jordan	1516–1918	402
Kuwait	1869–1899	30
Lebanon	1516–1918	402
Libya	1551–1911	360
Macedonia (Skopje)	c.1371–1913	542

	DATES	DURATION
Palestine/Israel	1516–1918	402
Romania		
Wallachia	1476–1829	353
Moldavia	1504–1829	325
Serbia	1389–1829	440
Syria	1516–1918	402
Tunisia	1574–1881	307
Turkey	c.1420–1923	503
Yemen	1517–1636	
	c.1870–1918	167

Note: The above data are only approximate. Borders change over time. Dates of the Ottoman conquests (and losses) do not neatly follow the present borders. Nor are the different administrative arrangements within the Ottoman Empire (ranging from autonomy and virtual independence to complete central goverment control) adequately reflected.

Brief Overview

Albania: independence at time of first Balkan War, 1912.

Algeria: beginning of French occupation, 1830.

Bosnia: administered by Austria from 1878, annexed by Austria, 1908.

Bulgaria: autonomous within Ottoman Empire from 1878; declared independence 1908.

Crete: Europeans forced Ottoman evacuation 1898 following insurrection and war with Greece.

Crimea: vassal state from 1475, lost de facto to Russia in 1774; annexed by Russia in 1803.

Croatia: only eastern portions (essentially between the Save and Drave rivers) came under Ottoman rule; remainder of Croatia, including Zaghreb, remained linked to Hungary and the Hapsburgs.

Cyprus: administered by Britain from 1878, annexed by Britain, 1914.

Egypt: 1882, British occupation; 1914, establishment of British Protectorate.

Greece: Ottoman penetration much earlier, but 1456 date of definitive conquest.

al-Hasa: Ottomans had challenged Portuguese incursions into Persian Gulf in the sixteenth century and continued to claim sovereignty in all Arabia, but actual control was nonexistent in central Arabia (al-Najd) and sporadic in the Gulf area. Britain's nineteenth-century system of informal protectorates (by which the former "Pirate Coast" got named the "Trucial Coast") further limited Ottoman control. Later Ottoman efforts from time of Midhat Pasha in Baghdad (1869–1872) to institute serious, formal control were of limited success and later brought to naught by Ibn Saud's de facto absorption of al-Hasa in 1913.

Herzegovina: under Austrian administration from 1878; annexed by Austrian in 1908.

Hijaz: Ottomans assumed control of the Holy Cities of Mecca and Madina after conquest of Egypt; lost to Wahhabis 1802/3 until reconquest 1812 by troops of Egypt's Muhammad Ali. Sharif Husayn in alliance with Britain initiated "Arab Revolt" in 1916.

Hungary: absorbed by Ottomans following 1526 Battle of Mohacs; part of Hungary a shifting military frontier between Ottomans and Austria throughout sixteenth and seventeenth century; most of Hungary lost to Ottomans in 1699 Austro-Ottoman Treaty of Carlowitz.

Iraq: *see* chapter 7 for details of shifting Ottoman-Iranian boundaries.

Israel/Palestine: *see* Syria

Jordan: *see* Syria

Kuwait: probably Ottoman control or at least influence from Basra since 16th century. Explicit effort assert control from 1869 (when Midhat Pasha governed in Iraq until 1872). Secret agreement for British protection in 1899; unratified Anglo-Ottoman convention (1913) recognizing Kuwait as autonomous Ottoman *kaza*.

Lebanon: *see also* Syria. In 1861 European powers imposed settlement making Mount Lebanon an autonomous Ottoman province governed by a non-Lebanese Christian appointed by the Ottoman government with European approval. Ottomans revoked this autonomy on outbreak of World War I.

Libya: Ottoman conquest of Tripoli, 1551; autonomous Qaramanli dynasty, 1711–1835. Thereafter, Ottoman direct administration until Libya lost to Italian conquest beginning in 1911.

Macedonia: the "Former Yugoslav Republic of Macedonia" (the compromise UN name, use of "Macedonia" being protested by Greece). Incorporation into Bulgaria (Treaty of San Stefano, 1878), reversed by Treaty of Berlin (also 1878), and restored to Ottoman rule. Lost to Ottoman rule following second Balkan War (1913).

Palestine/Israel: *see* Syria

Romania: Autonomy achieved in 1829, de jure independence in 1878 (Congress of Berlin).

Serbia: 1389 Battle of Kosovo. Autonomy from 1829, de jure independence from 1878 (Congress of Berlin).

Syria: defeat of the Mamluks in 1516 essentially left all of geographical Syria (Israel, Jordan, Lebanon, and Syria today) in Ottoman hands.

Tunisia: 1881, beginning of French Protectorate.

Turkey: the Ottomans were established in parts of Anatolia by the late thirteenth century but then lost most of these lands following Timur's victory at the 1402 Battle of Ankara. Ottoman reconquest of Anatolia began with reign of Sultan Mehmed I (1413–1421); for calculating the Ottoman duration in Anatolia the arbitrary date of 1420 has been chosen.

Yemen: Ottoman control was sporadic and largely confined to the coastal and lowland regions.

Sudan: conquered by Egypt's Muhammad Ali beginning in the late 1820s and remaining under Egyptian control until the successful revolt of the Sudanese Mahdiyya in the 1880s, is not included even though technically a part of the Ottoman Empire during those years. Indeed, the Sudanese oral and historical tradition refers to the period as the "Turkiyya." Still, although Egypt was then juridically part of the Ottoman Empire the Muhammad Ali dynasty was virtually autonomous and the Sudan was very much an Egyptian concern.

✣ IMPERIAL LEGACY ✣

THE OTTOMAN IMPRINT ON THE BALKANS
AND THE MIDDLE EAST

CHAPTER ONE

THE SETTING: AN INTRODUCTION

L. Carl Brown

The Ottoman Empire was one of the world's great imperial systems. Its beginnings go back to the thirteenth century. It lived in good times and in bad until the third decade of the twentieth. Of the many imposing imperial systems that grew up around the Mediterranean only the Roman Empire at its peak was more extensive and not even the Roman Empire lasted as long. The longevity record for Mediterranean empires goes, instead, to that eastern extension of imperial Rome, the Byzantine Empire. The Byzantines, however, except for a brief period did not match the Ottomans in the extent of territories and the diversity of peoples ruled.

To cite the Ottoman Empire in comparison with the Roman Empire, presented in countless Western civilization textbooks as the foundation of Western legal and political institutions, offers a healthy challenge to venerable dichotomies of East and West. To include the Byzantine Empire as well acts in the same way, but in more attenuated form, the Byzantines being in Western European and North American eyes never quite so Western. Yet, there we have it: Roman, Byzantine, and Ottoman—all Mediterranean and all based on wide-ranging and long-lived multinational imperial institutions. Indeed, to a certain extent the Ottoman Empire can be seen as the successor state to the Byzantines, just as the Byzantine Empire was the successor to Rome.

From another perspective, the Ottoman Empire represented the fullest flowering of Islamic political institutionalization, building on the foundations put in place by the earlier Muslim polities such as the Umayyad, Abbasid,

THE FOUR GREAT EMPIRES—ROMAN, BYZANTINE, ABBASID, AND OTTOMAN
Each is shown at its height in its time. The maps are only approximate. They do not,
for example, indicate the different forms of rule from loose "protectorate" to central
control. Moreover, this "snapshot"-in-time gives an exaggerated picture of the
Byzantine Empire, which quickly receded from its peak to much more modest territorial holdings. The Ottoman Empire, on the contrary, lost significant territorial
holdings only over roughly the last century of its existence. These maps also serve to
remind us how much of the same Mediterranean lands formed part of three or,
indeed, all four empires. *Maps on pages 2, 3, 4, by John T. Westlake, Princeton, N.J.*

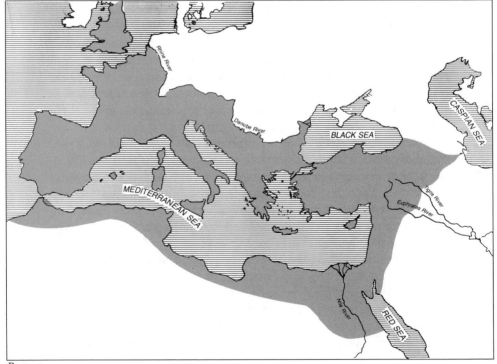

Roman

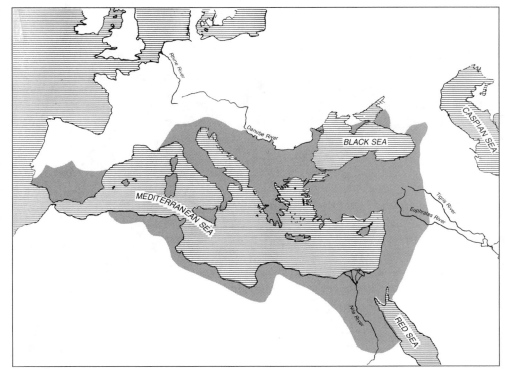

Byzantine

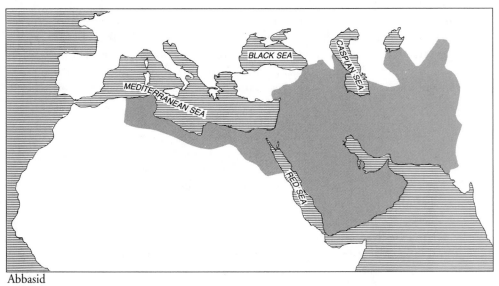

Abbasid

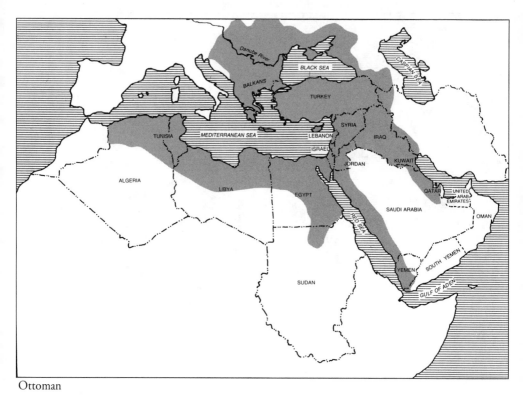

Ottoman

Fatimid, and Mamluk dynasties plus the Mongol heritage. In its heyday during the sixteenth century the Ottoman Empire shared the historical stage with two other Muslim imperial systems, the Safavid in Iran and the Mogul in India. These three contiguous empires represented an imposing expanse of Islamic civilization penetrating deeply into Asia, Europe, and Africa. In the long run, however, only the Ottoman Empire survived to the present century as a major force in international politics. By the late eighteenth century the Mogul empire was giving way to what became the extended period of British colonial rule in South Asia. The successor to the Safavids, the Qajar dynasty, did survive until the 1920s but with nothing like the geographical reach, political institutionalization, and military power possessed by the Ottomans. Vulnerable to the European state system as it was, the Ottoman Empire, that "sick man of Europe" in the classic textbook formulation, did manage to reassert central control in parts of North Africa and the Arabian peninsula during the nineteenth century. An Ottoman army also held a much larger Russian army in check for some six months in 1877.

The long-lived Ottoman Empire, in short, was the most extensive and most influential state system in the entire Muslim world during at least the last six centuries and quite possibly for any time since the rise of Islam itself.

From yet a third perspective the Ottoman Empire can be classified as the latest (perhaps the last?) and most institutionally elaborate of the many Western Asian imperial systems that reach back in time to the very beginnings of civilization. What might be labeled the millennial Western Asia/Mediterranean imperial tradition offers a historical chain through the ages from Pharaonic Egypt to the early states and civilizations of Mesopotamia (and the Hittites who loom large in the historical pedigree championed by Ataturk and his successors), to the Achaemenids, the Sassanians, the empires of Alexander and his successors, and then on to the Roman, Byzantine, Abbasid, and Ottoman eras.

Accordingly, in the Valhalla of past empires the Ottomans should rank high. In actual fact few major political systems have been so consistently ignored or misrepresented, not just in the West but in the many different states sharing an Ottoman past.

The West for its part has stubbornly refused to call the Ottoman Empire by its name, instead labeling this multireligious, multilingual, multiethnic polity as "Turkey" and its rulers "Turks." That those ruling from the banks of the Bosphorus themselves used the word "Turk" to mean "rustic" or "bumpkin" just did not penetrate Western perceptions. Ironically, the West since time out of mind has insisted that the Ottomans were "not like us" even while imposing, however unconsciously, a strictly Western ethnolinguistic rubric upon the Ottoman Empire, which was the very opposite of a nation-state.

Nor has the Ottoman Empire fared much better in the former Ottoman lands. As for the largely Christian peoples of the Balkans, plus Armenia in Southwest Asia, their modern nationalist orientations based on religion and language dictate a rejection of the Ottoman past as detested alien domination.

The Arabs, as well, have come to view the Ottoman period as one of alien rule, thereby anachronistically taking an Arab nationalism that is clearly a reality today and pushing it back into a time when no such political identification existed.

Even the Republic of Turkey approaches its Ottoman past with ambivalence. The Turkey of Mustafa Kemal Ataturk and his successors was to be a nation-state in the European mold. This new polity managed thus to become what Europe had always called its predecessor—Turkey. The word "Turk" instead of an epithet of disdain has become a nationalist badge of honor. Yet, in other ways today's Turks do identify with the Ottoman past, seeing its many centuries, somewhat anachronistically, as an era of Turkish national achievement. On balance, however, the major thrust of political ideology and institution building in the Republic of Turkey since the 1920s has been in the direction of a political community rooted in the notion of a common culture, language, and ethnicity, not an empire bringing together different cultures, languages, and ethnicities.

Thus, the Ottoman Empire today is generally viewed as either a burdensome heritage that must be expunged or as belonging to a bygone age that has been overtaken by events and is irrelevant to today's reality. That there may be some truth to this range of perceptions can be conceded. Not all ideas and institutions survive from one age to the next. It is, however, unacceptable to pass judgment on the Ottoman past and its possible influence on the present without a fair historical trial. This book may be seen as a collection of briefs for the court of history. The reader will find herein briefs for both the prosecution (Ottoman legacy lying somewhere between the negative and the noisome) and the defense (continuing importance of certain Ottoman ideas and institutions). All agree, however, on the need for a more balanced account of the Ottoman Empire and its legacy today.

Aiming more for broad themes than discrete detail the following chapters also seek to present interpretations that, while passing muster with the specialist, are readily accessible to the nonspecialist.

Even the issue of specialization was not without its problems in the planning that produced this book. It is revealing of the situation we seek to redress that most of the contributors were at first reluctant to take on the assignment of discussing the continuing Ottoman legacy in today's world. Almost all identified themselves as either Ottomanists with a less than specialized competence in the post-Ottoman period or vice-versa. Others claimed knowledge of some part of the lands and peoples once under Ottoman rule (e.g., the Arab world, the Balkans, Turkey) but not of the Ottoman entirety. Yet, only by breaching these arbitrary barriers separating the Ottoman and modern periods or Arab from Turk or Middle East from Balkans will a more accurate appraisal of the continuities and contrasts characterizing the Ottoman period and what came after be put in place.

It is also important to transcend the tendency to see only the Republic of Turkey as successor to the Ottoman legacy. Yes, in public perceptions of both Turks and others, Turkey replaced the Ottoman Empire, but certain of the states and peoples most inclined to reject their Ottoman past also reveal continuing cultural patterns linked to those Ottoman centuries. The authors assembled in this book are not straining to find Ottoman survivals at all cost. Rather, the operative principle is that the question of Ottoman legacy should be placed on the agenda, not dismissed by default.

Defining Terms

British Civil Secretary in Palestine during the 1920s, Sir Harry Luke, writes in his memoirs of a Palestine Arab delegation that came to protest in 1928 (this was the early phase of the "Wailing Wall incident," the struggle between Muslims and Jews over their respective holy sites that shared the same space). Having earlier served in Anatolia while the Ottoman Empire was still in existence, Luke knew some Turkish, but no Arabic. He decided to dispense with his Arabic interpreter and "found, winding up a rather heated discussion in what little remained of my Turkish, that this met with far greater acceptance than anything I had said before through the interpreter in Arabic. This was interesting as showing that there still lingers in this country among the older Arabs the tradition of Turkish as the language of authority." [1]

This account can be interpreted in two quite different ways. It suggests that those Palestinian Arab leaders who had spent the formative years of their lives as Ottoman subjects were shaped by the Ottoman political culture, but their children would not be so conditioned. The next generation of Palestinians would grow up never having heard Turkish used as "the language of authority." Thereafter, with each passing generation whatever might be said to remain of the Ottoman legacy would become ever fainter.

On another level, however, the incident illustrates the centuries-old separation between rulers and the ruled. Luke, just like the long chain of his Ottoman predecessors, did not speak the mother tongue of his Palestinian subjects and was not native to the area he administered. Indeed, this meeting fits right into the pattern of politics presented in Ivo Andric's *The Bridge on the Drina*, set not in Palestine but in Bosnia. The protagonists in Andric's novels, those Bosnian villagers on the one hand and the Ottoman officials on the other, represented two different political cultures—that of the rulers and the ruled—just as was the case with Luke confronting the Palestinians in his office.

Thus, the lines are drawn, On the one hand, the transition from Ottoman to post-Ottoman times represents such a sharp break that only those who had experienced the former in their daily lives bore traces of its influence after the Ottoman Empire was no more. On the other hand, the argument is that the millennial pattern of Middle Eastern politics with its sharp separation of the few rulers from the many ruled continued after 1918 and perhaps continues to this day. Just as the Ottomans built on and adapted attitudes and mores developed in earlier centuries so the present day post-Ottoman countries are adapting Ottoman ways, even if unconsciously.

Critics might attack this latter position as an egregious example of essentialist thinking with its image of the unchanging East. Yet, doesn't the discounting of a continuing Ottoman influence belittle the historically shaped cultural specificity of the Middle East? To imply that ideas and institutions developed over centuries, indeed over millennia, could so readily disappear comes dangerously close to accepting that the only really dynamic variable in the modern history of this part of the world has been the impact of the West on the non-Western world.

Such methodological problems confront the historian seeking to interpret any period, and the best working answer can be stated as a maxim: Never total change, never total continuity. For each specific historical case, one must carefully weigh how much change and how much continuity. Wide variation can be expected according to the subject being examined. For example, changes in settlement patterns need not correlate with changes in "the language of authority" and changes in the relative prestige of different occupations would probably not be irrelevant to changing patterns of marriage but the two might not follow the same rhythm. That being the case, the reader can expect different appraisals according to the different subjects treated in the essays that follow.

There is also the problem of defining what we mean by Ottoman. For example, certain institutions can best be classified as Islamic rather than Ottoman, for the pre-Ottoman centuries had produced a panoply of Islamic institutions manned by religious specialists dedicated to guarding and transmitting the faith.

Another question is whether the Ottoman Empire was becoming less Ottoman during the last century and a half of its long life when Ottoman rulers attempted to cope with a threatening Europe. This undeniable reality of European pressure on the Ottoman world has often pushed scholars to envisage the principal dynamic variable of the modern period as being the exogenous European West, not the indigenous Ottoman East. If one is inclined to follow this line of thought then "Ottoman" is best defined narrowly to embrace those ideas and institutions developed during the period of Ottoman self-sufficiency while excluding the cultural hybridization that seemingly set in once the neighboring European state system dominated the Ottoman lands.

Many other such deletions from what is to be deemed strictly Ottoman could be suggested. For example, institutions described as Ottoman might perhaps be seen as Byzantine or Abbasid survivals. Or the underlying environmental reality might in many instances be presented as more influential than the varying cultural adaptations taking place in Ottoman times. Or should Ottoman be defined in narrowly political terms, thereby separating out Islamic ideas and institutions?

For this book we have chosen the inclusive approach. Ottoman is used broadly to cover all aspects of the culture existing from the time of the eponym, Uthman, in the latter years of the thirteenth century to 1923, when the remaining Ottoman lands were parceled out and the Republic of Turkey was born. Ottoman is used to cover developments religious and secular, public and private.

It is to be expected that the legacy carried over from the last years of Ottoman existence will figure more strongly than that of earlier Ottoman centuries, and most of the essays bear out this expectation. All the more reason, therefore, to see as still very much a part of Ottoman history the turbulent period of wrestling with Western pressures that may be said to have begun in the late eighteenth century and did not end until Istanbul lost its millennial role as an imperial capital, becoming a provincial city in a Turkish nation-state.

Moreover, to depict those latter decades as being just as Ottoman as the age of Sulayman the Magnificent or of Mehmed the Conqueror keeps attention riveted on the actions of Ottomans, not just on intrusive outsiders, thereby avoiding the failing attributed to early modernization studies of viewing the complex process of change in terms of a dynamic outside society impacting on a passive traditional society.

Nor is it always true that the closer the past age was to the present the stronger the legacy. All people have certain behavior patterns that have existed for generations. These stable aspects of culture are not adequately identified with a single age, including the most recent. A tentative list might well include gender relations, land ownership, urban attitudes toward the rural population, aesthetic expressions,[2] the arrangement of sociopolitical groupings according to religious affiliation or what came to be called the millet system, and the sharp ruler/ruled distinction.

There is yet another way in which the remote past may offer more important legacies than later times. This can happen when a society formulates its past in service of its present values, when a people select—or even invent—a past to justify their present.

Applying the "usable" history approach to the study of the Ottoman period and thereafter as a tool for tracing surviving Ottoman legacies in the post-Ottoman period opens up important and at times contradictory vistas. In certain cases earlier Ottoman periods loom larger as legacies than more recent times as the following examples indicate:

> All the world knows that since the first days of the Ottoman State, the lofty principles of the Quran and the rules of the Seriat were always perfectly observed. Our mighty Sultanate reached the highest degree of strength and power, and all its subjects (the highest degree) of ease and prosperity.[3]

These are the opening lines of the famous 1839 Hatt-i Sharif of Gulhane, the first great Ottoman Westernizing imperial rescript. This programmatic statement presented an interpretation of the past that was to become a principal explanatory tool for statesmen and ideologues seeking to make Westernizing reforms palatable to a skeptical constituency. The lines managed to evoke a double golden age —1) that of the early Ottoman Empire and 2) the period of the Prophet Muhammad and the immediately following generations during which the Quran was revealed and the Shari'ah established. The reformers thus presented themselves not as borrowing from alien sources but as recapturing both that era when the Ottoman state was strong as well as the time of the Prophet Muhammad and "the rightly guided caliphs."

Variants on this theme were later developed, as the provenance of the new institutions and ideas became too obvious to be denied. Several Muslim spokesmen, for example, argued roughly as follows: We Muslims passed on the light of civilization to then barbarous Europe, and now we are taking back in part what we had earlier bestowed upon them. A complementary theme was that the Prophet Muhammad, himself, did not shy away from borrowing ideas developed by the infidels. All these themes amount to a selective use of the past for programmatic purposes.

The changing importance of the caliphate is another example of reworking the historical record. Although the word "caliph" had never completely dropped out of use as an honorific term the notion of a "Muslim pope" or, in keeping with the Byzantine legacy, a Muslim Caesaropope did not exist. With the reign of Sultan Abdulhamid (1876–1909) and the rise of Pan-Islam it became good politics to breathe new life into this old title. Sultan Abdul-hamid embraced the movement that came to be called Pan-Islam and pre-sented himself as the leader of all Muslims everywhere, not just those Muslims living within the shrinking Ottoman political boundaries. The repercussions of that idea were felt during the First World War, for when the Ottoman Empire joined the Central Powers and the Sultan in his capacity as caliph declared a jihad, the Allied colonial powers ruling over Muslim populations felt compelled to react. This was one important link in the chain of events leading to British negotiations with an Ottoman official ruling in Mecca, Sharif Husayn (great grandfather of the present King of Jordan). During the First World War he turned against his sovereign, allied with the British, and led the "Arab Revolt"—all of which produced a major turning point in mod-ern Middle Eastern history.

The symbolism of the caliphate—based on an idealized reading of early Islamic history—had become so important that Ataturk's abolition of that office in 1924 sent shock waves throughout the Muslim world. The reaction was especially strong among the Muslims of British India even though no part of that vast territory had ever been under Ottoman control or even contigu-ous to lands that had experienced Ottoman rule. The confused Muslim efforts to select a new caliph in the years immediately following Ataturk's bold move demonstrated anew the vast difference in difficulty between recreating an office presumed to be traditional and simply keeping alive what already exists, but note how Hamidian Pan-Islam had managed to "rewrite" the history of the caliphate.

Is it farfetched to see a direct line connecting Ottoman-led Pan-Islam and the many strands of political Islam today? At the very least even if direct influence of the former on the latter is not beyond dispute then certainly the structural parallelism bringing together the selective use of history in the nineteenth-century Ottoman world and its successor territories today (not to mention other Muslim lands) is readily apparent.

The other side of the "usable history" phenomenon is the strong proclivity, both among those living in lands once under Ottoman rule and elsewhere as well, to deplore or discount (or both) the Ottoman era. Does this screen us from a more accurate reconstruction of what really took place? One further question: If today's ideologues chose to champion new values would they in the process discover a different Ottoman past?

For example, throughout the eastern Arab world today the received wisdom is that the Ottoman era amounted to four centuries of alien domination.[4] Many present-day ills are explained by the double imperialism of first the Ottomans and then Europe. Yet, careful historical scholarship reveals that even as late in the last decade or so of the Ottoman period the overwhelming majority of Arabs living in geographical Syria (the "beating heart" of Arabism) did not regard Ottoman rule as alien and were either politically quietist or supportive of the government led by the sultan/caliph. Those who joined with Sharif Husayn and his British allies in the so-called Arab revolt were viewed askance by most of the people they presumed to represent.

The end of the First World War brought in its wake the end of the Ottoman Empire, Ataturk's Turkey turning its back on the Arabs (and for that matter Turkic peoples to the East) and the establishment of alien control in the form of British and French mandates. It then made good political sense to rewrite history, to construct an impeccably Arab nationalist genealogy extending back into the Ottoman period. This, by the way, is quite normal. Contrast the average American citizen's image of the American Revolution with the much more nuanced interpretation of what happened as presented by historians.

Arabs, in short, have interpreted the Ottoman era in Arab nationalist terms. The political community to be "imagined" is based on a common Arab language and culture. Anything that frustrates the development of that natural community, be it Ottoman or British, is alien. Again, no surprise in this. Witness how the rise of nationalisms in Europe undermined the earlier notion of Christendom and the legitimacy of the Holy Roman Empire.

Today, however, throughout the Arab world a counterelite is claiming that Islam is the answer. Notions, often quite vague, of a polity ruled by and for Muslims according to the shariah are challenging the Arab nationalist paradigm. What if the ideologues of an updated form of Pan-Islam, which parallels that championed by Sultan Abdulhamid a century ago choose, to rewrite the history of that reign?[5]

Alternatively, what if community leaders throughout the Fertile Crescent, or for that matter disintegrating Yugoslavia, choose to remember the Ottoman period as one that provided religious, linguistic, and ethnic autonomy within a political framework strong enough to protect life and limb of those under its sovereignty? A quite different image of the Ottoman past would then emerge.

With a broad definition of what is meant by Ottoman and a wide ranging examination of possible Ottoman legacies, this book seeks to encourage more scholarly attention to a still underdeveloped historical field and to mitigate overly arbitrary divisions between such specializations as Ottomanist, Arabist, and Balkanist. We believe as well that the history of this long-lived imperial system is instructive not just for the understanding of those lands once under Ottoman rule but for world history as well. The workings of major imperial systems East and West, ancient and modern, and the institutions and ideas they pass on to their successors should attract the attention of all seeking to make sense of their past and plan their future. Not the least of those imposing imperial examples was the Ottoman Empire.

NOTES

1. Sir Harry Luke, *Cities and Men: An Autobiography,* vol 3 (London: 1956), pp. 24–25.
2. Gibb suggests "what may be a universal psychological law in human societies. On the one hand, natural science and technology are indefinitely transmissible, and constitute the only truly international elements in human culture. On the other hand, art, aesthetics, philosophy, and religious thought retain their distinguishing characteristics within each separate culture. Every society jealously guards its own, and although not wholly impermeable to influences from other cultures only within a limited range and in forms adapted to its own temperament and psychological structure." H. A. R. Gibb, "The Influence of Islamic Culture on Medieval Europe," in Sylvia Thrupp, ed., *Change in Medieval Society: Europe North of the Alps, 1050–1500* (New York: Appleton, 1964), p. 167.
3. An English translation (originally by Halil Inalcik) of the entire rescript is in J. C. Hurewitz, ed., *The Middle East and North Africa in World Politics: A Documentary Record,* vol. 1 (New Haven: Yale University Press, 1975), pp. 269–71.
4. A theme not echoed in the Maghrib, where memories and the reality of the last years of Ottoman rule were not so traumatic as in the Fertile Crescent. Ottoman Algeria was lost to French colonialism beginning in 1830. As for Tunisia, oral tradition has it that after France imposed its protectorate in 1881 Tunisians scanned the coast hoping to see Ottoman ships arriving to repel the French. Libya was lost late to European colonialism (1911), but the Ottomans did militarily resist the Italian conquest.
5. Note, for example, the four-volume work by the late Egyptian historian Abd al-Aziz Muhammad Al-Shinnawi, entitled *Al-Dawla al-Uthmaniyya: Dawla Islamiyya Muftara 'Alayha* (The Ottoman Empire: A Maligned Islamic State). Reference to the Ottoman Empire as being both "Islamic" and "maligned" is significant.

→ PART ONE ←

PERCEPTIONS AND PARALLELS

The concept of legacy, Halil Inalcik points out, is liable to be both ethnocentric and excessively weighted in terms of the present. Both nationalists from the many different Ottoman successor states and Marxists see the Ottoman influence as decidedly negative. Added to this is the age-old Western perception rooted in the notion of Christendom defending itself against Islam and carried over to the still lively sense of two different, sharply divided civilizations—West and East. Yet, since modern history has been significantly shaped by Western domination of all the rest of the world—not just the lands of the Ottoman Empire—it is illogical to blame Ottoman backwardness. Western advances caught the rest of the world off balance too.

Several major characteristics of the Ottoman system, Inalcik maintains, influenced later developments. For example, the Ottoman Balkans and Anatolia possessed an agrarian social structure based on small peasant-family farms, unlike the Arab lands where the Ottomans maintained the preexisting large landholdings characteristic of the Nile valley and the Fertile Crescent.

Ottoman relations with Europe went through different phases. In the sixteenth century, a Europe still seeking to create states out of its feudal past viewed the strong centralized Ottoman state with fear and admiration. Later in the age of European hegemony the Ottoman Empire played a role in the working out of such notions of statecraft as concert diplomacy.

Since the Ottomans, more than most political systems, certainly more than Europe in general, accepted religious minorities and did not press for conversion to Islam (the *devshirme* system while it lasted being an important exception) and offered non-Muslims access to high office the Ottoman Empire can hardly be charged with threatening the cultural integrity of its non-Muslim, or for that matter, non-Turkish subjects. Rather, the Ottoman millet system served to keep in existence these protonations that later became, for better or worse, nation-states.

The Ottomans, Inalcik insists, were not all that economically inert but in the end it was "the triumph of the West's superiority in sciences and technology over the East's more pragmatic knowledge"—a thought-provoking twist to an old argument.

As for the Arabs, the Ottomans kept Arab lands out of European hands from the sixteenth century until the nineteenth century. Even thereafter Ottoman military and diplomatic resistance slowed European domination. Inalcik also sees Ottoman influence on the various strands of religious modernism and political Westernization present in the Arab world from the late Ottoman period to this day.

Norman Itzkowitz concentrates on the psychological aspect of the Ottoman legacy treating the question of how peoples of the Ottoman successor states perceive themselves and others. He also addresses Western perceptions of the Ottomans, always described as Turks. Evoking Gladstone's image of "the Turk" in the 1870s, Itzkowitz observes that if this great liberal statesman could have such a Manichean notion of Ottoman evil then the potential for general Western opinion to view dispassionately the Ottoman legacy would seem remote indeed.

Given the generally accepted idea that only the Republic of Turkey is successor to the Ottoman Empire the stage is set for nationalist ideologies to push back into bygone times the political struggles of the last Ottoman years. Arabs can blame Turks for having held back Arab development, and Turks can blame Arabs for having committed treason during the First World War. In the process, both have distorted a complex history. Equally, the tragic final Ottoman years of Armenian-Turkish relations (by this time the ethnic rubrics are apt) cause later generations to forget that earlier Ottoman statesmen regarded Armenians as the most loyal millet.

Itzkowitz's pessimistic interpretation does offer a ray of hope. What if the coming generation were taught to recapture the reality of past ages and not read back the present into the past? What if Turks ceased viewing the

Ottoman Empire as a Turkish nation-state? What if Serbs stopped conjuring up the fourteenth-century Battle of Kosovo whenever confronting someone from Anatolia, just as the British do not usually see their present political identities in terms of Celt, Saxon, and Norman? What if the West could transcend those old East–West stereotypes that overlay the earlier Christendom–Dar al-Islam dichotomy? Group myths will never be the same as scientific history, but perhaps the two can be brought closer together.

CHAPTER TWO

THE MEANING OF LEGACY:

THE OTTOMAN CASE

Halil Inalcik

How should we understand legacy in history? Today, it is in fashion to talk about the legacies of great cultures. A cursory look at the legacy literature is telling: heritage or legacy is expected to trace the contributions of a particular culture to our modern world, or more specifically to modern civilization. In other words, we look to the past selectively, picking out events and structures that have shaped a particular worldview and lifestyle represented today by Western culture. Even if we agree that Western culture achieves a rational approach to other cultures, still it is essentially Eurocentric. Our belief in the value system of Western culture, one can argue, is not in essence different from the attitude non-Western cultures have toward Western culture. It is an exception, for instance, to find in Islamic literature an unbiased study of non-Muslim cultures. This is because it is believed that Islam superseded all other cultures. Until recently, another's culture was considered meaningful and worth studying only in relation to one's own culture.

The first edition of the history of mankind, sponsored by UNESCO,[1] was deemed a failure and is to be replaced by a new history, because critics thought the book was too Eurocentric and oblivious of other world cultures. While no historian can write a "culture-free" world history we can depict today's world as an accumulative end-result of a long historical evolution embracing all past human experience. With this in mind I will attempt to discuss what influence the Ottoman Empire had in shaping our present world.

Questions Asked About the Ottoman Legacy

If one removed the Ottoman Empire from the panorama of history, the picture would be drastically different. The Ottoman impact on the Middle East; Eastern, Central, and Western Europe; North Africa and India is so important and pervasive that the histories of these regions cannot be adequately written without reference to the Ottomans. In regions such as the Balkans and the Middle East the impact was direct and decisive. In other areas—Western Europe and India—it was more indirect. Present conditions in the approximately twenty states that emerged from the disintegration of the empire, however, are certainly influenced by their Ottoman past. Their capital cities (such as Sofia, Belgrade, Sarajevo, Skopje) offer myriad examples of Ottoman architecture and urbanism. Their languages contain thousands of words and expressions borrowed from the Turkish language. Their popular cultures, cuisines, and lifestyles, as well as the general behavior of their peoples, also offer evidence of the Ottoman centuries. Yet it is often asserted that the Ottoman period contributed to the area's backwardness vis-à-vis other cultures.

A similar perspective is advanced in Turkey as well. During the last three decades certain intellectuals in Turkey have reviewed the extensive literature on modernization in terms of such questions as: Why has Turkey remained backward? Why have we struggled without success to modernize our country for the last one hundred and fifty years? An answer has been sought in the social structure of the Ottoman Empire. The empire is seen as a feudal state or a state at the stage of the *Asiatic Mode of Production* as Marxist historians claim. Those who argue the former say it was feudal because society was divided then into two principal classes, the ruling military elite on the one hand and the masses of dependent *reaya*, with no political or civil rights, on the other. The elite appropriated by force the surplus production of the *reaya*.

Those who identify the Ottoman Empire as one of the Asiatic empires possessing a strong centralist bureaucracy and a command economy believe that in this sociopolitical structure there was no possibility for change which could lead to economic growth and social evolution. Marxist scholars argue that the fundamental cause of the stagnant character of Ottoman economy and society was state ownership of arable lands, which resulted in the complete control of peasant production and labor. This left no opportunity for the agricultural economy to change into a market economy. For centuries a stagnant subsistence economy prevailed in agriculture. Similarly, a rigid regulatory regime imposed upon the crafts prevented urban industries from developing.

My own empirical studies on Ottoman social structure,[2] based on archival evidence, support the theory that the Ottoman state's control of agricultural land and peasant labor was an important factor in its failure to change both socially and economically. Even so, while accepting that the Marxist and other systemic approaches to the study of the Ottoman Empire offer new insights, they have tended to be presented in a reductionist manner, ignoring all the other fundamental cultural and economic conditions which made possible— even favored—the development of a capitalist world economy among the Western societies in a particular period of their history.[3] It may also be argued that Ottoman bureaucrats who favored reform were not unaware of Western secrets that contributed to this development. Indeed, they attempted to introduce reforms in this direction perhaps earlier than any other Asiatic society.

Thus, the question remains whether we can attribute the causes of the stagnant, undeveloped or slowly developing economies of the Middle East and the Balkans solely to a specific social structure shaped by (or inherited directly from) their Ottoman past. How, then, can we explain the failure of other Asian and East European societies to show dynamism? The question of backwardness thus ceases to be one associated with the Ottoman heritage, becoming instead a question common to all non-Western, traditional societies. Then the issue to discuss is why some countries were able to make more rapid progress in modernization than others—a question posed and discussed by development theory. The question of backwardness—or progress—bears a racist form, however, if posed as a claim that the Turks were responsible for the backwardness of certain societies. It amounts to an absurdity or to racism to claim that a particular Arab or Balkan nation remained backward or unable to progress as rapidly as some other societies because they remained part of the Turkish empire for so long. The term itself distorts historical reality. The Ottoman Empire was not a "Turkish empire." It was a multilingual, multireligious, and multicultural political system that is most appropriately to be compared to other empires that have existed throughout history. That Europeans consistently referred to the Ottoman Empire as Turkey and the Ottomans as Turks is revealing of European thought categories, but this venerable usage provides a procrustean mindset that seriously distorts Ottoman reality.

The Ottoman social system corresponded to certain specific conditions and circumstances in history and fulfilled certain functions under those conditions. It can be argued that in its time the Ottoman sociopolitical system represented an effective adaptation to circumstances. It served the particular society embraced by the Ottoman Empire and enabled it to survive for so long. Can the historian maintain that a political system which lasted so long as did the Ottoman Empire was based on disfunctional institutions?

It is difficult, in any case, to reach a balanced view of the reality of the Ottoman system in the face of theories loaded with intense nationalistic or doctrinaire presuppositions.

Basic Features of the Ottoman Social and Political System

Perhaps the most important legacy of the Ottoman Empire was the particular agrarian-social structure it maintained throughout its history in the
Balkans and Anatolia. Maintaining an agrarian system based on small peasant family-farms (the *çift-hane* system) was of vital importance for the whole
Ottoman socialpolitical structure. *Çift-hane* was an economic and fiscal unit
consisting of a peasant household with a farm of a size workable by a pair of
oxen, sufficient to sustain the household and meet reproduction and tax
obligations. The Ottoman bureaucracy took every necessary measure to
maintain such agrarian-fiscal units, and they were basically successful in
eliminating the trends that aimed at converting peasant farms into big
estates. The policy designed to ensure this consisted of putting all arable
land under state ownership, called *miri*. Thus, those many separate societies
in the Balkans and Anatolia that later formed their own independent
national states, including Turkey, all inherited basically a social structure
consisting of small peasant exploitations. The agrarian reforms introduced
under new nations did not have to make revolutionary changes. The contrast in agrarian landholding structure between Turkey and the Balkan
countries on the one hand, and Iran on the other, is striking. So, too, is the
contrast with the Arab lands, for there the Ottomans did not interfere with
the land regime established long before their rule. In addition, irrigation
agriculture prevalent in Egypt and lower Iraq required different arrangements in landholding.

The Ottomans created an almost ideal type of centralist monarchy at a
time when European royal dynasties in Spain, France, and England were
engaged in a formidable struggle against the feudal lords in order to establish
a centralized monarchy. By eliminating all local feudal lords and employing
only their personal retainers as public servants, Ottoman sultans created a
near perfect absolutist monarchy. Sixteenth-century theoreticians of absolutism in Europe, notably Jean Bodin,[4] believed that the Ottoman polity represented an ideal political system.

How the Ottomans were able to achieve such a perfect autocracy and a
powerful empire became the subject of wide interest in Europe at that time,
and hundreds of books and pamphlets on Ottoman history and political organization appeared throughout the century. Although Europe's view of the
Ottomans became rather scornful during the seventeenth century,[5] in the sixteenth century there was admiration of the Ottoman system of government
even in the Republic of Venice. It has also been suggested that Ivan IV followed certain Ottoman principles and institutions in his effort to establish an
autocratic regime in Russia.[6]

European States System and the Ottomans

In cultural and political ideology the Ottomans always professed to be the vanguard of the Islamic world, representing its militancy against a crusading, threatening Christendom. In practice, however, the Ottomans clearly distinguished the state and religion, dealing with issues that concerned political power and administration independently from religion. Let us focus here on these practical realities of the Ottoman history in its relations with Europe.

Between the mid-fifteenth and the nineteenth century large areas at the crossroads of the ancient continents were unified under the Ottoman Empire, including Asia Minor, the Balkans, and Arab lands. At the zenith of the empire's power, the Ottoman sultans extended their rule into the heart of Europe, annexing Hungary (1526–1699), Slovakia (1596–1699), and Kamieniec-Podolski in southern Poland. At the same time the Ottoman vassal state of the Crimean khans included in its dominions the southern Ukraine and the steppe area all the way to the northern Caucasus. Territorially, then, the Ottoman Empire could be considered more a European state than was the Russian Empire.

During the last half-century, historical research on the Crusades has shown that in the fifteenth and sixteenth centuries, the idea of a Europe unified on the basis of Christian ideology and a holy war against the Ottomans was either a myth or an effort to exploit public opinion in Europe in order to legitimize the policies of the individual states.[7] During the fourteenth and fifteenth centuries, a crusade was possible only when Venice and Hungary supported such an enterprise because of their own political interests. Every European state participating in a crusade had a specific goal, along with their common support for the fight against heresies. Despite the efforts to stir Western Christendom against Turks at critical moments, the Greek emperors in Constantinople and despots in the Morea more than once sought Ottoman cooperation in their hostility to the Latins, whose political and economic exploitation of the Greek peoples was hated.

Thus, the idea of *Respublica Christiana* was long dead, and in modern times *realpolitik* and the newly rising national monarchies of France, England, and Low Countries, and the Protestant princes in Germany all benefited from pressure placed on the Hapsburgs by the Ottomans (in certain cases they even sought their direct assistance). Ottoman military and political power provided an element of balance against the dominance of the Emperor and the Pope in Europe. It is clear that Protestantism benefited from Ottoman pressure on the Catholic Hapsburgs.[8]

Furthermore, documentary evidence suggests that in 1494, when Charles VIII of France was preparing to invade Italy, even the Papal States expected to receive assistance from the Ottomans.[9] In short, at the threshold of modern times, instead of the unity of Europe under the pope and the emperor, *realpolitik* and a new political order based on independent national monarchies called for a system based on a balance of power, and the Ottoman state played an important role in this emerging European states system.

In the following centuries Ottoman power remained a necessary component of the European states system. Ottoman alliances, although officially denied, were significant aspects of the foreign policies of the French and English monarchies in their struggle against the Hapsburg supremacy in Europe. When Elizabeth I of England sent her ambassador, William Harborne, to the Ottoman Porte in 1580 she expected to obtain not only commercial privileges but more importantly Ottoman pressure in the Mediterranean against Philip II of Spain, who was preparing his Great Armada to invade England. As late as the eighteenth century, when Austria, Russia, and Prussia partitioned Poland, it was the Ottoman Empire that did not recognize the fait-accompli and acted in concert with Western European states in a sustained effort to reestablish the balance of power in Europe.[10]

In the nineteenth century, when Western powers established their economic and political hegemony in the world, the Ottoman Empire—then reduced to a secondary power—depended on Western European powers in its struggle against the military imperialism of Austria and Russia, which were attempting to legitimize their anti-Ottoman policy in the name of European civilization and Christendom. This new situation was known to Western public opinion as the "Eastern Question," which consisted of maintaining the Ottoman Empire as part of an established order against the expansionist ambitions of Austria and Russia in southeastern Europe. Change in the existing order was of vital concern to the West because it might have upset the balance of power not only in the Middle East but also in Europe.

Throughout its history, the Ottoman Empire played a vital political role in the European states system. Although conditions have changed, it can be said that modern Turkey has the same strategic importance for Europe. The uncompromising attitude against the Ottomans, in the name of Christianity and European civilization, was only a myth or a legitimation effort on the part of those states that had a vested interest in its destruction. While imperialist Russia still persisted in its denial of the existence of the Ottoman state, Western European states profited from the commercial privileges granted by the sultans to expand their industrial economy and commerce. It is to be remembered that the Ottoman Empire formed the third largest market for British manufactures by the 1850s.[11] Ottoman membership in the European family of nations was first acknowledged in 1693 by William Penn, founder of the city of Philadelphia and the commonwealth of Pennsylvania. (Consistent with

Western usage Penn referred to Turks and Turkey.) Bernard Lewis has drawn attention to Penn's proposal,[12] which stated that Turkey should be invited to join an organization of European states to be responsible for arbitrating disputes and thus preventing wars.

Only in the period of the *Tanzimat* reforms, when the Ottomans decided to introduce Western-inspired reforms aimed at ensuring equality among all subjects before the law, was there an attempt to accept the Ottoman Empire into "the concert of Europe." First, at the convention of the Straits in 1841, the Ottoman Empire was considered a member of the community of nations. The Ottoman Empire was not formally accepted into "the concert of Europe" until following the Crimean War of 1853–56. It can safely be said that Great Power efforts over the past half-century or so to prevent a drastic change in the Middle Eastern political order is a legacy of the Great Power diplomacy toward the Ottoman Empire in the nineteenth century.

Indeed, the pattern of multilateral diplomacy and interstate cooperation according to set rules, which ultimately led to the creation of the United Nations, certainly has its links to the earlier Great Power conferences repeatedly held throughout the nineteenth century to resolve the so-called Eastern Question concerning Ottoman lands.

Despite these realities the Crusader ideology has lingered on, and the question continues to be asked whether the Islamic empire of the Ottomans could be called a component of the European states system. Crusading Europe, faithful to the medieval ideology of the *Respublica Christiana*, never quite accepted the existence of an Islamic state on European territory. When hundreds of thousands of Muslim Turks, Circassians, Tatars, Bosnians, and Albanians were forced to emigrate from the Balkans, the Crimea, and the Caucasus in the nineteenth century, the West remained approvingly silent. An intense propaganda for holy leagues, crusades to expel the Turks from Europe had created an image of the Turk as an Anti-Christ among the masses in the West. Recently some members of the European community have been attempting to exploit this feeling for their national purposes, against the secular Republic of Turkey.

Non-Muslim Communities Under the Ottomans

Let us now ask whether the Ottomans represented a culture that was hostile to and irreconcilable with Western cultural traditions. It must be remembered that historical Islam was different from the Islam preached in rigid canonical sources. True, as a universal religion Islam preached that the whole world would eventually convert to the "True Religion." So too, for that matter, did Christianity. In fact, however, even in the time of the Prophet compromises were made and guarantees were given to Christians and Jews allowing them to freely exercise their religion and live as a autonomous community under Islamic rule.[13]

The Ottomans, building their empire under special conditions, became particularly tolerant and conciliatory toward Christians and Jews. With millions of Christian subjects in the Balkans, they needed to win over the Christian masses through maintaining not only their church organization but also their preconquest customs, taxes, and local institutions.[14] Even members of the Greek, Serbian, Bulgarian, and Albanian military class who cooperated with the conquerors were incorporated as Christian timar-holders into the Ottoman military class, in most cases with the same privileges they had enjoyed previously.[15] Nor did they have to convert to Islam. Islamization among them came about as a social process.

The Ottomans also employed Greek or Serbian Christians and Jews as scribes and tax farmers or in other state services. The Greek, Latin, Hungarian, and Serbian languages were used in the Ottoman official correspondence. These non-Muslim elements in Ottoman state service should not be confused with the boys who were levied and trained to become the Sultan's *kuls*, or servitors. These levy-boys (*devshirme*) were to have an Islamic education and later to serve the sultan as soldiers, commanders, governors, and vezirs.

In any case, under Ottoman rule there was, in one way or another, considerable social and cultural intercourse, even integration, between the conqueror and the conquered. In the countryside, the Turkish dervishes and sipahis visited or lived in Christian villages, producing an exchange of customs and beliefs among Muslims and Christians to such extent that popular Islam in the Balkans became quite different from conservative urban Islam found in the old Muslim world.[16] At the same time, the Ottomans respected the autonomy of the communities under their respective churches, a procedure known as the *millet* system.[17] Subsequently, the Christian Balkan nations would develop their own nationalist movements and eventually—at different times throughout the nineteenth century—form their own independent states. The venerable Ottoman policy of providing the several religious communities, non-Muslim and Muslim for that matter, considerable autonomy facilitated this development.

Western Economic Development and the Ottomans

In general, mutual cultural borrowings between the Ottoman Muslim East and Christian Europe were frequent and became part of daily life. It is now a commonplace that the Ottomans were responsible for the spread of coffeehouses in Europe. We learn from the Ottoman records, for instance, that in

Thomas Allon's early nineteenth-century engraving entitled "Interior of a Turkish Caffinet." Robert Walsh, *Constantinople and the Scenery of the Seven Churches of Asia Minor.* (London: Fisher, 1838)

A military band in present-day Turkey wearing the traditional Ottoman uniforms. Photo by Joseph Szyliowicz

the Polish city of Kamieniec there were ten coffeehouses in the year 1681.[18] Not as widely known is that the Ottomans introduced rice cultivation into Hungary, that the tulip was introduced to the Low Countries in the middle of the sixteenth century by Busbecq, the imperial Hapsburg ambassador to Istanbul, and that the military band in European armies originated with the Ottomans.

The Middle Eastern contribution to Western economic development was not only indirect, through trade, but also direct, through certain industries. Syria's influence in particular on Europe's economic and technological development in the Middle Ages cannot be ignored, and this influence continued in modern times under the Ottomans.

Perhaps more important were the weaving and dyeing techniques and designs borrowed first by Italians and then by other Westerners from the Middle East and used in the manufacture of cotton and silk textiles.[19] Silk industries did not develop in Western European countries until the sixteenth and seventeenth centuries, thanks to the large supplies of cheap and fine raw silk from Iran through Anatolia.[20] The Levant market, also, was responsible for the development of woolen industries in the West. The English, for example, felt the need to improve the quality of woolen manufactures, shifting from a coarse kersey type to broadcloth to meet the demands of the Ottoman market in the last decades of the sixteenth century.

The rise of cotton industries and the Industrial Revolution in the West were directly linked to the Indian and Ottoman markets. The Ottoman Empire continued to compete and even to export its cheap cotton products to the European markets, and to France in particular during the seventeenth and eighteenth centuries. White and blue coarse cotton goods, exported from Izmir (Smyrna), were in great demand in Marseilles, and exported from there to Spain to be used as inexpensive clothing for slaves on American plantations and colonies—the origin of blue jeans.[21]

Mercantilistic England was as concerned as France when Indian cotton goods such as chintz, calicoes, etc., were so cheap and attractive that massive amounts began to flood the English markets. The dilemma for Western mercantilistic countries was how to compete with the growing demand at home for cheap products from the East. The first method, employed around 1700, was to impose high tariffs and even outright prohibition of imports in order to curb the flight of specie from the country. The competitive advantages the Ottoman Empire and India held over Western countries were technological— weaving and dyeing and design, but above all the low prices resulting from the production of raw material in Ottoman lands and India and, more importantly, the cheaper labor.[22] Even when France and England made rapid developments in the cotton industries, they were unable to curb the growing import levels from the East. India became the dominant exporter of cotton goods in the world. While the Ottoman Empire—western Anatolia and Syria in particular—specialized in cheap coarse cottons, India excelled in fine cottons, especially muslins. The Ottoman Empire was drained of its bullion for imports of these expensive Indian cottons beginning as early as the fifteenth century.

For France and England, the vital question was how to lower labor costs—a challenge that supported the new liberal views advocating low tariffs for wheat imports. But in the search for a solution to the most important economic problem of the day, namely the high cost of labor, the discovery of the machine was made and an answer was provided. In the last analysis, this was the triumph of the West's superiority in sciences and technology over the East's more pragmatic knowledge. For us, however, the most important point is that there can be no explanation of Western achievements without consideration of the social and economic symbiosis between East and West.

The Arab World and the Ottomans

If there had never been an Ottoman Empire the map of the Islamic world today would be drastically different. By the end of the fifteenth century the Spanish had brought their *Reconquista* into the Maghrib and had begun to capture coastal cities. That the *Reconquista* failed to cross the Mediterranean is due in no little measure to effective Ottoman resistance. Forces from within Morocco led the resistance there, it is true, but elsewhere along both the southern and eastern shores of the Mediterranean it was Ottoman power that not only preserved the territories of Dar al-Islam but pushed deep into Europe, even to the outskirts of Vienna in 1529.

In 1517, when the Portuguese fleet attacked Jidda in an effort to capture the Holy Cities of Islam, it was the Ottoman admiral Selman Reis who repulsed them. Within twenty years the Ottomans had built up a defense line from Aden to Abyssinia, which foiled repeated Portuguese attempts to enter the Red Sea. The Arab lands began to receive Indian goods through the Persian Gulf and the Red Sea, which were under Ottoman protection, and there was a full revival of spice trade in the Middle East in mid-sixteenth century. Syrian and Egyptian cities recovered their prosperity and expanded.[23] Aleppo, in particular, became the center of the caravan roads from Hijaz, Basra-Baghdad, and Iran and thus became the principal trade center for the whole Middle East in that same century.

The Ottoman period in the history of Arab lands, lasting for four centuries undoubtedly constituted a decisive factor in the present conditions of the Arab world today. Excluding Syria and upper Iraq, the Ottomans erected in the Arab lands two pashaliks of Egypt and Baghdad under governors with extraordinary powers.

The Pasha of Egypt was responsible for the administrative, military and financial affairs not only in Egypt itself but also in Hijaz, Yemen, Sudan, and Habesh (Abyssinia), as well as the Indian Ocean. The governor of Egypt, Suleyman Pasha, organized quite independently an ambitious expedition against the Portuguese, which resulted in the conquest of Aden, the reorganization of the province of Yemen, and the siege of Diu in India in 1538. Consistent with this tradition Muhammad Ali of Egypt sent troops into Arabia in 1812 to put down the Saudi-Wahhabi threat.

The Pashalik of Baghdad, on the other hand, not only controlled Iraq but also had supervision in Gulf countries including Qatif, Al-Hasa, and Kuwait. An Ottoman navy under his supervision based at Basra struggled to expel the Portuguese from Bahrain and the whole Gulf area by attempting to capture Hormuz in the 1550s. During the Saudi-Wahhabi rebellion from the mid-eighteenth century and on, the governor of Baghdad supported the Arab tribes in Kuwait that were fighting against the Saudis. As a result, the Egyptian and Iraqi policies toward the Arab peninsula today have a tradition reflecting back to the position of the Ottoman Pashaliks of Egypt and Baghdad in bygone centuries.

When we turn to social evolution, recent studies show that the rise of indigenous Arab notable families and dynasties was the result of a specific Ottoman tax-farming system in the eighteenth century.[24] In Arab cities the leadership was monopolized by either the powerful *multezim* or the ulama families. The third in line for local leadership was provided by the local Ottoman military command, the janissary commanders or other high officers who, over time, became incorporated into the local elite. It is clearly a distortion of historical reality to find in these notable families leaders of national resistance or awakening in the Arab lands during so early a period.[25] Instead of being the hero of Egyptian nationalism, Muhammad Ali appears to have been an Ottoman *ayan* pasha competing with his archrival, the Grand Vizier Husrev in Istanbul.[26] Muhammad Ali's modernization efforts, also, were directly connected with the Ottoman reform measures introduced by Selim III.

The most important legacy of the Ottoman Empire is undoubtedly the modern nation-state of Turkey. The ideas and developments, including the basic idea of a secular Turkish republic, go back to the shifts erupting into Ottoman society during the last century of the empire. Today, the secular Turkish republic is an example and a source of controversy for the whole Islamic world. To survive and to assert themselves in the face of the challenges posed by the Western world, Muslim countries today are oscillating between Ataturk and Khomeini for a solution.

NOTES

1. *History of Mankind: Cultural and Scientific Development*, by an international commission, UNESCO, (New York: Harper and Row, 1963).
2. See H. Inalcik, *The Middle East and the Balkans Under the Ottoman Empire* (Bloomington: Indiana University Turkish program, 1993).
3. See H. Inalcik, ed., *An Economic and Social History of the Ottoman Empire* (New York: Cambridge University Press, 1994).
4. *Six Books of a Commonweale* (London, 1962), Index: Turkey.
5. L. Valensei, *Venise et la sublime Porte: La naissance du despote* (Paris: Hachette, 1987).
6. J. Pelenski, *Russia and Kazan* (The Hague: Mouton, 1974).
7. See K. M. Setton, *The Papacy and the Levant, 1204–1571*, 4 vols. (Philadelphia: American Philosophical Society, 1976–1984).
8. K. Brandi, *The Emperor Charles V*, trans. V. Wedgewood (New York: Knopf, 1939); S. Fisher-Galati, *Ottoman Imperialism and German Protestantism, 1521–1555* (Cambridge: Harvard University Press, 1959); C. M. Kortepeter, *Ottoman Imperialism During the Reformation* (New York: New York University Press, 1972).
9. H. Inalcik, "A Case Study in Renaissance Diplomacy: The Agreement Between Innocent VIII and Bayezid II on Djem Sultan," *Journal of Turkish Studies* (Harvard University) 3 (1979–1980): pp. 209–30.
10. A. Sorel, *The Eastern Question in the Eighteenth Century* (New York: Ferrig, 1969).
11. F. E. Bailey, *British Policy and the Turkish Reform Movement* (Cambridge: Harvard University Press, 1942).
12. B. Lewis, *Islam and the West* (New York: Oxford: Oxford University Press, 1993), p. 33.
13. M. Hamidullah, *Documents sur la diplomatie musulmane* (Paris, 1935).
14. H. Inalcik, "Ottoman Methods of Conquest" *Studia Islamica* 3 (1954), pp. 103–29.
15. H. Inalcik, "Stefan Duşan dan Osmanli Imperatorluguna: xv. Asirda Rumeli de Hiristiyan Sipahiler ve Menşeleri," *Mélanges Fuad Köprülü* (Istanbul, 1953), pp. 207–48.
16. F. W. Hasluck, *Christianity and Islam Under the Sultans*, 2 vols., ed. Margaret Hasluck (Oxford: Clarendon Press, 1929).
17. B. Braude and B. Lewis, eds., *Christians and Jews in the Ottoman Empire* (New York: Holmes and Meier, 1982).
18. I am indebted for this information to Dariusz Kolodziejczk, who is preparing the source for publication.
19. M. F. Mazzaoui, *The Italian Cotton Industry in the Later Middle Ages, 1100–1600* (Cambridge: Cambridge University Press, 1981).
20. H. Inalcik, "Bursa and the Commerce of the Levant," *Journal of Economic and Social History of the Orient* 3 (1960): pp. 131–47.
21. H. Inalcik, "Osmanli Pamuklu Pazari, Hindistan veIngiltere: Pazar Rekabetinde Emek Maliyetinin Rolu," *ODTU, Gelisme Dergisi*, special issue 2 (1979–80) pp. 1–65.
22. Ibid.
23. F. Braudel, *The Mediterranean and the Mediterranean World in the Age of Philip II*, vol. 1 (New York: Harper and Row, 1972), pp. 543–68; on the cities see A. Cohen and B. Lewis, *Population and Revenue in the Towns of Palestine in the Sixteenth Century* (Princeton: Princeton University Press, 1978).
24. H. Inalcik, "Centralization and Decentralization in Ottoman Administration" in *Studies in Eighteenth-Century Islamic History*, eds. T. Naff and R. Owen (Champaign: University of Illinois Press, 1977), pp. 27–52.
25. H. Inalcik, "Tax Collection, Embezzelment, and Bribery in Ottoman Finances," *Turkish Studies Association Bulletin* (1992).
26. "Husrev Pasa," *Islam Ansiklopedisi* 5, pp. 609–16.

CHAPTER THREE

THE PROBLEM OF PERCEPTIONS

Norman Itzkowitz

I would like to step outside the realm of the history of ideas and institutions to discuss

- perceptions and what Europeans and other have thought of the Ottomans and what of those views still survive
- what the Ottomans thought of the Arabs and vice versa—and what of those views still inhabit the mutual perceptions of Arabs and Turks
- what the non-Muslims of the empire thought of others and still think of others within a framework I prefer to call the millet mentality rather than the millet system.

I will also address issues raised by requited and unrequited nationalist urges. Not every group over whom the Ottomans exercised dominion is evoked, but the examples chosen represent the general trend.

It may be useful to reflect on what is meant by Ottoman and the vicissitudes in the meaning of that term over time. To those early warriors on the Seljuk/Byzantine frontier, Osmanli most likely meant someone who had thrown in his lot with the founder of the dynasty, Osman or his successors. In time the independent warlords who had entered the local struggle on the side of Osman and his Osmanlis or Osmanlilar came to recognize that calling themselves, and being called Osmanlis, adherents of Osman, signified an act of loyalty and legitimacy.

From that humble beginning the term "Ottoman" soon took on a dynastic meaning as in Al-i Osman—the family of Osman, that is, the Ottoman dynasty. By the mid-sixteenth century in the reign of Suleiman the Magnificent the terms "Osmanli" and "Osmanlilar" took on cultural overtones, referring to the Muslim Turco-Arabo-Persian culture of the elite class of Ottomans—those who served the state and religion, and knew the Ottoman way. That is, they were Muslims and had positions in the service of the state as bureaucrats—men of the pen, military men—men of the sword, the ulama, men of *'ilm* (religious knowledge) or who held significant positions in the palace.

In the Ottoman Empire the term "Turk" was used by members of the Ottoman group to refer to peasants and country bumpkins, not to themselves. Europeans, on the other hand, referred to people on the other side of the Islamic curtain as Turks, regardless of their status as Ottomans or non-Ottomans. Most Turks they came into contact with were people of the Ottoman group, consequently Ottoman and Turks were one and the same for them. When Richard Knolles in 1603 described the Turks as "the present ter-

A CONSULTATION ABOUT THE STATE OF TURKEY.

A consultation about the state of Turkey. Note that the Ottoman Empire is always "Turkey" to Europe. Cartoon from *Punch* (1853).

ror of the world," he meant the armies of the Ottoman sultan officered by Ottomans and comprising Turks and others as cavalrymen and infantry.

By the time of Tsar Nicholas I on the eve of the Crimean War, this former terror of the world had been reduced to the sick man of Europe and there was no lack of claimants to the sick man's inheritance. This in its simplest terms was what the Eastern Question.was all about. In the course of this discussion I will used the terms Ottoman and Turk interchangeably as did their European adversaries early and late.

The next distinction we need to make is what of this legacy is Ottoman and what is Islamic. There is no question that in most of the institutions of the empire the Ottomans were indebted to earlier Islamic models. In many areas, however, the Ottomans made their own particular contributions. Indeed, as a general rule it can be said that the long-lived Ottoman Empire represented the fullest development of Muslim political and religious institutionalization ever achieved. The degree of continuity or change during the Ottoman period is a proper and important concern for the historian. At another level of analysis, that adopted here, the distinction between the Ottoman and Islamic is of less relevance. The Ottoman state as well as the larger Ottoman culture and civilization within which it was situated was necessarily viewed as a whole by contemporaries both within the borders of the empire and beyond. For purposes of this discussion when I use the term "Ottoman" with regard to an institution, unless it is important to distinguish it from earlier Islamic models, assume that is includes but adapts and elaborates on earlier Islamic material.

From the moment Ottoman power made itself felt first in Asia Minor and then in the Balkans, there were those who vilified it. As the Ottoman yoke descended upon the Balkan peoples, it was initially found to be lighter than that imposed upon them by their previous rulers, who exacted the meta or fifty-fifty split of the fruits of the peasants' labors. The local populaces often found themselves carrying a lighter tax burden and enjoying the exercise of their religion and security for their lives and property. Ottoman rule was often preferred to indigenous rule which may have been of the same religion, but which was confiscatory both of the crops and the labor of the peasantry, and harsh. Some of these feelings and perceptions have come down to us in the form of subtle comments and quips which if not ever really uttered still are illustrative of attitudes people could easily have held. For example, as Protestantism spread into some areas of the Balkans that were Catholic, we are told that the populace expressed their anti-Catholic position in the comment "Better the turban of the sultan than the tiara of the pope."

As long as Ottoman rule and the economy remained strong and people were unburdened by ideas like nationalism and self-determination that would bring into question the very essence of the empire, life continued in its timeworn ruts. What disrupted all that and changed the way people looked at each other was the arrival in the Balkans of nationalism, but not just nationalism. It was nationalism associated with changes wrought in Europe by the demise of the old pre-Congress of Vienna balance of power that completely changed the environment in which the Ottoman Empire had been living. The partitions of Poland in the last quarter of the eighteenth century did away with the remnants of significant territory available for compensation, the equalizer that kept the old balance of power alive. The major territory available for future compensation would be the Ottoman Empire.

One by one, peoples who had lived within the empire under the principle that in the empire everyone was equal, but the Muslims were more equal, now turned their backs on the old rules and sought to realize their manifest destiny of nationhood. The European powers were drawn into this internal disintegration from at least the time of the Greek War of Independence in the 1820s and even more after the Crimean War. As the Ottomans lost the capacity to direct from the center the effort against emerging nationalism, the burden fell upon local elements in the field. Most of those elements were irregulars. In this confrontation neither side behaved with decorum or with restraint. With the various contenders throughout the unraveling Ottoman Empire supported by their outside European patrons, the struggle took on the color of a religious war. It was not simply the constituent elements of the Ottoman Empire seeking to become nations, it was Christians against Muslims. But even more than that, the struggle took on racial overtones which unleashed a vicious attack upon the character of the Turks. This is seen in its pristine glory in the case of Bulgaria.

In 1876 unrest in Bulgaria exploded into confessional strife. The Bulgarians found a champion in William Gladstone, whose expressions of outrage were directed at both the Turks (i.e., the Ottomans) and at his own government, which he attacked for protecting the Turks since his archrival, Disraeli, was committed to a policy of the defense of both the territorial integrity and independence of the Ottoman Empire. In his pamphlet *The Bulgarian Horrors*,[1] Gladstone characterized the events in Bulgaria as the "basest and blackest outrages upon record within the present century, if not within the memory of man." He accused the Ottoman government of "crimes and outrages so vast in scale as to exceed all modern example, and so unutterably vile as well as fierce in character, that it passes the power of heart to conceive, and of tongue and pen adequately to describe them." Warming to his task, Gladstone continued: "Let me endeavor very briefly to sketch, in the rudest outline, what the Turkish race was and what it is. It is not a question of Mahometanism simply, but of Mahometanism compounded with the peculiar character of a race. They are not the mild Mahometans of India, not the chivalrous Saladins of

Syria, nor the cultured Moors of Spain. They were upon the whole, from the black day when they first entered Europe, the one great anti-human specimen of humanity. Wherever they went a broad line of blood marked the track behind them; and as far as their dominion reached, civilization disappeared from view."

Gladstone here joined the ranks of many who in the past and in the present have dubbed the Turk the terrible Turk, or, as Thomas Carlyle insisted, "the unspeakable Turk," and who see the Turks as engaged solely in rape and rapine, unpossessed of any socially redeemable virtues. One perception held over from Ottoman times is the characterization of Turks as vicious people driven by their religion and culture to acts of murder and wantonness. To this outcry on behalf of the Bulgarians we need only add those strident voices raised on behalf of the Armenians, the Greeks, and even the Arabs, whom many view through the eyes of Lowell Thomas as he helped to champion Lawrence of Arabia.

This is not to say that the Ottomans were blameless, a totally high-minded and peace-loving people. But Christian Europe's unending pursuit of victory over Islam in any age has poisoned the atmosphere and continues to do so today. Moreover, from 1300 to 1923, the standard-bearer happened to have been the Turk. A single example will make the point. With the retreat of Communism from Central and Eastern Europe and the lessening of tension between the United States and the USSR, Turkey faced reduced international importance and a decline in U.S. aid. Then with the Iraqi problem taking center stage, the Turks shut down the oil pipeline from Iraq and supported the embargo. These actions are seen in Turkey as chips in the game of gaining admission into the European Economic Community. The Turks may well find these chips of little value in overcoming the centuries-long hostility that Christian Europe has harbored for the Muslim Turks.

Gladstone ended his 1876 anti-Turkish pamphlet with a call for the states of Europe to extinguish Turkish rule in Bulgaria: "Let the Turks now carry away their abuses in the only possible manner, namely by carrying off themselves. Their Zaptiehs and their Mudirs, their Bimbashis and their Yuzbachis, their Kaimakams and their Pashas, one and all, bag and baggage, shall, I hope, clear out from the province they had desolated and profaned."

Recent revelations about the inhuman behavior of the Bulgarians toward their Turkish minority have not brought forward any Gladstones to defend the virtues of the Turks and they will again be asked to go to the end of the queue as Poland, Hungary, and others elbow their way to the front of the European Community waiting line. Support of U.S. policy in Arabia may avail them little in Europe. Such is the Ottoman legacy.

Another Ottoman legacy alive and well in the realm of perceptions is the lack of esteem in which the Ottomans held the Arabs and the Arabs in turn held the Turks. The central Islamic world of the Fertile Crescent had hardly recovered from the shock of the incursion of the Mongols into their daily lives when the Ottoman Turks took over most of the Arab world beginning early in the sixteenth century. The Ottomans did not make much room in their military, bureaucracy, or religious establishments for Arabs until late in the life of the empire. The Arabs largely hold the Turks responsible for their back-wardness, and the Turks consider the Arab behavior in World War I and the proclamation of the Arab Revolt as treachery. The Arabs counter that when the Ottoman governor in Syria, Jemal Pasha, hanged several Arabs in Beirut early in the war, the Turks forfeited any Arab support.

Arabic and Ottoman literature offer examples of the hostile attitudes they held toward each other. Katib Chelebi writes of an archconservative member of the ulama,[2] who condemned innovations as the path to hell and who objected to the use of eating utensils since Muhammad had no such instruments. He was then ridiculed by his friend who suggested that according to such thinking it would be best for everyone to get rid of their underwear and run around with bare-behinds like desert Arabs.

Such attitudes continue to this day. When in the 1960s and 1970s the Turks experienced a series of revolutions and military takeovers, it is widely report-ed that a member of the Turkish parliament beseeched his fellow Turks to behave better, saying, "one more revolution and people will think we are Arabs." These attitudes, born of centuries of being the dominators and the dominated, form another part of the Ottoman legacy.

Another Ottoman legacy relates to issues stemming from requited and unrequited nationalism. The Ottoman Empire was a multiethnic, multina-tional, multireligious, multilingual state. Once nationalism reared its head first in the Balkans and then elsewhere within the empire, pressures developed which the Ottomans could not contain. In the European part of the empire, ethnic or national groups filtered out of Ottoman control, often with the sup-port of one or another European power, to become nation states—Yugoslavia, Bulgaria, Romania, Greece, to mention just a few. Arab nationalism, Armen-ian nationalism, Kurdish nationalism were thwarted. The Arabs of Asia (those of Northern Africa having already come under British, French, Italian, or Spanish colonial rule in different forms) emerged from World War I under the control largely of Britain and France in the form of "mandates." The Armeni-ans and the Kurds did not even get that far up the ladder of independence, more the fault of European power diplomacy than Ottoman machinations, but among these peoples the blame was attached to the Turks. Memories of bloody engagements with the Ottoman Turks, and cries of genocide, coupled with feelings of inadequacy that accompany the failure to achieve nationhood, poisoned and continue to poison the relationships between Armenians and Turks, and Kurds and Turks.

Even where nationhood was achieved, relationships can be uneasy at best as in the case of the Greeks and the Turks. The Greeks will do everything they can to keep Turkey out of the European Community, while both Greeks and Turks nurse their wounds over Cyprus and fail to find a workable solution to the island's woes. This continuing hostility between Greek and Turk can be attributed to the Ottoman legacy, but it is more accurately to be seen as the deadly interaction of European imperial ambitions, nationalist ideologies made in Europe and the Ottoman system.

Identifying elements of the Ottoman legacy that are still alive in our world today is easier than accounting for the continued virulence of these attitudes so long after the presumed perpetrator of these crimes and misdemeanors—the Ottoman Empire—has disappeared and is no longer available as a target for retribution. I believe that these situations continue to be so virulent and so intractable because they partake of the psychology of ethnic conflict. There are seven elements at work here.

1. the increasingly strong connection between self and nation. If you have no nation you have no self. We know from clinical data that people will do anything in defense of the self, so it is not surprising that over the years since nationalism first infected the Balkans and the other areas of the Ottoman Empire nationalism has resulted in vast quantities of bloodshed, and unrequited nationalism continues to unleash terror in the world.

2. the concept of the list of historical grievances. Each side in ethnic conflicts can submit their own list of historical grievances, lists that grow longer with the passage of time.

3. the intergenerational transmission of attitudes. You need to be carefully taught to hate and the older generation acts as the initiator of the young into this venomous business. (I had an Armenian student who would berate me for teaching the history of the Turks and for assigning certain books he felt were anti-Armenian. One day I asked him where he got all these notions. Did he know any Turks, had any Turks ever done anything to him? No and No. Where did he get his information? He thought for a moment and then said, from his grandmother.)

4. each side generally knows little about the other. They have each created a demon that represents the other, and it is the demons that speak to each other. They not only do not know anything about each other—they do not wish to know anything about each other.

5. what we can call the egoism of victimization. Only my suffering is important. The suffering of the other person is meaningless.
6. war or some sort of action is seen as therapy. It restores the sense of mastery over the situation and temporarily cools the heart.
7. with the inability to mourn their loss there is little hope for the sides involved in ethnic conflict to negotiate their differences.[3]

We see these seven points operating in ethnic conflicts current today around the world—the Arab-Israeli situation, northern Ireland, and South Africa are only three such situations. They are also at work in the elements left over from Ottoman times, the Greeks and the Turks, the Turks and the Armenians, and the Turks and the Kurds.[4]

Is there any hope that these tragic elements left from the Ottoman legacy can be expunged from our midst and laid to rest? Not much. Yet, we have to start somewhere. We cannot kill all the grandmothers, so we must start with the children and educate them at very early ages to forestall their being infected by the bitterness of ethnic conflict.

One more element of the Ottoman legacy has been newly placed at the doorstep of the defunct Ottoman Empire. This is the concept of the "Ottomanization" of the Soviet Union, by which is meant the fragmentation of a multinational empire resulting from the combination of pressures from outside and within.

As with most similarities, some of them are far-fetched, some simple, some profound, and some simply misleading. The central issue for those who think in these terms is whether disintegration works for freedom, or whether it produces instability. Optimists noting this parallel can point out that the end of the Ottoman Empire resulted in the creation of the modern Turkish republic. Turkey, due to its origins in the ruins of an empire shorn of its imperial domains and ethnic tensions, became able to pursue economic development, democratization, and social progress in better fashion. Accordingly, it is to be hoped that the former Soviet Union may yet emerge as a number of more cohesive unitary states reduced in size and power and ready to take their proper place as peace-loving, democratic states in the family of nations.

The bald fact remains, however, that the Ottoman Empire is not the Soviet Union. The differences between the two are perhaps more instructive than the similarities. The Ottomans controlled their non-Muslims peoples through the millet system whereas the Soviets have handled their ethnonational problem through autonomous republics, autonomous provinces, and autonomous regions. Instead of allowing the nationalities to deal with their own affairs in their own language, the Soviet state cyrillicized the alphabets of some of those nationalities, and sent them Russian teachers, officials, and soldiers, in effect treating them as old-fashioned colonies. Under Stalin there was a greater push for centralization, cultural Russification, and the repression of non-Russian national elites. National histories were rewritten to give a greater sense of progressivism to Great Russian imperialism.

None of this happened with the millets under the Ottoman Empire. There was nothing comparable to Russification. The Armenians, Jews, and Greeks did not have to write their languages in the Arabic script. The Russians reserved all the choice jobs for themselves and were definitely not equal opportunity employers. But the major difference was that the Soviet Union did not experience the foreign intervention into its internal affairs that the Ottomans endured.

In one important way, comparison between the breakup of the Ottoman and Soviet empires can be useful if it directs attention to the larger historical question of what changes and what survives when empires that once held together peoples of different religions, races, and languages are broken into presumably constituent parts called nation-states. Perhaps then the best comparison at hand is with the Hapsburg Empire, that old neighbor and enemy of the Ottomans. In any case, beyond the historian's essential task of reconstructing what actually caused the deconstruction of these empires lies the equally imposing task of taking the measure of what the later generations, insiders and outsiders, perceive as having taken place.

NOTES

1. William Ewart Gladstone, *Bulgarian Horrors and the Question of the East* (London: J. Murray, 1876). The quotations are from pages 9, 11–13, and 61–62.

2. Katib Chelebi, *Mizan ul-Haqq* (*The Balance of Truth*), tr. Geoffrey L. Lewis (London: Allen and Unwin, 1957). Katib Chelebi was a seventh-century Ottoman bureaucrat who commented widely on Ottoman political and fiscal matters.

3. These psychological issues represent the ideas of the work of Dr. Vamik D. Volkan, professor of Psychiatry, University of Virginia Medical School, and director of the Center for the Study of Mind and Human Interaction, University of Virginia Medical School, Charlottesville, Va. See his pioneering study on psychopolitical history, *Cyprus: War and Adaptation* (Charlottesville: University Press of Virginia, 1979).

4. Helpful in understanding the psychodynamics of ethnic conflict is the concept of the need to have enemies and allies as brilliantly elaborated by Dr. Vamik D. Volkan in his study *The Need to Have Enemies and Allies* (Northvale, N.J.: Jason Aronson, 1979). On the individual level in the human passage through the psychosexual and psychosocial stages of development, the oedipal stage offers insight into later group dynamics as the individual shares a group identity. The first enemy is the father and the first ally is the mother in the oedipal drama. Mental representations of these images are carried over into later life. We resolve the conflict with the leader by transforming it into loyalty and devotion (p. 56) and "the psychology of group formation that includes oedipal connections and leader/follower dynamics helps to crystallize the individual member's sense of belonging to the group, and it fosters recognition of some other group as inimical irrespective of any real danger it may pose" (p. 59).

PART TWO

THE ARAB WORLD AND THE BALKANS

Maria Todorova describes two diametrically opposed interpretations of the Ottoman legacy in the Balkans. One regards the Ottoman period as an alien intrusion. The other sees this long era more nearly as "a symbiosis of Turkish, Islamic, and Byzantine/Balkan traditions." The former, being more in line with Balkan nationalisms, is the prevailing orthodoxy among Balkans scholars, opinion molders, and the people at large. This orthodoxy needs to be significantly modified, but to see the Ottoman period too much in terms of continuity from Byzantine times risks "trivializing the Ottoman phenomenon." A more subtle historical reconstruction would uncover both alien intrusion that did not strike root and a symbiosis that did, the emphasis depending on time, place, and subject.

The problem of legacy can also be divided in two, as seen by 1) the objectivist outsider or 2) the subjectivist insider approach. Todorova treats first the Ottoman legacy as continuity (or history as reconstructed reality) and second as perception (or history as constructed ideology).

She finds a limited Ottoman political legacy because the Balkans had little elite continuity. The Ottoman legacy in high culture was also limited, not only because the Balkan opinion-molders from the early nineteenth century on stressed their Europeanness and Christianness but also because the extent to which Ottoman high culture moved out of Istanbul into the Balkans was limited, even though a considerable number of the Ottoman elite over the centuries came from the Balkans.

In popular culture and everyday life a more persistent Ottoman legacy can be discerned, which has even resisted later state-directed efforts at de-Ottomanization. This is especially the case in such matters as cuisine and music.

In the socioeconomic field the Ottoman legacy includes the absence of a landed nobility, a pattern of small peasant holdings, limited urban autonomy, a weak bourgeoisie, and a strong state. The most important legacy may be in the demographic sphere. The Ottoman period of Balkan history was characterized by massive population movements from the earliest days of the empire to the very end (and immediately thereafter, e.g., the Greek and Turkish "repatriations" in the early 1920s) leaving a juxtaposition of religious, linguistic, and ethnic groups with their overlapping irredentia. Sadly, the "Macedoine" salad of demographic diversity that characterizes the Balkans was not all that inconsistent with the pluralist, imperialist Ottoman pattern of political organization, but for narrow nationalism it remains a nightmare.

Balkan intellectuals offer a strikingly similar image of the Ottoman legacy, seeing their nation as having reached before the Ottoman era a civilizational level equal to, if not above, that of Western Europe, only to have been held back by the Ottoman centuries. The only exception to these narrow nationalist histories has been the work of certain Marxists who have achieved advances in such fields as economic history and class analysis. Even the Marxists, however, have tended to view the Ottoman Empire as having hampered the needed move toward economic and technological "progress."

As long as nationalism remains the dominant discourse, Todorova concludes, the Balkan perception of the Ottoman legacy will remain remote from the reality of that legacy.

Dennison Rusinow, examining Yugoslavia's disintegration, asks to what extent the Ottoman past has contributed to the tormented present. He finds that the Ottoman period played a role in arranging the demographic arena insofar as the crazyquilt of ethnic, linguistic, and—most of all—religious groups in former Yugoslavia was elaborated during the centuries of Ottoman rule. The Ottoman era increased earlier diversity and added two new groups—Jews (now numerically insignificant) and Muslims (still significant especially in beleaguered Bosnia).

Even so, the real cause of the present troubles is neither "ancient hatreds" nor the Ottoman legacy. Disintegration and brutal conflict set in when nationalist theory and programs were imposed upon a country of "ethnic and religious fragmentation, mixed populations, and overlapping historical or competing historical and ethnic claims."

Only Slovenia, 90 percent Slovene and with 99 percent of the total Slovene population to be found in all Yugoslavia, has a chance to create a homogeneous mini-state without irredenta. As for the others, 26 percent of the Serbs live outside of Serbia, 20 percent of the Croats outside of Croatia, and 19 percent of the Muslims outside of Bosnia-Herzegovina.

Surveying population patterns of disintegrating Yugoslavia, with special attention to Bosnia, Rusinow traces the major changes during the Ottoman, Austro-Hungarian, and Titoist Communist period, to the extent that history documentation (generally incomplete and bitterly disputed) permits.

As for the Bosnian Muslims, Rusinow lays to rest the charge that these "notoriously undogmatic, even heterodox, and often hard-drinking, pork-eating Muslims" are closet Muslim fundamentalists seeking to create a theocratic state. More to the point, Bosnian Muslims are still a predominantly urban and Serbs a predominantly rural people, which makes the present Serb-Muslim war also in large measure "a war of the country against the city." The Bosnian Muslims were naturally more attracted to the notion of loyalty to a multinational Ottoman Empire and were slow to develop a sense of nationalism as did their Christian neighbors. To this extent, their situation was comparable to the Muslim Arabs and Turks of the Ottoman Empire. Still, Rusinow concludes that even Bosnian Muslims were "well on their way to self-identification as a distinct national as well as (or instead of) a confessional 'imagined community' by the time Ottoman rule formally ended in 1908."

The Ottoman centuries set the stage for what might have developed into a multinational pluralistic polity. The Austro-Hungarian influence worked essentially in the same direction. As for the Titoist experiment, it is perhaps to be understand less in terms of Communism than of an updated Ottoman model (pluralist or transnational rather than nationalist). All of this legacy is now being swept aside by narrow nationalisms. Given the near impossibility of realizing these conflicting nationalist dreams the ethnic cleansing has been brutal and massive. More of the same seems likely.

Karl Barbir begins his "Memory, Heritage, and History: The Ottoman Legacy in the Arab World" with the haunting citation from Thucydides: "It was a case of people adapting their memories to suit their sufferings." This sets the theme of his essay, which is the distinction between the past as reality and as ideology. One can understand that the peoples of the Balkans, overwhelmingly Christian and also European by accident of geography, would reconstruct their history to condemn the Ottoman period. It is not so straightforward for the Arabs, overwhelmingly Muslim and Afro-Asian. The we/they polarities of identity-formation might have dictated Arab identification with their Ottoman past or at least a more nuanced use of the past for present purposes.

Barbir considers why the Arabs have approached their Ottoman past negatively and why that earlier adapting of memories may now be changing. He first summarizes the Arab world's Ottoman past as reality and then addresses the changing Arab reconstruction of the past for present purposes.

Most of the Arab world came under Ottoman rule during the sixteenth century, and the first two centuries or more was not a period of decline (pace Ranke and a whole school of Western historians). Even less was it perceived as such, but the Ottomans were seen in decidedly pre-national terms as territorially and culturally remote. This distinction was enhanced by the relatively small number of Arabs integrated into the Ottoman ruling elite.

It was the eventual radical change of institutions and ideologies throughout the Middle East growing out of the Ottoman response to the European threat from the late eighteenth century to the end of the empire after the First World War that produced the Arab historiography of Ottoman oppression. The ideal of an integrated, centralized, and modernized polity made up of different ethnic, linguistic, and religious groups broke on the shoals of narrow nationalisms. During the Young Turk period even the rulers in Istanbul seemed bent on imposing an ethnolinguistic criterion of political affiliation. The intriguing idea of an Arabo-Turkish empire modeled on the Austro-Hungarian Empire never really caught hold. The harsh Ottoman rule in the Fertile Crescent during the World War I years, the "Arab revolt," and Atatürk's subsequent opting for a Turkish nation-state finished the process. In formulating an appropriate nationalist past Arabs picked up the very European idea of the Ottoman Empire as being Turkey and of the Turks as alien oppressors who were succeeded by yet another group of alien oppressors (European colonialism). Thus, the fully elaborated nationalist myth was that Arabs have been struggling for centuries to be free—a nationalist historical reconstruction hauntingly similar to that of Balkan nationalisms.

Today many Arabs, reacting against what is seen as "the failure of secular and nationalist models of reform and progress" could view the Ottoman Empire, the last great Islamic empire, more favorably. Yet, they would ignore much that was distinctively Ottoman, including the capacity to tolerate and protect different religious, linguistic, and ethnic groups.

More encouraging are those few Arab scholars seeking to see the Ottoman centuries in their entirety as characterized by an amazingly long-lived political system whose very durability poses questions that cry out for answers. The centuries before the "impact of the West" were neither an idyllic golden age nor a period of stagnation, but an era no less dynamic than what followed and quite relevant to our study of possible Ottoman legacies.

For all the attention given by scholars to ideologies and institutions, human history is set in terrestrial space. States have boundaries. Moreover, the notion of natural boundaries is as pervasive as that of natural nations (and just as arbitrary). Irredentist claims are usually based on the charge that outside forces have sundered some part of the nation from its territorial patrimony.

Most of the Arab world formed part of the Ottoman Empire for some four centuries, and Andre Raymond discusses the Ottoman legacy in delimiting Arab political boundaries.

His more important findings are the following: French North Africa tended to accept the boundaries worked out in Ottoman times (thus Tlemcen, for example, remaining Algerian, not Moroccan, territory) except for the Sahara. The Ottomans, for good ecological reasons, viewed the Sahara as a no-man's-land. France saw to it that most of the Sahara became Algerian, thereby largely cutting off both Morocco and Tunisia from its time-honored cultural and commercial hinterland. This is the background to the post-independence Saharan border disputes dividing the three Maghrib states.

What is now the Iran-Iraqi border was arrived at after some two centuries of Ottoman-Iranian warfare (c.1530s to 1746), and later warfare brought no appreciable changes. "If lessons could be drawn from history . . . Iraq would probably have been wise in 1980 not to try to modify the limits that the Ottomans had bequeathed to Iraq after a protracted, and useless, conflict with its Eastern neighbors."

The Ottoman Iraqi-Kuwait border was imprecise because before the discovery of oil the matter was not that important. This, however, "establishes no later Iraqi right over Kuwait."

The earlier Ottoman provincial borders in Anatolia and the Fertile Crescent followed more nearly economic than ethnolinguistic realities. Aleppo and Mosul thus formed the natural urban termini of a major trading zone now divided among three sovereign states. What then emerged as the border between the Republic of Turkey and the Arab states of Syria and Iraq resulted from the ability of Atatürk's Turkey to absorb most of the largely Turkish-speaking areas.

Raymond's overall conclusion is that, generally speaking, the Ottomans managed to work out both external and internal boundaries in pragmatic fashion consistent with the Ottoman tradition of incorporating autonomous local power structures. In none of the border problems facing today's Arab world "is the responsibility of the Ottomans engaged."

CHAPTER FOUR

THE OTTOMAN LEGACY IN THE BALKANS

Maria Todorova

Deconstructing the Title

In 1794 the British traveler Morritt, then fresh out of Cambridge, set off on a journey through the Levant. His fervor for the "wrecks of ancient grandeur" led him from London and across Europe to Constantinople, and from there to the sites of Troy, Mount Athos, and Athens. While on his way from Bucharest to Constantinople he crossed the Balkan mountains at the Shipka pass and described his feelings in a letter to his sister: "We were approaching classic ground. We slept at the foot of a mountain, which we crossed the next day, which separates Bulgaria from Romania (the ancient Thrace), and which, though now debased by the name of Bal.Kan, is no less a personage than the ancient Haemus."[1]

It is only natural that for one of the "Levant lunatics" and future prominent member of the Society of Dilettanti, the territories of the Ottoman Empire were first and foremost "classic ground" and any reminder of the present was annoying and debasing the illustrious ancient tradition. "Balkan" was, of course, the Turkish word for "wooded mountain," which was applied as a noun also to other mountain formations but stuck as a permanent name to the mountain range that ran through Bulgaria. Later, although contending for primacy alongside such appellations as "Turkey in Europe," "Rumelia," "Southeastern Europe" etc., it came to be applied to the whole peninsula.[2]

The Ottoman retreat from the Balkans, 1814–1913. Map by Blaine R. Walker, University of Pittsburgh.

It is, therefore, preposterous to look for an Ottoman legacy *in* the Balkans. The Balkans *are* the Ottoman legacy.

There have been two main and completely different approaches to the problem of the *Ottoman* Empire in the Balkans on the one hand, and to the problem of the Ottoman *legacy*, on the other. In a word, how do we define Ottoman? What do we mean by legacy?

The definition of *Ottoman* posits at least two interpretations of the Ottoman legacy. One has it that it was a religiously, socially, and institutionally alien imposition on autochthonous Christian medieval societies (Byzantine,

Bulgarian, Serbian, etc.) whose remnants can be traced, but they are treated as nonorganic accretions on the indigenous natural body of these societies. The central element of this interpretation is the belief in the incompatibility between Christianity and Islam, the incompatibility between the essentially nomadic civilization of the newcomers and the old urban and settled agrarian civilizations of the Balkans and the Near East. Most nineteenth-century European assessments and most assessments emanating from within Balkan historiography (contemporary included) are based on this widely held belief.[3]

This view in its extremes has been dispelled from serious scholarly works (mainly outside the Balkan historiographical tradition). This interpretation, however, is sometimes (often unconsciously) reproduced in what can be described as the mechanical (or separate spheres) approach to the Ottoman legacy, i.e., the attempts to decompose it into its supposed constituent elements, and the ensuing efforts to trace the Ottoman legacy in separate spheres, e.g., in language, in music, in food, in architecture, in art, in dress, in administrative traditions, political institutions, etc. Within this approach, no matter whether the research emanates from the Balkans, from Turkey proper, or from outside the region, Ottoman becomes synonymous with Islamic or Turkish (and to a lesser extent Arabic and Persian) influences in different spheres, usually subsumed in the heading "Oriental elements."[4] It is the lack of a theoretical framework, rather than deliberate attempts at isolating constituent elements, which brings about this mechanistic division in otherwise excellent, but usually exclusively empirical, works.

Within the Balkan historiographical tradition itself, which continues to insist on the existence of completely distinct and incompatible local/indigenous and foreign/Ottoman spheres,[5] the danger lies not so much in overemphasizing "the impact of the West" and overlooking the continuities and the indigenous institutions, but rather in separating artificially "indigenous" from "Ottoman" institutions and influences.

This interpretation of the Ottoman presence in the Balkans, however flawed, has a certain rationale behind it. It rests on the not-so-erroneous perception of segregation of the local Christian population within the empire. For all the objections to romanticized heartbreaking assessments of Christian plight under the infidel Turk, a tendency that has been long and rightly criticized, the Ottoman Empire was, first and foremost, an Islamic state with a strict religious hierarchy where the non-Muslims occupied, without any doubt, the back seats. The strict division on religious lines prevented integration of this population, except in cases of conversion.

At no time, but especially in the last two centuries, did the Ottoman Empire have strong social cohesiveness or a high degree of social integration. Not only was there no feeling of belonging to a common Ottoman society but the population felt that it belonged to disparate (religious, social, or other) groups that would not converge. The Ottoman state until well into the nineteenth century was essentially a supranational (or, even better, nonnational) empire with strong medieval elements, where the bureaucracy seems to have been the only common institution linking, but not unifying, all the population. That the Ottoman Empire did not create an integrated society is beyond doubt; what some Balkan historians seem unable to understand is that this empire did not strive to achieve such integration.

Once the emerging Balkan nations had embarked on efforts to attain self-identity (beginning in the eighteenth century but achieving a high degree of intensity in the nineteenth), they tried to delineate boundaries between themselves and their rulers. This was done in a nationalist discourse that was inherently incongruous to the imperial principle, but that had become the dominant discourse in Europe. In this light, the belated attempt to forge an Ottoman consciousness after the middle of the nineteenth century was a doomed utopian experiment. This process of alienation was something that long predated the disintegration of the empire, and is thus a systemic element of the Ottoman past. The question is not whether such alienation existed but how strong it was in different periods, and what populations it encompassed.

Whereas for modern Turkey and the Middle East the Ottoman legacy is one which can and has been considered organic (despite often vehemently negative assessments), in the Balkans the persistent attempt to depict it as alien is based on more than mere emotional or political conjecture. While the Ottoman period has consistently been the *ancien régime* for Republican Turkey, the Balkan perception is more complicated. Analytically, it is *also* the *ancien régime* but, based on the specific position of Christianity within a Muslim empire, it has been perceived almost exclusively as foreign domination or, as the Ottoman *yoke*.

This brings in a completely different framework of assessment: that of struggles for national emancipation and the creation of nation-states thought of not only as radical breaks with the past, but the negation of this past. To some extent this element of negation holds true also for the Turks (and to an even greater degree for the Arabs), but in the Balkan case this break was facilitated by the double boundary of language *and* religion, the two central foci around which Balkan ethnicity and nationalism were constructed. Whereas Islam provided an important link to the Ottoman past in both the Turkish and Arab cases, language served as an important delineator for the Arabs. It took Kemal's political genius to realize the centrality of language in the transmission of traditions, and in the formation of nationalism and to strike decisively with his language reform.[6]

The second interpretation treats the Ottoman legacy as the complex symbiosis of Turkish, Islamic, and Byzantine/Balkan traditions. Its premise is that centuries of coexistence must have produced a common legacy, and that the history of the Ottoman state is the history of all its constituent populations (notwithstanding religious, social, professional, and other divisions and hierarchies). The facts underlying this interpretation are the early syncretism in the religious, cultural, and institutional spheres, as well as the remarkable absorptive capacity of the conquerors.

An institution like the Orthodox Church which, in the first interpretation, must be depicted as the only genuine institution of the conquered and subject Balkan people, as a preserver of religion, language, and local traditions, can be seen, in the second interpretation, as a quintessentially Ottoman institution. Benefiting from the imperial dimensions of the state, the Church's oecumenical character and policies are comprehensible only in an Ottoman framework. The Patriarch, as *millet-bashi*, is a very Ottoman figure. It is revealing that the secession of the emerging nations from the empire meant also an almost simultaneous secession from the Constantinople patriarchate, i.e., from the Orthodox church of the Ottoman Empire. In the Bulgarian case this preceded the political separation by almost a decade, and was played out in a discourse of national emancipation from the Greek clergy. The Bulgarian exarchate evolved as a veritable national organization, and in the critical circumstances of the 1870s there was no possibility for it to become an Ottoman institution. In the Greek case the break with Constantinople followed slightly over a decade after the outbreak of the war for independence, and coincided with the beginnings of the independent state. The expropriation of the "dedicated monasteries" in the newly unified principalities of Wallachia and Moldavia was part of the same process.

It is interesting to speculate whether imperial success and bureaucratic power in the first centuries of Ottoman expansion attracted to some extent the loyalty of the Balkan population. There is good reason to believe that this was the case. Even the much-discussed *devshirme* and the ambiguous attitudes it generated in the population can be seen as an integrative mechanism. The emotionally burdened question of conversions to Islam can also be approached in this light. These conversions began immediately after the arrival of the Ottomans and continued until the nineteenth century, but the crucial period was the seventeenth century. Although there were obvious cases of enforced conversions, most were nonenforced. These, often euphemistically called "voluntary," were the result of indirect economic and social, but not administrative, pressure. They were stimulated primarily by the desire to achieve a distinct kind of integration. This is to be contrasted with the conversions of the Orthodox peasantry to Protestantism in Transylvania, which offered no social or political advantages, and can be better compared to the conversions to Catholicism or rather to the Uniate church, most of which also occurred during the seventeenth century.

As in the instance of the first interpretation of the Ottoman legacy, which insists on the mechanical separateness of the alien Ottoman element from the development of the indigenous populations, this second, or organic, interpretation also has its caveats. One of them, for example, is the approach which focuses exclusively on the continuity from the Byzantine period, thus trivializing the Ottoman phenomenon, as was done in Iorga's famous and influential work. Although the way Iorga's theory about Byzantium after Byzantium was argued and developed may be today no more than an exotic episode in the development of Balkan historiography, his formulation *Byzance après Byzance* will be alive for much longer, not only because it was a fortunate mot but because it reflects more than its creator would intimate.[7] It is a good descriptive term, in particular for representing the commonalities of the Orthodox population in the Ottoman Empire, but also in general, in emphasizing the continuity of the imperial tradition where, in certain aspects, the cultural fracture delineated by the advent of nationalism might have been more profound, and in any case intellectually more radical, than the one brought in with Ottoman conquest.

It has to be emphasized, at the same time, that both interpretations—the organic and the separate—when cleansed of their emotional or evaluational overtones, can be articulated in a moderate and convincing fashion. The preference for either one is dictated not only by philosophical or political predispositions, but also by methodical considerations.

It seems that in the macro-historical domain (economics, demography and social structure, and other phenomena of a *longue durée* nature) the second interpretation is more relevant, but it is not entitled to exclusive validity. Some long-term developments in the religious and cultural sphere, as well as the history of institutions, are more adequately explained within the separate spheres approach. Likewise, in the micro-historical sphere (political history, biography, art, and literary history, etc.) both interpretations can be evoked. Figures like the famous mystic and revolutionary, Şeyh Bedreddin (Simavi), who preached the union of Islam, Christianity, and Judaism in the early fifteenth century; the conqueror of Constantinople, Sultan Mehmed II Fatih; the Serbian-born Grand Vizier Sokollu Mehmed pasha (Mehmed Sokolović), who had risen within the *devshirme* system and successfully served three consecutive sultans during the time of the greatest Ottoman expansion; the Moldavian Prince Dimitrie Cantemir, who had been brought up in Constantinople and was an accomplished diplomat, the first modern historian of the Ottoman Empire, and a renowned figure of the Enlightenment; and even figures who were active during the "nationalist" eighteenth and nineteenth centuries, like the great Greek patriot and revolutionary, Rhigas Velestinlis, who had been in phanariote service in the Danubian principalities and provided an all-Balkan vision for the future of the peninsula; or the great Ottoman reformer and father of the first Ottoman constitution, Midhat pasha—all can be understood and described only within the organic approach, although it is necessary to distinguish between dominant and less-important traditions in the shaping of their outlook and activities, as well as in the extent of their influence on different groups.

Other cases warrant a predominantly separate spheres interpretation, like the fifteenth-century chronicler Aşikpasazade; the brilliant author of the acclaimed "Habname" Veisi; "the greatest polyhistor of the Ottomans," Kâtib Çelebi;[8] the fiery monk and author of the "Slavo-Bulgarian history" (very influential among the Bulgarians), Father Paisii; the remarkable Serbian writer and promoter of South Slav unity, Dositey Obradović; the prominent figure of the Greek political and intellectual enlightenment, Adamandios Koraïs. These examples can be continued *ad infinitum.*

Both views have their rationale, and both have produced, within their own confined approach, works of great quality, as well as works of ephemeral significance. These two interpretations of the Ottoman legacy are not merely possible scholarly reconstructions (although I have argued at some length for their methodological rationale). They actually existed side by side throughout the whole Ottoman period. Although the national discourse of the last two centuries dramatically escalated the feeling of separateness, it by no means invented the separate spheres approach. In fact, the two attitudes are clearly identifiable from the very beginning of the existence of the Ottoman Empire in Europe and, to ground them for example in late Byzantine assessments, one could probably speak of a Sphrantzes-Khalkokondyles-Doukas paradigm on the one hand, and a Kritoboulos paradigm on the other.[9]

Given the character and the scarcity of material, it is difficult to speculate about the relative weight of these outlooks. It is more difficult to hazard how deep they had been diffused throughout society. Risking a simplified generalization one could hypothesize that, as a whole, the first view was expounded by the outgoing elites of the independent medieval states (aristocratic and clerical), and was later picked up and developed within the national discourse by a substantial part of the new commercial and secular intellectual elites of the eighteenth and nineteenth centuries, who not only felt alienated from but severely hindered by the Ottoman polity; whereas the second was shared by significant numbers of the newly created elites within the non-Muslim millets which were part and parcel of the Ottoman structure or had achieved an acceptable modus vivendi (high clergy, phanariotes, local notables, etc.).

At the same time, even within the national discourse one can trace the

works of the two *Weltanshauungen* (or *Ottomananschauungen*). One was represented by a group within the national movements which took a gradualist
and evolutionist approach to the problem of emancipation within the
Ottoman Empire. In the early nineteenth century the Greek society *Filo-
mousos Etaireia* set its priorities on education and believed in the peaceful penetration and subsequent transformation of the Ottoman Empire into a Greek
state through the hegemony of the Greek commercial and cultural element.
Likewise, in the 1860s and 1870s significant strata of the Bulgarian commercial and educational elites espoused evolutionist convictions and saw the ideal
future of Bulgaria as achieving administrative autonomy within a strong and
reformed empire. Others advocated the creation of a dualist Turko-Bulgarian
state, inspired by the Austro-Hungarian *Ausgleich*. This position of acquiring
autonomy but without breaking away from the empire was dominant among
the Albanians, who not only became its strongest champions but staunchly
supported it to the end.

Attempts to explain these positions simply on the grounds of vested economic interest and social conservatism are unsatisfactory. While in the Greek
case the strong motive was, among others, the preservation of the territorial
unity of the Greek ethnic element and of the Greek *Kulturraum* with visions
of a resurrected Byzantium, in the Albanian case one can discern, alongside
the fear of encroachments by the newly formed neighboring nation-states, a
political affinity based on religion and the special status Albanians had
acquired in the empire. Likewise, the creation of a Bulgarian elite in Constantinople, although far from occupying the privileged positions of the former phanariot circles, prompted the search for legalistic and nonradical solutions. This certainly is not an exhaustive analysis of the numerous visions and
subtle differences within the national movements; the important issue is that
considerable groups were, whether prompted by political expedience or not,
essentially advocates of the organic approach.

It was, however, the revolutionary alternative of a complete break with the
Ottoman Empire that in the long run "made history." It is doubtful whether,
in an atmosphere in which the nation-state was imposed as the gold standard
of "civilized" political organization throughout the nineteenth and twentieth
centuries, the imperial alternative could be viable.

Accordingly, the revolutionaries' attitude, although at the time espoused by
those seen as marginal and extremely radical intellectuals, has become in a
period of Balkan nationalism practically the exclusive approach.

If we now address the problem of the *legacy*, there are again two possible
interpretations. One is the approach of the objectivist outsider whose central
observation point is chronologically situated within the Ottoman period
(usually at its end), and who takes a linear view following historical time: from

the past to the present. This approach has produced the bulk of the historical literature. This does not mean that the scholars employing this approach are either apologists for the Ottoman Empire or are identifying with their subject matter (although there are certainly examples of this type). What seems to be common to such writers is their assumption that the Ottoman legacy can be objectively defined and that, even after the disintegration of the Ottoman Empire, there are elements of this legacy that can be objectively analyzed in the different regions comprising the former Ottoman Empire.

The other is the highly subjective insider's approach, which can be defined as the evaluative and retrospective assessment of the Ottoman legacy from the present viewpoint.

Thus are to be distinguished two different approaches: the Ottoman legacy as *continuity* and the Ottoman legacy as *perception*. This is by no means an exhaustive treatment of the subject nor even a synthesis of the many valuable empirical works dealing with aspects of the larger problem. Still, both the vastness of the theme and the lack, to my knowledge, of any elaborate theoretical or generalist framework in the field of Balkan studies,[10] permits only a tentative methodological approach to the tantalizing question of the Ottoman legacy in the Balkans.

The Ottoman Legacy as Continuity

Any legacy can be understood as something received from the past, as historical continuity. This presupposes a distinct point in historical time after which a historical process can be rationalized as legacy. It also means that at different points in time the same unfolding process can be said to have produced different legacies. In this respect, the Ottoman legacy is not simply the bulk of characteristics accumulated from the fourteenth to the twentieth century. The Ottoman period in Balkan history was a continuous and complex process, which ended during the nineteenth and early twentieth centuries. The moment at which this process ended and became a legacy bears, first and foremost, the characteristics of the historical situation of the eighteenth and nineteenth centuries. The Ottoman legacy is treated here as the cluster of historical continuities after the secession of the Balkan states from the Ottoman Empire.

Furthermore, the significant regional differences within the empire, not only between the Rumelian, Anatolian, or North-African possessions but within the Balkans themselves, precludes attempts to speak of a single Ottoman legacy. How can the political legacy of the Ottoman Empire in the Romanian principalities, for example, be compared to that in Serbia or Bulgaria or Albania? How can the economic situation in the areas of large estates

(Bosnia, Thessaly, Albania) be compared to areas of quasi-independent small-proprietors in most of the rest of the Balkans? When assessing the Ottoman legacy one must avoid both uncritical overgeneralizations and the truism that a characteristic of Ottoman rule and, thus, a central aspect of the Ottoman legacy, was great interregional variability.

On a more general level, the central problem in dealing with the Ottoman legacy in the Balkans is the question of continuity or break. The important subquestions to be asked are: 1) Which are the possible "spheres of influence" or continuities of the Ottoman legacy? 2) To what extent is there an Ottoman legacy today? 3) Is there a temporal watershed marking the time after which the workings of the legacy as continuity are transformed into legacy as perception, or do the different spheres follow their own chronology?

Beginning with the *political sphere*, in one of its important aspects, the formation of state boundaries, there were several contending factors: the Ottoman administrative tradition, which had shaped the region for several centuries; the aspirations of the national movements, which were based on two (often incompatible) criteria: historic rights and self-determination; finally, the strategic interests of the European powers, which saw in the Ottoman Empire a pillar in the European balance of power, and the young Balkan states as threatening that balance.

The internal Ottoman provincial divisions had followed closely the boundaries of the numerous Balkan principalities existing in the fourteenth and fifteenth centuries, and the stages of the Ottoman conquest. To this extent they provide a clear, though not immobile, continuity from the pre-Ottoman period (down to preserving the toponymy), and are a *par excellence* example of the Ottoman legacy as the complex product of local Balkan, Islamic, and Turkish components.[11] In some instances, internal provincial frontiers later became state boundaries (like the vassal provinces of Wallachia and Moldavia, or Albania and Montenegro). In other cases (e.g., the Serbian) an administrative unit, the Belgrade pashalik, became the nucleus for the future nation-state.

Still, neither historic rights (based on the territorial zenith of the medieval Balkan states) nor issues of self-determination were, in the final account, instrumental in delineating frontiers. At the very most, these elements shaped the controversial and incompatible Balkan irredentist programs of the nineteenth and twentieth centuries. The size, the shape, the stages of growth, even the very existence of the different Balkan states were almost exclusively regulated by great power considerations following the rules of the balance-of-power game. As Bismarck told the Ottoman delegates at the 1878 Berlin congress: "If you think the Congress has met for Turkey, disabuse yourselves. San-

Stefano would have remained unaltered, if it had not touched certain European interests."[12] The other Balkan delegates were not given even this attention. The Treaty of Berlin (1878) determined the political development of the Balkans in the century to follow.

Bosnia at first glance seems to illustrate the workings of the Ottoman legacy in the political field. It was an important administrative unit (*vilayet*) within the empire formed on the basis of the medieval kingdom of Bosnia. Its complex religious/ethnic structure is comprehensible only within the Ottoman framework, although even in the pre-Ottoman period, "Bosnia was the only country in the Balkans where membership in the community was not dependent on a common religion," where in fact different religions could peacefully coexist (in this particular case the Bosnian church, Catholicism and Orthodoxy), and belonging to the dominant religion was not a necessary criterion for political status.[13] Yet, the Bosnian problem as a political issue should be attributed not to the Ottoman legacy but to great and small power considerations. It was upheld not because of the precarious mixture of its population, but because, first, Austro-Hungary was looking for an outpost in the Balkans, and later, because its quasi-independence prevented the upsetting of a precarious power balance between Serbs and Croats.

To a great extent, the Albanian case presents similar considerations. Albania, without an irredenta against the Ottoman Empire was not a clear-cut secessionist case like all other Balkan nations. The reason for this was the special status of the Albanians in the empire and their comparatively later effort to attain cultural autonomy. By the first decade of the twentieth century, when their movement for emancipation had gained a considerable momentum, they themselves had become the object of expansionist aims on the part of their already independent neighbors. Thus, while chronologically Albania's birth coincided with the passing away of the empire, its struggle for survival and its irredenta developed against the other Balkan nations, particularly Serbia and Greece. It was first and foremost the pressure of Austria-Hungary and Italy that guaranteed Albania's independent existence.

The Ottoman legacy in the political sphere (as far as foreign policy and the question of boundaries are concerned) extends from the beginning of autonomous or independent statehood in the Balkans until World War I, which ended the Ottoman political presence in the Balkans. Thus, the Ottoman political legacy lasted from a few decades to almost a century for the different regions (with the chronological exception of Albania). After 1912–1923 (the common terminus post quem), the anti-Ottoman irredentist programs (though not the national ones in general) were, more or less, attained. Henceforth the Ottoman period in the self-consciousness of the Balkan political elites became only a matter of historical reflection with consequences in relation to the modernization process, and to attitudes toward the minorities.[14] In fact, this latter remained the only continuing real element of the legacy. In all other aspects it had turned into perception.

The creation of autonomous and independent Balkan states was both a break with and a rejection of the political past. This is evident particularly in the attempt to substitute new European institutions for those of the past: the combination of Ottoman/Muslim state institutions and forms of local self-government. This process was more abrupt or more gradual in different regions. In Greece the Bavarian regency immediately launched an elaborate program of educational, judicial, bureaucratic, economic, military, and religious reforms on a society "in which men did not in practice differentiate between spheres of human affairs, such as political, economic, social, or religious."[15] Autonomous Serbia for more than a decade under Miloš Obrenović remained a pashalik, and only in the 1840s, during the reign of Alexander Karageorgiević, began to lay the basis for a Western-type state apparatus.[16] In Bulgaria, despite the efforts for an immediate break, it took nearly two decades to consolidate the new institutions.[17] Because of its peculiar position toward its Ottoman suzerain Romania's Europeanization drive was not immediately related to its political break from the empire but preceded it. In general, as far as political institutions were concerned the Ottoman legacy was insignificant and overcome at differential speed by the separate Balkan states.

Moreover, there was almost no continuity of political elites in the Balkans, at least of elites that had participated in the Ottoman political process. The Balkan Christian locals were integrated in the bureaucracy only at the lowest level, if at all, and then mostly as intermediaries between the self-governing bodies and the Ottoman authorities. This was almost entirely the case for Bulgaria and Serbia, not to speak of Montenegro, which was practically independent.

The unique position of the phanariots, who were simultaneously Ottoman bureaucrats and Greek cultural elites, does not significantly change the picture among the Greeks. Their sphere of influence was primarily in Constantinople (and for a century the Danubian principalities), and despite their commanding cultural authority, their political ideals and goals set them apart from the mainstream Greek national movement. Even if the assertions that the phanariotes were cherishing a Byzantine ideal and nourish the dream of restoring the Byzantine Empire are groundless, their political instincts made them rely heavily on the unifying authority of Orthodoxy and Russian support, thus effectively making of them representatives of the ecumenical imperial tradition which estranged them from the newly espoused ideals of the nation-state. Even while an important segment of the phanariote elite took an important part in the political and literary accomplishments of the newly erected independent Greek state, it did so on an individual basis and not as a social group. In fact, the rhetoric of the break with the phanariote past was as vehement in modern Greece as the one with the Ottoman past.

The only real exception was Romania, which had retained its local aristocracy despite a century of phanariot predominance, but this is to be explained by the special status of the Danubian principalities as vassal territories. which also accounts for the peculiarities in their social and economic structure.

Aside from the patriarchate and the phanariots, the Ottoman Empire did not create or support political elites among the non-Muslim subject population that would have a strong vested interest in its existence, and even these two most loyal institutions were alienated after the 1820s. It was mostly the Muslim Balkan population which saw its allegiences primarily associated with the empire, although the fact that so many Muslims remained in the Balkans suggests that localism was a dominant loyalty more powerful than the imperial attachment. This was the case of the Muslim Bosnians, who constituted the social elite of their region, as well as of some other non-Turkish Muslims. They did not develop a national ideology aspiring for a separate state and their fluid consciousness bore the features of the millet structure.

At first glance, the situation looks similar to the Albanians, who were the only Balkan ethnic group consistently preferring a compromise solution under the shelter of the Porte. Despite the Muslim majority among the Albanians, however, Albanianness proved to be a stronger integrative force. In fact, the Albanians developed a strong ethnic nationalism very much in line with the other Balkan nations (as well as the Turks), and the link with the Ottoman Empire and Turkey should be seen not as the result of the workings of the Ottoman legacy but as a pragmatic move on the part of the Albanian leadership in its search for political allies.

In the *cultural sphere,* the most visible and immediate break occurred in elite culture, a break facilitated by the combination of two extremely important boundaries: the religious and the linguistic. Ottoman culture, i.e., the high culture of the Ottoman Empire, was produced and consumed exclusively by educated Ottoman, Arabic, and Persian-speaking Muslims. This group, concentrated in Istanbul and not so numerous in the Balkans, disappeared entirely from the newly seceded states leaving behind only the presence of Ottoman architectural monuments. The exception in this respect are the Bosnian Slavic-speaking Muslims who, unlike their counterparts in Bulgaria, Greece, or Macedonia, occupied the highest places in the social hierarchy of the region.[18]

On the other hand, there was a lack of local elites integrated in Ottoman culture who saw themselves as representatives of the respective ethnic groups they had come from. In fact, there was a lack of local Christian elites altogether (always with the exception of the Constantinople patriarchate and the phanariots) until the eighteenth and nineteenth centuries. The aristocratic and clerical elites of the medieval Christian Balkan states, who were the potential creators of a local high culture, had for the most part emigrated or perished. After the conquest only a small part of the Balkan Christian aristocracies was integrated into the lower echelons of political power, but ceased thereby being ethnic or religious leaders.

The Ottomans did not create or tolerate local Balkan political or cultural elites and, outside the institution of the Patriarchate and the phanariots, no high Christian elites were integrated in the empire, which was constructed around its Muslimness. Partial exceptions are the Danubian principalities and especially Dubrovnik, the vassal Ottoman territories, whose cultural elites, although not integrated were at least tolerated. One can thus speak of a double break: one, occurring at the time of the conquest; and a second at the time of political independence in the nineteenth century.

This leads to the important question of the channels of intellectual and ideological penetration in the Balkans. Because of the crucial division between Islam and Christianity, ideas in the Christian Balkans came almost exclusively from the *Christian* West and Russia. This is true both for the more traditional clerical and administrative elites as well as for the commercial and educational elites (i.e., the local middle class), who emerged during the eighteenth and the nineteenth centuries.

These latter consumed mostly the ideas of the European Enlightenment and later those of nineteenth-century romanticism and nationalism. The ideological conflict with the more conservative circles was never so sharp as in the Greek case where, by the nineteenth century, the patriarchate and the phanariots, despite their ecumenical claims, were perceived as belonging exclusively to the Greek ethnic sphere. The phanariots were not simply an Ottoman institution; they were also the main link to, and preservers of, the Byzantine continuity. Thus, the passionate break with the phanariot tradition at the outset of independent Greece, the pronounced enmity to everything Byzantine, the attempt to wipe out a millennium of historical development (at least in the dominant discourse of the followers of Koraïs) grew out of a realization of how much of the Byzantine legacy was built into the Ottoman Empire. The desire for a break with the medieval past and for a development along the lines of the European Enlightenment in some cases overrode the purely ethno/religious opposition to the empire.

On the level of popular culture and everyday life, the Ottoman legacy proved more persistent.[19] One can look for it in authentic Ottoman elements (architecture and urban structure, food, music, the institution of the coffeehouse, etc.). One can follow it up through its influence via direct cultural contact (on language, religious syncretism, etc.). Finally, one can trace it in the reactive response and adaptation of indigenous institutions and cultural trends to the Ottoman system.[20]

The zealous efforts at de-Ottomanization succeeded primarily in the material (visible and public) sphere. The most radical changes occurred in the overall appearance of the cities, in architecture, in clothing. All Balkan countries (although with different degrees of intensity, stronger in Bulgaria, weaker in Serbia, for example) resorted to attempts at purifying their language and their toponymy from Turkisms. As a whole, the existence of bi- and multilingualism expired with the passing of the generations having direct knowledge of life in the empire. More important was the socialization of the broad masses of people as citizens of nation-states through such state institutions as schools and the army, which promoted the standardized literary language and were central in the process of national homogenization.[21]

In food and diet, as well as music, the Ottoman legacy was more tenacious. As regards food, there is an interesting observation about Bulgaria that could be probably successfully generalized for the whole of the Balkan area. The greater abundance and diversification of food made dishes previously confined only to the Muslim urban elites increasingly part of the diet of the whole urban population and of large segments of the rural population. Thus, while the haute cuisine of the limited Bulgarian urban elites tended to become more Europeanized in the last decades of the nineteenth century, the general cuisine of Bulgaria (Christian and Muslim alike) became increasingly Ottomanized after the end of the Ottoman rule.[22]

In popular beliefs, customs, attitudes, and values the efforts to de-Ottomanize proved to be much more strenuous. De-Ottomanization meant achieving the coveted ideal of the polar opposite of being Ottoman (or Oriental), namely a steady Europeanization, Westernization, or modernization of society. It was supposed to bring in a new set of relations both in the family and in society as a whole, based on individuality and rationality, an entirely different position for women, a revised role for children and childrearing, a new work ethos.

To take but one of the most exploited themes, the position of women, it had been and continues to be almost exclusively attributed to the influence of Islam. Yet, it is practically impossible to distinguish among the workings of traditional (not necessarily only Balkan) patriarchal peasant morality, the influence of Orthodox Christianity, and the role of Ottoman culture per se (in this case the role of Islam).[23] The difficulty of differentiating between Ottoman and traditional local cultures has led to methodological solutions such as the treatment of "de-Ottomanization," "de-Orientalization," "de-Balkanization," and "de-patriarchalization" as synonyms.[24] Yet, as long as research continues to ignore the axis Balkan–Ottoman, and instead follows exclusively the two bipolar axes traditional Balkan culture–the West, and Ottoman culture–the West,[25] this important aspect of social history will be trivialized into the traditional–modern dichotomy.

There is no doubt that the Balkans represent a cultural region, possibly a subregion of the larger eastern Mediterranean area. This is not simply an ascriptive category; the Balkan peoples themselves, although often reluctantly and with pejorative accents, accede to belonging to it. Whether and to what extent one can attribute its existence to the workings of the Ottoman imperial legacy (or earlier to the Byzantine legacy), the least that can be asserted is that the Ottoman Empire played a crucial role as mediator in the course of several centuries, which permitted broad contacts, mutual influences, and cultural exchange in a large area of the eastern Mediterranean.

In the *economic/social sphere* the empire left a more tangible legacy. There are at least three characteristics common to almost all Balkan societies that can be attributed directly to the Ottoman presence. The first is the lack of a landed nobility. It is not merely the question of having obliterated the old local feudal Christian aristocracies but also of hindering the tendency to form a landowning class that could evolve independently from the strong centralized state. The absolute control of the state over the land, resources, and subjects meant that "private large estates, even when the owner was a member of the ruling elite, could not attain predominance in agricultural production, chiefly because the working force had to be won over from a relatively free peasant class, whereas the produce would be sold at low prices fixed by the mechanisms of a command economy."[26] The existence of a relatively free peasantry (at least free from a system of personal dependence and serfdom) and the consequent predominance of the small peasant holding as the basic unit of production is the second characteristic trait with which all Balkan societies (with the exception of Romania) entered on the road of independence.

The absence of an aristocracy, however, did not guarantee a quick and intensive capitalistic development that, in theory at least, would not have been inhibited by the domination of the aristocracy over the bourgeoisie as in parts of Eastern Europe.[27] Although urban life in the Balkans had an uninterrupted tradition, it never acquired the autonomous role it had in the West, with a strong independent commercial and industrial class. The Balkan city was incorporated in the Ottoman system as a completely constructed feudal category and was entirely subordinated to the state.[28]

The argument that the existence of a relatively free peasantry is an Ottoman legacy and that the Ottoman Empire spared the Balkans the so-called second edition of serfdom is plausible. Less plausible is the argument that this particular result in the long run "proved to be an obstacle to substantial increases in agricultural productivity and rendered more difficult the transition to the capitalistic mode of production."[29] The only Balkan exception, Romania, which did not spare its peasantry the second serfdom, which retained a powerful landowning nobility, and which even experienced a certain degree of urban administrative and political autonomy, equally lingered on in the periphery of European capitalist development. In any case, this whole debate transposes the emphasis from the Ottoman legacy as continuity to the perception of the Ottoman legacy as an agent of backwardness—to be addressed later.

This social legacy of a de facto free peasantry, the lack of an aristocracy, a weak bourgeoisie and the presence of a strong centralized state was doubtlessly important for the political development of the post-independence period. Yet even this strong common legacy produced different results due to factors extraneous to the Ottoman legacy but typical of local developments in the post-Ottoman era. For example, even in the case of the closest social parallel, Bulgaria and Serbia, the different role of the peasants (extremely important in the Bulgarian case, rather docile and dependent in the Serbian) was due to the different time these peasantries became politically active in the late nineteenth century.[30]

To put the question differently: did the central place of the peasants in the Ottoman state, which saw its primary social function in the support of this class to the detriment of other productive classes (particularly the nascent bourgeoisie), remain a living legacy? was the presence of strong state bureaucracies in practically all Balkan independent states an Ottoman legacy? In both cases the correlation is dubious. Despite the central place of the peasantry in the economic and social structure of all Balkan countries nowhere did the new ruling political elites champion peasant interests. Even in the only instance of a genuine advocacy of the peasant cause and a real peasant political experiment, that of Stamboliiski in Bulgaria, there was no intrinsically anti-industrial or antimodernizing policy (despite the strong antiurban overtones).[31] The similarities, as far as they exist, rather than being attributed to the common Ottoman legacy, can be seen as similar responses to challenges presented by agrarian societies being integrated into an urbanized and industrialized Europe. Likewise, the existence of statism, the overwhelming role of state bureaucracies and the grip they exerted over society was certainly not confined in Europe to the counties of the Ottoman *Kulturraum* and should be interpreted in the larger context of European history.

Probably most important in the social domain is the Ottoman legacy in the *demographic sphere*. This was not only a long-term development over several centuries but one which proved difficult to undo, and has immediate repercussions today. It merits, therefore, a survey of the whole Ottoman period, not only the last century.

The demographic history of the Ottoman Empire comprises problems pertaining to the geographic movement of the population (colonization, both voluntary and forced; migrations, economic or political, internal and external); to the demographic processes and characteristics (fertility, mortality, nuptiality, population size and structure, household and family structure, etc.); as well as to other types of population movements (religious shifts, different aspects of social mobility, etc.).[32] As far as long-term demographic processes and characteristics are concerned, such as fertility, mortality, marriage patterns, family and household size and structure, there is no indication that the empire has left a unique imprint which requires us to speak of a specific Ottoman legacy.[33]

The fundamental consequence of the establishment of the Pax Ottomana in the Balkans was the abolition of state and feudal frontiers, which enhanced population movements and the interpenetration of different population groups. Although there are no reliable aggregate figures on population shifts before the nineteenth century, attempts have been made to assess the character and effects of these movements.

One of the interesting problems of Ottoman demographic history is the question of Turkish, or rather Turkic, colonization. As with the great majority of similar problems, its interpretation (and, in fact, the impetus for this type of research) has been to serve other issues, especially to give an explanation for the Ottoman conquest, the long-term Ottoman presence and the sizeable Muslim population in the Balkans. Turkish historiography, in particular, postulated that, among the variety of factors accounting for the Ottoman success, the size of the Turkish masses arriving from Anatolia was decisive. Thus, the history of the Ottoman Empire, in this view, could be re-interpreted as the history of migrations of great masses of people who had a numerical superiority over the indigenous population. In this interpretation the conscious and planned colonization of the Balkans on the part of the Sultan's government held a central place.[34]

In contrast, Balkan historiography has made considerable efforts to refute, or rather relativize, the essential significance of Ottoman colonization in explaining both the success of the Ottoman conquest, and the significant size of the Muslim population by the last centuries of Ottoman rule. This attempt has centered on the process of conversions to Islam as chiefly responsible for the growth of the Muslim population in the Balkans.[35]

The careful review of existing sources shows that between the fourteenth and sixteenth, but especially during the fifteenth century there were population transfers from Anatolia to the Balkans, populations shifts within the peninsula, and also some transfers from the Balkans to Anatolia. These comprised both nomads, as well as settled groups of peasants and urban dwellers. The rationale behind these transfers was based on both strategic (political and military) and economic considerations. The practice of *sürgün* (deportations or population transfers) was not an Ottoman invention. It had been utilized with the same rationale by Romans, Persians, and Byzantines. The Ottomans, as successors to the Byzantine Empire, inherited this practice and incorporated it as a significant element in the policy of the central government.[36]

It is extremely difficult to give a numerical value to the adjectives used by different historians in describing the deportations from one place to another: "massive," "huge," "significant," "large-scale." One of the few cases where one can speculate within a framework of realistic figures is the repopulation of Istanbul with a skilled work force by Mehmed II after the conquest of 1453.[37] Alongside this great political move, which aimed at creating a flourishing economic and administrative center, most of the Muslim colonization in the Balkans shows a concentration in strategic locations along military roads and around fortified places.

In the eastern part of the Balkan peninsula Muslim colonization formed an almost uninterrupted line that reached the Danube and, thus, achieved contact with the Tatar masses on the northern Black Sea coast. There were considerable numbers of Muslim settlers along two of the main river routes in the Balkans that had exceptional strategic importance: the Maritsa valley, and the Vardar valley. The nomad population from Anatolia was transferred primarily to Eastern Thrace as *müsellem* (a special tax-exempt settled category serving in the military) or *yürük* (the category of continuing Turkoman nomads).[38] There is little doubt that the Muslim colonization as well as the mass conversions in this period (primarily those in the Western Balkans, especially Bosnia and Albania) concentrated on areas strategically vulnerable to the potential attacks of the anti-Ottoman coalitions.

The sixteenth century did not witness significant colonization and, in fact, by the end of the century population moves from Anatolia to the Balkans had stopped. At the same time, even during the period of the highest concentration of Turkish settlers in the Balkans, which also coincided with the temporary withdrawal of the local population to less accessible or outlying regions, the ratio between Muslims and non-Muslims showed the significant numerical preponderance of the non-Muslims in practically all provinces.[39]

Yet, the first reliable statistical data from the nineteenth century demonstrated considerable changes in the ratio between Muslims and non-Muslims although non-Muslim predominance was preserved. This had occurred even though the flow of colonizers had stopped, and significant losses both in the wars of the seventeenth and eighteenth centuries and from the plague epidemics had mostly affected the Muslim population. Growth of the Muslim population in these circumstances can only be credibly explained by conversions to Islam. Most numerous during the seventeenth century, the vast majority of the Balkan conversions were individual. The nonenforced conversions grew out of efforts to improve social or economic status. It is moreover the individual character of these conversions that explains why integration into the new religious (and social) milieu was accompanied with subsequent loss of the native tongue. The exceptions are those cases where conversions occurred en masse in larger or smaller groups, irrespective of whether they were voluntary or enforced: Bosnia, Albania, the Rhodopes (the Pomaks), Macedonia (the Torbesh), etc.

The outcome of the debate between the two contending interpretations need not necessarily serve either one of the political causes they can be used to legitimize. The issue in both cases is the attempt to prove the "blood-kinship" of the contested groups to the larger nations in the area. The fact that the Islamization thesis can be supported far better than the colonization one by no means gives support to any of the anti-Muslim or anti-Turkish manifestations, which at one time or other have been pursued in different parts of the Balkans. This is especially true for the renaming campaign in Bulgaria in the 1980s, which sought to return the "stray converts" to the main body of the nation completely disregarding aspects like self-perception and self-consciousness. Conversely, even if the colonization thesis had been the only explanation for Muslim presence in the Balkans, thus laying claim to a direct ethnic connection, it still should not be a justification for an, at times, overactive, even aggressive, policy on the part of different political circles in Turkey.

Although the nineteenth century witnessed the beginnings of a modern census system, the official statistics do not give a completely dependable picture of the size and character of migrations. Many of the seasonal workers, nomads, and immigrants were not registered. With a few exceptions (for example, the Danube vilayet in the 1860s) the number of migrations (both external and internal) began to be reflected in the censuses only at the end of the century.[40] For the most part, the substantial shifts in population during the nineteenth century were due to political events: the wars between the Ottomans and Russia, which resulted in outmigrations (like the Bulgarian emigration to the Danubian principalities and Russia), or immigrations (the most numerous of which was the settlement of huge masses of Tatars from the Crimea and of Circassians both in the Balkans and in Anatolia).[41]

The most substantial changes, however, were the result of the secession of the Balkan nation-states from the Ottoman Empire. It has been estimated that over one million Muslims left the Balkan states during the last three decades of the nineteenth century and relocated in Constantinople, the remaining European possessions of the Porte and Anatolia. In the same period, as a result of the Eastern crisis of 1875–1878, a million Christian inhabitants exchanged their residence with the outgoing Muslims. Even more drastic were the migrations in the long war decade, 1912–1922 (the two Balkan wars, World War I, and the Greek-Turkish war). Close to two and a half million people were affected by dislocations (among them close to a million and a half Greeks from Asia Minor, around half a million Muslims who left the Balkans for Turkey, a quarter million Bulgarian refugees, etc.).[42]

Despite these drastic population shifts, not a single Balkan country achieved the cherished ideal characteristics of the nineteenth and twentieth century European nation-state: ethnic and religious homogeneity. Greece and Albania came closest to monoethnic states but they, too, had to handle minority problems: Greece that of its so-called Slavic-speaking and its multiethnic Muslim minorities; Albania its tiny Greek minority. Bulgaria was left with over 13 percent of different ethnic and religious minorities (Turks, Pomaks, Gypsies, Tatars, Armenians, Jews, Russians, etc.). Yugoslavia had close to 15 percent of national minorities (Germans, Magyars, Albanians, Romanians, Turks, etc.) but its national majority of 85 percent itself was composed of three recognized constituents (Slovenes, Croats, and Serbs, who at that time included also the separately unrecognized population of Macedonia as well as the Serbo-Croatian-speaking Bosnian Moslems). Romania had the largest minority of about 27 percent (Magyars, Germans, Jews, Ukrainians, Russians, Bulgarians, Turks, Tatars, Gypsies, etc.). Turkey itself, which emerged from the Ottoman Empire reduced and revolving around an ethnic nucleus after the expulsion of the Greeks and the Armenian massacres, had to deal with substantial minorities, to mention but the largest, the Kurds.[43]

Most complex was the situation in the so-called contact zones: Macedonia, Bosnia, Dobrudzha, Kosovo, Vojvodina, Transylvania, Constantinople itself. Just the enumeration of these zones shows that some of them were contact zones within the Austro-Hungarian Empire. This suggests that the question of the Ottoman legacy in the demographic sphere has to be approached on a higher level of generalization: the problem of imperial legacies in a nation-state context. If compared to the other multi- or supranational imperial European legacies of the time, the Austrian and the Russian, the Ottoman legacy displays some fundamental differences.

Apart from the obvious fact of being a Muslim empire, the crucial distinction was that, at a time of burgeoning nationalist ideas, the dominant groups in the Austrian and the Russian empires were composed of the ethnic elements with the highest degree of ethnic/national consciousness, whereas in the Ottoman Empire the case was the reverse. The Turks, from a Balkan (but not from a Middle Eastern) perspective, were the last group in the empire to develop their own Turkish nationalism. When this began in the last decades of the nineteenth century, the greater part of the Balkans was already outside the Ottoman sphere and was not directly affected by it, except for Macedonia and Albania at the time of the Young Turk revolution. Yet, the Ottoman Empire shared with its two imperial counterparts other fundamental similarities created by the incompatibility between the imperial system and the nation-state criteria of self-determination as well as ethnic and religious homogeneity.

All Balkan countries (Turkey as well) have resorted to similar solutions in trying to solve their minority problems in the new context: emigration and assimilation. The culmination of the first solution were the major population shifts following World War I but there were also substantial population waves in the interwar period and after World War II, both interstate and internal ones: the Greek emigration from Istanbul in the 1950s, the German and Jewish emigrations from Ceausescu's Romania, the Turkish emigrations from Bulgaria in the 1950s and again in the 1980s, etc. As for the second option, assimilation, one could point to several relatively successful outcomes: the integration and assimilation of the so-called Slavophones and other non-Greek minorities in Northern Greece; the similar fate of the remaining Greek population on the Bulgarian Black Sea coast, etc. Still, one can easily indicate many more failures. The unresolved minority issues include the existing and potential crisis points in the Balkans: Bosnia, Macedonia, Kosovo, Transylvania, Thrace, Cyprus, etc.

Insofar as the complex ethnic and religious diversity is a continuity from the Ottoman period, the apparent conclusion would be that in the demographic sphere the Ottoman legacy (both in its specifics and as an imperial legacy, in general) is persistent. Yet, the issue becomes more complex when taking into account the question of different and competing ways of shaping group consciousness in general, and ethnic and national consciousness in particular; it becomes even more complicated when exploring the problem of whether, when, and how the Ottoman legacy as historical continuity in this sphere turns into the perception of the Ottoman legacy; and it becomes downright confusing when one tries to draw the delicate line between the workings of the Ottoman legacy and the influence of Turkish nationalism.

Nationalism in the Balkans in the nineteenth century had been constructed primarily around languistic and religious identities. Language was perceived by practically all national and cultural leaders as the mightiest agent of unification. Nowhere has this been more evident than in the Albanian case, where it comparatively easily overcame religious divisions between Muslims, Orthodox, and Catholics. The efforts of the new states centered on the creation of secularized, centralized, and uniform educational systems as one of the most powerful agents of nationalism, alongside the army and other institutions. Yet this very emphasis on the unifying potential of language stressed at the same time its exclusiveness and the rigidity of the ethnic boundaries it delineated. This precluded the integration (except in the cases of assimilation) of different linguistic groups into a single nation: Albanians in Serbia, Turks in Bulgaria and Greece, Greeks in Albania, Magyars in Romania, Kurds in Turkey, etc.

Moreover, not only did groups of different linguistic background from the dominant ethnic group in the nation-state prove impossible to integrate; so also did groups of identical ethnic background and speakers of the same language, like the Pomaks in Bulgaria, the Slavic Bosnian Muslims, the Torbeshi in Macedonia, etc. Although language had become the nucleus of different ethnic and national identities among the Balkan Christians (Orthodox for the most part), it could not raze the fundamental boundary between Muslims and Christians established during the centuries of Ottoman rule. The reason for this was not, as the great bulk of Balkan and foreign historiography maintains, that Orthodoxy played a major and crucial role in nation-building.[44] In fact, "religion came last in the struggle to forge new national identities" and in some cases "did not become a functional element in national definition until the nation-states had nationalized their churches."[45] It never could be a sufficient component of national self-identity, and even in the national struggles, its primary contribution was to strengthen the opposition to the Muslim rulers. Again, the exception is the Albanian case, possibly because nationalist ideas developed simultaneously among its different religious components of which the Muslims were the majority, and because the perceived danger from without came from Christian quarters (Greeks and Serbs) rather than from the Muslim center. Within the Orthodox ecumene, the process of nation-building demonstrated "the essential incompatibility between the imagined community of religion and the imagined community of the nation."[46]

This does not mean that the religious boundary between Christianity and Islam was the only divider. Clearly, the different Christian denominations, and particularly the opposition between Orthodoxy and Catholicism, presented additional frontiers of tension. Yet, these frontiers did not prove unsurmountable. This is especially true of the coexistance and cooperation between the Romanian Uniate and Orthodox churches where Romanianness became the dominant link. Despite the anti-Catholic prejudice in Bulgaria, the small Bulgarian Catholic community (as well as the even smaller group of Bulgarian Protestants) were considered and perceived themselves an organic part of the Bulgarian nation. The unbridgeable division between Catholic Croats and

Orthodox Serbs can be explained not by irreconcilable religious differencies but by different historical traditions within which the two communities had developed, the Croats essentially outside the Ottoman sphere. During the nineteenth century the notion of separateness, although not irreversible, had become internalized by significant groups of Croats and Serbs who were cherishing separate state-building ideals, despite the substantial appeal and support for the Yugoslav idea.

Ironically, Balkan nationalism, which irrevocably destroyed the imagined community of Orthodox Christianity, managed to preserve a frozen, unchangeable and stultifyingly uniform image of the Muslim community, and consistently dealt with it in *millet* terms. In other words, the Christian populations of the Balkans began speaking among themselves the language of nationalism. whereas their attitudes toward the Muslims remained in the realm of the undifferentiated religious communities discourse. A manifestation of this Christian attitude was the continuous and indiscriminate use of the name "Turk" to refer to Muslims in general, a practice still alive in many parts of the Balkans.[47]

On the other hand, it could be maintained that the Balkan Muslims, because they could not adapt to the national mode and were practically excluded from the process of nation formation in the Balkans, retained a fluid consciousness that, for a longer time, displayed millet mentality characteristics, and thus the bearing of the Ottoman legacy. This does not mean that Islam became an alternative form of national consciousness. A "Muslim nation" emerged, at least theoretically, only in the case of the highly secularized Bosnian Muslims, under Tito's specific administrative arrangement. The type of political nationalism which they seem (at least officially) to espouse is distinctly different from the organic nationalism of other groups in the region. The Muslims, marginalized in the face of a sphere that excluded them, were induced to view the Muslim sphere as an acceptable alternative.[48]

Yet, it would be incorrect to describe this Muslim sphere as part of the Ottoman legacy. The Ottoman legacy was possibly alive in the consciousness of a generation after World War I, but the immediate memories of a living Ottoman Empire were more or less extinguished by the eve of World War II.

With the creation of the Turkish republic, however, the Ottoman legacy vanished increasingly into the realm of perception. Thereafter one should speak of the influence of Turkish nationalism on Balkan Muslims. Still, the conflation of Ottoman with Turkish, stemming from the undifferentiated Christain perceptions of the Muslim sphere, makes this distinction difficult. Because of the predominant view of a complete break with an alien culture and polity, the Balkan countries willingly relinquished any claim to the Ottoman past, and saw Turkey as its sole heir. Therefore, when dealing with

Turkish nationalism they often ascribe to it imperial, Ottoman ambitions. At the same time, despite the rejection of the Ottoman imperial past, the Turks still view themselves as the genuine successors to the Ottoman legacy. The present active Balkan policy of Turkey, which is articulating its geopolitical interests in the form of protection of the Muslims, certainly does not help to refute these perceptions.

The influence of Turkey itself, not passive but also consciously promoted, is complex. It affects primarily the Turkish-speaking population of the Balkans, living mostly in Bulgaria and in lesser numbers in Greece, Romania, and the former Yugoslavia. This influence also affected part of the Slavic-speaking Muslims (particularly the Pomaks in Bulgaria), as well as part of the Gypsies, many of whom felt that they could be more easily integrated into an ethnically and linguistically alien but religiously familiar dominant group. The complicated mechanism of this attraction deserves study. [49] What marks the transformation from Ottoman legacy to Turkish influence is that the new twentieth-century emigration from the Balkans does not enter and remain in Turkey simply as Muslims, but becomes assimilated as Turks. At the same time, the influence of Turkey is not to be reduced simply to an emigration appeal. It enters, as a potential ally or opponent, in the complex game of Balkan international relations. To see in this elements of nostalgia, Muslim solidarity, and the appeal of the Ottomam legacy is, to say the least, naive.

To summarize, the Ottoman legacy as continuity displayed different degrees of perseverance. In practically all spheres, except the demographic and that of popular culture, the break came almost immediately after political independence and was completed by the end of World War I; thereafter it was relegated to the realm of perception. In the demographic sphere, however, the Ottoman legacy continued for some time and became intertwined with the influence of the Turkish nation-state.

The Ottoman Legacy as Perception

Any tradition is a *process* of interaction between an ever-evolving and accumulating past, and ever-evolving and accumulating perceptions of generations of people who are redefining their evaluations of the past. Whether in historiographical or literary works, it is a question not of reconstructing, but of constructing the past, with more or less pronounced allegorical motifs. This important development is at the center of securing present social arrangements, and above all legitimizing the state and searching for identity at all times, the present included. It cannot, therefore, be dismissed on grounds that it is the distortion or falsification of history. A characteristic of tradition is that it is being constantly invented and reinvented.[50]

The perception of the Ottoman legacy, in the above-defined sense, has been and is being shaped by generations of historians, poets, writers, journalists and other intellectuals, as well as politicians. What we are dealing with is, on the one hand, the evolving perception of the Ottoman past within a specific social group and, on the other hand, the transmission and dissemination of this perception to broader strata of the population. The first can be reconstructed from the output of historiographical works, textbooks, belles lettres, journalistic pieces, and art. It represents the dominant views of the intellectual and political elites of the moment. The second problem is more difficult to analyze as there are no systematic studies of how deep and successful the penetration of these hegemonic views has been. Even more elusive is the important question of possible counter- or alternative perceptions coming from different ethnic, social, or age groups within the several nation-states. That there have been no systematic studies whatsoever indicates the strength of the hegemonic discourse.

Probably the most striking feature of the dominant discourses in the different Balkan countries is the remarkable similarity between them (although with different degrees of intensity) and the amazing continuity over time. Briefly summarized, the argument runs as follows:

On the eve of the Ottoman conquest the medieval societies of the Balkans had reached a high degree of sophistication that made them commensurate with, if not ahead of, developments in Western Europe. Despite the political fragmentation of the peninsula, a characteristic, among others, typical for the latest and most developed stages of European feudal medieval societies, there were signs of developments in the direction of the consolidation of medieval nations (perceived as proto-nations),[51] of humanism and national cultures. The arrival of the Ottomans was thus a calamity of unparalleled consequences because it disrupted the natural development of the southeast European societies as a substantial and creative part of European humanism and the Renaissance. Ottoman rule left the Balkans untouched by the great ideas and transformations of the Renaissance and the Reformation. It further brought a deep cultural regression and even barbarization and social leveling. The conquerors put an end to the Balkan political and intellectual elites, either by physically annihilating part of the aristocracy and the clergy (in practically all Balkan historiographies the beloved term is the nineteenth-century concept "intelligentsia"), or by forcing them to emigrate or, finally, by integrating them into their political structure thereby denationalizing them. The only institutions that kept the religion and ethnic consciousness alive were the Orthodox church and the self-governing bodies, chief among them the village commune.

The only redeeming feature in the first centuries of Ottoman rule was the possible relaxation of the economic plight of the peasantry with the introduction of a uniform and regular tax burden of the centralized state. But, according to a widespread assertion, although difficult to substantiate, the pressure of foreign rulers is something drastically different from the exploitation by one's own elites. The Ottomans have been unanimously described as bearers of an *essentially* different and alien civilization characterized by a fanatic and militant religion, which introduced different economic and societal practices and brought about the pastoralization and agrarianization of the Balkans. Emphasis has been laid on the excesses of violence, crimes, and cruelty that reached unbearable proportions at the time of Ottoman decline, especially during the eighteenth century, and triggered the struggle for national emancipation.

This picture of "the saddest and darkest period"[52] in Balkan history makes the five centuries of Ottoman rule the historiographical counterpart of the Western European "Dark Ages" before the advent of historical revisionism. Modern Balkan historiographies were shaped in the century of the national idea and under the strong influence of the then dominant trends of romanticism and positivism. These historiographies acquired their institutional standing and became one of the most important pillars in the different independent nation-states. The predominantly ethical-didactic and religious orientation of historical writing until the eighteenth century was translated into an equally single-minded mission: to shape national consciousness and legitimize the nation-state. That Balkan historiographies developed primarily as national historiographies accounts for their relative parochialism with scant knowledge of the history of their neighbors in the same period. It is, moreover, not a simple ignorance of the history of the neighboring nations but a conscious effort to belittle, to ignore, to distort, to deride, and even to negate.

In this effort the mutual enmity of Balkan historiographies, which developed into a passionate polemical tradition against each other, very often overshadowed even the hostility against the Ottoman Empire and Turkey. At the same time, for all the stereotypes about virulent Balkan nationalism, it has to be recognized that most Balkan nationalisms are, in fact, essentially defensive, and their shrillness is the direct result of problems of unconsolidated nation-states and social identities in crisis. This nervousness about identity accounts for the unique preoccupation with ethnogenesis in the Balkans. Within the persisting continuum of the nation-state and with different degrees of intensity (the shrill nationalism of many works of the interwar decade having remained, luckily, unsurpassed), this is the predominant mode of historical writing in the Balkans.

One of the few exceptions from this hegemonic national(ist) historiography has been the work of Marxist and neo-Marxist scholars, i.e., scholars using the Marxist *approach,* not the Marxist *lingo* in which a host of traditional works in the former communist countries were written. These authors have made considerable contributions, especially in the field of economic history, social structures, class analysis, etc. Yet, curiously enough, although very differently formulated from the overwhelming concerns of the romantic nationalist agenda, the Marxist approach achieved a meeting point and common ground with the national in treating the Ottoman Empire as the quintessential *inhibitor.* In the nationalist case it was seen as inhibiting the natural evolution of the organic nation. In the Marxist case the Ottoman Empire and its legacy had hindered "progress." The verdict over the empire was articulated in terms of hindrances to modernization, chiefly but not exclusively in the economic sphere: regionalism, parochialism, familialism and clan orientation, indifference to the European technology, activities, and values that produced capitalism, the subordination of women, corruption, conformism, conservatism, religious obscurantism, fatalism, etc.[53]

One specific social phenomenon served to bridge the two discourses. Throughout the eighteenth and nineteenth centuries, the social transformations accompanying the economic changes resulting from the gradual integration of the Ottoman Empire into the European economy did not significantly affect the activities of the Ottoman ruling class. Most of its aspirations were channeled toward higher military and administrative positions, which led to its almost complete bureaucratization.

Conversely, the non-Muslim population of the Balkans produced an important stratum of merchants and entrepreneurs who not only controlled "the wholesale export trade but also the wholesale trade of the outlying markets of the empire earmarked for the largest consumer of goods, the capital Istanbul."[54] The growth of a home market created conditions favorable to the setting up of the first scattered and centralized manufactures, again initiated almost exclusively among the non-Muslim subjects of the empire (primarily Greeks but by the mid-nineteenth century also considerable numbers of Bulgarians).

That the Ottoman system remained rigid and unsupportive of these new social groups created a profound tension which had a cumulative effect on the rising national feelings. "The sharpening of the contrast between the economic role and the political disenfranchisement of the newly emerging national bourgeoisies was reflected in the increasing unwillingness to endure any national oppression."[55] Although recent research exonerates the Ottoman legacy from exclusive blame for Balkan backwardness, the older perception remains intact not only in historiography but also in literature. One can mention in this respect the works of Ivo Andrić, Dimitûr Talev, Dobrica Čosić, and Nikos Kazantzakis.

The important questions are why this perception persists and how long it will last. It has been argued that tradition is "an actively shaping force" and, at the same time, a "deliberately selective and connecting process which offers an historical and cultural ratification of a contemporary order."[56] The contemporary order, despite claims to the opposite, has us still firmly rooted in the age of the nation-states with nationalism as the central ideology and dominant discourse. Moreover, the last decade of the twentieth century is witnessing a profound economic and social transformation, especially acute in Eastern Europe, and the Balkans are no exception. The concomitant multiple crises of legitimacy and identity of the political systems, of the intellectual elites, of ethnic groups, of personal loyalties, etc. insures, that the vision of a "new post-nationalist theoretical culture" will long remain utopian. Meanwhile, for all its perniciousness, nationalism "provides men deprived of their niche in the old stable local structures with an identity in a high culture, one that confers dignity."[57]

NOTES

I wish to thank Engin Akarlı of Washington University at St. Louis who offered valuable critical comments.

1. John B. S. Morrit of Rokeby, *A Grand Tour: Letters and Journeys 1794–96*, ed. G. E. Marindin (London: Century, 1985), p. 65.
2. Karl Kaser, *Südosteuropäische Geschichte und Geschichtswissenschaft* (Wien, Köln: Böhlau Verlag, 1990), pp. 91–103.
3. For comprehensive surveys on the perception of the Ottoman Empire in Balkan historiographies, see Basilike Papoulia, "Die Osmanenzeit in der griechischen Geschichtsforschung seit der Unabhängigkeit," *Die Staaten Südosteuropas und die Osmanen*, Hrsg. Hans Georg Majer (Munich: Selbstverlag der Südosteuropa-Gesellschaft, 1989), pp. 113–26; Maria Todorova, "Die Osmanenzeit in der bulgarischen Geschichtsforschung seit der Unabhängigkeit," *Die Staaten Südosteuropas*, pp. 127–62; Selami Pulaha, "Wissenschaftliche Forschungen über die osmanische Periode des Mittelalters in Albanien (15. Jahrhundert bis Anfang des 19. Jahrhunderts), *Die Staaten Südosteuropas*, pp. 163–78; Olga Zirojević, "Die Bewahrung und Erforschung der osmanischen Hinterlassenschaft in Jugoslawien: Archive und Forschungseinrichtungen," *Die Staaten Südosteuropas*, pp. 187–204; Gunnar Hering, "Die Osmanenzeit im Selbstverständnis der Völker Südosteuropas," *Die Staaten Südosteuropas*, pp. 361–71.
4. How arbitrary and mechanistic these divisions are can be seen from the utilization of "Oriental." Oriental languages in the curricula of the Balkan universities are, of course, Turkish, Arabic, and Persian, besides the recently appearing languages of the Far East. Accordingly, following the linguistic criterion, Oriental are the influences transmitted by the Ottoman polity (Ottoman, and less so Arabic and Persian). The pre-Ottoman Byzantine influence, although emanating from the same geographical area, and despite the fact that it left its distinctive imprint on Ottoman society and institutions, is not considered Oriental. Nor are the pre-Byzantine Turkic and Iranian influences considered Oriental. But these are inconsistencies not necessarily attributable only to the Balkans. Throughout the present century Slavic languages, for example, continued to be taught in Paris as part of the curricula of L'Institut des Langues Orientales, reflecting geopolitical divisions as much as institutional traditions.
5. For a recent example of this premise, see the following statement in an otherwise excellent study

on the spread of Islam in the Balkans: "The Ottoman conquerors swept over the lands of the formerly independent principalities and kingdoms, bringing with them an alien militant ideology. For a lengthy period of time the subjected peoples were detached from the natural milieu of their development—the Christian European world, and existed within the boundaries of the Ottoman empire, where a nation of an alien faith ruled." Antonina Zhelyazkova, *Razprostranenie na islyama v zapadnobûlgarskite zemi pod osmanska vlast, XV-XVIII vek* (Sofia: Bulgarian Academy of Sciences, 1990), p. 255.

6. See Semih Tezcan, "Kontinuität und Diskontinuität der Sprachentwicklung in der Türkei," *Die Staaten Südosteuropas*, pp. 215–22.

7. Nicolae Iorga, *Byzance après Byzance: continuation de l' "Histoire de la vie byzantine"* (Bucharest: A l'institut d'etudes byzantine, 1935). Elements of his vision can still be encountered in many, but especially in Greek, historical works. I am grateful to Paschalis Kitromilides for pointing out the utility of Iorga's notion, independent from the original intention of its author. I also wish to thank him for urging me to rethink and refine some of my pronouncements on the phanariotes; the responsibility for the final formulation falls, obviously, on me.

8. Franz Babinger, *Die Geschichtsschreiber der Osmanen und ihre Werke* (Leipzig: Harrassowitz, 1927).

9. Sphrantzes (Phrantzes), Khalkokondyles (Chalkcocondyles), Doukas (Ducas) and Kritoboulos (Critobulos, Kritovoulos) were the last great Byzantine historians of the fifteenth century who described the Ottoman conquest, and at the same time kept closely to the pattern of the ancient models, especially Herodotus and Thucydides. While the first three deplored the Ottoman advance and described it as a singular tragedy, Kritoboulos accepted it with a calm determinism. He not only served under Sultan Mehmed II but his Greek "History of Mehmed the Conqueror" was dedicated to him; see Kritovoulos, *History of Mehmed the Conqueror*, tr. Charles T. Riggs (Princeton: Princeton University Press, 1954).

10. There have been several general treatments of the problem of the Ottoman legacy in the Balkans, some of high quality and with significant insights, but with the exception of the important contribution of Gunnar Hering, "Die Osmanenzeit im Selbstverständnis der Völker Südosteuropas," *Die Staaten Südosteuropas*, pp. 355–80, none has attempted a comprehensive methodological approach. See the concluding chapter of Peter Sugar, *Southeastern Europe Under Ottoman Rule, 1354–1804* (Seattle: University of Washington Press, 1977); the comparative chapter 3 "Balkan People Under Ottoman and Habsburg Rule: A Comparison," in Barbara Jelavich, *History of the Balkans*, vol 1: *Eighteenth and Nineteenth Centuries* (Cambridge: New York: Cambridge University Press, 1983); Wayne S. Vuchinich, "Some Aspects of the Ottoman Legacy," *The Balkans in Transition: Essays on the Development of Balkan Life and Politics Since the Eighteenth Century*, ed. Charles and Barbara Jelavich (Berkeley/Los Angeles: University of California Press, 1963).

11. See H. J. Kornrumpf, "Zur territorial Verwaltungsgliederung des Osmanischen Reiches, ihrem Entstehen und ihrem Einfluss auf die Nachfolgestaaten," *Ethnogenese und Staatsbildung in Südosteuropa*, Hrsg. K. D. Grothusen (Göttingen, 1974), pp. 52–61.

12. Cited in R. W. Seton-Watson, *Disraeli, Gladstone, and the Eastern Question* (London, 1935; New York: Barnes and Noble, 1963), p. 450.

13. John V. A. Fine, Jr., *The Late Medieval Balkans: A Critical Survey from the Late Twelfth Century to the Ottoman Conquest* (Ann Arbor: University of Michigan Press, 1987), p. 484.

14. Gunnar Hering, "Die Osmanenzeit," *Die Staaten Südosteuropas* p. 361.

15. John Petropulos, *Politics and Statecraft in the Kingdom of Greece, 1833–1843* (Princeton: Princeton University Press, 1968), p. 501.

16. M. B. Petrovich, *A History of Modern Serbia, 1804–1918* (New York: Jovanovich, 1976).

17. Bernard Lory, *Le sort de l'heritage ottoman en Bulgarie: L'exemple des villes bulgares, 1978–1900* (Istanbul: Isis, 1985), pp. 62–78.

18. Darko Tanasković, "Les thèmes et les traditions Ottomans dans la littérature Bosniaque," *Die Staaten Südosteuropas*, pp. 299–307.

19. For a comprehensive attempt at a theoretical approach to this problem, see Klaus Roth, "Osmanische Spuren in der Alltagskultur Südosteuropas," *Die Staaten Südosteuropas*, pp. 319–32. Although dealing only with Bulgaria one has to mention here the excellent study of Bernard Lory, *Le sort de l'heritage ottoman en Bulgarie.*

20. For this classification, see Klaus Roth, "Osmanische Spuren in der Alltagskultur Südosteuropas," *Die Staaten Südosteuropas*, pp. 321–22.

21. Maria Todorova, "Language as Cultural Unifier in a Multilingual Setting: the Bulgarian Case During the Nineteenth Century," *Eastern European Politics and Societies* 4:3 (1990).

22. Bernard Lory, *Le sort de l'heritage ottoman en Bulgarie*, p. 138.

23. Lory, *Le sort de l'heritage ottoman*, pp. 166–67.

24. Klaus Roth, "Osmanische Spuren in der Alltagskultur Südosteuropas," *Die Staaten Südosteuropas*, p. 323.

25. Lory, *Le sort de l'heritage ottoman*, pp. 194–96.

26. Fikret Adanır, "Tradition and Rural Change in Southeastern Europe During Ottoman Rule," *The Origins of Backwardness in Eastern Europe: Economics and Politics from the Middle Ages Until the Early Twentieth Century*, ed. Daniel Chirot (Berkeley/Los Angeles: University of California Press, 1989), p. 155.

27. Jacek Kochanowicz, "The Polish Economy and the Evolution of Dependency," *The Origins of Backwardness in Eastern Europe*, p. 119.

28. Nikolay Todorov, *The Balkan City, 1400–1900* (Seattle: University of Washington Press, 1983).

29. Adanır, "Tradition and Rural Change," p. 156.

30. Gale Stokes, "The Social Origins of East European Politics," *The Origins of Backwardness in Eastern Europe*, p. 238.

31. John D. Bell, *Peasants in Power: Alexander Stamboliski and the Bulgarian Agrarian National Union, 1899–1923* (Princeton: Princeton University Press, 1977).

32. M. Todorova, N. Todorov, "Problemi i zadachi na istoricheskata demografiya na Osmanskata imperiya," *Balkanistika* 2 (1987): 35.

33. This argument has been developed at some length in Maria Todorova, *Balkan Family History and the European Pattern: Demographic Developments in Ottoman Bulgaria* (Washington, D.C.: American University Press, 1993).

34. Ömer Lûtfi Barkan, "Osmanlı imparatorluğunda bir iskân ve kolonizasyon metodu olarak sürgünler," Istanbul Üniversitesi *Iktisat Fakültesi Mecmuası* 11, 13, 16 (1949–1951); "Rumeli'nin iskâni için yapılan sürgünler," Istanbul Üniversitesi *Iktisat Fakültesi Mecmuası* 13 (1950).

35. See, among others, Elena Grozdanova, *Bûlgarskata narodnost prez XVII vek. Demografsko izsledvane* (Sofia, 1989); Antonina Zhelyazkova, *Razprostranenie na islyama v zapadnobulgarskite zemi pod osmanska vlast, 15–18 vek* (Sofia: Bulgarian Academy of Sciences, 1990); Sami Pulaha, *Aspects de démographie historique des contrées albanais pendant les XVe-XVIe siècles* (Tirana, 1984); M. Sokoloski, "Islamizatsija u Makedonija u XV i XVI veku," *Istorijski Casopis* 22 (1975). During the campaign against the ethnic Turks in Bulgaria in the 1980s the Bulgarians produced an immense amount of propaganda literature amidst which there are also some valuable contributions, particularly source publications.

36. Speros Vryonis, *The Decline of Medieval Hellenism in Asia Minor and the Process of Islamization from the Eleventh Through the Fifteenth Centuries* (Berkeley/Los Angeles: University of California Press, 1971); Peter Charanis, *Studies on the Demography of the Byzantine Empire* (London: Variorum reprints, 1972).

37. Marie Mathilde Alexandresku-Derska Bulgaru, "La politique démographique des sultans à Istanbul (1453–1496)," *Revue des études sud-est européennes* 28, nos. 1–4 (1990): 45–56.

38. M. Tayyib Gökbilgin, *Rumeli'de Yürükler, Tatarlar ve Evlâdi Fatihan* (Istanbul, 1957); Strashimir

Dimitrov, "Za yurushkata organizatsiya i rolyata ï v etnoasimilatsionnite protsesi," *Vekove* (1982), pp. 1–2; Antonijević D., "Prilog proučavanju stočarskih migracija na Balkanu," *Balcanica* (1976).

39. Nikolay Todorov, Asparukh Velkov, *Situation démographique de la péninsule balkanique (fin du XVe s. début du XVIe s.)* (Sofia, 1988); Ömer Lûtfi Barkan, "Osmanlı imparatorluğunda bir iskân ve kolonizasyon metodu olarak sürgünler."

40. Kemal Karpat, *Ottoman Population, 1830–1914* (Madison: University of Wisconsin Press, 1985), p. 27.

41. Mark Pinson, "Ottoman Colonization of the Circassians in Rumili After the Crimean War," *Etudes balkaniques*, 3 (1972); "Russian Policy and Emigration of the Crimean Tatars to the Ottoman Empire, 1854–1862," *Güney-Doğu Avrupa Araştırmalari Dergisi*, vol. 1 (1972).

42. Dimitrije Djordjević, "Migrations During the 1912–1913 Balkan Wars and World War One," *Migrations in Balkan History* (Belgrade: Serbian Academy of Sciences and Arts, 1989), pp. 115–29.

43. According to the calculations of the Soviet Turkologist G. I. Starchenkov, based on statistical figures and indirect measurements, in 1985 Turkey had about 18% ethnic and religious minorities (of a population of 51,430,000, Turks - 42 million, Kurds - 8 million, Arabs - 700,000, Armenians - 180,000, Greeks - 150,000, Circassians - 40,000, Georgians - 30,000, Laz - 20,000, Jews - 10,000, others -300,000; cited in Cengiz Hakov, "Natsionalniyat vûpros v republikanska Turtsiya," *Aspekti na etnokulturnata situatsiya v Bulgariya*, vol. 1 (Sofia: Tsentür za izsledvane na demokratsiyata i fonadatsia "Friedrich Naumann," 1991), p. 69.

44. For a general exposition defending this view and based mostly on the Greek case, see George G. Arnakis, "The Role of Religion in the Development of Balkan Nationalism," *The Balkans in Transition: Essays on the Development of Balkan Life and Politics Since the Eighteenth Century*, ed. Charles and Barbara Jelavich (Berkeley/Los Angeles: University of California Press, 1963), pp. 115–44.

45. Paschalis Kitromilides, "Imagined Communities and the Origins of the National Question in the Balkans," *European History Quarterly* 19, no. 2 (April 1989): 184.

46. Paschalis Kitromilides, "Imagined Communities," p. 177.

47. Eran Fraenkel, "Urban Muslim Identity in Macedonia: The Interplay of Ottomanism and Multilingual Nationalism," *Language Contact—Language Conflict*, eds. Eran Fraenkel and Christina Kramer (New York: Peter Lang, 1993), pp. 29–44.

48. Eran Fraenkel gives examples of this process in Macedonia where "there have been no Macedonian Muslims who have forsworn Islam for the sake of *Makedonstvo* whereas, consciously or not, they have abandoned the "Slavicness" of their identity in favor of a non-Slavic (Albanian) expression of their Islam"; or else when both Albanians and Gypsies would declare themselves Turks in order to avoid the scorn of the Slavic neighbors. "Turning a Donkey Into a Horse: Conflict and Paradox in the Identity of Macedonian Muslims," Paper for the 23d National Convention of the AAASS, Miami 1991 (cited with the permission of the author).

49. An attempt in this respect has been undertaken in the past few years in Bulgaria where two conferences were held discussing recent research on the ethnocultural situation in Bulgaria. See the relevant papers in *Aspekti na etnokulturnata situatsiya v Bûlgariya* (Sofia: Tsentur za izsledvane na demokratsiyata i fonadatsia "Friedrich Naumann"), vol. 1 (1991); vol. 2 (1992).

50. Eric Hobsbawm and Terence Ranger, *The Invention of Tradition* (New York: Cambridge University Press, 1983).

51. Depending on the local terminology, the assertion is that Greece witnessed the uninterrupted evolution of its "*ethnos*," while in the domains of the hegemony of the Marxist discourse it was the consolidation of the folk ("narodnost") as a primary stage of the "nation."

52. This specific formula was used by Constantine Jireček, the Czech historian and minister of education of post-Ottoman Bulgaria, *Geschichte der Bulgaren* (Prague, 1876), p. 448. His immense authority secured the perpetuation of many more similar cliches in Bulgarian historiography, although they were certainly not confined to this particular national historiography.

53. Gunnar Hering, "Die Osmanenzeit im Selbstverständnis der Völker Südosteuropas," *Die Staaten Südosteuropas*, p. 367.
54. Nikolay Todorov, "Social Structures in the Balkans During the Eighteenth and Nineteenth Centuries," *Etudes balkaniques* 4 (1985): 57–58.
55. Nikolay Todorov, "Social Structures in the Balkans," p. 62.
56. Raymond Williams, *Marxism and Literature* (New York: Oxford University Press, 1977), pp. 115–16.
57. Ernest Gellner, "The Mightier Pen? Edward Said and the Double Standards of Inside-Out Colonialism," *The Times Literary Supplement* (February 19, 1993), p. 4.

CHAPTER FIVE

THE OTTOMAN LEGACY IN YUGOSLAVIA'S

DISINTEGRATION AND CIVIL WAR

Dennison Rusinow

In 1991 the Socialist Federal Republic of Yugoslavia, a successor state of the Ottoman and Hapsburg empires and lately an increasingly loose federation of six republics and two autonomous provinces, disintegrated. Declarations of independence by two of the republics (Slovenia and Croatia), followed by two more (Bosnia-Herzegovina and Macedonia), provoked a combination of civil war and aggression from "rump" Yugoslavia (Serbia and Montenegro) in Croatia and later in Bosnia-Herzegovina. The horrors of massacres and mass rapes to speed "ethnic cleansing," refugees by the hundreds of thousands fleeing devastated or besieged towns and villages, and deliberate destruction of the cultural and spiritual legacies of a thousand years of intertwined lives and civilizations filled the media and tortured the conscience of most of the world.

The explanation of these horrors, that Orthodox Serbs, Catholic Croats, and Muslim fellow-Slavs "cannot live together"—which they have been doing for centuries, mostly in peace if not in harmony—was becoming a self-fulfilling prophecy. A plethora of external national and international actors proved unable to find or unwilling to enforce a way to stop the violence and multiple violations of international law and human-rights covenants. There was widespread apprehension that this failure could lead to an expansion of the conflict into the twentieth century's third Balkan War (or its fifth, if the Balkan portions of two world wars are also counted) and to attempted emulation of the aggressors' methods and success elsewhere.

The trauma of disintegration and the tragedy of civil war and "ethnic

The Ottoman Empire, 1739–1913, in Yugoslavia's successor. Map by Blaine R. Wallace, University of Pittsburgh.

cleansing" that have been ravaging the ex-Ottoman lands and peoples of ex-Yugoslavia constitute the latest episode in the classic "Eastern Question," also known as "After the Ottomans, What?" The central argument in the following pages is that particular changes in ethnic, religious, political, and social maps and relationships, which qualify as "Ottoman legacies" because they occurred during and as consequences of the long Ottoman chapter in the region's history, are essential to understanding and explaining why, where, and how the conflicts that led to civil war, and the war itself, occurred.

The primary focus is on three pieces of former Yugoslavia that have been the territories most in dispute and most prone to violence on a massive scale in the War of Yugoslav Succession. These are the former Hapsburg Military Frontier in Croatia (almost all of which was Ottoman in the sixteenth century, and most of it until the end of the seventeenth), Bosnia and Herzegovina (Ottoman from the fifteenth century until 1908, although occupied and administered by Austria-Hungary after 1878), and Kosovo (Ottoman from

1389 to 1912). Their current grim fate—war in Croatia and Bosnia-Herzegovina and war waiting to happen in Kosovo—is because of particular mixes of national communities whose current leaders' competing nationalist programs and territorial claims cannot be satisfied without war and (except for the national program of the nation in Bosnia-Herzegovina called "Muslim") without massive involuntary population movements or physical elimination, together lately known as "ethnic cleansing."

This is not to "blame" Ottoman demographic, religious, and social legacies for contemporary evils, which have other and more relevant roots. Yugoslavia disintegrated primarily because of megalomanic and ruthless demagogic politicians (most of them ex- or pseudo ex-Communists) and nationalist intellectuals (often also ex-Communists) who discovered that nationalism was a more potent tool to mobilize support and to gain or retain power than Marxism had ever been. To these ends they incited painful remembrance of ancient and recent wrongs, frustrated national ambitions, and reasons to fear for communal survival. These were "things" that "slumbered in the hearts of many Serbs [and also Slovenes, Croats, et al.], but it took an industry of hate to revive them,"[1] and to infect critical masses of people in their several national communities.

At that point disintegration of their common state became inevitable. Its disintegration was violent because the exclusivity and inclusivity of nation-states, as posited by nationalist theory and in their leaders' national(ist) programs, conflicted with ethnic and religious fragmentation, mixed populations, and overlapping or competing historical and ethnic claims. Given the scattering of "diaspora" communities of most Yugoslav nations outside their "homeland" republics (including 26 percent of 8.5 million Serbs outside Serbia, 20 percent of 4.6 million Croats outside Croatia, and 19 perceent of 2.4 million Muslim Slavs outside Bosnia-Herzegovina),[2] only Slovenia (90 percent Slovene and with 99 percent of Yugoslavia's Slovenes) could become an independent nation-state without including large minorities of another nation or nations, and without leaving large minorities of its own in other successor nation-states. Each would similarly include portions of others' "historic" territories and exclude portions of its own. In longer-term historical perspective, the dubious honor of "blame" for the Yugoslav catastrophe therefore belongs to any attempt, which current events reveal as a disastrous absurdity, to implement Western and Central European doctrines concerning national self-determination in "ethnic shatterbelts" like southeastern Europe.

It merits repetition that the basic cause of the conflict is *not*, as often alleged to explain its particular brutality or to soothe the outside world's conscience, "ancient hatreds" between Balkan ethnic and religious communities, whose urge to kill each other has periodically been restrained only by an imperial regime alien to them all (the *pax ottomanica*) and the Serbian-royal and Titoist-communist dictatorships that succeeded it. Without exaggerating and romanticizing the conviviality that has frequently characterized their long cohabitation, or minimizing frequent violent confrontations, there seems to have been at least as much of the former as of the latter in their histories.[3]

Ottoman conquest, colonization, conversions, and later fighting retreat from the Balkans also did not create the "ethnic shatterbelt" and confrontational religious heterogeneity that already characterized pre-Ottoman southeastern Europe and that would defy later attempts to establish homogenous ethnonational or confessional-national states. The Ottoman contribution was to add to and rearrange the pieces, thereby further complicating the ethnic and religious kaleidoscope. In addition, the Ottoman system, with its separation of subject peoples on a confessional rather than territorial basis while granting considerable local autonomy, inhibited the homogenization through assimilation to a hegemonic language and culture that was creating larger proto-national and national communities in other parts of Europe and also, through assimilation to the Turkish language and culture, in central Anatolia. These Ottoman legacies thus shaped the demographic and social basis that determined where, for whom, and how national(ist) mobilization at the time of Yugoslavia's disintegration would tend to be most effective and most violent in its consequences.

During the century and a half between the Battle of Mohacs (1526) and the second siege of Vienna (1683), all of later Yugoslavia was under Ottoman rule except Hapsburg Slovenia, a small portion of Croatia (north and west of Sisak) that the Hapsburgs held or recovered after Mohacs, some scattered Venetian possessions in Istria and Dalmatia, and the tributary Republic of Dubrovnik. Ottoman Croatia-Slavonia and the Sanjak (Banat) of Temesvar were permanently lost to the Hapsburgs in the treaties of Sremski Karlovci (Carlowitz: 1699) and Požarevac (1718), but Ottoman sovereignty was maintained south of the Sava-Danube line—except for eventually Hapsburg Dalmatia and Dubrovnik and briefly (1718–39) in Sumadija—until full independence for Serbia and Montenegro and Austro-Hungarian administration of Bosnia-Herzegovina were conceded at the Congress of Berlin in 1878. Kosovo ("Old Serbia") and Macedonia ("South Serbia") were lost only in 1912, in the First Balkan War.

It is in this geographic framework, and in the context of almost continuous frontier or more general warfare, that the Ottoman ethnodemographic and religiodemographic legacy took shape. Post-1945 internal Yugoslav political boundaries that are also crucial issues in the current War of Yugoslav Succession, in particular the boundaries between the former Socialist Republics of Bosnia-Herzegovina, Croatia, and Serbia, are also part of that legacy.

The pre-Ottoman distribution of peoples, faiths, and even states in these lands is in many particulars still a matter of dispute. Documentary and archeological evidence tends to be scarce, contradictory, and inadequately explored. Most research and writing on these subjects has been in the service of romantic national historiography and pseudoscientific nationalist ethnography, designed to legitimize one or another of the region's competing national claims. Many disputes and apparent contradictions also arise from the fact that these peoples, faiths, and states all tended to be movable feasts, over space and time, in a region of frequently ephemeral political communities and confessional allegiances that lies astride the perennially contested and also movable boundary (first drawn by Emperor Diocletian in the third century) between Western and Eastern Roman and later Roman-Catholic and Byzantine-Orthodox cultural worlds.

This much is clear: Most of the people the Ottomans encountered and conquered in their northward march through what would one day become Yugoslavia spoke one or another of a variety of South Slavic dialects (or languages?) and were variously and sometimes sequentially Roman Catholic, Orthodox, and heretical or heterodox Christians. Those in the north and west, closer to Rome, were mostly Catholic; those in the south, closer to Constantinople, were mostly Orthodox; and those in the middle zone, an independent Kingdom of Bosnia when its Ottoman conquest began in 1463, were a mixture of all three. Most had lived for some period or periods, usually corresponding to periods of Byzantine or Hungarian weakness, in small states or short-lived empires "of their own." Each such moment in their respective histories would later be remembered as a golden age, and the territories of these states as just as rightfully theirs as the partly or largely different territories they presently inhabited.

These peoples called themselves and were called by a number of names, the eventually most widespread of which corresponded to the names of the largest and most enduring of their native (but movable) medieval states: Bulgaria, Croatia, and Serbia. However, assimilation of the peoples of these pre-Ottoman Balkan states to the dialect or language and other cultural attributes of governing elites or power-centers—the kind of "nation-building" through cultural homogenization then taking place in more enduring and stronger kingdoms in other parts of Europe[4]—was repeatedly interrupted by their disintegration or renewed transformation into peripheral territories of geographically and culturally external powers.

Colonization and *conversion* during the first centuries of Ottoman rule added two numerically and culturally significant non-Christian religious communities, both already present but in previously insignificant numbers,[5] to the region's religious mosaic. Sephardic Jews, welcomed in the Ottoman Empire after their expulsion from Spain in 1492, became an economically and culturally important part of the population in Sarajevo, Salonika, and other Balkan towns until they were decimated by German Nazis and Croatian Ustashe during World War II. A much larger Muslim community initially consisted of Turkish and other Muslim colonists but soon included what most scholars agree were far more numerous native converts. (See Maria Todorova's contribution to this volume for the debate over whether colonization or conversion accounts for the greater part of the Muslim community in the Balkans as a whole.) Muslims soon constituted the majority of the urban population almost everywhere (100 percent of 1,024 households in Sarajevo, an Ottoman foundation, were recorded as Muslim in the Ottoman census of 1520–30, as were 630 of 842 households in Skopje/Üsküp and 640 of 845 households in Bitola/Monastir),[6] but also among the rural population in some districts. The location of these last indicates which peoples in the western Balkans converted to Islam in large numbers: Slavs in the late medieval Kingdom of Bosnia; and Albanians, especially in the northern (Gheg) regions of Albanian settlement.

Meanwhile, Ottoman-imposed or Ottoman-induced *migrations* were producing new distributions and mixtures of ethnolinguistic and religious communities, particularly in districts that became post-1991 focuses of tension, competing claims, and tinder for "ethnic cleansing" and civil war. The combined consequences of conversions and migrations in these last— Bosnia-Herzegovina, Kosovo,[7] and much of Croatia—therefore merit closer examination.

The gradual, interrupted Ottoman advance through the lands of future Yugoslavia between the first Battle of Kosovo (1389) and the battles of Mohacs and Sisak (1526 and 1593) set in motion an almost continuous wave of migrations by Orthodox Serbs and Serbianized or Serbianizing Vlachs,[8] and then Croats, from conquered or threatened regions. Much of it was from valleys and principal lines of communication into nearby mountains that attracted less Ottoman interest and attention, but a more significant portion was in the direction of territories for the moment or permanently still under Christian rulers. The demographic "centers of gravity" of both Serbs and Croats thus continued to move northward, a displacement that had begun for the Croats several centuries earlier.

A second major wave was a by-product of later campaigns in the long Hapsburg-Ottoman war of 1683–99, during which Hapsburg armies penetrated deep into the Balkans before withdrawing toward the future (1699) Ottoman-Hapsburg frontier on the Sava and Danube. Serbs who had risen in support of this foray, fearful of Ottoman vengeance, followed the Hapsburg withdrawal and were given sanctuary in newly "liberated" but war-ravaged and depopulated southern Hungary and Croatia. The most important episode of this second wave was a first mass exodus (*seoba*) of Serbs, led by Serbian Orthodox Patriarch Arsenije III Crnojević, from Kosovo to newly "liberated" Hapsburg lands across the Danube and Sava in 1690. There Arsenije established a Serbian Orthodox Metropolitanate at Sremski Karlovci, under Hapsburg protection. It would in effect substitute for the patriarchate at Peć, where Albanians recently converted or in process of conversion to Islam posted guardians or "chieftains" (*vojvode*) to protect the old patriarchal complex, other Orthodox monasteries in Kosovo, and the priests and monks who stayed on.[9]

The net results of these migrations and religious conversions can be summarized for territories contested in the War of Yugoslav Succession of the 1990s as follows.

Kosovo and Krajina

Kosovo ("Old Serbia") and parts of Croatia and Slavonia that became the expanding Hapsburg Military Frontier (*Militärgrenze* or *Vojna krajina*) against the Ottoman Empire are linked through the consequences of Serb migrations from the former to the latter during and after the 1683–99 war. Although disputed by Serb nationalists, Albanians as descendents of Illyrians were certainly and probably continuously present in Kosovo since before Slavs even reached the Balkans. Serb and Vlach migrations after 1530 had with equal certainty established an Orthodox population of peasant-warriors, many of them formerly in Ottoman service, among the Catholic Croats of the Croatian and Bosnian *krajine*. Still, the magnitude and social diversity of the Serb exodus in 1690 and an apparently larger one in 1730 was what actually created both "the Albanian question" in Kosovo and "the Serb question" in Croatia.[10]

As many of Kosovo's Serbs departed, Albanians of the northern (Gheg) highland clans, still in the process of conversion from predominantly Catholic Christian to Sunni and more specifically Bektashi Islam, descended in growing numbers to join their kin and a diminishing number of Serbs in the more fertile plain of Kosovo that Serbs regard as the sacred cradle ("our Jerusalem") of their culture, state, and church. Smaller-scale net out-migration by Serbs and in-migration by Albanians continued until the end of Ottoman rule in 1912. Briefly reversed by state-sponsored Serb colonization and expulsions of Albanians between the two world wars, it resumed when Kosovo became part of Italian-occupied "Greater Albania" from 1941 to 1943 and after 1945, when interwar Serb colonists were in turn expelled by the new Yugoslav regime. As a result, and with later assistance from an enormously high Albanian birthrate, this historically Serb land was by 1990 90 percent Albanian in population.

After 1945 in form but initially not in substance an Autonomous Region (later Province) of the Republic of Serbia in federal Yugoslavia, Kosovo passed from Serb to local Albanian political domination (in both cases by Communists) after genuine autonomy within Serbia was dictated by Tito in 1968. At that point the demographic legacy of migrations largely induced by Ottoman rule became a double irredentist as well as a double minority problem: for Albanians as a minority in Yugoslavia and for Slavs (predominantly Serbs but also Montenegrins) as a minority in Kosovo. The unconstitutional elimination of autonomy by a new Serbian regime under Slobodan Milošević in 1989–90, bringing Kosovo again under direct Serbian rule, marked at least the temporary triumph of Serb irredentism over Albanian. It also set the stage for the potential extension of the War of Yugoslav Succession to Kosovo and beyond, a prospect that was generating serious international concern by 1993.

In addition to making room for an eventual Albanian majority in Kosovo, the exodus of Serbs from "Old Serbia" and their resettlement north of the Sava and Danube rivers in and after 1690 greatly enlarged Croatia's Orthodox and Serb minority, which became a majority in many Military Frontier districts.[11] Most were settled and remained as free warrior-peasants, pledged to drop their plows and seize their guns to confront Ottoman incursions. The enemy would change in the twentieth century, but the tradition persisted. Their special status as Hapsburg frontier militiamen, which included communal and church autonomy and freedom from feudal obligations, often represented Hapsburg confirmation of privileges originally granted by the Ottomans to the Serbian Orthodox millet or to Serbs in Ottoman service. Their Croat neighbors did not share these privileges. This became a source of Croat resentment, and of Serb determination to defend their communal autonomy, that were eventually articulated in nationalist sentiments and ideologies. Meanwhile, the two communities generally lived in peace with one another, if not in harmony, until 1941 and from 1945 to 1990.

By the time the Hapsburg Military Frontier was gradually dismantled in the nineteenth century, Serbs were an overwhelming majority in the mountainous and sparsely populated western districts, where they proclaimed an Autonomous Krajina Republic in 1990. In the Yugoslav census of 1991, taken just before civil war and "ethnic cleansing" began, they were 89,551 (77 percent) of 117,000 inhabitants of the Knin region, and 73,481 (65 percent) of 113,000 in nearby Banija and Kordun. Memories of genocide by the Croatian fascist Ustashe, who ruled Croatia and Bosnia-Herzegovina as Axis clients during World War II, are particularly strong in Banija and Kordun, where some of the worst wartime atrocities occurred; Serb-Croat competition for the

Knin region's scarce arable land and jobs has made it a breeding ground for intense nationalist sentiments since at least the early twentieth century. In Slavonia, where actual civil war began in May 1991, 83,558 Serbs constituted minorities of more than 25 percent in six central and eastern counties (but outnumbered Croats in only one of these), with an additional 116,902 as smaller minorities in the rest.[12]

In the violence that ensued when these Serbs and their mentors in Belgrade refused to accept their reduction to a potentially discriminated minority in a nationalist-ruled and by late 1991 independent Croatian nation-state, this Ottoman demographic legacy would produce bitter fruit. A local revolt by Croatian Serbs in the western portion of the former *Vojna krajina* that began in August 1990 set the stage for the combination of civil war and aggression by the Yugoslav Army and irregulars from Serbia that was to follow. It would engulf all of the Croatian *krajina* after the Croatian government declared independence (with symbols and rhetoric that not only Serbs regarded as recidivist Ustashe) in the summer of 1991. In April 1992 the same combination of civil war and external aggression, this time from Croatia as well as Serbia, would also engulf and ultimately destroy tri-national Bosnia-Herzegovina, which had won international recognition as a state and member of the United Nations that same month.

Bosnia-Herzegovina

When Yugoslavia was reestablished as a federal (and Communist-ruled) state in 1945, five of its six federated republics were constitutionally defined as the national homelands, or nation-states, of their nominative South Slav nations: Serbs, Croats, Slovenes, Macedonians, and Montenegrins.[13] Successive constitutions declared that each of these possessed an inalienable right to national self-determination, including separation, but that all five had already expressed their desire to form a common federal state by jointly participating, along with the other peoples of reborn Yugoslavia, in the Communist-led "National Liberation Struggle" during World War II. (Whether their purported wartime exercise of this right was irrevocable, and whether it could in future be exercised by the republics as their nation-state homelands or only through plebescites by members of these nations, wherever they lived, ceased to be moot questions at the end of the 1980s.)

The sixth republic, Bosnia-Herzegovina, was explicitly defined as a "historic" rather than "national" state, and as the shared homeland of three peoples: its Muslims, Serbs, and Croats, in the 1991 census respectively 44, 31, and 17 percent of its 4.4 million population at that time (5.5 percent recorded themselves as "Yugoslavs" and 2.1 percent were "others" or "unknown").[14] Its boundaries, challenged as an arbitrary Communist invention when Yugoslavia disintegrated, deviated only minutely from its Ottoman boundaries at the end of the eighteenth century or as much as two centuries earlier.[15]

Its Slavic Muslim community, another Ottoman legacy whose right to call itself a nation (and even to physical existence) would also be challenged when Yugoslavia disintegrated, had already suffered a prolonged official national-identity problem under the Communist regime that had recognized its separate *communal* identity in 1943. In the first postwar census (1948) its members could declare themselves as Serbs, as Croats, or as "Muslims nationally undesignated" (*muslimani nacionalno neopredeljeni*), and in the census of 1953 as Serbs, Croats, or "Yugoslavs undesignated" (*Jugosloveni neopredeljeni*). The 1961 census offered them a new category: "Muslims (ethnic adherence)" (*Muslimani [etnička pripadnost]*). This became "Muslims in the sense of nationality" (*Muslimani u smislu narodnosti*) in the census of 1971—although the regime had finally recognized them as a fully separate "nation" in January 1968. The census of 1981 was thus the first to list them as "Muslim" without qualification and in alphabetical order, between Macedonian and Slovene, as one of Yugoslavia's six (until then five) equal and constitutive "nations." Some of the reasons for this prolonged and hesitant "affirmation of a Muslim nation" were contemporary and political, but even these incorporated the more basic question of whether and why these Muslim Slavs were indeed a nation.[16]

As previously noted, the population of the pre-Ottoman Kingdom of Bosnia was partly Catholic, partly Orthodox, and partly adherents of what seems to have been a cross between folk religion and a Bosnian "state" church, often but according to most recent scholarship incorrectly called Bogomil. The practice of this last and its basically Christian dogmas (if it had any), which are largely undocumented and therefore also a matter of dispute, were apparently at least heterodox if not heretical.[17] The distribution and size of these three religious communities are also uncertain and matters of dispute, although late pre-Ottoman Catholic and Serbian Orthodox ecclesiastical jurisdictions and sites of monasteries suggest that Orthodoxy was then thinly represented west of the Drina River (then and now the Bosnian–Serbian border), except for western Herzegovina.[18] All seems to have been underendowed with clergy, churches (they were almost exclusively represented by monasteries), hierarchies, and informed believers.

Mehmet II's conquest of this kingdom, which began in 1463 and was seriously contested (with corresponding devastation and depopulation) only west of the Vrbas River, would radically alter both the composition and geographic distribution of its religious and subsequently proto-national and national communities. The Bosnian church, already weakened and with its clergy mostly in flight or converts to Catholicism shortly before the conquest, simply disappeared—perhaps also because its raison d'etre as a "national" church defying the power as well as dogmas of both "East" and "West" (a kind of medieval Titoism) vanished with the Bosnian state. However recent scholarship tends to reject the traditional view that its adherents, beginning with the nobility, converted to Islam quickly and en masse, and that today's Bosnian Muslims are for the most part their descendants.

Instead, most now agree with John Fine that Islamization was a gradual process, which drew recruits from all the Christian churches, and which occurred as part of a general melee of conversions between as well as out of Orthodoxy, Catholicism, and the dying Bosnian church. In this view, the basic reason why conversion to Islam was notoriously more common in Bosnia (and Albania), creating large native Muslim communities there, was because none of this religious borderland's competing and poorly endowed Christian faiths enjoyed the kind of monopoly and coherence of creed and organization, with numerous clergy, churches, and full hierarchy, that fortified Christian resistance to Islamization in other Balkan states conquered by the Ottomans. Easier in these circumstances, conversion (or adaptation) to Islam also entailed privileges in an Islamic state but did not require abandonment of practices like celebration of Christian holidays and favorite saints, who could be identified with Muslim (especially Bektashi) equivalents. Bosnian Christians, noble and peasant, and Catholic, Orthodox, or adherents of the Bosnian church, thus had little to lose and much to gain by converting or "adapting" to Islam. According to generations of outside and fellow-Muslim observers, their and their descendants' observance of Islamic doctrine and practices has with few exceptions been as relaxed as their ancestors' various Christian observances.

Whatever the disputed motivations and timing of these conversions, the consequences included the creation of a situation unique in Ottoman Europe: native and predominantly Slavic Muslims ruling Christian and Muslim Slavs alike and in the name of a distant sultan. So great was the power of these Slavic Muslim notables that they were for a long period able to prevent the sultan's official representative from residing in the capital of his pashalik, Sarajevo; he could come within its walls only one day a year, as an honored guest, but otherwise had to live at Travnik, sixty miles away.

The descendants of those who did not convert, and who were subject to the legal and other disabilities suffered by most non-Muslims in the empire, would come to regard those who did, and their descendants, as opportunistic traitors to their nation or race. This view is frequently cited as a rationale by Serbs and Croats engaged in or seeking to excuse the genocidal "ethnic cleansing" of Bosnia-Herzegovina's Muslims that began in April 1992.

With the Bosnian church eliminated, Bosnia-Herzegovina was still a contested frontier between Catholic and Orthodox Christianity, and thereby between Croats and Serbs, whose religion-based communal identity would gradually be transformed into what Emanuel Turczynski calls "confessional-nationality."[19] At first the balance of comparative advantage may have alternated between the competitors. Catholics did not have a separate millet, and religious subjects of the popes were often viewed by the Ottomans with greater suspicion than were other Christians. However, the Catholic Church in Bosnia-Herzegovina initially benefited from a patent of protection and privilege (*Milodraška ahdnama*) granted by Mehmet II on May 28, 1463, to its widespread network of Franciscan monasteries and priests. The order's presence in the Franciscan province of Bosna Srebrena subsequently (and consequently?) increased from 80 members in the second half of the sixteenth century to 1,623 in the first half of the seventeenth.

Meanwhile, the Serbian Orthodox Church was subordinated to the Patriarch of Constantinople, and thus to a Greek hierarchy in an initially single Orthodox millet. This Catholic comparative advantage seems to have persisted until the Peć patriarchate was restored in 1557 by Suleiman the Magnificent, under the influence of Grand Vizier Mehmet Pasha Sokolli (Sokolović), the most successful and famous Bosnian-born product of the *devshirme*, whose brother was installed as patriarch. The Serbs thus acquired their own *millet-bashi*, with all the rights and powers accruing to that office in the Ottoman system. This seems to have marked the beginning of a transfer to the Orthodox of whatever advantage Mehmet II's *Milodraška ahdnama* had initially given to the Bosnian Catholic Church. The border between Orthodox and Catholic Christianity was moving west, from the Drina to the Una (the Bosnian-Croatian frontier), but with numerous Catholic and therefore Croatian islands in between.

As in southern Hungary and Slavonia after their devastation in the war of 1683–99, repopulation of Bosnia west of the Vrbas, similarly depopulated by death or flight as Ottoman armies slowly reduced the last bastions of Bosnian and later also Hungarian resistance,[20] further complicated an already complex ethnic and religious map. Here the newcomers were Muslim as well as Orthodox, with the former eventually a solid majority in the extreme northwest, where Bihać fell to the Ottomans only in 1592, and the latter a majority, surrounding Muslim and Catholic pockets, in most of the rest.

By the end of the sixteenth century the distribution of Bosnia-Herzegovina's three religious and (proto-) national communities probably closely resembled the extraordinarily complex one recorded by the 1991 census, one year before Serbs, followed by Croats and Muslims where they could do so, began simplifying it with "ethnic cleansing."[21] The proportions, however, may have changed. Classified by religion as lately synonymous with national-ity, Orthodox Serbs were on most but not all calculations more numerous than Muslims (with Catholic Croats then and now in third place) until their ranks were decimated by attempted genocide at the hands of the Ustashe dur-ing World War II, and by their consequently greater participation and losses in Partisan and Serb-royalist Chetnik wartime resistance movements. The other principal difference is in cities and large towns. Predominantly (and in Sarajevo entirely) Muslim in the sixteenth century, by the twentieth century the cities were as mixed, in varying proportions, as the country as a whole (e.g., Sarajevo: 49.3 percent Muslim, 29.9 percent Serb, 6.6 percent Croat, and 10.7 percent "Yugoslav" in early 1991).[22] Muslims, however, were still pre-dominantly urban and Serbs predominantly rural, which made the Serb-Mus-lim war in the 1990s also in large measure a war of the country against the city. Following former Belgrade Mayor Bogdan Bogdanović, Bogdan Denitch calls this "urbicide" and "the revenge of the local red-necks who have always hated the cities."[23] Their rural predominance also provided the rationale for Serb claims that as farmers they have a right, although only 31 percent of Bosnia-Herzegovina's population, to up to 70 percent of its territory.

Their Serb and Croat enemies and some outside observers have accused the dominant Muslim political party in post-Communist Bosnia-Herzegovina and Alija Izetbegović, its president and since 1990 also president of Bosnia-Herzegovina's collective and tri-national state presidency, of being "Muslim fundamentalists" who are seeking to establish "an Islamic state." Those mak-ing these accusations point to Muslim insistence on a unitary Bosnian state, which they could hope to dominate with their 44 percent of the population and the likelihood that their higher natural increase rate would soon make this an absolute majority. (By early 1992 Bosnian Serb and Croat leaders were cor-respondingly insisting on the solution they would soon seek to impose by force: division of Bosnia-Herzegovina into three states, based on segregated national and religious communities and linked in a loose confederation as a cover for de facto annexation of its Serb and Croat mini-states by Serbia and Croatia.) They also cite a treatise, entitled *The Islamic Declaration*, written in 1970 by Izetbegović and the principal evidence in his trial and sentencing in 1983, under the Communist *ancien regime*, for "acting from the standpoint of Islamic fundamentalism and Muslim nationalism."

Most of *The Islamic Declaration*,[24] which is subtitled "A Program for the Islamization of Muslims and the Muslim Peoples," in fact belongs to the mainstream of late nineteenth- and twentieth-century Muslim concern with "Islamic renewal," a term Izetbegović uses interchangeably with "Islamic renaissance." His "Program" aims to rescue Muslims, their society, and their faith from what he regards as a prolonged nadir of dependency, backwardness, and loss of historic creativity and high culture. He attributes this deplorable state of affairs to debasement of the Quran and Islam in general, from an all-pervasive and correct but inherently flexible and progressive guide ("more than a religion") to rote repetition of texts in "a religion without faith" dominated by those he describes with undisguised sarcasm as "theologians." Equal guilt is ascribed to "our Westerners" and "so-called progressives" with their adulation and emulation of the wrong things: "They cannot see that the power of the Western world does not lie in how it lives, but how it works; that its strength is not in fashion, godlessness, night clubs, a younger generation out of control, but in the extraordinary diligence, persistence, knowledge, and responsibility of its people."

He is therefore both anti-Zealot and anti-Herodian: equally critical of "conservatives who want the old forms, and modernists who want someone else's form." The first are exemplified by "our theologians," who would condemn Muslims to continued backwardness, ignorance, and superstition. Mustafa Kemal, who took Turkey down a false path to secularization, uncritical Westernization, and the status of a backward, "plagiary" nation, is an example of the second error. The Japanese, by contrast, amalgamated the best of their traditional culture and the best the West had to offer to achieve their present success.

The answer for Muslims is analogous: the creation of a modern but again truly "Islamic society," which must precede rather than follow the establishment of "Muslim governance" or an "Islamic state" (which must also have an "Islamicized" Muslim majority) if the latter are to be based on democracy and consent rather than autocracy and coercion. For Izetbegović the creators of Pakistan, otherwise a praiseworthy achievement, made a grave mistake in reversing this order. "Islamic activist" is clearly a better label for these views than "fundamentalist," although endorsement of the principle of "Muslim governance" for a state with an "Islamicized" Muslim majority can still alarm non-Muslims and also Muslims who prefer a secular state.

Subsequent Serb and Croat actions based on the argument that the political goals and behavior of Bosnia's notoriously undogmatic, even heterodox, and often hard-drinking, pork-eating Muslims are inspired by "Islamic fundamentalism" may be making that falsehood into a self-fulfilling prophecy. For present purposes more to the point, this argument implicitly denies that "Muslim" might be a national identity (a nation) as well as a religious identity. It ignores the possibility that Muslims, by demanding a unitary state in which their numbers would make them the dominant "state people," might be seeking to establish a modern, secular nation-state "of their own," corresponding to Serbia for Serbs, Croatia for Croats, etc. Although such a state would still be objectionable to its Serbs and Croats, who would become national minorities rather than "co-nations" in a tri-national state, it would not be a theocratic Islamic one.

The underlying question is the ideological and sociological justification of the "Muslim nation" that Titoist-Yugoslav theory and law fully recognized in 1968 as Yugoslavia's sixth separate and equal nation.[25] Is this Muslim nation merely "Tito's invention," as critics of its legitimacy call it? According to this view, his regime "proclaimed" a nation that did not exist in order to spite both Serb and Croat nationalists and eliminate a historic and acutely dangerous Balkan bone of territorial contention. "Proclamation" of this fictitious nation was thus a device to subvert the principal basis for both Serb and Croat claims to Bosnia-Herzegovina by denying the Muslim Slavs to both Serbs and Croats, who respectively claim them as Islamicized Serbs or Islamicized Croats. If they are the former, they and Bosnia-Herzegovina's other (Christian Orthodox) Serbs are an absolute majority, and Bosnia-Herzegovina "belongs" to Serbia. If they are Croats, they and the other (Roman Catholic) Croats are an absolute majority, and Bosnia-Herzegovina "belongs" to Croatia.

Or was formal recognition in fact (as the regime claimed) an "affirmation" of a completed process of nation-building with numerous analogues in older European and contemporary third world history, and therefore an "imagined community" as "real" as other nations?[26]

In descriptions of their "ethnogenesis" and definitions of their nationhood written by contemporary Bosnian Muslim and some foreign historians and social scientists,[27] the Muslim Slavs of Yugoslavia have indeed if only lately become a modern and essentially secular nation—*Muslimani* as a national community, distinguished by a capital "M" from *muslimani* as a religious community. Its national specificity and consciousness are said to be products of a combination of factors. The impact of Islam as culture and ethos as well as religion is one of the most important of these, but so is the fact that the impacted culture was a distinct (Bosnian) one before Ottoman rule and influence led to the conversion of most Bosnian nobles and many peasants to Islam.

The role of Islam was to add new dimensions to a process of differentiation and individualization that was thus already underway in the medieval Bosnian state, as in the medieval Croatian and Serbian states, and as capable of further development into a separate *national* culture and identity. The product of this dynamic synthesis of Islamic and Bosnian Slav cultural elements was a society distinct from both other Slav and other Muslim communities—a culture *sui generis*, which is one way of defining a nation. The growth and penetration of this distinctiveness was enhanced by the growing and fiercely defended local authority and autonomy of the Bosnian Muslim nobility (the only "native" and Slavic aristocracy in the Ottoman Balkans), who ruled over Christian and Muslim *reaya* alike.

The emergence of a national or even proto-national consciousness appropriate to this specificity was delayed, however, by multiple inhibitions. The Slavic Muslim nobility, despite its own "Bosnianism," closely identified with the Ottoman Empire as protector of the Islamic faith and embodiment of the antinational or at least nonnational concept of a universal Islamic community (*umma islamiyya*) and Islam as both state and religion (*Islam din wa dawla*). In this context the Ottoman millet system, which tended to encourage a transition "from millets to modern nations" among Orthodox Balkan peoples with their own "national" churches,[28] may have had the opposite effect among Slav Muslims. It is indicative that until the twentieth century most of them continued to call themselves "*Turci*" (Turks), a term they understood to mean "adherents of Islam" rather than "ethnic" Turks, whom they called "*Turkuši*" (Turkics?) or "Osmanli."

Equally important were the consequences of Bosnia-Herzegovina's proximity to the European "West," its geographic marginality to the rest of the Muslim world, and the timing and way that (central) European concepts of nation and nation-state came to Bosnia, primarily from Austria-Hungary and Serbia, where language and common ancestry (real or mythical) were regarded by most nationalists as the primary and necessary defining characteristics of a nation. With a nation defined in this way, the Slav Muslims, speaking the same štokavian dialect as their Orthodox and Catholic neighbors (although with more Turkish and Arabic loan-words) and sharing the same origins (or myths of origin), must be either Serbs or Croats. And that, of course, was what they were hearing from both Serb and Croat nationalists. The only alternative then on offer was the idea of a multireligious "Bosnian nation," based on common language and history, which was promoted by Benjamin von Kallay (Austro-Hungarian governor of Bosnia-Herzegovina from 1882 to 1903) as a counter to both Serb and Croat nationalist proselytism.

A number of Muslim intellectuals responded to the political program of Serb nationalists and the Serbian government, who also (but for the sake of their own aspirations to Bosnia-Herzegovina) supported the maintenance of nominal Ottoman sovereignty in the Hapsburg-occupied province, by identifying themselves as "Serbs of Muslim faith." An apparently larger number, attracted by Croat cultural flattery (e.g., in a "Turcophilic" and pro-Islamic literary vogue) and educated in an expanding network of schools largely staffed by Hapsburg Croats and Zagreb-educated Muslims, similarly called themselves Croats. However, "all sources agree that the identification of Bosnian Muslims with either the Serbian or the Croatian *nation* remained limited."[29] Kallay's promotion of a tri-communal Bosnian national identity, the third option, attracted the support of some Muslim intellectuals but could not compete with the appeal and programs of already widespread Serb and Croat national consciousness or with most Muslims' still basically religious self-identification and Ottomanist nostalgia.

Meanwhile, however, other developments under Hapsburg rule were contributing to the wider penetration and secularization of Bosnian Muslim communal identity, and thereby laying the basis for its eventual translation into what looked increasingly like a national identity. The first decades of Hapsburg rule brought a dramatic expansion of secular primary and secondary education and of Muslim cultural societies, reading clubs, and economic and political organizations. The same developments had provided a basis for the earlier spread of Slovene nationalist consciousness. Here they performed an additional function by contributing to a secularization of the foundations of Muslim identity. Especially revealing in this regard are descriptions of members of the first post-1878 generation of "Westernized" Muslim intellectuals, living in *fin de siecle* Vienna, calling themselves "*Muslimani*" rather than "*Turci*," and seeking to develop a secular but distinctive Bosnian-Muslim literature in their native (South Slavic štokavian) dialect or language, which they initially wrote in (Islamic) Arabic and later in ("European") Latin script.

With these new "secular, cultural-educational bases of the Bosnian Muslim community," Steven Burg concludes,

> Bosnia became, in large part, a "divided society": Serbs, Croats, and Muslims each could live their lives wholly within the framework of Serb, Croat, and Muslim organizations. There can be no doubt that the development of such parallel organizations hastened the transformation of the meaning of self-identification as a "Muslim" from the narrowly religious to the national.[30]

Bosnian Muslims were thus apparently well on their way to self-identification as a distinct national as well as (or instead of) a confessional "imagined community" by the time Ottoman rule formally ended in 1908. Its precise formulation (the "mix" of Islamic and Bosnian elements in its definition and as perceived by its members) would continue to be uncertain, and the penetration of secular national consciousness among elites as well as ordinary Muslims would be incomplete and fragile, even after it was fully "affirmed" by Tito's Communist regime in 1968. By 1990, however, Muslim "national consciousness" was a fact that even Serbs and Croats who continued to deny it must live with, to the peril of their own ambitions in Bosnia-Herzegovina.

The Ottoman Legacy in Yugoslavia's Internal Boundaries

The internal (interrepublican) boundaries of "Tito's Yugoslavia" were also hotly disputed in anticipation of and during the War of Yugoslav Succession.

As governmental demands and popular support for a confederation, "a league of sovereign states," or complete independence increased in Slovenia and Croatia after 1988, President Milošević of Serbia issued public warnings that Serbia would insist on changes in interrepublican borders if any of these things should come to pass or seem imminent. Leaders of the Serb minorities in Croatian *krajina* and then in Bosnia-Herzegovina issued and later acted on similar warnings. Only thus, Milošević and those who preceded or followed him on this issue declared, could most if not all Serbs in other republics continue to live in and enjoy the protection of a single state. This was the reason Serbs had wanted Yugoslavia and why Serbia had sacrificed so much to create it.

To support and legitimize these territorial demands, Milošević and company further argued that these internal boundaries never had been internationally recognized, historic, or ethnic borders between states. They were merely "administrative" borders between federal units that Tito and his inner circle of other anti-Serb Croats and Slovenes had drawn when they came to power. As in their creation of Kosovo and Vojvodina as autonomous provinces within Serbia, their primary purpose was to divide the Serb nation and weaken Serbia.[31]

The argument that Yugoslavia's interrepublican boundaries did not demarcate nationally homogenous communities is true (except for Slovenia) and the crux of the problem. The claim that these were not borders between internationally recognized sovereign states, and therefore not subject to international laws and conventions prohibiting unilateral and especially violent changes in international borders, was arguable at least until 1992, when Slovenia, Croatia, and Bosnia-Herzegovina were admitted to the United Nations and recognized by numerous UN member-states.[32] However, the argument that these were "arbitrary" borders, without historic and in the past internationally recognized roots and rationale, is simply false. Almost all portions of the most seriously contested frontiers—those of Croatia and Bosnia-Herzegovina—are older than Yugoslavia, in large part by several centuries.[33] They are in equally large part Ottoman legacies, drawn at some point during centuries of war and diplomacy between the Ottoman Empire and its Venetian, Ragusan (Dubrovnik), and Hapsburg neighbors.

With minor exceptions in the Bihać area, the post-1945 border between the Yugoslav Republic of Bosnia-Herzegovina and the Croato-Slavonian portion of the Republic of Croatia had been the border between the Ottoman and Hapsburg empires from 1699 (the Treaty of Sremski Karlovci) until 1878 (the Congress of Berlin) and legally until 1908 (Austro-Hungarian annexation of Bosnia-Herzegovina). Its eastern portion, downstream from the junction of the Vrbas and Sava rivers, had been the border between Ottoman Bosnia and

Ottoman Slavonia (Hungary) since the sixteenth century. Except for its southern end, where the Bay of Kotor and territories south of there were transferred to Montenegro, the post-1945 border between the Dalmatian portion of Croatia and Bosnia-Herzegovina—challenged by both Serbs and Croats in the 1990s—had been the border between the Ottoman Empire and the Venetian and Ragusan republics in its final form, established by 1718 and inherited by the Hapsburg Empire after both republics were extinguished by Napoleon. This included one of two outlets to the Adriatic Sea for Ottoman Bosnia, the northward one at Neum,[34] which the Republic of Dubrovnik ceded to the Ottoman Empire in 1699 to avoid territorial contiguity with its then more threatening Venetian neighbor, and which now separated the Dubrovnik region from the rest of Croatia. These borders, also in large part an Ottoman legacy, are thus among the oldest and most continuous in Europe.[35]

These pages are an exercise in what Maria Todorova calls "evaluative and retrospective assessment of the Ottoman heritage from the present viewpoint." My excuse is the manifest importance of a better understanding, as a prerequisite for effective remedy or at least containment, of the roots and reasons for the present tragedy in former Yugoslavia that may be replicated elsewhere. I have argued that the nature and consequences of changes in the region's ethnic, religious, cultural, and political maps during and as results of the advance, presence, and retreat of the Ottoman Empire in the Balkans are essential ingredients of such an understanding. It is not coincidental, but not often noted, that the districts most seriously affected by additions to and changes in the mix of their ethnic, religious, and cultural communities in the Ottoman period—in Croatia, Bosnia-Herzegovina, and Kosovo—are now the districts most seriously contested in the War of Yugoslav Succession.

NOTES

1. Gordana Knezović (Serb deputy editor of the Sarajevo daily *Oslobodjenje*), as quoted by John Burns, "Hate Was Just an Ember, But Oh, So Easy to Fan," in the *New York Times* (January 17, 1993).

2. These and data cited later from the 1991 Yugoslav census are from Ruža Petrović, "The National Composition of Yugoslavia's Population, 1991" in *Yugoslav Survey* 33, no. 1 (1992): 3–24.

3. This is a central theme, at times somewhat exaggerated, in three important new books on Bosnia-Herzogovina, published since this chapter was written, that are highly recommended for both historical background to and the proximate causes and course of the war there: Noel Malcolm, *Bosnia: A Short History* (New York: Columbia University Press, 1994); John Fine and Robert Donia, *Bosnia and Herzogovina: A Tradition Betrayed* (New York: Columbia University Press, 1994); and Mark Pinson, ed., *The Muslims of Bosnia-Herzogivina: Their Historic Development from the Middle Ages to the Dissolution of Yugoslavia* (Cambridge: Harvard University Press, 1994).

4. The process described by Hugh Seton-Watson, in *Nations and States* (London: Methuen, 1977), as distinguishing "the old, continuous nations" of Western Europe from discontinuous and modern types. Cf. Eric Hobsbawm's chapter on "proto-nationism" in *Nations and Nationalism Since 1780*, 2d ed. (Cambridge and New York: Cambridge University Press, 1992).

5. A Jewish presence in the Balkans dates at least from the early Roman period, and Saracen raiders in the eighth century reportedly left some converts to Islam behind them. *Muslims in Yugoslavia*, a handbook published by the Council of the Islamic Community of Bosnia and Herzegovina, Croatia, and Slovenia in 1978, cites Arabic-language sources in claiming that Islam is as old as Christianity in Yugoslavia.

6. Kemal Karpat, *An Enquiry Into the Social Foundations of Nationalism in the Ottoman State: From Social Estates to Classes, From Millets to Nations* (Princeton University Center of International Studies Research Monograph No. 39, July 1973), p. 42 and table II-A.

7. Along with adjacent parts of Montenegro and western Macedonia, which also acquired Albanian majorities at some point and possibly earlier.

8. Who these were another matter of dispute. "Vlach" usually and otherwise refers to people speaking Romance dialects, sometimes including Romanians but more frequently herdsmen of different ethnic origins, who are supposedly descendants of more or less Romanized Paleobalcanic peoples who literally took to the hills when the dam of the Roman *limes* was breached by barbarian hordes. Drago Roksandić, a Croatian Serb historian and specialist on the Serbs of Croatia, describes *these* Vlachs as follows: "Since many question the ethnic identity of Vlachs of Orthodox faith and Serbian speech, who comprised a large part of emigrants from the Ottoman Empire, it should be noted that even if, as herdsmen-warriors until the thirteenth, fourteenth, [and] fifteenth century, they were incorporated as a *corpus separatum* in medieval Serb society (which they were not), in the period of Ottoman rule they had abundant reason to integrate themselves into the Serb Orthodox community" (my translation from an unpublished paper for a symposium on "Christianity and Islam in Southeastern Europe" at Airley House, Virginia, in September 1992).

9. My meetings in 1965 and 1979 with the latest (and last?) Albanian Muslim *vojvoda* of Peć Patriarchate, Rame K. Nikçi of the Kelmendi clan and also a member of the Yugoslav League of Communists, are described in *The Other Albanians*, American Universities Field Staff Reports, Southeast Europe Series 12:2 (November 1965) and *The Other Albania: Kosovo 1979, Part II*, ibid., 1980/No. 6). On the first occasion he proudly recited the names and biographies (invariably ending in violent death) of twelve generations of ancestors, arriving in the tenth at the one who converted from Catholic Christianity to Islam and migrated to Kosovo. In 1965 he was additionally a school administrator and in 1979 head of the Peć district employment office.

10. Thus Drago Roksandić (in the unpublished paper cited in note 8) notes that the exodus of 1690 "greatly strengthened the older Serb communities, who with varying (dis-) continuity lived in east-central Europe from the 15th and 16th centuries at latest. But these were not only former Turkish *martolozi* and mercenaries who became Hapsburg 'militiamen,' frontiersmen (*krajišnici*), and similar, but also merchants, craftsmen, and above all, for the first time on such a scale, the church hierarchy, headed by the Patriarch. Therefore that exodus, although only one of many, is the most important." The following, including the section on Bosnia, draws on that paper and other works by the same author: *Srpska i hrvatska povijest i "nova historija"* (Zagreb: Stvarnost, 1991), and *Srbi u Hrvatskoj* (Zagreb: Vjesnik "posebno izdanje," 1991).

11. It also created a Serb plurality in what briefly (1848–60) became the Serb *Vojvodina* (duchy) in southeastern Hungary, just across the Danube from Ottoman and later autonomous Serbia. In Vojvodina these *prečani* (across-the-river) Serbs came to occupy positions across the social spectrum, from peasants to intellectual and commercial elites, and became the fountainhead of Serb cultural renaissance and national(ist) aspirations in the 18th and early 19th centuries.

12. Adolf Karger, "Die serbischen Siedlungsräume in Kroatien," in *Osteuropa* 42, no.2 (February 1992): 141–46, with tables and map based on results of the 1991 Yugoslav census.

13. Macedonians and Montenegrins were classified as Serbs when the first Yugoslav state was created as the Kingdom of the Serbs, Croats, and Slovenes in 1918. Their "elevation" to separate nation status by Tito's Communist regime remains hotly disputed, especially by many Serbs. Equally disputed was the later promotion of Muslim Slavs to the same status.

14. Petrović, "The National Composition" in *Yugoslav Survey*, which provides a useful presentation and analysis of data on nationality in all of the republics from the 1991 census.

15. These and other postwar border adjustments are described in Miodrag Zečević and Bogdan Lekić, *Frontiers and Internal Territorial Division in Yugoslavia* (Belgrade: Ministry of Information of the Republic of Serbia, 1991).

16. Recent historical and postwar political historical reasons for this hesitation and their reflection in postwar censuses are described in Dennison Rusinow, *Yugoslavia's Muslim Nation*, in *UFSI Reports* 8 (1982).

17. John Fine, whose *The Bosnian Church* (New York: Columbia University Press, 1975) is generally considered the most authoritative, is one of those who disputes the traditional view that the Bosnian church was "Bogomil" and Manichaean. Cf. his contributions to Fine and Donia (1994), and to Pinson (1994), and the balancing of both views in Malcolm (1994).

18. As argued by Roksandić, in the paper cited in note 8 above, with maps of pre-Ottoman and Ottoman Catholic and Orthodox ecclesiastical jurisdictions and monasteries.

19. Emanuel Turczynski, *Konfession und Nation: Zur Frühgeschichte der serbischen und rumänischen Nationsbildung* (Dusseldorf, 1976) as cited by Peter Sugar, "Nationalism and Religion in the Balkans Since the 19th Century" (unpublished paper for the previously cited Airley House symposium, see note 8).

20. A history of the Croatian Catholic Church compares the fate of Catholics in central and western Bosnia in the fifteenth and sixteenth centuries as follows: "The inhabitants of more central parts of Bosnia remained on their ancestral properties because the war here was quickly over, but the indigenous population between the Vrbas and Una disappeared because here the war lasted a long time; they partly perished and partly emigrated." As quoted by Roksandić, in his Airley House paper, from Josip Buturac and Antun Ivandija, *Povijest Katoličke Crkve medju Hrvatima* (Zagreb: HKD Sv. Cirila i Metoda, 1973), pp 142f; my translation.

21. The 1991 census was also the basis for the proposed division of Bosnia-Herzegovina into ten autonomous provinces—three each for the Croats, Serbs, and Muslims plus Sarajevo—in the "peace plan" drafted by Cyrus Vance and Lord David Owen for the United Nations and the European Community in January 1993 and rejected by the Bosnian Serbs, then controling an estimated 70 percent of the republic, in April–May.

22. Kemal Karpat's explanation (*An Enquiry*, pp. 40–48) of the rise and decline of Muslim preponderance in Ottoman cities, which he attributes to changing trade and occupational patterns, uses Sarajevo as one of his examples and probably applies to most other Bosnian cities.

23. Bogdan Denitch, "The Death of Yugoslavia: A Personal Report and a Beginning of An Analysis," mss. for forthcoming publication in *Dissent*, p. 7.

24. The following observations are based on an English translation published in *South Slav Journal* 10, no. 1 (1987).

25. The remainder of this section is partly based on Rusinow, *Yugoslavia's Muslim Nation* (note 16) and adapted from my chapter, "The Yugoslav Peoples" in Peter Sugar, ed., *East European Nationalisms in the Twentieth Century* (Washington, D.C.: American University Press, forthcoming).

26. The concept of nations as "imagined communities" is by Benedict Anderson, *Imagined Communities* (London: Verso, 1983).

27. The Bosnians, who differ about highly significant matters like the weighting of Islam and other factors in "making" a Muslim nation and the extent and content of this achievement, include Salim Cerić, *Muslimani srpskohrvatskog jezika* (1968), Atif Purivatra, *Nacionalni i politički razvitak Muslimana* (1969), and Muhamed Hadžÿahić, *Od tradicije do identiteta: geneza nacionalnog pitanja bosanskih Muslimana* (1974), all published in Sarajevo (by Svjetlost) after full official

recognition of the Muslim nation in 1968. Non-Yugoslav authors on whom I have also drawn include Steven L. Burg, *The Political Integration of Yugoslavia's Muslims: Determinants of Success and Failure* (Pittsburgh: Carl Beck Papers in Russian and East European studies, No. 203, 1983), and Ivo Banac, *The National Question in Yugoslavia* (Ithaca: Cornell University Press, 1974), pp. 359–77.

28. The central and persuasive argument in Karpat, *An Enquiry.*

29. Burg, *Political Integration*, p. 11. Cf. Banac, *National Question*, pp. 364–66.

30. Ibid., p. 12.

31. A "memorandum" drafted by members of the Serbian Academy of Science and Arts in 1986 (*Memorandum SANU*), first published without authorization in several non-Serbian periodicals and later widely regarded as the Milošević regime's basic ideological and programatic text, includes a forceful early articulation of these arguments (relevant portions are translated in my chapter in Sugar, *East European Nationalisms*). Cf. Zečević, *Frontiers and Internal Territorial Division*, for their reiteration in 1990, and Ljubo Boban, *Hrvatske granice 1918–1992* (Zagreb: Skolska knjiga, 1992), for counterarguments.

32. The Serb counterargument is that internal borders cannot be "grandfathered" into international borders by international recognition of secessionist states designed to prevent border changes that are already in progress.

33. The serious exception is the short but highly controversial and violently contested border between Croatia and Vojvodina (Serbia). It was drawn after considerable controversy and largely but not entirely along ethnic lines (between predominantly Croat and predominantly Serb or Magyar districts and even villages) in 1945.

34. The southern one, at Sutorina on the Bay of Kotor, was transferred to Montenegro, along with ex-Venetian territories around and south of Kotor, in 1945.

35. See *Granice Hrvatske na zemljovidima od 12. do 20. stoljeća* (Zagreb: Museum of Arts and Crafts, 1992), a richly illustrated catalog for an exhibit in Zagreb (December 1992–February 1993) of maps of Croatia and environs dating from the twelfth to the twentieth century. The selection is designed to substantiate both the antiquity of Croatia's 1945–91 borders within Yugoslavia and designation of parts of Bosnia-Herzegovina in the Ottoman period as "Turkish Croatia" and "Turkish Venetia/Dalmatia."

CHAPTER SIX

MEMORY, HERITAGE, AND HISTORY:

THE OTTOMAN LEGACY IN THE ARAB WORLD

Karl K. Barbir

Thucydides offers this description of how the Athenian people looked back at an event of the Peloponnesian War: "it was a case of people adapting their memories to suit their sufferings."[1] The Athenians were by no means alone in this. People from that time to this day have adapted their memories to suit not just their sufferings but their prejudices, hopes, and fears. A recent example comes from the American journalist P. J. O'Rourke. In a best-selling collection of essays (many of them concerning the 1991 Gulf War), O'Rourke directs his sarcasm at the Ottoman background of the modern Middle East: "Until 1918 the Arabian peninsula was ruled by the Ottoman Empire, so called because it had the same amount of intelligence and energy as a footstool."[2] O'Rourke is simply repeating a theme of nationalist historiography which has held sway since the rise of nationalism around the world during roughly the last century and a half.[3] This nationalist view of the past adapts a people's memories to suit their sufferings, as Thucydides would have it.

How the Arab peoples have approached their Ottoman past—negatively, much in the spirit of O'Rourke—is now a familiar theme of modern Arab history.[4] But why was that theme so long enshrined as orthodoxy, and why has it begun to change, if ever so slowly, during the last two decades? My suggested answer to these questions falls into two parts. The first part summarizes what is known about the past as "reality," in the common-sense understanding of that term—what the experience of the Arabic-speaking peoples was like in Ottoman times and how those peoples responded to it. The second part looks at the ways in which the past serves present purposes, and how those uses have changed since the end of the Ottoman Empire following the First World War.

The Past As Reality

The Ottoman era of Arab history is almost exactly four centuries, a long time span for any people. Much of that period remains shrouded in mystery, scantly studied and little understood. This is especially the case for what might be called the early modern period of Arab history corresponding to the "middle centuries" of Ottoman history (roughly 1600–1800). That those middle centuries were the point of departure for the modern experience is now beyond doubt, but there is still relatively little known about them and shared in common by the peoples of the successor states, even compared to what is known about the Middle East from the nineteenth century on.

There are many reasons for this situation. The most notable of them is that the notion of Ottoman "decline" became a staple of European historiography by the early nineteenth century. When Leopold von Ranke, the father of professional history in Europe, published his history of the seventeenth-century Ottoman and Spanish empires,[5] his main theme was that the Ottoman and Spanish empires were declining as the European middle classes were rising. That notion was incorporated into nationalist writings in the Middle East during the late nineteenth and early twentieth centuries, and it became a commonplace of both Turkish and Arab historiography, echoing the European view uncritically and for entirely different reasons.

The recent past became an object of derision and contempt; the remote past, the age of glory and empire (particularly the Umayyad and Abbasid periods) was held up as a standard to which modern Arabs might aspire. For those who now began to think of themselves as Turks, the ancient Hittites, among others, provided an important model.

In a different vein, the Young Ottomans, mid nineteenth-century reformist intellectuals who were deeply influenced by European science and knowledge, directed their efforts toward creating a modernized Ottoman Empire. Nationalist and ecumenical visions were thus engaged in a struggle for the soul of the Ottoman state. That the ecumenical vision lost out was by no means inevitable.

Another reason for the relative neglect of the middle centuries of Ottoman history was the assumption that the dramatic changes of the nineteenth century—domestic reform, social unrest, nationalist agitation, and European economic and political ascendancy—made the earlier Ottoman period appear irrelevant, qualitatively no different from the more remote, medieval past.

Over the last generation, however, scholarship in both the Middle East and in the West has begun to take a different approach, assuming that those middle centuries possessed a dynamic of their own, that living societies within an Ottoman framework actually did evolve and change (although admittedly not at the pace of the nineteenth century), and that there is much to be learned from the experience of those middle centuries.

As for the Arabic-speaking peoples of the empire, concentrated for the most part in some one-third of the Ottoman provinces as late as the eighteenth century, they maintained a certain reserve, sometimes even indifference, punctuated by periods of open resistance to their Ottoman masters. Such resistance most often coincided with periods of uncertainty and unrest in the imperial capital, when factions of the ruling elite vied to control the Ottoman imperial house for their own purposes.

There are several vivid examples of this phenomenon. The famed "Edirne Incident," a coup d'etat in 1703, resulted in the overthrow of Feyzullah Efendi, the empire's chief mufti, at the hands of another faction of the ruling elite that resented the mufti's influence over the sultan. In particular, that other faction blamed Feyzullah for his disastrous interference in the war the Ottomans had prosecuted against the Austrians and their brilliant general, Prince Eugene of Savoy, from 1683 to 1699, and which that general continued well into the eighteenth century.[6] Shortly after this revolution, an uprising occurred in Jerusalem that had little to do with the issues dividing the ruling elite in the capital, and more to do with local politics and factionalism among the local elite.[7] The same held true for disturbances at the same time in other places.

Similarly, very few primarily Arabic-speaking persons participated in the ruling elite of the empire. Perhaps two or three individuals of Arab ethnic background served as grand vizier and, by one estimate, for the sixteenth and seventeenth centuries, no more than three or four percent of the official religious-legal hierarchy, the ulama, were of Arab background.[8]

Arabic literary sources by the eighteenth century distinguished the practices and values of the imperial capital from those of the Arab provinces. The former's customs were referred to in a stock phrase, "as was their custom or habit," *ka-'adatihim*. This phrase emphasized a sense of difference, not just the separation implied by geographic distance.[9]

Learned Arabs who visited the Ottoman capital were impressed, to be sure, by much of what they saw; but they rarely enjoyed the benefit of belonging to the ruling elite, of becoming Ottomans, those who served both the Islamic faith and the universal Islamic state. For example, the bitter disappointment of the Egyptian, al-Khafaji, who was well steeped in Ottoman letters and spent much time in Istanbul, is very much in evidence in his mid-seventeenth century work, *Rihanat al-ahibba'*, and it was probably typical of most Arabic-

speaking individuals (not to mention other provincials) who found themselves frozen out of the highest rewards of patronage and power controlled by
the Ottoman state.[10]

Also illuminating the perception of a cultural distance between periphery
and center was Muhammad Khalil al-Muradi, chief Hanafi mufti of
Damasacus between 1778 and 1791, historian of that city and an important figure in Damascene social and intellectual life. Muradi's case illustrates the complex relationships tying a provincial figure—albeit an important one—to the
center of Ottoman politics and society in Istanbul. He clearly fit the standard
scholarly definition of an Ottoman as an individual who served the faith and
the state (*din ve devlet*) and practiced the language and etiquette of the
Ottoman elite (*edeb-i Osmani*).[11] Muradi did know Ottoman Turkish,
although he was primarily Arabic-speaking; he observed a different, though
no less sophisticated, etiquette marked by the gravity and sobriety for which
provincial Arab or Turkish ulama were generally recognized; and he served the
faith and the state while also exercising social leadership in an urban setting,
a common practice outside the empire's capital.

When he encountered his Ottoman counterparts in the imperial capital,
Muradi sensed the cultural differences distinguishing him (and, by extention
others from the Arab provinces) from his Istanbul hosts. That sense of difference appears often in the works of this eminent Arab intellectual. He always
took pains to emphasize it by referring to Ottoman practices with the stock
phrase already mentioned, "as was their custom."[12]

For their part, Muradi's Ottoman colleagues, the elite in the capital,
regarded both provincial and especially rural peoples of whatever ethnicity—
Turkish or Arab—with suspicion and contempt. The Turkish term "Arap"
even carried with it a pejorative racial connotation of "black," which has been
preserved in the modern Turkish language.[13] An example illustrates the mentality involved. In 1757, the newly named grand vizier Raghib Pasha, who had
briefly served as governor of Aleppo and then even more briefly as governor
of Damascus, referred to his colleague and predecessor at Damascus, the
Arab As'ad Pasha al-'Azm, as "peasant, son of a peasant" (*fallah ibn fallah*)
when the latter refused to assist Raghib to proceed quickly to Istanbul and to
assume his new duties as grand vizier.[14] The irony here is that Raghib's derision was expressed in Arabic, a language he knew well as a member of the
Ottoman learned and bureaucratic elite and which he had studied when he
was earlier governor of Egypt. Moreover, in that very year the official
Ottoman register of outgoing edicts, the *Mühimme Defteri*, referred to Damascus, an Arab city then dominated by the 'Azm family, as *haram-i rabi'*, or
the fourth holiest city of Islam. This was a novel formulation, which may well
have had political significance.[15]

Clearly there was ambivalence in even the cultured, Ottoman-speaking Arab's perception of the Ottoman Empire and things Ottoman. The distinction was not solely ethnic or a matter of language, but was textured by personal experience, social solidarity, and professional identification. Here, it was familiarity which bred discontent; it was not ignorance and deliberate rejection which did so, as was to be the case in much of the twentieth century, after the empire's demise. Even so, it is important to keep in mind that in this early modern period, before the nineteenth century, the sociopolitical context remains firmly imperial, which is to say pre-nationalist.

What changed this ambivalent and occasionally hostile relationship over the course of the nineteenth century? Other than the well-known impact of Europe, it is clear that Ottoman reform movements, in their successive stages (Selim III, 1789–1807; Mahmud II, 1808–1839; the Tanzimat period, 1839–1876; the reign of Abdulhamid II, 1876–1909; and the period when the Young Turks dominated, until 1918), did much to undermine the self-understanding of Middle Eastern peoples who had been part of the Ottoman Empire. New currents of thought, primarily from the West, came in torrents, making for a heady ideological brew. Islamism, reformism, decentralization, and nationalism were all bandied about as possibilities for the future by an increasingly vocal and literate elite, regardless of their ethnic or religious backgrounds. That the many different nationalisms were to prevail, as it appears so understandable from today's vantage-point, was by no means seen as assured by those generations who wrestled with these contending ideas at the time. The Ottoman reformers worked to preserve the empire that Tsar Nicholas I of Russia called "sick," probably terminally ill, shortly before the onset of the Crimean War. Ironically, the Russian Empire predeceased the Ottoman by a few years. It was an unhealthy time for eastern empires.

Despite the defeat of the Young Ottoman ideal with the imposition of Sultan Abdulhamid II's despotism after 1878, a modified reformism persisted among segments of the Ottoman elite, both at the center and in the provinces. This reformism attempted to respect the particularities of Ottoman peoples within an overarching Islamic-Ottoman framework. This conception of variety-within-unity (a rough nineteenth-century Middle Eastern equivalent of today's "diversity" in American public discourse) continued to exercise a powerful attraction, particularly because it offered legal and civic equality (at least in principle) to all Ottoman subjects and was thought by the reformers to be the only way to save the state by retaining the loyalties of all its peoples. The reformers, however, had formidable opponents both within the ruling elite and among the nascent nationalist groups everywhere in the empire.

It was not until the Young Turks appeared to abandon the reformists' pluralistic vision in the years just before World War I that some Arabs seriously began to contemplate a separate destiny of their own, even though a cultural and literary revival had begun among them as early as the middle of the nineteenth century.[16] World War I made the realization of the Arabs' dream seem possible. And it was the horror of that war which helped to entrench the nationalist historiography of the 1920s and 1930s among Arabs. This was particularly the case with Arabs of the Fertile Crescent. Finding themselves divided into the separate European mandatory states of Syria, Lebanon, Iraq, Trans-Jordan, and Palestine, these Arabs could easily "suit their sufferings" with the idea that the Arabs had had the bad luck of finally escaping one retrogressive imperialism (Ottoman) only to fall prey to another imperialism (European). Indeed, this became the standard version of Arab nationalism.

The classic Arab statement of this view appeared, ironically, in English in 1938. This was *The Arab Awakening*, written by George Antonius, a Palestinian Christian Arab. Later historical research has, however, demonstrated the weaknesses in this interpretation of Arab-Ottoman relations. Among the corrections presented by subsequent historical research are the following: 1) The role of Christian missionaries and the schools they created (such as the Syrian Protestant College, later American University of Beirut), while important in

Sultan Abdulhamid II. Topkapi Palace Museum.

stimulating Westernization, pale in comparison to the Ottoman Empire's much more pervasive modernizing educational efforts begun during the period of the Tanzimat. 2) Sultan Abdulhamid was not anti-Arab. Indeed, his reign brought several Arabs to high office. Abdulhamid's Pan-Islam can be seen, in part, as a plausible strategy of relying more on the (largely Arab and Turkish) Muslimness of the empire, after having lost most of the largely Christian territories in Ottoman Europe. 3) The World War I Arab revolt under Sharif Husayn in alliance with Great Britain was supported by only a small number of Arabs, most of whom remained either favorably disposed to the Ottoman government (the last remaining Muslim state of any significance) or at least prudently neutral.

Arabism, in short, came late, and it is poor history to read back into earlier times an Arab nationalism seeking liberation from Ottoman imperialism. The final break was also in large measure a response to the increasingly pronounced Turkish nationalism emanating from Istanbul with the advent of the Young Turk period.[17]

Moreover, the clear point of no return was Kemal Atatürk's forging a successful Turkish nationalist alternative to the imperial legacy. This necessarily ruled out any prospect of an Arabic-Turkish political entity. In the period after World War I, rejection of the Ottoman past, expressed most virulently by those who were themselves formed during the last decades of Ottoman rule, prevailed.[18]

The Past as Ideology

A willed ignorance of and an inability to come to terms with the past as reality is one of the difficulties of writing history. In this human activity there are relatively few settled matters; and historians' choices, commitments, and times tend to shape what they find significant in the past. In other words, each historian is "hooked" to a particular field or subject, whether the hook is personal experience, curiosity, or ideological predilection. Today, however, historians' hooks have changed with the passage of time and with the increasing distance between our own day and the last days of the Ottoman Empire.[19] It should be admitted that not so long ago, nonspecialist historians, even more so the general public, saw little of value in the Ottoman legacy; and it is unfortunate that there are still many who make that judgment today. Why is that the case?

Despite professional historians' protestations to the contrary, ordinary human beings still define history in terms of their own personal experiences. A glance at the history titles displayed in bookstores will convince any skeptic that people are solipsists: the books one sees primarily concern wars, biographies, revolutions, the stuff of ordinary experiences and dreams, in which one can identify with events through which one has lived or with persons with whom one shares values or, in contrast, with whom one differs substantially.

The Ottoman Empire now stands as an interesting example of such solipsism. Few remain alive to whom the empire's life, its realities, are vivid memories. With the passage of time the Ottoman Empire is now truly a part of history, and as such it must be dealt with realistically rather than denied or condemned, as it has been when nationalism among the former peoples of the empire became the dominant ideology, and when, for Arabs, a personal memory of the empire's last rulers, the Young Turks, was vivid and painful, associated with Turkish nationalism and the disasters of World War I and its aftermath. How much more remote are the "middle centuries," which, as has been indicated, were of importance in the formation of the modern Middle East!

With the passing of the first generation of post-Ottoman nationalists, the Arab world witnessed in the 1970s the beginnings of a movement covered by the rubric of *turath*, or legacy. Those involved in this effort have reacted to what they see as the failure of secular and nationalist models of reform and progress. Intellectuals have attempted to define a non-Western, nonsecular identity, couched in Islamic terms. The Ottoman past has figured ambivalently in this redefinition of identity. The Ottomans were one of the last universal Islamic empires, but they are seen as having failed in their encounter with the West. Thus, among authors of the *turath* school, there has been an appreciation of the Islamic aspect of the Ottoman experience, but also a reluctance to consider the *secular* experience of that empire in its contact with the rest of the world and in its everyday responses to the realities of power, of having to contain the aspirations of both Muslim and non-Muslim peoples whose identities could be defined in more than one way. Likewise, the *turath* authors tend to elide over the middle centuries, jumping from the sixteenth century, when much of the Arab world became part of the Ottoman Empire, to the nineteenth century, when the West became so deeply involved in the region.

The Ottoman Empire was more accepting of diverse ethnic, religious, economic, and occupational groups than its modern successors. This may be said without romanticizing the past. The practical considerations which faced Ottoman rulers meant that they had to respect this diversity. Consider, for example, André Raymond's appraisal of urban life in the Arab part of the Ottoman Empire during the early modern period:

> Arab cities in the Ottoman era were characterized by the existence of a great diversity of community organizations (*ta'ifa*, pl. *tawa'if*) that played a very important role in the most varied domains: professional communities . . . , religious and national communities . . . , and geographical communities. . . . These *tawa'if* provided a framework that ensured the inner cohesion of urban society

while enabling the authorities to exercise firm control (in an indirect way). . . . The subjects were thus integrated in a series of networks that covered every aspect of their lives and that, in most cases, were superimposed: a given individual belonged to a craft guild in the course of his professional activity in the suq where he worked during the day, and he belonged to the community of the quarter in which he lived with his family.[20]

Thus, the millet system is only one of several elements of the Ottoman legacy, regardless of the regret and hostility this has raised in the minds of nationalists. Several political movements in the Ottoman successor states, the Arab Ba'th party most notably, regard the millet system as a relic of an Ottoman and European policy of *divide et impera*. Alongside this nationalist view, however, there is an earlier, mid-nineteenth century ideal, the Young Ottoman model, which conceived of a federated empire of peoples and religious communities within an overarching, universal Islamic-Ottoman framework. This was the ideal promoted by the reforming chief minister of the empire, Midhat Pasha (1876–77), by the Lebanese polymath Butrus al-Bustani in the preceding two decades, and promoted in the twentieth century by the Syrian jurist Yusuf al-Hakim, plus others and a minority of contemporary Arab intellectuals.[21]

An example of this view was brought out in a talk by a Christian Lebanese academician at the onset of the Lebanese civil war, in late 1976. Speaking at the United Nations in New York, Elie Salem, an Orthodox Christian, said that Lebanon was "a lost star from the Ottoman galaxy." This was a remarkable statement for a Lebanese, for Lebanon's historiographical tradition (contested as it has been) has emphasized the uniqueness of Lebanon in Middle Eastern history and has sought to detach it from the broader currents (read Islamic) of the region's past.[22]

Lately, a few Arab scholars have addressed their Ottoman heritage in the realization that four hundred years of history cannot be swept aside so neatly. To illustrate the magnitude of this difficulty of coming to terms with a historical legacy, compare the Arab nationalist historiography of the period roughly 1952–1980 with the recent interest in the Ottoman past as demonstrated by the establishment of associations for Ottoman studies in several Arab countries. Although the new Ottoman studies associations have not engaged in a complete reassessment of the Ottoman past, they have begun the process.

A representative sample of this new thinking may be found in the first numbers of a new journal, *Arab Historical Review for Ottoman Studies* (*AHROS*), edited and published by Abdeljelil Temimi of the University of Tunis, the Ottoman Studies Association of Beirut, founded in 1986, with members drawn from several religious-ethnic communities; the Center for

Turkish Studies at the University of Mosul, Iraq, founded in 1988; the Moroccan Association of Ottoman Studies, founded in 1989; and the Egyptian Center of Ottoman Studies, founded in 1990.[23]

One implication of these recent efforts, not yet widely recognized or acknowledged, is that the Ottoman peoples and society may eventually come to be regarded as "normal," not exotic. This is the thrust of Rifaat Abou-El-Haj's argument in *Formation of the Modern State: The Ottoman Empire, Sixteenth to Eighteenth Centuries*. There, he decries the historiography that "continues to emphasize the peculiarities, oddities, and particularism of Ottoman history and civilization."[24] The sooner students of the Ottoman legacy agree that their subjects of study are "normal," comparable to other subjects in other times and places, the better off scholarship will be. The hooks of "exoticism" and of "revulsion" toward the Ottoman past need to be rejected.

One further difficult question facing those who investigate the Ottoman legacy is the persistence of the Ottoman Empire despite all the difficulties. If the empire was in such difficulty, if it suffered so grievously from internal and external challenges, how did it survive? If the Ottomans were so tyrannical, how did individual ethnic/religious/national groups survive? To answer these questions is to go beyond the usual generalizations about lack of alternative structures, or the canceling out of European rivalries concerning the Ottoman patrimony. In regard to the internal situation of the empire Rifaat Abou-El-Haj argues that during the seventeenth and eighteenth centuries, there were apparently contradictory forces of centralization and decentralization at work. The way they interacted might well have preserved at least the essentials of the empire, but they also introduced enormous changes: in the system of tax collection, the composition of the ruling elite, the factionalism within that elite; and so on.[25]

This is a more elaborate and empirically informed hypothesis than that suggested by scholars in the past, an indication of the progress that has been made and which has been the work of many hands. It has the merit of suggesting a dynamic process, rather than headlong decline or stagnation, the previous alternatives. How this hypothesis is treated by future specialized research will be of considerable importance to students of the Ottoman legacy. Will they take a comparative view, within an Ottoman framework, struggling with the main lines of Ottoman history, learning Ottoman Turkish, doing research in the Ottoman archives, and seeking common ground among peoples of the successor states?

Another difficulty facing the successor states is the role of the West. That this role was enormous from the late eighteenth century on must be accepted. Still, there remains the need to see the clash of cultures as involving action and reaction from both sides. It is not as if the Ottoman Empire, even though beleagured, was an inert state and society on which intrusive Europe could work its will. This would be to marginalize Ottoman history as seen from within, to define the Ottoman legacy solely in terms of Europe. It would ignore not only the many initiatives coming from within the Ottoman world from the time of Selim III to the end of empire but also the changes taking place in that important early modern period of c. 1600–1800 before European pressure became predominant.[26]

There was, after all, a vigorous discussion among Ottoman elites from the seventeenth century onward dealing with the problem of Ottoman "decline," or change, as their viewpoints dictated. The extent of change already taking place before the period of European dominance are suggested by such observations as those of Alexander Russell, physician to the Levant Company in Aleppo during the middle decades of the eighteenth century. Russell mixed freely with the local population, unlike many other Europeans resident in Aleppo during his time. His remarks, contained in a large work about Aleppo reveal a dynamic society. For example, Russell reports: "Religion, not reverenced as formerly, retains little more than its outward form: not having influence sufficiently to restrain the numerous vices, which modern luxury, and the frivolous spirit of the age, have universally introduced."[27]

Here one may detect the degree to which Western tastes and goods had become popular among the better-off segments of Aleppine society by the middle to late eighteenth century. A clearer indication of the economic and social implications of the diffusion of Western consumption habits, and of important changes going on within this one segment of Ottoman society, is contained in the following remark made to Russell by a mufti of Aleppo, whom Russell knew intimately: "If you take . . . the reverse of what you have seen daily practiced by us, to be the actual law, you will be nearer the truth and in less danger of misleading your countrymen."[28]

This lament, which has become a staple of contemporary Muslim activist writing in the twentieth century, is also the product of a confrontation between two cultures, two ways of life, two systems of values, a confrontation that would appear to be two centuries old! Russell and the mufti were not exceptional or unusual in perceiving the disruptive changes of their times. In regard to the heedless pursuit of wealth and status, and the consequent neglect of the study of the past, the Egyptian historian 'Abd al-Rahman al-Jabarti (d. after 1826) has much to say. Chronicler of the eighteenth and early nineteenth centuries, witness to Napoleon's occupation of Egypt and to the establishment of Muhammad 'Ali's dynasty in that country, Jabarti was a busy correspondent with important scholars elsewhere in the Ottoman world, from Istanbul to Damascus. In the introduction to his famous history, Jabarti writes:

Things in this age have been turned upside down; [history's] prestige has declined; the foundations of judgment have become unsteady. Events are recorded neither in registers nor in books. The concerns of the moment that are not of [immediate] benefit are lost. What has passed and gone cannot be recovered except when some poor wretch, secluded in the corners of obscurity and neglect, withdrawn from what others do, occupies himself in the time of his isolation and consoles his solitude by counting the wickednesses of fate and its blessings.[29]

Russell's and Jabarti's experiences suggest that students of the Ottoman legacy are challenged, as other historians are, to view the experience of their subjects of study as normal, to evaluate the relative importance of continuity and of change, linking the middle centuries with the modern era, and to make the whole process meaningful to contemporary readers.

One final example of the relevance of the Ottoman past, and of the universal order implied in the nineteenth-century reformist Ottoman ideal of variety-within-unity, is the tragic experience of Bosnia-Herzegovina, and of Sarajevo in particular, the site of the incident in 1914 that sparked the first world war, which hurried the Ottoman Empire to its final disintegration. The suffering of Croats, Muslims, and Serbs in what once was part of the Ottoman world has made painfully relevant *The Bridge on the Drina*, the novel that won Ivo Andric, a Bosnian Serb, the Nobel Prize for Literature in 1961.[30] Andric vindicates Julien Benda, who wrote in the 1920s, "The notion that political warfare involves a war of cultures is entirely an invention of modern times, and confers upon them a conspicuous place in the moral history of humanity," adding his famous phrase that ours is "indeed an age of the *intellectual organization of political hatreds.*"[31]

In the final section of his novel, treating the period after 1878 when Austria-Hungary supplanted the Ottoman Empire in ruling Bosnia, Andric relates a discussion between two university students. One of them, Toma Galus, is a German Austrian whose father had moved to Bosnia; the other, Fehim Bahtijarevic, is a Muslim Bosnian. Their arguments, sometimes vehement and sometimes hesitating, evoke the principal themes of this essay:

The subject was Bahtijarevic's choice of studies. Galus was proving to him that he would be making a mistake in taking up oriental studies. . . .

Bahtijarevic remained silent, and that silence, like the most lively and eloquent speech, provoked Galus. . . . With all his natural vivacity and all the vocabulary then prevalent in nationalist literature, he set out the plans and aims of the revolutionary youth movement. All the living forces of the race must be awakened and set in action. Under their blows the Austro-Hungarian monarchy, that prison of the peoples, would disintegrate as the Turkish Empire had disintegrated. . . . Modern nationalism will triumph over religious diversities and outmoded prejudice, will liberate our people from foreign influence and exploitation. Then will the national state be born.[32]

We live today with the consequences of this way of thinking. From the bridge on the Drina, to Sarajevo, to Beirut, to Jerusalem's heights, to the mountains of Kurdistan, the Ottoman legacy lives on. How it is understood and how it is interpreted will help to determine how human beings will live in this "new world order," indeed whether they can live at all in Julien Benda's age "of the *intellectual organization of political hatreds.*"

NOTES

I thank participants at the First Skilliter Colloquium in Ottoman History held at Newnham College, Cambridge University, in April 1992 and also Professors William Ochsenwald and F. Robert Hunter for their comments and insights. For more than twenty years, one person inspired me to pursue the scholarly directions that have issued in this essay. It is therefore dedicated to the memory of Albert Habib Hourani (1915–1993).

1. Thucydides, *History of the Peloponnesian War*, tr. Rex Warner (London and New York: Penguin Classics, 1972) p. 156.
2. P. J. O'Rourke, *Give War a Chance* (New York: Atlantic Monthly, 1992) p. 167.
3. For a stimulating assessment of nationalism, see Benedict Anderson, *Imagined Communities: Reflections on the Origin and Spread of Nationalism* (rev. ed.; London: Verso, 1991). People in formulating national ideology have devised whole traditions, which they invested with ancient memory, even when not warranted. See Eric Hobsbawm and Terence Ranger, eds., *The Invention of Tradition* (New York: Cambridge: Cambridge University Press, 1984).
4. An influential assessment of this problem is Albert Hourani's "The Ottoman Background of the Modern Middle East," in his *The Emergence of the Modern Middle East* (Berkeley/Los Angeles: University of California Press, 1981), pp. 1–18. Perhaps the best scholarly treatment of the problem in the Arab context is 'Abd al-'Aziz al-Duri, *Al-Takwin al-tarikhi li-al-ummah al-'arabiyyah* (Beirut, 1984), translated into English by Lawrence I. Conrad as *The Historical Formation of the Arab Nation: A Study in Identity and Consciousness* (Durham, N.C.: Duke University Press, 1988).
5. Leopold von Ranke, *The Ottoman and Spanish Empires in the Seventeenth Century*, tr. Walter K. Kelly (London, 1843).
6. For a recent account of this affair, see Rifaat Abou-El-Haj, *The 1703 Rebellion and the Structure of Ottoman Politics* (Istanbul: Nederlands, Archaeological Institute, 1984).
7. A recent study of this incident is Minna Rosen, "The Naqib al-Ashraf Rebellion in Jerusalem and Its Repercussions on the City's *Dhimmis*" *Asian and African Studies* 22 (1984): 249–70.
8. Rifa'at Abou-el-Haj, personal communication, September 1992.
9. See Karl Barbir's discussion in *Ottoman Rule in Damascus, 1708–1758* (Princeton: Princeton University Press, 1980), pp. 75–77.
10. See Rifaat Abou-El-Haj, *Formation of the Modern State: The Ottoman Empire, Sixteenth to Eighteenth Centuries* (Albany: State University of New York Press, 1991) p. 25; and, for more information, his "Ara' 'arabiyya 'an al-inhitat al-'Uthmani fi al-qarn al-sabi' 'ashar," *Al-Majalla al-Tarikhiyya al-Maghribiyya* 57/58 (1990) pp. 17–21.
11. This working definition originated with Lewis V. Thomas and was followed by Norman

Itzkowitz and Max Mote in *Mubadele: An Ottoman-Russian Exchange of Ambassadors* (Chicago: University of Chicago Press, 1970), p. 11. One important advantage of this definition is that it is derived from an Ottoman self-view. A more recent formulation of this definition is in Norman Itzkowitz, "Political Structure," *Modernization in the Middle East: The Ottoman Empire and Its Afro-Asian Successors*, ed. Cyril E. Black and L. Carl Brown (Princeton: Princeton University Press, 1992), pp. 46–47.

12. For example, in his *Silk al-durar fi a'yan al-qarn al-thani 'ashar* (4 vols.; reprinted Baghdad, 1972?), vol. 2, p. 25.

13. Cf. *Redhouse Yeni Türkçe-Ingilizce Sözlük* (Istanbul: Redhouse Press, 1968), p. 69.

14. Barbir, *Ottoman Rule*, pp. 59–60.

15. The reference to the fourth holy place is in Istanbul, Osmanli Arsivi, Mühimme Defteri 160, dated 20 Saban 1171 (April 30, 1758), p. 377.

16. A recent study of these trends, in the Damascus context, is David Dean Commins, *Islamic Reform: Politics and Social Change in Late Ottoman Syria* (New York and Oxford: Oxford University Press, 1990).

17. Pioneering studies on Arab-Ottoman relations, correcting the premature Arab nationalist orientation are C. Ernest Dawn, *From Ottomanism to Arabism* (Champaign: University of Illinois Press, 1973) and Zeine N. Zeine, *Arab-Turkish Relations and the Emergence of Arab Nationalism* (Beirut: Khayats, 1958). *The Origins of Arab Nationalism*, ed. Rashid Khalidi, Lisa Anderson, Muhammad Muslih, and Reeva S. Simon (New York: Columbia University Press, 1991) offers a thorough examination of this issue.

18. For biographies of two prominent individuals who took this stance, but in strikingly different ways, see William L. Cleveland, *The Making of an Arab Nationalist: Ottomanism and Arabism in the Life and Thought of Sati' al-Husri* (Princeton: Princeton University Press, 1971); and his *Islam Against the West: Shakib Arslan and the Campaign for Islamic Nationalism* (Austin: University of Texas Press, 1985).

19. Instructive on this point is J. H. Hexter's famous essay, "The Historian and His Day," in *Reappraisals in History* (Evanston, Ill.: Northwestern University Press, 1961), pp. 1–13.

20. André Raymond, *The Great Arab Cities in the 16th-18th Centuries: An Introduction* (New York: New York University Press, 1984), p. 18.

21. Yusuf al-Hakim, *Suriyya wa al-'ahd al-'Uthmani*, vol. 1 (Beirut: Dar al-Nahar, 1966). Hakim, a Syrian Christian, was formed in the last decades of Ottoman rule and rose to be Chief Justice of independent Syria. For an assessment of Butrus al-Bustani (d. 1883), also a Christian, see Leila al-Imad, "Butrus al-Bustani: A Literary Genius and Social Prophet" *AHROS* 3–4 (December 1991): 39–46.

22. For a sensitive treatment of the problem of reworking Lebanese history within an Ottoman framework, or at least acknowledging the Ottoman dimension of Lebanon's past, see Kamal Salibi, *A House of Many Mansions: The History of Lebanon Reconsidered* (Berkeley/Los Angeles: University of California Press, 1988), chs 8 ("Ottoman Lebanon: How Unique?"), 11 ("The War Over Lebanese History"), and 12 ("A House of Many Mansions").

23. Rifaat Abou-El-Haj, "The Social Uses of the Past: Recent Arab Historiography of Ottoman Rule," *International Journal of Middle East Studies* 14 (1982): 185–201; Abdeljelil Temimi, "Problématiques de la réchèrche historique sur les provinces arabes à l'époque ottomane," *AHROS* 3–4 (December 1991): 111–17 (Arabic version, pp. 23–30). The list of new Ottoman studies centers is given on p. 115. It should be noted that Morocco was not part of the Ottoman Empire, although it had intensive trade and diplomatic contacts with it. For western Arabia, specifically the Hijaz, which was under Ottoman rule, see William Ochsenwald, "The Recent Historiography of Western Arabia: A Critical Examination," to appear in volume 23 of the *Proceedings of the Seminar for Arabian Studies*.

24. *Formation of the Modern State* p. 1. As Suraiya Faroqhi and Cornell Fleischer point out in their preface to this work (p. xi), "such relatively innocuous statements may stop being innocuous

when one considers the context in which they are made," namely the tradition that continues to see the experience of other civilizations as exotic, strange, and not necessarily subject to trends and forces similar to those found elsewhere.

25. See Abou-El-Haj, *Formation of the Modern State*, particularly the Epilogue, pp. 61–72.

26. This point is made most forcefully by Roger Owen in "The Middle East in the Eighteenth Century—an 'Islamic' Society in Decline: A Critique of Gibb and Bowen's *Islamic Society and the West*," *Review of Middle East Studies* I (1975): 101–12. Owen (p. 108) criticizes the obsession of some Western scholars with the notion of Ottoman decline; in his view, that conception is "clearly ideological and stems directly from the initial project of examining the Middle East in terms of an entity called 'Islamic' society, something which can only be compared with another entity—Western society."

27. Alexander Russell, *The Natural History of Aleppo*, vol. 1, 2d ed. revised by Patrick Russell (2 vols.; London, 1794), p. 336.

28. Russell, *Natural History*, p. 337.

29. 'Abd al-Rahman al-Jabarti, *'Aja'ib al-athar fi al-tarajim wa al-akhbar* I (4 vols.; Bulaq, 1879), p. 5.

30. Ivo Andric, *The Bridge on the Drina*, translated from the Serbo-Croatian by Lovett F. Edwards (Chicago: University of Chicago Press, 1977). Andric was earlier a student of Slavic languages at the University of Vienna. His doctoral thesis has recently been translated into English: *The Development of Spiritual Life in Bosnia Under the Influence of Turkish Rule*, ed. and tr. Zelimir B. Juricic and John F. Loud (Durham and London; Duke University Press, 1990).

31. Julien Benda, *The Treason of the Intellectuals*, tr. Richard Aldington (New York: Norton, 1969) pp. 20 and 27 respectively (emphasis in original).

32. Andric, *The Bridge on the Drina*, pp. 242, 244–45. .

CHAPTER SEVEN

THE OTTOMAN LEGACY IN

ARAB POLITICAL BOUNDARIES

André Raymond

Most of the Arab world formed part of the Ottoman Empire, having been absorbed in a process of conquest and expansion that began in 1514 (Iraq) and ended in 1574 (Tunisia), with the definitive inclusion of Iraq finally settled only in 1639 following several Ottoman-Safavid wars. Only Morocco, Mauritania, and parts of the Arabian Peninsula completely escaped one form or another of Ottoman rule, for even the Sudan came under Egyptian rule beginning in 1820 at a time when Egypt was nominally part of the Ottoman Empire.

Moreover, the Arab world constituted a major segment of the expansive Ottoman Empire from the sixteenth century onward, growing in importance in the nineteenth century as Ottoman holdings in Europe were lost, one after the other, to independence movements supported by the European state system.

These Ottoman Arab lands later fell under British, French or Italian (Libya) rule beginning as early as 1830 (Algeria) with the last to be colonized being those Arab lands of the Fertile Crescent divided between Britain and France as League of Nations mandated territories after World War I. The only parts of the Ottoman Arab lands to escape a period of European colonial rule were the western and central portions (the Hijaz and the Najd) of what later became Saudi Arabia and Yemen. It was only after a process beginning very slowly as early as the 1920s and reaching a crescendo in the 1950s and 1960s that these Arab regions, which had been Ottoman provinces and then colonial territories, achieved full independence.

During the process of this accession to independence, and after, the problem of boundaries played an important role. It has been a constant Arab assertion that colonial boundaries, dividing the Arab *umma*, had been one of the reasons for the difficult development of a united Arab nation, or of regional regroupments. Several conflicts that arose during the first decades of the post-independence period confirm the importance of the problem: the Algerian-Moroccan war of 1962–1963 (with its Sahara war extension); boundary disputes and conflicts between Saudi Arabia and its neighbors; conflict between Libya and Chad; the eight-year war between Iraq and Iran; and lately Iraqi aggression against Kuwait.

Therefore one has to think seriously about these conflicts, their importance and their origin. And, of course, one must avoid a condescending European attitude of assuming the futility of such conflicts, for this would be to ignore four or five centuries of wars for boundaries that shaped today's Europe or to ignore those struggles over boundaries now brewing in various parts of the European continent, and exploding in the case of the former Yugoslavia. Political boundaries are neither irrelevant nor out of date. It is worth asking how these modern Arab state boundaries developed, and what was the role of the Ottomans who governed this area for so long.

I shall first deal with the "external" boundaries of the empire and then with the "internal" boundaries, although this classification is not totally operative.

The External Boundaries of the Empire

For the Arab part of the empire the problem of establishing external boundaries arose in the west (between the deylik of Algiers and Morocco) and in the east (between Iraq and Persia).

In the west, before the installation of Ottoman power, the Abd al-Wad dynasty with its capital in Tlemcen, which loosely dominated the "Central Maghrib," was neighbor to the Marinid Moroccan empire. Turks first appeared in this region as sea warriors (*ghazis*) fighting against the Christians, who were threatening the Muslim Mediterranean cities. Arûj, a bold Turkish privateer, who was waging a naval jihad against the Christians, was called in to help by the autonomous Algerians then threatened by the Spaniards. He settled in Algiers (in 1515). His brother and successor, Khayr al-Din, soon realized that the only way to establish his authority and contain the Spanish expansion was to place himself under Ottoman suzerainty. He recognized the authority of Sultan Selim (1518) and in return he was appointed *beylerbey* (governor), received substantial military support (two thousand men), and was authorized to levy four thousand volunteers in Anatolia. It is in this manner that the Ottoman authority got a foothold in North Africa. After Khayr al-

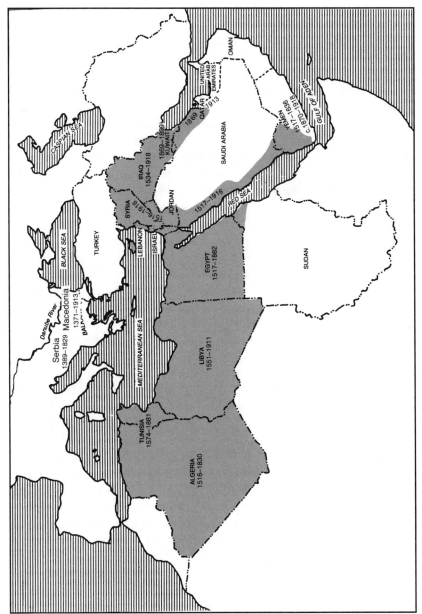

The Arab world in the Ottoman Empire. Map by John T. Westlake, Princeton, N.J.

Din's occupation of Bone, Constantine, and Algiers, Salah Ra'is, pasha of Algiers, was able to occupy Tlemcen, in 1555. The ujaq of Algiers was now in direct contact with imperial Morocco, where the internal political difficulties which had accompanied the accession of the sharifian dynasty of the Sa'dians had no doubt hindered reactions against the development of a powerful empire on Morocco's eastern borders.

The Sa'dian empire (1550–1660) was to stay aloof from Ottoman influence, although, at times, the formal inclusion of Morocco in the empire was contemplated. But as soon as the Sa'dians were able to develop an active policy in the east, they tried to bring Tlemcen into the Moroccan orbit. The establishment of a lasting delimitation between the sharifian empire and the semi-autonomous state of the ujaq of Algiers was implemented through a series of conflicts in which the janissaries of Algiers generally had the upper hand, thanks to the excellent military organization they had received from the Ottomans. In 1557 Mulay Muhammad Sharif invaded the province of Tlemcen, but was driven back by the *beylerbey* Hasan and his 6,000 "musketeers" who advanced thereafter against Morocco until they pitched their tents under the walls of Fez.

Around 1574 Mulay 'Abdallah allied with the Christians. Ulj Ali, *beylerbey* of the Ottoman Maghrib then gave permission for a campaign in Morocco; Ramadan lead his 7,000 janissaries to Fez and placed the Ottoman protege, Mulay Muluk, on the throne. An Ottoman protectorate was thus very nearly established in Morocco but, in 1578, Mulay Muluk was killed at the famous battle of Qasr al-Kabir. The tribute the Ottomans had succeeded in imposing on Morocco was later refused by the reestablished Sa'dians.

At the end of the seventeenth century the Alawites (the dynasty that still rules Morocco) again failed to extend Moroccan control into the province of Tlemcen. In 1692 at the Muluya River, the dey of Algiers crushingly defeated the powerful sultan Mulay Isma'il, who, according to the Algerian sources, acknowledged his defeat in humiliating terms. He presented himself to his victorious enemy, kissed the earth three times and said "You are the knife, I am the flesh which you can cut."[1] After a century of unsuccessful struggle the Moroccans had to recognize the military superiority of the Algerians, and resign themselves to a boundary that left Tlemcen on the Algerian side.

The French conquest of Algiers in 1830 permitted a brief occupation of Tlemcen by Morocco (1831), but as soon as Abd al-Qadir had his authority recognized in western Algeria (convention of the Tafna, in 1837) the western province, and Tlemcen, fell under his authority. The backing Morocco gave to Abd al-Qadir in his war against France and the French expansionist policy produced a confrontation that was settled militarily at Isly, where the French army defeated the Moroccans (August 14, 1844). The convention of Lalla Maghnia (March 18, 1845) defined the limits between French Algeria and

Morocco. On the whole this settlement conformed to the "Turkish" boundary in the northern region,[2] where a precise limit could be drawn. Further south the tribes were shared between both powers, the Sahara being considered a no-man's-land.

The settlement was unfavorable to Morocco. It was aggravated by the encroachments of French colonial administration on the Algerian border, but even more severely by the French colonial policy of "penetration" in the Sahara from Algiers, which established the French dominated Algeria in the Sahara. Out of necessity (the "Turks," established in the coastal regions of Algeria and Tunisia, had been unable to control the far hinterland of the Maghrib), but also in a logical manner, the Ottomans had considered the Maghrib interior as a kind of common hinterland, loosely tied to the Mediterranean regions. This conception also had the advantage of leaving the local nomad Berber population (the Tuaregs) free to roam in vast areas in which no formal boundaries existed, and in which oil was still to be discovered. For the sake of their imperial African policy the French annexed all this vast zone to Algeria, which they supposed definitely tied to France, thus depriving Morocco and Tunisia of their traditional outlets toward the southern regions.

Thus, the conflicts following Maghrib independence in the Maghrib resulted more from European than Ottoman policy. A few years before the end of the Algerian war of independence (1962), the Tunisian authorities tried to obtain from the French a rectification of Saharan boundaries which they deemed, quite reasonably, unfair, since they severed Tunisia from regions with which the country had had traditional (mainly commercial) relations, and deprived it from an eventual share in the rich oil fields recently discovered in the "Algerian" Sahara. The battle engaged for delimitation in the last period of "French" Algeria stopped abruptly because little Tunisia did not have enough political and military power to back its claims.

The serious incidents that turned to open war between Morocco and recently independent Algeria, in 1962 and 1963,[3] and the continuing conflict about the ex-Spanish Sahara are directly linked to the colonial boundaries which clearly gave the advantage to Algeria at the expense of Morocco and of its traditional relations with the Sudan. In the northern region, where an Algerian-Moroccan delimitation had been traced in the Ottoman period, and roughly confirmed in 1845, the two contending countries have finally agreed to keep the traditional delimitation. But a conflict is still raging in the desert areas. The Tuaregs, divided by boundaries put in place by French colonial authorities, try to keep their cultural identity uneasily tolerated by nationalist governments that would prefer to absorb them into centralized nation-states. The Tuareg case is not very different from that of the Kurds, but the Tuaregs are a small, scattered, and rapidly diminishing community.

The eastern boundaries of the Arab provinces of the Ottoman Empire were fixed after long and difficult conflict between the Ottoman Empire and Iran. At the beginning of the sixteenth century, Arab Iraq, long dominated by Iranian influences, had fallen under the authority of the Safavids. Even before turning against the central Arab lands (Syria and Egypt) Selim the conqueror launched a campaign in the east, and after the victory of Chaldiran he was able to occupy Mosul (1514). But it was Suleiman who, in 1534 and 1535, conquered Baghdad. With the occupation of Basra some years later, the fate of Iraq would apparently have been settled, with eastern limits very similar to today's frontiers had it not been for the "folie des grandeurs" of both parties.

In 1623 the Iranians occupied Baghdad (but not Mosul and Kirkuk) and a third Ottoman sultan, Murad IV, had to launch a powerful campaign, in 1638–39, to recapture the whole of Iraq. The treaty signed in 1639 agreed on a border that could have remained definitive.

When however the Afghans conquered Iran (1722) the Ottomans supposed that the internal difficulties of their neighbors afforded them a good opportunity to settle to their advantage the longstanding quarrel. This was not to be the last example of political forces on the Iraqi side of the Iraq-Iran border misjudging the presumed vulnerability of its eastern neighbor. Things began well for the Ottomans with the conquest of Karmanshah and Hamadan but then evolved into a nightmare with a crushing defeat in 1726. There was a short lull, but this "perverse and needless war" was revived when the Safavids returned to power in Iran.[4] After alternate successes and defeats, a treaty was concluded in 1732 on the basis of a return to the 1639 (Murad IV) provisions.

By then, however, a new conqueror had arisen in the east, Nadir Shah, who proclaimed his ambitions in 1733: "Be it known to you, the Basha of Bagdat, that we claim an indubitable right of visiting the tombs of the Imams Ali . . . and Husein. . . . We are going soon at the head of our victorious army to breath the sweet air of the plains of Bagdat, and to take our repose under the shadow of its walls."[5] In effect, Nadir Shah's expedition was no "promenade de santé." It inaugurated a thirteen-year period of desultory but vicious warfare (30,000 Iranians killed in one of the several bloody battles) until finally the two sides, perceiving the stalemate, concluded a peace in 1746 that again endorsed the boundaries of 1639. Later warfare between the two states brought no appreciable border changes, and the next major peace treaty between the Ottomans and Iran (Erzurum in 1823) also accepted the boundaries agreed upon in 1639.[6]

Perhaps the historical lesson is that the boundaries established in 1639 were realistic, and a more judicious Iraq in 1980 would have refrained from trying to modify the limits that the Ottomans had bequeathed to Iraq after a protracted and useless conflict with their eastern neighbors.

The problem of Kuwait has of late been much discussed but without any clear conclusion. It is probable that the Ottomans exerted some sort of control on the lands adjoining Iraq, but they did not exercise sovereignty over Kuwait when the Al-Sabah dynasty appeared in the eighteenth century. It was much later, when Midhat Pasha governed Baghdad (1869–1872), that the Ottoman government tried to strengthen its authority over Kuwait: it was then organized as a district (*kaza*) attached to Basra.

The rulers of Kuwait were eager to obtain formal British protection, which was granted but not made public: the agreement of 1899 was to remain secret. In the end (1913) an Anglo-Ottoman convention recognizing Kuwait as an autonomous *kaza* was negotiated and concluded, but never ratified. The Ottoman suzerainty in Kuwait was thus indisputable, but this establishes no later Iraqi right over Kuwait. In any case, World War I allowed Kuwait to step out of the empire and to engage in a separate existence under British protection: its boundaries, which had been outlined in 1913, were recognized in 1922 by the Saudis, and in 1932 by independent Iraq. The Ottomans never found time to delimit the border, which was not then a matter of great concern. The oil fields were not yet exploited.

The boundaries of northern Syria (eyalets of Aleppo and of Raqqa) were internal limits that became international boundaries after 1918. Aleppo, which was the main center in the region and which exerted an economic attraction on southeastern Anatolia, was the capital of a province that comprised Turcophone regions (Iskanderun, Kilis, and Ruha/Urfa), extending as far as the Euphrates. The Sèvres treaty of 1920 left Iskanderun, Urfa, and Mardin to Syria, but the successes of the Kemalist movement allowed Turkey to recover obviously Turcophone regions. French policy in 1939, directed at keeping Turkey neutral, did the rest. Iskanderun and also Antioch were given back to Turkey. In this case Turkey gave the Ottoman heritage a little twist. On the whole, nevertheless, the Ottoman boundaries have stood fast against the great upheavals in the area since the end of World War I.

The Internal Boundaries: The Near East

It is true that many of these "internal" (provincial) boundaries became international in the years following 1918 when the Arab world was carved into nine states after the defeat, and destruction, of the Ottoman Empire. Even so, the earlier Ottoman organization of these provinces was an internal process which, for that reason, should be examined separately.

The shaping of the provinces in the Near East took into consideration practical and historical factors. In Iraq, the subdivision of the country probably followed the stages of the Ottoman conquest: the province of Mosul (the first to be conquered) became a sancak in 1546. Baghdad, occupied by Suleiman, became an eyalet in 1535. Basra, annexed somewhat later, was made an eyalet in 1552, Shehrizor (Kirkuk) after 1549.

In this manner the region that became Iraq constituted four provinces around the important cities of Basra, Baghdad, Mosul, and Kirkuk, a provincial organization that took into consideration the religious and ethnic elements into which the country was (and still is) divided. The province of Basra had a large population of Shiites. The province of Shehrizor (Kirkuk) was inhabited by Kurds and the Ottoman government frequently appointed Kurdish beys or acknowledged hereditary Kurdish rulers.[7]

The Mamluk empire, which Selim annihilated in 1517, had been composed of Egypt/Misr (the central province) plus the seven *niyabat* of Syria: Ghazza, Safad, al-Karak, Sham (Damascus), Tarablus, Hama, and Aleppo. The Ottoman organization of Bilad al-Sham (today's Syria, Lebanon, Israel, occupied Palestine, and Jordan) was much simplified: four provinces were created: Aleppo (1521), Sham (Damascus, with lesser territorial subdivisions for the Lebanese mountain and Jerusalem, 1516–17), Trablus al-sharq (c.1570), and Raqqa (c. 1594). Egypt, of course, did not pose any problem and constituted the province of Misir (1517).

As in the case of Iraq, the provincial organization seemingly aimed at creating relatively coherent territorial subdivisions of limited size and thus easy to administer. Such divisions were, however, only administrative, within the framework of a unified empire. They should not be compared with the rigid boundaries dividing modern states. The subjects of these provinces were Arabic-speaking people, sharing an Arab culture, inside a vast Muslim empire that took in charge the interests of the *umma*. In commerce as well as in culture there was constant coming and going from one province to another, from one city to another, as appears clearly in the biographies of merchants and shaykhs.

The Ottoman delimitation was no obstacle to later local or large unifications: they were negotiated in wartime agreements (1914 to 1918) between Great Britain and the Arabs, clearly demanded by the populations when consulted by the American King Crane Commission of 1919, and partially carried out, in the case of Iraq by Great Britain, and in the case of Syria by France, although France, at times, thought of dividing Syria to more easily subdue it.

But France and Britain, in the process of reconstituting the Near East after the disruption of the empire, introduced elements that were to lead to its later decomposition. France was pledged to organize the autonomy of a Christian Lebanon that had already been prepared with the *Règlement organique* of 1861, promulgated by the Ottoman government under heavy pressure from the European powers. The French decision to expand the tiny Lebanese mountain state and to create a "Grand Liban" (Greater Lebanon) to meet Maronite demands was a fatal one. With the adding of Sunnis and Shiites the Maronites were no longer the majority. They became only the most important minority in Greater Lebanon. A later demographic evolution—with the non-Christian population increasing much more rapidly than the Christian—further diminished the Maronite position. The long Lebanese civil war partly derives from that 1920 French decision to create Greater Lebanon.

Equally disastrous was the British decision to divide Palestine in order to settle Jewish immigrants in its western part. The policy of the Jewish National Home as announced in the Balfour declaration of 1917, and as carried out by the British Mandate, has brought the consequences we know too well: a displaced people, four wars (1948, 1956, 1967, 1973), and instability in the whole region.

The Internal Boundaries: The Maghrib

In the Maghrib the Ottomans resorted to a boundary policy that completely reversed the existing situation. The pre-Ottoman Maghrib had been divided, like Caesar's Gaul, into three parts:

1. A Hafsid empire the center of which was Ifriqiyya (present day Tunisia) with two wings, the region of Trablus al-gharb (Tripoli) in the east, and the region of Constantine in the west.[8]
2. A western Maghrib including Morocco and the Abd al-Wad state (1239–1554), around Tlemcen.
3. A central Maghrib, a rather shapeless ensemble that may be more easily defined as a transition zone than as a political construction.

Merinid Morocco and Hafsid Ifriqiyya were, with Mamluk Egypt, the three powerful empires that dominated the Arab Mediterranean at the beginning of the sixteenth century; the Ottomans succeeded in absorbing and reorganizing the last two.

In this region the establishment of Ottoman authority was mainly a response to the Christian attempts to settle in the ports of the Maghrib, the activity of the Portuguese being directed against Moroccan ports, and the Spaniards being mostly at work in the central and eastern Maghrib. The reaction to this "crusade" was at first individual, Turkish privateers taking the initiative of the jihad. Later the Ottomans were called in to help, and their intervention brought about the progressive organization of the provinces: they were in Algiers as early as 1519, in Constantine by 1535, in Tripoli in 1551, in Tunis in 1574. This chronology played a great part in fixing boundaries that were later to be those of independent states, Algeria, Tunisia, and Libya. The Ottomans organized their new territories from Algiers, their first conquest, and inevitably to its benefit.

This delimitation was a long and progressive process. On the eastern side, the problems centered around the island of Jerba, long disputed between the provinces of Tripoli and Tunis. Before the sixteenth century Jerba was a prosperous region, relying upon commercial activities and enjoying a large autonomy under the authority of hereditary shaykhs and the distant tutelage of the Hafsids. Often threatened by Christian incursions, Jerba was used at the beginning of the sixteenth century as a base by the Turkish privateers, Aruj and his brothers, and later Turgut Reis (Dragut). When the Spanish threat was too pressing, Turgut engaged in the Ottoman sultan's service (1551), just like Khayr al-Din had done a few decades earlier. It is in this way that Jerba entered in the Ottoman orbit: in 1552 Suleiman granted his investiture to the shaykh of Jerba, and when Turgut was appointed *beylerbey* of Tripoli (in 1554) he extended his authority over Jerba.[9] The province of Tripoli was thus organized twenty years before Tunis became an Ottoman province.

Turkish rule was probably heavy in Jerba, the more so as the inhabitants of the island had been accustomed to the remote suzerainty of Tunis. Hence a series of revolts and of calls for protection from Tunis with which the Jerbans had close commercial relations. There was a Jerban community in Tunis and a sûq (market) of the Jerbans, near the Great Mosque of Zaytuna. As long as Turgut was present in Tripoli the Tunisians were unable to make their influence felt in Jerba, the more so as Tunis remained more or less under Spanish control until 1574.

In 1605, at last, Uthman Dey of Tunis sent soldiers to Jerba and the island was annexed to Tunis. But the imperial government was slow to accept this situation. Only in 1613 did Istanbul recognize the *fait accompli*. Nevertheless Jerba kept a particular status and paid an annual tribute to Istanbul, largely symbolic to be sure (a modest sum of 5,350 piasters).[10]

Several incidents during the eighteenth century indicated moreover that the Porte had not totally given up hope of reestablishing its authority in Jerba, which was hardly recognized in the practically autonomous Tunisia. In 1704 a supposed attempt to make the island a pashalik provoked a war between Tunis (which objected to the idea) and Algiers and Tripoli,[11] and in 1794 Istanbul took the island away from the authority of Tunis for a short time.

On the western wing of the Hafsid state the delimitation was carried out in the wake of a progressive extension of the ujaq of Algiers, eastward, and of the Regency of Tunis, westward. But whereas Ottoman rule had been established in Algiers in 1519, and in Constantine in 1535, it was only in 1574 that Sinan Pasha definitively took over Tunis. For that reason Constantine was put under Algerian authority and, between the two pashaliks, the demarcation line was established far to the east.

Its precise definition was the result of a long and difficult process because the two janisssary ujaqs met in a region inhabited by unsettled tribes whose allegiances shifted from one side to the other, according to their interests, and the relative strength of the two rival powers. The strong autonomy enjoyed by the ujaq of Algiers, and by Muradid, and later Husaynid Tunisia, limited the possibility of Ottoman central government intervention in these local problems.

The first serious conflict occurred in 1612–1614, about the control of the tribes wandering in the intermediary zone between the two regencies.[12] The disputed area was patrolled by the Tunisian ruler Ramadan Bey in 1612, and the Algerian military expedition (*mahalla*), in 1613. But there was no open conflict. A mediation of murabits and muftis brought about negotiations that ended in 1614 with a formal treaty between the two provinces: the Wadi Sarrat was designated as the line of separation, the city of Le Kef remaining in Tunisian territory.[13] This first approach was to remain the basis for the boundary settlement. In 1628 conflict recurred in spite of mediation attempts by the sultan. The Tunisians took the offensive, arrived before Constantine (which had been a province of the Hafsid empire), but were routed and had to fight their way back to Le Kef. The treaty which was then concluded on the whole confirmed the previous agreement.

Numerous conflicts occurred during the seventeenth and eighteenth centuries, the ujaq of Algiers constantly intervening in the affairs of the Tunisian Regency and several times occupying Tunis, but the two provinces always reverted to the delimitation line of wadi Sarrat. In this long enumeration of conflicts (1680, 1684, 1685, 1694, 1700, 1705, 1735, 1756, 1807), noteworthy are those of 1700 and 1807, when the Tunisian army reached Constantine only to be driven back.

In the eastern Maghrib (as in the west) establishing boundaries was thus difficult and provoked numerous conflicts ending only in 1821, shortly before the French occupation of Algiers in 1830. The equilibrium that was painfully reached was largely linked with the chronology of Ottoman conquest. Quite logically, the Ottomans first organized in separate provinces the province of Algiers (with the addition of Constantine) and then that of Trablus. When, much later, Tunis became a province there was no reason to revert to the organization which had been that of eastern Maghrib during the Hafsid dynasty. In this case the Ottoman innovated and their delimitation was totally different from the organization they had found at their arrival in the Maghrib.

The Ottoman intervention in the region was not originally planned from Istanbul, but was the result of a call for assistance from local populations threatened by the crusade and from locally active Turkish warriors (the 'Aruj brothers and Turgut). Later the Porte, while leaving considerable autonomy to the actors on the spot, intervened directly on several occasions. In 1552 Suleiman gave his investiture to the shaykh of Jerba, which resulted in the annexation of the island to Trablus.[14] After conquering Tunis the Porte contributed to the organization of the Regency of Tunis, in 1579 and 1588, in confirming that Kairawan, Sousse, and Sfax would be included in the province.[15] The final attribution of Jerba to Tunis was decided in Istanbul in 1613. This put an end to the island's ambiguous situation.

It is not quite clear whether the Porte gave its sanction to the delimitation of 1614 between Algiers and Tunis, but it is likely: a few years later the Porte tried, unsuccessfully, to mediate in another Algerian-Tunisian conflict (1628). Although not able to prevent numerous conflicts between the two regencies the Porte did use its influence in 1821 to settle the problem definitively. After a local incident that could have stirred up the fire, the imperial government sent an envoy to North Africa, calling upon both regencies "to put an end to their rivalry and to live henceforward in good harmony."[16] A treaty signed March 20, 1821, confirmed the previous agreements between the two regencies.

The Ottoman delimitation of eastern Maghrib was interestingly a total reversal of the situation that had prevailed in North Africa before the Ottoman conquest. A new settlement which placed Tlemcen (on the west) and Constantine (on the east) under the influence of Algiers, and which separated Trablus from Tunis, could have proved unworkable. Nevertheless three centuries of Ottoman rule in North Africa consolidated the situation. The existence of an Algeria is the result of Ottoman rule in the Maghrib. While the French colonial authorities introduced modifications favorable to Algeria in fixing the Tunisian boundary (Randon, 1844; Senatus Consulte of 1863; delimitation of 1883) they kept the organization that the Ottomans had left them.[17] The stable and homogeneous political communities which were thus organized constitute today's Algeria, Tunisia, and Libya.

Through a series of conflicts which lasted until the end of the eighteenth century, the Ottomans established what we may call the external limits of the Arab world, but, of course, the boundary between Morocco and Algeria has become an "internal" boundary. The limits were defined by the equilibrium of forces between the Ottoman Empire and the two great empires of Morocco and Iran. These limits varied little after the sixteenth century and recent attempts in modifying them were quite unhappy.

The internal boundaries were drawn with an empiricism characterizing Ottoman organization. Moreover, the central Ottoman government was often content to ratify an equilibrium reached by local forces. Such an attitude is in conformity with the Ottoman tradition of decentralization and the acceptance of local autonomous powers. Although quite anomalous, the division of Maghrib into its four components, as organized by the Ottomans and the local powers, did bear the test of time. The very looseness of Ottoman provincial administration proved to be positive factors. Unfortunately, in the Sahara region, European colonization modified and gave rigidity to a system that would have made the Sahara an open field for cooperative development.

In the Middle East, the Ottomans created a provincial framework that could be modified in the direction of a stronger national concentration. One should not confound the delimitation of provinces, which could easily unite, and the creation during the European colonial period of separate states with rigid limits. In this case as in the case of Maghrib, the "separated" states had the time needed to unite across "artificial" boundaries. They often tried, but without success.

In none of the border problems that have often torn the Middle East is the responsibility of the Ottomans engaged. The difficulties of Lebanon and the problem of Palestine stem from actions taken by the European colonial powers, France and Britain. It seems appropriate to conclude that as regards boundaries the Ottoman legacy was positive.

NOTES

1. H. de Grammont, *Histoire d'Alger* (Angers, 1887), p. 262.
2. C.-A. Julien, *Histoire de l'Algérie contemporaine* (Paris: Payot, 1964), p. 200.
3. *Annuaire de l'Afrique du Nord* (Aix-en-Provence: NRS, 1964), pp. 143–49.
4. S. H. Longrigg, *Four Centuries of Modern Iraq* (Oxford: Oxford University Press, 1925), p. 134.
5. Ibid., p. 137.
6. P. M. Holt, *Egypt and the Fertile Crescent, 1516–1922: A Political History* (Ithaca: Cornell University Press, 1966), p. 248.
7. D. E. Pitcher, *An Historical Geography of the Ottoman Empire* (Leiden: Brill, 1972), p. 141.
8. R. Brunschvig, *La Berbérie orientale sous les Hafside* (2 vols.; Paris: Adrien Maisonneuve, 1940–47), 1: 283.
9. G. Veinstein, "Apercus sur l'entrée de l' île de Djerba dans l'orbite ottomane," *Revue d'Histoire Maghrébine* 31–32 (1983): 397ff.
10. M. H. Cherif, *Pouvoir et Société dans la Tunisie de Husayn Bin Alî* (2 vols.; Tunis: University of Tunis, 1984), 1: 154.
11. Ibid., 1: 115.
12. T. Bachrouch, *Formation Sociale Barbaresque et Pouvoir à Tunis* (Tunis: University of Tunis, 1977), p. 160.
13. Wazîr al Sarrâj, *al-Hulal al-Sundusiyya* (2 vols.; Tunis: al-Dar al-tunisiyya lil-nashr, 1970–1973), 2: 178.
14. G. Veinstein, "Apercus," pp. 402–8.
15. T. Bachrouch, *Formation Sociale*, pp. 163–64.

16. A. Rousseau, *Les Annales Tunisiennes* (Tunis: Bouslama, 1980, reprint. of the first edition), pp. 343–43; A. Ibn Abî l-Dhiyâf, *Ithâf Ahl al-Zaman bi Akhbar Muluk Tunis wa 'Ahd al-aman* (8 vols.; Tunis: Secrétariat d'Etat aux Affaires Culturelles, 1963–1965), 3: 134.

17. Ch. Monchicourt, "La frontière algéro-tunisienne dans le Tell et dans la Steppe," *Revue Africaine* 82 (1938).

PART THREE

THE POLITICAL DIMENSION

Ergun Ozbudun integrates one of the oldest themes in Ottoman studies and a leading issue in modern political science. The former is the idea that the Ottoman Empire with its bureaucratic elaboration, state autonomy, central control of society, and the weakness of civil society represented the polar opposite of, first, European feudalism and, later, the European nation-state. The second is the interest of today's political scientists in weighing the different patterns of state/civil society relations to determine what combination best fits the requirements of modern times, the assumption being that a powerful civil society granting the state a high degree of legitimacy represents the ideal.

Was the Ottoman Empire an "Oriental Despotism"? Or was it an impressive example of effective marshaling of societal resources, outpacing Europe and others in its early years, that was rendered anachronistic by later global developments? Was the Ottoman Empire ahead of its time in fulfilling the first part of Madison's political dictum—"You must first enable the government to control the governed, and in the next place oblige it to control itself"—but laggard in the second?

Ozbudun sees as one of the most important Ottoman legacies the tradition of "a strong and centralized state, reasonably effective by standards of the day, highly autonomous of societal forces . . . and highly valued for its own sake." The Ottoman ruling elites were not seriously checked by either commercial or agricultural interests. Indeed, the overall weakness of nonstate corporate structures produced the "strong state, weak society" syndrome.

A significant distinction separates post-Ottoman Turks from Arabs. The former have continued to grant the state high legitimacy; the Arabs, by contrast, have a much more pessimistic view of the state.

For all subjects of the Ottoman Empire, Turks, Arabs, or others, there was no nation-state tradition. This grew up later and disjunctively during the modern period of direct or indirect Western domination. Here, again, Ozbudun detects a distinction between Arab and Turkish adaptation. The Turks blended ethnolinguistic nationalism with the Ottoman tradition of the strong, legitimate state. The Arabs, however, have wavered between Pan-Arabism and local nationalisms while being less than sanguine about the strong state as such. Even the Arab successor states tend to have strong state autonomy but with low legitimacy, hardly a formula for stability.

Ozbudun cautions that "two recent tendencies, the rise of the big bourgeoisie and the resurgence of political Islam, although leading to a less autonomous state, do not justify much optimism for the development of liberal democracy in the region." On balance, however, he sees the political legacy of state autonomy as being still very much alive, for better or for worse.

The hallmark of a centralized empire is a well-elaborated body of bureaucratic institutions, ideas, and personnel. Carter Findley, in posing the question of whether the Ottoman administrative legacy is still alive in today's Middle East, concentrates on that period of Westernization and reform extending from the late eighteenth century to the end of the empire after World War I. Many present-day bureaucratic institutions and attitudes, Findley observes, bespeak an Ottoman past.

Reform, for all its ups and downs from the 1790s to the 1920s, consistently involved efforts to increase centralization and enhance state authority. Borrowing their ideas more from central European concepts of government than from classical British liberalism, the Ottoman reformers sought to bring into being a *rechtsstaat*, an Ottoman Prussia. This was consistent with greater authority for the administrative class vis-à-vis the sultan. Thus, one finds even under the authoritarian Sultan Abdulhamid the establishment of European-style civil service regulations.

The period was also the first in which Ottoman statesmen found themselves depending "more on the good will of foreign powers than of their own people." To the extent that the Ottoman Empire during its last century and a half of existence was obliged to rely more and more on diplomacy instead of—or at least in addition to—war, those in the civilian bureaucracy knowledgeable in the ways of Europe gained greater influence and authority.

During this period the numbers of civil officials expanded from perhaps 2,000 at the end of the eighteenth century to as many of 35,000 in 1908. This last period of Ottoman history thus constituted the heyday of the bureaucratic state with the bureaucracy increasing greatly in numbers, functions, and authority. Moreover, it was largely within the ranks of this growing bureaucratic class that debates about Ottoman reforms and political ideologies took place.

Findley shows the historical roots of certain characteristics existing in many Ottoman successor states. Today's large bureaucracies, the preference for public sector over private and for command as opposed to market economy, and the ideal of a body of administrative guardians—the Ottoman Prussia motif—may not be completely attributable to the Ottoman legacy. Many states in many parts of the world have similar characteristics. Still, the close historical connection brought out in Findley's essay does suggest that survivals from the Ottoman past are part of the answer.

Roderic Davison's essay is organized around four questions: 1) What was the situation of the Ottoman Empire during roughly the last century or so of its existence? 2) What strategy did the Ottomans develop during this period? 3) What did the Near East as a whole inherit from this? and 4) What, more specifically, did the Republic of Turkey inherit?

The Ottoman diplomacy that Davison describes was a defensive strategy adopted by a beleaguered empire resisting European pressure. There is no need to look for earlier Ottoman practices or principles.

Davison identifies twelve different principles or practices characterizing Ottoman diplomacy during this period of the Eastern Question. Many of these can be subsumed under the general rubric of seeking acceptance into the European state system and attempting to hold the European states to their own rules of diplomatic conduct, e.g., territorial integrity, legitimacy of existing states, the sanctity of treaties, and the virtue of balance of power politics to maintain the peace.

The Ottomans sought to deter the most threatening European states by lining up with their rivals. It was, on balance, a sophisticated and consistent policy. Ottoman statesmen skillfully played the very weak hand they had been dealt in what was fated to be eventually a losing game.

Less successful was the Ottoman practice of borrowing needed funds from Europe, a practice that led to state bankruptcy and further European infringement on an already badly compromised sovereignty. More successful for a time was the Ottoman sponsoring of Pan-Islam from roughly the 1860s on. At least this caught the attention of those European powers exercising colonial domination over many Muslims, especially Britain, but also France and the Netherlands.

Davison is more inclined to see a similarity of diplomatic circumstances in the period before and after World War I than direct Ottoman influence on the successor states. For example, Middle Eastern states today seek to play off the great powers (or during the cold war the two superpowers) but probably do so more in response to the logic of the situation than with a memory of Ottoman statecraft. Even so, it may well be a matter of both Ottoman legacy and response to similar conditions.

The Ottoman legacy to the Republic of Turkey is more in evidence, but often as explicit rejection of Ottoman ways, e.g., opting for an ethnolinguistic nation-state and refusing the burden of empire, rejection of Pan-Islam, and resistance to the idea of becoming indebted to foreigners. Yet, in other ways Davison finds that the Turkey of Atatürk and his successors adapted the most effective aspects of the Ottoman diplomatic practice vis-à-vis the Western state system, placing these methods in service of a nation-state, not a multi-national empire.

CHAPTER EIGHT

THE CONTINUING OTTOMAN LEGACY AND THE STATE TRADITION IN THE MIDDLE EAST

Ergun Özbudun

One of the most important legacies of the Ottoman Empire is a "state tradition." By this I mean a strong and centralized state, reasonably effective by the standards of its day, highly autonomous of societal forces, and occupying a central and highly valued place in Ottoman political culture. This tradition, we argue, continues to affect politics in Turkey and in the other successor states, albeit in modified form.

The first section elucidates the key concepts related to state autonomy and state capabilities. In the second section, the politico-cultural conditions that created a distinctive Ottoman state tradition are briefly set out. The third section discusses specifics resulting from the Ottoman state tradition and shared by the contemporary successor states. In the fourth and fifth sections, respectively, two dimensions of state strength, autonomy and capabilities, are discussed with reference to the successor states, with particular emphasis on Turkey, Egypt, Syria, and Iraq. In the concluding section, prospects for the development of democratic government in the region are examined.

Beyond the scope of this essay but of particular interest to comparativists would be to study the Ottoman impact on the contemporary Balkan states. The different trajectories of democratic development in the formerly Ottoman Balkan countries as opposed to other East European states that had never been under Ottoman occupation, or only briefly as with Hungary, suggest that this would be a fruitful line of research.

State Autonomy and Capabilities

State autonomy refers to the insulation of the state from societal pressures and to its freedom to make important policy decisions. Autonomy should not be confused with state strength or capabilities. Strong states are those with high capabilities "to penetrate society, regulate social relationships, extract resources, and appropriate or use resources in determined ways."[1] A state that is nonautonomous in the sense of being the instrument of a particular social class or group may be quite strong in terms of these capabilities. Conversely, an autonomous state may be quite weak in such capabilities.[2] Furthermore, states may be strong in some capacities but weak in others. For example, the Egyptian, Syrian, and Iraqi states have been impressively strong in terms of penetration into society and mobilization of human resources, but failed conspicuously in extracting financial resources from their societies, regulating social relationships, and appropriating resources in ways determined by their top leaderships.[3] State capabilities, in turn, depend among other things, on stable administrative-military control over the territory, loyal and competent officials, and plentiful financial resources.[4]

Another confusion surrounding the notion of autonomy derives from the difference between its minimalist and maximalist definitions. The former posits that autonomy requires only that state leaders follow their own preferences rather than responding to societal pressures. If, however, the state is the instrument of a particular social force leading to an identity of preferences between the two, it is meaningless to talk about state autonomy. The maximalist definition sees the test of autonomy as "the willingness of the state to impose policies against the resistance of the dominant social class." In fact, this is a rare case. The notion of autonomy does not preclude alliances between the state apparatus and other social groups or the pursuit of policies by the state that objectively serve the interests of such groups.[5] "It is, of course, one thing to argue that the state is an autonomous, non-class, actor. It is quite another thing to argue that it is the only actor."[6]

A further point sometimes neglected in state autonomy discussions is the cultural dimension. State autonomy is not simply hegemony of an omnipotent state over a weak, obedient, and unincorporated society. The state is not only a matter of certain specialized political structures, but also one of beliefs, values, and attitudes. An autonomous state is one that is central to the thinking of members of its society and also is cherished and valued by them for its own sake as an independent entity.

The term "state autonomy" is not always used in a value-free fashion. "The autonomy of the state," Binder notes, "is ambiguous depending upon whether we are considering Western, 'developed' states, or 'underdeveloped' states. In the case of advanced capitalist states, the autonomy of the state is employed to explain and to justify the resistance to pluralist demands." State institutions "represent a public interest and an historical-cultural consensus which lend stability and continuity" to the system. "In contrast, the autonomy of the state, when applied to developing systems, is used to explain the arbitrariness of government, the apparent absence of a ruling class, the irrelevance of social structure, or even culture, to the explanation of politics."[7]

Autonomy will be used here as a strictly empirical variable with neither positive nor negative connotations, equated with neither the public interest nor arbitrary autocracy. State autonomy is compatible with a great variety of political regimes.

The Ottoman Political Legacy

The Ottoman state tradition might be characterized as follows: the state possessed a high degree of autonomy. Status-oriented values, rather than market-oriented values, were dominant. The relationship between economic and political power was the reverse of its equivalent in Western Europe. Instead of economic power (ownership of the means of production) leading to political power, political power (high position in the state bureaucracy) gave access to material wealth. The wealth thus accumulated, however, could not be converted into more permanent economic assets because it was liable, both in theory and practice, to confiscation by the state.

The Ottoman state, unlike its Western European counterparts, did not favor the emergence of a powerful merchant class. The much-referred to "ethnic division of labor" meant that international trade was dominated by non-Muslim minorities, but such economic power could not be converted into a significant political role because of the Islamic nature of the state.

As regards land ownership as another potential source of economic power, the state retained the theoretical ownership of all cultivable land and, until the decline of central authority, its effective control as well. The fief-holders (*sipahi*) were not a land-based aristocracy, but a military service gentry who were paid by the state in the form of a portion of taxes they collected from peasants. Their titles could always be revoked by the central authority. The rise of a class of local notables (*ayan*) in the eighteenth century, who often combined local social and military power with connections to central government and tax-farming privileges, did not fundamentally alter this state of affairs. The status of the *ayan* can in no way be compared to that of feudal aristocracy in Western Europe, since it remained essentially a de facto situation lacking the legal basis and political legitimacy of the latter. Besides, the effective centralization drive under Mahmud II (1808–1839) deprived the *ayan* of much of their political influence.

In short, the power of the state elites in the Ottoman Empire was not seri-ously threatened. Neither the mercantile bourgeoisie nor the landowners developed into a class that could effectively control and limit, much less cap-ture, the state. Thus, the fundamental social cleavage in the Ottoman Empire was based on a strictly political criterion. On the one hand, there was the rul-ing military (*askeri*) class, which "included those to whom the Sultan dele-gated religious or executive power through an imperial diploma, namely, offi-cers of the court and the army, civil servants, and ulema." On the other hand, there was the ruled (*reaya*) who comprised "all Muslim and non-Muslim sub-jects who paid taxes but who had no part in the government. It was a funda-mental rule of the empire to exclude its subjects from the privileges of the military."[8]

Accompanying the excessive centralization of state authority and its con-centration in the hands of the state elites was civil society's weakness. This means the fragility or absence of corporate, autonomous, intermediary social structures that, in the West, operated independently of the government and played a cushioning role between the state and the individual.

In Europe, the church was the foremost of these corporate structures, and it may have provided a model of organization for other corporate structures such as the guilds, autonomous cities, and the like. These had no parallels in the Islamic Middle East. Islamic law does not, as a rule, recognize corporate identities. For all the theoretical supremacy of the shari'ah, the religious class does not have a corporate identity, but depends on the state (i.e., secular authority) for its appointments, promotions, and salaries.

Similarly, neither the cities nor the artisan guilds played an autonomous role comparable to their counterparts in Western Europe. The *ahi* guilds (arti-san organizations with a strong religious coloring), which played some role in the formative years of the empire, were later deprived of their corporate priv-ileges and put under strict government controls.[9]

In short, no autonomous structure stood between the political authority and the community of believers. It is in this sense that Moore characterizes Egypt as an "unincorporated" society.[10] In fact, the same adjective holds true for all Islamic Middle Eastern societies, past and present. This does not mean, of course, that the premodern Islamic Middle Eastern society was totally undifferentiated, atomized, or regimented. One can speak of a high degree of pluralism of craft guilds, the clergy, religious brotherhoods, endowments, mutual aid groups, religious organizations of non-Muslim communities, nationalities, sects, tribes, clans, extended families, etc.[11] The penetrative capabilities of the Ottoman Empire, although quite high by the standards of its day, were still too limited to allow it to regulate the whole range of social relationships. Moreover, the strict separation between the rulers and the ruled, and the absence of a representative system, did not permit this traditional pluralism to evolve into the pluralistic infrastructure of a modern democratic state. Furthermore, the nineteenth-century drive of the centralized state to reaffirm its corporate exclusivity in response to European challenges further weakened traditional pluralism. Thus, "today a good number of the early modern corporate and moral communities are gone, and among the new ones those of medium size are still thinly represented."[12]

This absence of powerful economic interests that use the state to serve its own interests, plus the absence or weakness of corporate intermediary bodies, produced a high degree of state autonomy. Not the captive of any particular social class, the state could make decisions that would change, eliminate, or create class relationships.

As for the cultural dimension of state autonomy, it has often been observed that the state is given a salient role in both Ottoman-Turkish political thought and in the perceptions of the people. The state is valued in its own right, is relatively autonomous from the society, and plays a tutelary and paternalistic role. This paternalistic image is reflected in the popular expression of "father state" (*devlet baba*). Another interesting popular saying is "May God preserve the State and the Nation" (*Allah Devlete, Millete zeval vermesin*). Ottoman writings on politics and government are replete with such terms as "the Sublime State" (*Devlet-i Aliye*), "raison d'état" (*hikmet-i hükümet*), or "the sublime interests of the State" (*Devletin ali menfaatleri*). Such notions readily found their place in the political discourse of the Turkish republic. Indeed the Preamble of the 1982 Turkish constitution described the State (always spelled with a capital S) as "sacred" (*kutsal Türk Devleti*), adding that no thoughts or opinions could find protection against "Turkish national interests," presumably meaning state interests as defined by the state apparatus.

This exaltation of the state has been consistently fostered through the educational system and the military.[13] Indeed, the military and (at least until quite recently) the civilian bureaucracy have traditionally seen themselves as the guardians of the state and the protectors of public interest. Consequently, they have viewed with suspicion all particularistic interests and political parties which represented them.[14]

With respect to the cultural dimension of state autonomy, there seems to be a significant difference between Turkey and the Arab successor states. It has often been observed that the state does not occupy such a lofty place in Arabic political thought. Morroe Berger, in his analysis of Egypt, Syria, Iraq, Lebanon, and Jordan found "no agencies to inculcate a civic spirit in the Near East. . . . Between fidelity to family and Islam there appeared to be no room for loyalty to a body, the city, or state, which was neither a kinship nor a religious group. Indeed, through most of Arab history the city or state has not been sufficiently differentiated from the religious community to permit the growth of civic or secular loyalty."[15]

Ben-Dor blames many of the ills in the region (conflict, instability, lack of legitimacy, despotic governments) on the absence of a "state logic" or "raison d'état," which he defines as "a filter through which interests related to social, national, or particularistic ideologies and interests are sifted, refined, aggregated, and perhaps moderated. . . . The very stateness of a country and particularly its political elites create the basic condition for a conception of common interest." Ben-Dor, however, distinguishes Turkey (and Egypt) from the rest of the Arab world. "The Egyptian case is unique, perhaps comparable among the Islamic countries of the Middle East only to Turkey, not only in its strength of statehood but even in the resemblance to a Western-type nation-state."[16]

Just as Turkish popular sayings reflect a feeling of respect for a strong but benevolent state, a recent study on Arab popular sayings or proverbs indicated a sense of helplessness, submission, self-abasement, cynicism, and mistrust.[17]

Such submissive attitudes toward political authority in the contemporary Middle East cannot be explained only by the legacy of the Ottoman state tradition. Closely intermingled with that centuries-old tradition is the Islamic legacy that exhorts believers to obey earthly authority. Here one is faced with two different points of view. The first holds that:

> In the traditional Islamic society, the power of the state was in both theory and practice limited. . . . The traditional Islamic state may be autocratic; it is not despotic. The power of the sovereign is limited by a number of factors, some legal, some social. It is limited in principle by the holy law, which, being of divine origin, precedes the state. The state and the sovereign are subject to the law and are in a sense created and authorized by law and not, as in Western systems, the other way around. In addition to this theoretical restraint, there were also practical restraints. In traditional Islamic societies, there were many well-entrenched interests and intermediate powers that imposed effective limits on the ability of the state to control its subjects.[18]

On the other side of the coin, however, is the tradition of unquestioned obedience and submission to political authority justified, among others, by the famous dictum of Ibn Taymiyya: "Sixty years under an unjust imam are better than a single night without a ruler,"[19] or that of Ibn Jama'a of Damascus who said that "the sovereign has a right to govern until another and stronger one shall oust him from power and rule in his stead. The latter will rule by the same title and will have to be acknowledged on the same grounds; for a government, however objectionable, is better than none at all, and between two evils we must choose the lesser."[20] Vatikiotis maintains that "since the eleventh century, the only political theory of Islam has been that of passive obedience to any de facto authority, government by consent remains an unknown concept; autocracy has been the real and, in the main, the only experience."[21]

One way to reconcile these two opposing views is to distinguish between the ideal Islamic state and the reality of the state in different Muslim communities. It should be added, however, that the weight of the historical evidence favors the pessimistic point of view.

The Specificity of the Ottoman State and Its Implications for Contemporary Middle Eastern States

The fundamental difference between the Ottoman state system and the states of Western Europe has been remarked on by a host of classical political theorists including Machiavelli, Bodin, Bacon, Harrington, Bernier, Montesquieu, and Karl Marx, as well as by contemporary authors.[22] Two extreme positions should be avoided. One is insistence on the uniqueness of the Ottoman or Islamic experience, a position advocated interestingly both by Orientalist scholars and fundamentalist Muslim thinkers.[23] The second is to engage in sweeping universal generalizations on political development. A more middle-of-the-road approach allows us to take into account historical specificities, while making meaningful comparisons with other world regions, especially those with a strong state tradition such as Latin America, Russia, and East Asia.

Three components of the Ottoman state tradition seem to have influenced the structure and behavior of the successor states: the absence of a nation-state tradition; the capacity of the state to accumulate and use political power; and the absence of a representative tradition.

THE ABSENCE OF A NATION-STATE TRADITION

The Ottoman Empire was anything but a nation-state. It was a multinational, multiethnic, multireligious, multisectarian state. What has to be explained, therefore, is the surprising resilience of Ottoman successor states in the absence of a nation-state tradition.

Again, there seems to be a significant difference between Turkey and the Arab states, with Egypt occupying a middle position somewhat closer to Turkey. While Turkish nationalism was a relative latecomer,[24] the Young Turks first (1908–1918) and then the Kemalists were successful in building a new collective identity around Turkish nationalism to replace the Ottoman-Islamic identity. This was helped by the loss of Arabic-speaking lands of the empire at the end of World War I, the traumatic experience of the Turkish War of Independence (1919–1922), the religious and linguistic homogeneity of the new

Turkish republic, the charisma and the prestige of Kemal Atatürk, and perhaps the strong sense of statehood in Turkish political culture alluded to above. Of all the successor states, Turkey has made the easiest transition to a nation-state.

The picture is considerably different in the Arab successor states. There is an interesting debate among Arab scholars on whether Arab nation- (or territorial) states represent a historical reality or are alien translations to the Arab world. Bahgat Korany, for example, argues the second view:

> External factors predominated in the territorial definition of Arab states. . . .
> The present Middle Eastern borders and thus the whole of the modern Middle
> Eastern state system are products of this mandate period. Because of its "alien"
> origins, the implementing of the inter-state system was to face two pressures:
> internal strains within the polity at the time of the system's institutionalisation,
> and territorial disputes once the inter-state system was established.[25]

Naff agrees that the "post-medieval European idea of the state—a territorially defined entity apart from ruler or dynasty organised in accordance with man-made rules—was alien to Muslim political theory."[26]

Iliya Harik argues, on the other hand, that Arab countries are not only old societies, "but also old states. Except for three of them—Iraq, Syria, and Jordan—they all go back to the nineteenth century or a much earlier period." Arab nationalist belittling of the state system as a creation of colonialism is a "historical misperception. . . . Fifteen of the contemporary Arab states are the product of indigenous and regional forces mostly unrelated to European colonialism, and in most cases predate it."[27]

The contradiction between these two views may not be as great as it seems, however, since Harik admits that hardly any of the Arab states "unconditionally accepts the legitimacy of its own statehood" and that the crisis of legitimacy is particularly acute in the Fertile Crescent,[28] while Korany concedes that the Arab territorial state, despite its alien origins, "is becoming increasingly implanted and naturalized. It is not an indigenous phenomenon," he argues, "yet it no longer seems a foreign import. It is thus a hybrid product . . . People have become accustomed to its presence, it is now the order of the day, the standard frame of reference." And this is largely a victory by default, due to the inability of Islamists and Arab nationalists to elaborate an alternative operational formula of a "pan" state.[29]

Still the nation-state has never been as fully legitimized anywhere in the Arab world as it has been in Turkey. The nation-state in the Arab world has been under a three-pronged attack from Arab nationalism, Islam, and the substate ethnic and sectarian divisions. Harik notes that Arab states "have been caught up in the pull and push of conflicting forces, some coming from domestic centrifugal sources such as ethnic and sectarian divisions and some from the universal forces of pan-Arabism and pan-Islam, both of which draw away from the legitimacy of statehood enjoyed by these countries. Arab nationalism, more so than Islam, denies legitimacy to the state system."[30]

The idea of one Arab nation, from Morocco to the Gulf, is a powerful force in the minds of Arab intellectuals and masses. It is particularly strong in the Fertile Crescent countries where, interestingly, the legitimacy of the territorial state is weakest. A relatively recent large-scale survey of 6,000 persons in ten Arab countries indicated that 78.5 percent of the respondents believed in the existence of an Arab entity, and 77.9 percent believed that this Arab entity constitutes a nation (of which 53 percent believing that this nation is divided at present by artificial boundaries); 69.1 percent thought that Arab unity would be beneficial for them as individuals, and 81.7 percent beneficial for their children.[31]

Arab nationalism is not only the dream of a handful of intellectuals but an ideal valued among the masses. Even the different words in Arabic used to distinguish Arab nationalism from territorial state nationalism suggest that the former is valued more highly. Thus, "nation-station nationalism was often disparagingly described as *qutriyya*, or regionalism. . . . The more prestigious, resonant and historical meaningful term *qawmiyya* was reserved for Arab nationalism."[32]

A second challenge to the Arab territorial-nation states comes from Islam. Vatikiotis argues, for example, that "Islam and nationalism are mutually exclusive terms. As a constructive loyalty to a territorially defined national group, nationalism has been incompatible with Islam in which the state is not ethnically or territorially defined, but is itself ideological and religious."[33]

Moreover, Islam is supposed to guide and regulate not only the spiritual lives of the believers, but their total social and political lives as well. If the differentiation of the state from society (autonomy) is an important element of stateness, can an Islamic state be autonomous? In an Islamic society, "the very idea of the separation of church and state is meaningless, since there are no two entities to be separated."[34] Therefore, those authors who link the emergence of the modern state in Western Europe to the increasing differentiation of the state from society would understandably be skeptical about the possibility of the emergence of a true state in the Islamic world. Badie and Birnbaum argue, for example, that "as the product of a culture based largely on the principle of differentiation, the state has not been able to achieve institutional form in societies dominated by 'organic religions' such as Islam or Hinduism, which reject the idea of a temporal or secular domain distinct from the spiritual."[35]

One should distinguish, however, between the theory of the ideal Islamic state and the practical accommodations between temporal authority and the religious establishment in the past and present Middle Eastern societies. In many Islamic societies the secular authority has been sufficiently differentiated from the religious sphere. A good example would be the Ottoman state where the temporal authority dominated religion rather than the other way around. Ottoman sultans asserted from the outset their right to enact legislation, sometimes even in conflict with the express commands of Islamic law. One has only to remember that one of the greatest Ottoman sultans, Suleiman I, the Magnificent to Westerners, was called "Kanuni" (the law-giver or legislator) in Turkish. This notion of the autonomy and superiority of temporal authority helps explain the ease with which the *Tanzimat* reformers and then the Young Turks were able to regulate large areas of social life by secular legislation.[36]

As for fundamentalist Islamic rejection of the nation-state, again the practice is different from the theory. In many Arab countries as well as in Turkey, state and religion coexist in a more or less cooperative relationship. The state's incorporation of the religious establishment into its own structure enhances its power and legitimacy. Only in cases where the official religious establishment is unable to control the religious forces in the society does the universalism of the Islamic theory of state become a threat to the nation-state.[37]

The third challenge to the Arab territorial state comes not from such supranational ideologies as Arab nationalism and Islam, but from the substate level, namely ethnic and sectarian divisions. Lebanon is the archetypical example of this so-called "mosaic" model, with Maronite Christians, Druze, Sunni Arabs, Shiite Arabs, various other Christian Arab communities as well as non-Arab Armenians. Syria is divided along religious and sectarian lines among the Sunni, Shiite (themselves divided among the Alawites and Ismailis), Druze, and Christian Arabs, not to mention smaller Kurdish, Turkish, and Armenian communities. Iraq is divided linguistically into Arabs, Kurds, and Turks, and religiously between the Sunnis and the Shiites, with a small Christian minority. Even the relatively more homogeneous countries of the region have significant ethnic or religious minorities (Kurds in Turkey, Copts in Egypt, and Berbers in the Maghrib). Ethnic and sectarian loyalties are strong, and to the extent that modernization effects social cleavages and political loyalties, one observes a movement from local, family, or clan-based allegiances to larger sectarian allegiances, but not necessarily toward an overarching national identity.

In terms of the relative strength of nation-state identity vis-à-vis the competing loyalties of pan-nationalism, Islamic universalism, and substate group identities, Turkey is clearly the closest approximation of the Western-type nation-state model. In the Arab world, Egypt is the closest parallel to Turkey, with a socially homogeneous population produced by the ecological homogeneity of the Nile valley, its strong sense of Egyptianness, and a historical continuity extending over millennia.

Other Arab states with a long history of separate identity and reinforcing specificities are Morocco, Tunisia, and Oman, the first two of which have already approximated the nation-state model.[38] By the same criteria, the countries where the legitimacy of the nation-state is weakest are those of the Fertile Crescent: Syria, Iraq, Jordan, and Lebanon. The extent to which the nation-state has become legitimate has important implications for democratic development, as will be argued in the final section.

THE CAPACITY TO CONCENTRATE AND TO EXPAND POLITICAL POWER

As opposed to feudal systems where the amount of political power is small and dispersed, in bureaucratic empires like the Ottoman state, power is concentrated even though its total amount (i.e., the state's penetrative, extractive, and regulative capabilities) may be small. If, following Huntington, we identify the first stage of political modernization as the concentration of power and the second stage as the expansion of power,[39] the autonomous state apparatuses of bureaucratic empires have a greater capacity than feudal systems to concentrate and expand political power, unhampered by established class interests, and to use such power for the economic and social modernization of their countries.

The two reformist regimes in the nineteenth century (Ottoman Sultan Mahmud II and Muhammad Ali in Egypt) did so with relative ease and considerable success. The *Tanzimat* reformers and the Young Turks followed the path of reform while further expanding political power. Their twentieth-century counterparts were Kemalism, Nasserism, Bourguibism, and Baathism. All were able to carry out far-reaching changes in their societies without much effective opposition, and to expand power beyond the wildest dreams of the Ottoman sultans, penetrating into every remote corner of their countries and involving an ever-growing number of their people in the regulative network of the state.

THE ABSENCE OF REPRESENTATIVE INSTITUTIONS

The combination of factors that made the concentration and expansion of political power possible in the Ottoman Empire and its successor states makes its dispersal (i.e., the growth of democratic institutions) difficult. The case is often made that the development of modern democracy in Western Europe had its roots in the medieval feudal traditions. Western European feudalism implied a legally defined and mutually binding division of powers between a relatively weak central authority and well-entrenched local centers of power. It also implied some idea of representation in the form of estates, regardless of how frequently or infrequently assemblies of estates were in fact called. To this was added the corporate autonomy of the church, the cities, and the guilds. From this medieval social and political pluralism, Europe evolved toward constitutionalism, the rule of law, and modern representative institutions with only a relatively short interruption represented by the age of royal absolutism.

Bureaucratic empires may lack such facilitating preconditions for democratic development. The Ottoman Empire had no representative tradition until the last quarter of the nineteenth century. Although it was an established custom for the Ottoman government to convene an assembly of leading civil, military, and religious officials to discuss important matters of policy, especially in times of stress, this body, called the "general assembly" (*meclis-i umumi*) or the consultative assembly (*meclis-i mesveret*), had no representative character. Nor did the Grand Council of Justice (*meclis-i vala-yi ahkam-i adliye*), which was created by Mahmud II in 1838 and functioned as a de facto, but appointed, legislature in the *Tanzimat* period. The elective principle was first introduced into local government by the provincial law of 1864.[40] "While [Ottoman] central government had various means at its disposal for gathering information, opinion, and counsel, none of these ways seem to have been, even in embryo, a form of the principle of representative government."[41]

The first Ottoman constitution of 1876 was an important step in the development of representative institutions. It extended the representative-elective principle to the level of central government, even though it left some crucial powers in the hands of the monarch and remained in force for barely one year, to be followed by thirty years of absolutist rule by Abdulhamid II.[42] Reference should also be made in this connection to the Tunisian constitution of 1860, and to the efforts to develop a representational system in Egypt under the khedives Ismail and Tawfiq. Like the Ottoman experience, however, both proved to be shortlived.

The early twentieth-century experiments with constitutional and representative government were no more successful. Although the second constitutionalist period (1908–1913) in the [Ottoman] empire proved to be somewhat longer-lived and provided the first experience with organized political parties and competitive elections, it quickly degenerated into the single-party dictatorship of the Union and Progress Party. The Egyptian constitution of 1923 had no greater success. The "liberal experiment" in Egypt was neither truly liberal nor truly democratic. Effective political power remained in the hands of the king and the British authorities, and was exercised in a heavily authoritarian manner.[43] Kedourie describes the 1923 Egyptian constitution as:

> A model, a text-book constitution . . . full of checks and of balances, an ordered and intricate toyland in which everything was calm and beauty. Its radical fail-

ing . . . was that it assumed and took it for granted that elections in Egypt could possibly elicit . . . the will of the electorate. As the sequel, from 1923 to 1952, showed, they did nothing of the kind; Egyptian elections, rather, proved to be ratifications by the masses of decisions taken by the king, or else by the Cairo politicians, depending on which side had, for the time being, the upper hand.[44]

Among all the successor states to the Ottoman Empire, only three (Turkey, Israel, and Lebanon) have been able to maintain a competitive democratic system for any length of time. The Israeli democracy, created in large part by Jewish settlers from Europe, is necessarily less linked to an Ottoman past. The Lebanese democracy was even at its best highly "precarious" and oligarchical. Destroyed by the brutal civil war beginning in 1975, its recovery is by no means assured.[45] Turkey's relatively successful democratic record in the last forty-five years has been marred by three military interventions.

The Continuing Ottoman Legacy: State Autonomy

The autonomy of the state means the autonomy of the officials, bureaucrats, and military officers who occupy high posts in the state. Who are they in the contemporary Middle East? Do they come from a particular class background? Do they represent the interests and aspirations of a particular social class? Or do they themselves create or develop into a new class?

Manfred Halpern was one of the first to stress the rise of a new salaried middle class as the key to an understanding of modern Middle East politics. In his view, this class "constitutes the most active political, social, and economic factor from Morocco to Pakistan. Leadership in all areas of Middle Eastern life is increasingly being seized by a class of men inspired by nontraditional knowledge, and it is being clustered around a core of salaried civilian and military politicians, organizers, administrators, and experts." Unlike its counterpart in the industrialized states, this class

> uses its power not to defend order or property but to create them—a revolutionary task that is being undertaken so far without any final commitment to any particular system of institutions. . . . At this extraordinary moment when the traditional ruling class has been defeated and the peasants and workers have not yet organized themselves to make their own demands, politics has become a game played almost entirely within the new middle class.[46]

Whether this new middle class is as socially and politically homogeneous as the term "class" implies and whether being "salaried" is one of their defining characteristics is debatable.[47] Most probably, it displays greater cohesion prior to its seizure of power, but soon thereafter important policy differences within the leading cadres of the new regime become visible. Examples abound: divisions among the Young Turks after the constitutionalist revolution of 1908, among Kemalists after the victory of the War of Independence, among the Free officers in Egypt, within the Syrian Ba'th which were reflected in the coups of 1966 and 1970, in Iraq, Algeria, etc. The central fact for our purposes is that these new middle-class men, mostly with careers in government service, have come to political power in most of the Ottoman successor states, as political elite studies have convincingly shown.[48]

Despite the amorphous character of this "new middle class," several generalizations can be made about it. First, they owe their status to their training and modern skills, not to their wealth. Second, they are mostly, especially until quite recently, in government careers. Third, they are most likely the offspring of urban petite bourgeoisie or the rural middle class. The military in particular and to a lesser extent the civilian bureaucracy provided a channel of upward mobility to the sons of such modest families. This does not make them, however, an instrument or representative of petite bourgeoisie or of the rural middle class.

> The leaders of these alleged petit bourgeois regimes have often displayed considerable hostility toward the commercial and trading sectors of their society. . . . They reached accommodations with the petite bourgeoisie only because the state was incapable of nationalizing their activities with any reasonable degree of efficiency. [Although] many regimes in the Middle East in the 1960s were indeed of petit bourgeois origin . . . their leaders had, by and large, an antibourgeois (whether petit or grand) mentality. They were not the creatures of their class.[49]

A counter argument is that the Egyptian military elite taking power after 1952 had its roots in the rural middle class of rich peasants who owned between 10 and 50 *feddans*; that this rural bourgeoisie, unaffected by the land reforms and helped by the elimination of the largest landowners, became the new rural upper class; that they were the real beneficiaries of the policies of the revolutionary regime; that they were mobilized and participant, and constituted the "second stratum" in Egypt from among whom many important officials were chosen; that the "second stratum does not rule but is the stratum without which the rulers cannot rule"; and that, in this sense, the rural middle class embodied the Egyptian revolution.[50] On balance, however, the view that the rural middle class "never embodied the Egyptian revolution" and "official attitudes toward the rural middle class ranged from hostile to tolerant, but they were never supportive" seems sounder.[51]

The relationship between the post-1952 Egyptian state elites and the rural middle class resembles the post-1920 situation in Turkey, where the Kemalist state elites found it convenient to ally themselves with rural notables, keeping them as a junior and not very influential partner. Perhaps the price of this alliance was the absence of a far-reaching land reform in Turkey.[52]

Contemporary Middle Eastern states provide "extreme instances of autonomous state action—historical situations in which strategic elites use military force to take control of an entire national state and then employ bureaucratic means to enforce reformist or revolutionary changes from above."[53] The precondition for this "revolution from above" model is a relatively autonomous state apparatus where the bureaucrats "are not recruited from the dominant landed, commercial, and industrial classes; and they do not form close personal and economic ties with these classes after their elevation to high office. Relatively autonomous bureaucrats are thus independent of those classes which control the means of production." And the characteristics of the revolutionary process are:

> [a] the extralegal takeover of political power and the initiation of economic, social, and political change is organized and led by some of the highest military and often civil bureaucrats in the old regime. [b] there is little or no mass participation in the revolutionary takeover or in the initiation of change. Mass movements and uprisings may precede and accompany the revolution from above, but military bureaucrats who take revolutionary action do so independently from, and often in opposition to, such movements. [c] the extralegal takeover of power and the initiation of change is accompanied by very little violence, execution, emigration, or counterrevolution. [d] the initiation of change is undertaken in a pragmatic, step-at-a-time manner with little appeal to radical ideology. [e] military bureaucrats who lead a revolution from above—as opposed to a coup d'etat - destroy the economic and political base of the aristocracy or upper class. The destructive process is basic to both revolution from above and from below.[54]

Kemalist Turkey, for example, did not have to destroy powerful economic interests, because there were no such interests in Turkey of the 1920s, but it did attack and subdue a strong Islamic opposition even at the risk of breaking an alliance forged during the war of independence. As for the other successor states, "one cannot but be surprised at the ease with which the independent states of the Middle East contained or broke the power of significant economic interests in their societies." The only entrenched indigenous class in the region has been the landowners, and even if we grant that their historical roots are fairly shallow, it still remains interesting that they have "given up without a fight" in Egypt, Syria, and Iraq. The same is true for the relatively strong business interests in Syria.[55]

The Ottoman tradition of the benevolent father state with a strong concern for equity may well reinforce state autonomy.[56] This has created a political culture accepting the legitimacy of an interventionist state. "It is conceded in the abstract that the state and its leaders have a right and an obligation to set a course for society and to use public resources to pursue that course." Moreover, "the emphasis is on the ends of state intervention, and checks and balances are not seen as preventing abuse of power but rather as impeding the state's course toward its goal. Therefore, to some extent, there has been an acceptance of a high concentration of power —economic, administrative, and military." Nowhere in the region, save Lebanon and perhaps the present-day Turkey, do private sectors enjoy full legitimacy.[57]

The legitimacy of state interventionism is as much a cause of state autonomy as its result. The powerful role of the state as the initiator of industrialization, manager of state economic enterprises, purveyor of employment, holder of oil (and other) rent, instrument of investment, consumption, and distribution of revenue gives it strong leverage against all social groups.[58]

The phenomenon of the "rentier state," although quite unrelated to the Ottoman legacy, also contributes to state autonomy, by putting immense amounts of revenue at the service of the state since oil rents accrue directly to the state. Although not all Arab states are oil-rich states, it has been argued that a rentier mentality prevails in all of them.[59] For example, Syria is described as "an oil state by transference." Indeed, foreign grants and loans covered more than 50 percent of its budget in the late 1970s and only slightly less than 50 percent in the mid-1980s.[60]

The Continuing Ottoman Legacy: State Capabilities

The Ottoman Empire had an extensive and elaborate civil and military bureaucracy, highly developed by the standards of its day and certainly by those of most of the third world countries. This was the most direct legacy of the Ottoman state to the Turkish republic. Rustow has calculated that 93 percent of the empire's general staff officers and 85 percent of its civil servants continued their service in Turkey.[61] To a lesser extent some of the other successor states also inherited this legacy. Particularly in Iraq, ex-Ottoman soldiers and administrators constituted the first generation of ministers, politicians, and high administrators.

In the Arab states bureaucratization, in the sense of an increase in the number of administrative units and personnel, a rise in wages and salaries, and "an orientation whereby the administrative and technical dominate the social," has grown substantially in the last thirty years. In Egypt, at the beginning of 1978, the public sector was employing about 3.2 million officials and workers (i.e., a third of the total workforce and over half of the nonagricultural workforce). Total public expenditures in 1980 represented 60 percent of GDP, and total government revenues 40 percent of GDP.[62] In Iraq, total government employment in 1977 reached 410,000, or nearly half of Iraq's organized workforce.[63] Between 1976 and 1980, out of a total of 13,460 million Iraqi dinars of allocated investments 12,000 million (some 88 percent) were public investments.[64] In Syria, combined public sector and civil service employment (not including some 230,000 Syrians in uniform) totaled 350,000 out of a total workforce of 2.1 million.[65] Bureaucratic growth is just as marked in conservative Gulf states and in Jordan as in the self-proclaimed socialist states.[66]

> [Bureaucracy's] elaborate hierarchy and strict chain of command is . . . an invaluable instrument of control . . . Arab rulers appear to prefer a system of administrative authority in which all power emanates from a single political leader and where the influence of others is derivative in rough proportion to their perceived access to him or their share in his largesse. . . . To ensure competition among a leader's subordinates, they are endowed with roughly equal power and given overlapping areas of authority.[67]

Together with the growth of public bureaucracy and rise in government expenditures came an impressive growth in state capabilities, particularly in the areas of defense and internal security, but also in health, education, welfare, and public works.[68] Egypt, Iraq, and Syria "have managed to build some of the most formidable manpower mobilization systems for war of any states in the world . . . And these abilities have not been limited exclusively to the military sphere. These states also have placed other state personnel into even the most remote corners of their societies. For example, all have achieved some notable successes in fielding teachers in villages and towns."[69]

State capability, however, is not a unidimensional phenomenon. A state may be strong in some areas, but weak in others. Certain Middle Eastern states have shown impressive coercive, mobilizational, and penetrative capabilities, but have remained weak in regulating social relationships and using resources in determined ways. One good example is the thwarting of Nasser's goal to create a more egalitarian rural society where "the sum of social control local strongmen have exercised has prevented state leaders from developing the state's own mobilizational capabilities."[70]

Future Prospects: Retreating States and Expanding Societies?

The theme "retreating states and expanding societies" has recently become popular in Middle Eastern studies. Do these presumed trends represent a reduction in the age-old autonomy of the Middle Eastern state? Do they signify a meaningful step toward democracy? Two trends are unmistakably clear.

The first is increased emphasis on the private sector, greater reliance on market forces, a lessening of government controls over the economy, and opening to international markets. These shifts in economic policy have brought the rise of the big bourgeoisie in many Middle Eastern states. Even though it is questionable whether the bourgeoisie "dominates" or holds "hegemonic" power in any Middle Eastern Muslim country, "some of those regimes may be fairly described as 'bourgeois states' or at least emergent or embryonic bourgeois states."[71] Turkey under Özal has gone farthest in this direction toward full legitimation of the private sector. The Turkish entrepreneurial bourgeoisie "may now be ready, if the international economy is at all hospitable, to consolidate Turkey in the ranks of the NIC's (newly industrialized countries) and to make the Turkish state its instrument."[72] The Turkish version of *infitah* has been followed somewhat more timidly and cautiously by Egypt and Tunisia, and even by such "radical states" as Syria, Iraq, and Algeria to a lesser but still significant extent."[73]

The growth of the private sector and the rise of the entrepreneurial bourgeoisie can certainly be considered a reduction of state autonomy. This does not mean, however, that rising bourgeoisie will be in conflict with the state apparatus or able to establish hegemony over it. The state, even in Turkey, still has powerful leverage over the business community. A symbiotic and cooperative relationship between the two can benefit both. "The private sector growing up in the shadow of the state (and thanks to the public sector) certainly has an interest in gaining freedom of economic action, more access to credit, fiscal facilities, the freedom of cross-border traffic, but why should it have to undertake open political action when it can try to obtain all this at less cost to itself by remaining entrenched in bureaucratic or palace politics where the informal network of family, regional and factional solidarity is at the heart of the game."[74] It does not appear that the emergent big bourgeoisie can yet dispense with the protective domination of a very powerful state apparatus. The Lebanese and the Iranian cases suggest "that the failure of the two to cooperate may bring about a consequence which is far worse for both than the alternatives of mutual cooperation or the acquiescence in the domination of either."[75]

These observations indicate "what *infitah* does *not* mean. It does not mean that the state sector is about to be dismantled, even in Turkey. It does not mean that the state is ceding to 'civil society': This may happen, to some extent, in Turkey and Egypt; it is much less likely in Iraq or Algeria. Rather than a *retreat* of the state, *infitah* is better conceived as a *restructuring* of state activity, always mediating between society and international actors, still responsible for the basic welfare of the population, and continuing to formulate the goals and strategy of economic development and structural change."[76]

The second clear tendency observed in the entire region, including officially secular Turkey, is the resurgence of political (often fundamentalist) Islamic movements. Their growing power has forced many states to a more accommodationist policy.[77] Since such movements are an outgrowth of civil society, as opposed to the official religious establishments, they can be considered yet another aspect of the retreat of the state and the expansion of the society, or a further reason for the weakening of the state autonomy. Granting that there are many variations in the Islamic camp, any movement intent on establishing an "Islamic state" cannot be said to constitute a fertile ground for the development of genuine liberal and pluralist democracy in the region. For the Islamic radicals are intent on taking over the "modern state and use its own tools in order to Islamize society; there is no sense in dismantling this state" or dispensing with the modern technology it utilizes. "The liquidation of basic democratic liberties in the name of the *Shari'ah* follows necessarily. And that entails a restriction of civil society's sphere (even compared with the present situation)."[78]

Thus, the convergence of the two recent tendencies, the rise of the big bourgeoisie and the resurgence of political Islam, although leading to a less autonomous state, does not justify much optimism for the development of liberal democracy in the region. The rise of the bourgeoisie in itself is no guarantee for the installation of democracy since, as the experience has shown elsewhere, a bourgeois state can also be authoritarian or antidemocratic.[79] Since the bourgeoisie is not strong enough to create a liberal-democratic state alone, it needs political allies.

Two possible allies are the petite bourgeoisie (bureaucrats, small traders, shopkeepers, etc.) and the Islamic fundamentalists. Neither provides a fertile ground for democratic development.[80] Although Binder finds a common interest between the bourgeoisie and the fundamentalists in reducing the power of the autonomous state and some ground for convergence between Islamic fundamentalists and Islamic liberals (those who advocate the compatibility of Islam and political liberalism), he finds that "the liberal Islamic paradigm can hardly be said to be dominant in the Middle East at the present time . . . It is enormously difficult to develop liberalism outside of a sustaining bourgeois culture in which a high value is placed upon liberal education, individual dignity, the rule of law, freedom of the press, freedom of artistic expression and criticism . . . Until the circumstances render the concept self-evidently meaningful to mass and elite alike, the prospects for Islamic liberalism will remain dim."[81]

Similarly, Ben-Dor argues that "a golden path must be found in which *raison d'état* reigns supreme, but is tempered and refined by Islamic ethics. Islam does not invade, subvert, overwhelm, or capture the state; it accepts its supremacy (in its proper sphere) so long as the logic of state takes into consideration the ethical constraints of Islam . . . In his pursuit of the interests of the state, Christianity, Judaism, or Islam cannot tell him [the ruler] what to do, but they can tell him what not to do. Their ethics cannot dictate *raison d'état*, but they can restrict the means employed to pursue *raison d'état*."[82] This golden path seems to be even farther away today than it was in the Ottoman days.

On most issues touched upon in this chapter, Turkey's role has been emphasized. On the question of the relationship between the state and religion, however, Turkey's secularist model is not likely to be followed by any Arab country in the foreseeable future. In Turkey, however, despite certain encroachments by religious forces the essentials of the secular state have remained intact even after 50 years of multi-party politics. Secularism has never become an unacceptable idiom; on the contrary, it has completely dominated the political discourse. A variety of Islamic organizations, associations, parties, and brotherhoods, ranging from liberal-accommodationist to radical revolutionary, represent only a minority of Turkish public opinion.

Perhaps one of the reasons for this difference between Turkey and the Arab world is that Islam, while constituting an important element in Turkish identity, is a much more essential part of Arab identity. A pertinent testimony is the following words by Michel Aflaq, himself a Christian and the ideological father of one of the most secularist political movements in the Arab world, the *Ba'th*: "Islam in its pure truth sprang up in the heart of Arabism and it gave the finest expression of the genius of [Arabism], and it marched with its history and it mixed with Arabism in its most glorious roles, so it is impossible for there to be a clash between them."[83] On the contrary, it has been possible to build a secular nationalism in Turkey, based on the separate identity of Turks, without rejecting the ethical implications and cultural norms of Islam.

A final variable that will determine the prospects for democratic development in the Middle East is the degree to which the nation-state is accepted and legitimized. Those countries where the nation-state is most firmly established, have the best chance to create or maintain a democratic regime. National unity is a "background condition" for transition to democracy. This "means that the vast majority of citizens in a democracy-to-be must have no doubt or mental reservations as to which community they belong to. . . . Democracy is a system of rule by temporary majorities. In order that rulers and policies may freely change, the boundaries must endure, the composition of the citizenry be continuous."[84] As Ivor Jennings puts it, "the people cannot decide until somebody decides who are the people."[85]

Judged by these three criteria (the rise of the bourgeoisie, the tameness and accommodationism of the Islamic groups, and the legitimacy of the nation-state) the countries with the strongest potential for democracy are Turkey,

Egypt, Tunisia, and Morocco. Turkey once more leads the field with its half-century-old experiment with genuine multiparty politics. Having gone through a number of crises and military interruptions, Turkish democracy finally seems to have entered into a phase of consolidation. The most likely medium-term scenario for the other three countries seems to be a continuation of the present experiments with limited pluralism: the "controlled pluralism" in Egypt, the "manipulated pluralism" in Morocco, and the "emergent pluralism" in Tunisia.[86] Among the three, Egypt is the most genuinely pluralistic, with its somewhat marginal but true opposition parties and its hybrid, eclectic, unruly but still vibrant system of interest representation.[87]

In conclusion, the most important political legacy of the Ottoman Empire to its successor states is state autonomy. A combination of political, social, economic, cultural, and historical factors has produced a particularly strong and autonomous state tradition in this region. Since achieving independence, almost all successor states have retained this tradition. In certain areas, they have even strengthened it, due to oil rents and the growth of bureaucratic and coercive apparatus. The more recent countertrends—toward a market economy and the rise of Islamic groups—are working in the opposite direction, forcing the state to retreat to some extent. It is too early to say, however, that these trends are likely to lead to a major transformation of the Middle Eastern state in the near future.

NOTES

1. Joel Migdal, *Strong Societies and Weak States: State-Society Relations and State Capabilities in the Third World* (Princeton: Princeton University Press, 1988), pp. 4–5
2. Raymond A. Hinnebusch, "Authoritarian Power Under Pressure: Comparative Patterns of Persistence and Change in 'Post-Populist' Egypt and Syria," paper presented at the Conference on "Retreating States and Expanding Societies: The State Autonomy/Informal Society Dialectic in the Middle East and North Africa," Aix-en-Provence, France, March 25–27, 1988. Hereafter cited as "Retreating States."
3. Migdal, *Strong Societies and Weak States*, passim, "The Transmission of the State to Society," "Retreating States." See also Stephen D. Krasner, *Defending the National Interest: Raw Material Investment and U.S. Foreign Policy* (Princeton: Princeton University Press, 1978), p. 58.
4. Theda Skocpol, "Bringing the State Back In: Strategies of Analysis in Current Research," in Peter Evans, Dietrich Rueschemeyer, Theda Skocpol, eds., *Bringing the State Back In* (New York: Cambridge: Cambridge University Press, 1985), pp. 15–17.
5. Hinnebusch, "Authoritarian Power Under Pressure," pp. 30–31, n. 1, 2.
6. Leonard Binder, *Islamic Liberalism: A Critique of Development Ideologies* (Chicago: University of Chicago Press, 1988), p. 78.
7. Binder, *Islamic Liberalism*, p. 41.
8. Halil Inalcik, "The Nature of Traditional Society: Turkey," in Robert E. Ward and Dankwart A. Rustow, eds., *Political Modernization in Japan and Turkey* (Princeton: Princeton University Press, 1964), p. 44. For a good comparison of the Ottoman land tenure system with Western European

154 ERGUN ÖZBUDUN

feudalism, see Perry Anderson, *Lineages of the Absolutist State* (London: Verso, 1979), pp. 361–394.

9. Serif Mardin, "Power, Civil Society and Culture in the Ottoman Empire," *Comparative Studies in Society and History,* 11 (June 1969): 265–66.

10. Clement Henry Moore, "Authoritarian Politics in Unincorporated Society: The Case of Nasser's Egypt," *Comparative Politics* 6 (January 1974): 195, 207.

11. Peter Von Sivers, "Retreating States and Expanding Societies: The State Autonomy/Informal Civil Society Dialectic in the Middle East and North Africa," in "Retreating States," p 3.

12. Ibid., p. 4.

13. On the centrality of the state in Turkish political culture, see especially, Engin Deniz Akarli, "The State as a Socio-Cultural Phenomenon and Political Participation in Turkey," in Akarli and Gabriel Ben-Dor, eds., *Political Participation in Turkey: Historical Background and Present Problems* (Istanbul: Bogaziçi University Publications, 1975), pp. 135–38.

14. Ergun Özbudun, "State Elites and Democratic Political Culture in Turkey," in Larry Diamond, ed., *Political Culture and Democracy in Developing Countries* (Boulder, Colo.: Lynne Reinner, 1993), pp. 247–68.. See also Mehmet Ali Birand, *Emret Komutanim* (Istanbul: Milliyet Yayinlari, 1986), for a perceptive analysis of the military's attitudes toward civilian authority, the Kemalist legacy, and their perceptions of public interest.

15. Morroe Berger, *The Arab World Today* (Garden City, N.Y.: Doubleday Anchor, 1964), pp. 272–73.

16. Gabriel Ben-Dor, *State and Conflict in the Middle East: Emergence of the Postcolonial State* (New York: Praeger, 1983), pp. 18–20, 57.

17. Afaf Lutfi al Sayyid Marsot, "Popular Attitudes Towards Authority in Egypt," in "Retreating States."

18. Bernard Lewis, "Loyalty to Community, Nation and State," in George S. Wise and Charles Issawi, eds. *Middle East Perspectives: The New Twenty Years* (Princeton, N.J.: Darwin Press, 1981), pp. 15–16.

19. Cited in Charles E. Butterworth, "State and Authority in Arabic Political Thought," in Ghassan Salame, ed., *The Foundations of the Arab State* (London: Croom Helm, 1987), p. 98. Hereafter cited as Salame, ed., *Arab State.*

20. Cited in Ben-Dor, *State and Conflict,* p. vi.

21. P. J. Vatikiotis, *Islam and the State* (London: Croom Helm, 1987), p. 22.

22. Anderson, *Absolutist State,* pp. 397–400, 462–549.

23. Salame, "Introduction," in Salame, ed., *Arab State,* pp. 9–10. For the fundamentalist Muslim position on the uniqueness of the Islamic state, see Fehmi Jadaane, "Notions of the State in Contemporary Arab-Islamic Writings," Salame, ed., *Arab State,* pp. 124–25.

24. See David Kushner, *The Rise of Turkish Nationalism* (London: Frank Cass, 1977).

25. Bahgat Korany, "Alien and Besieged Yet Here to Stay: The Contradictions of the Arab Territorial State," in Salame, ed., *Arab State,* pp. 48, 62.

26. Thomas Naff, "The Ottoman Empire and the European State System," in H. Bull and A. Watson, eds., *The Expansion of International Society* (Oxford: New York: Oxford University Press, 1984), p. 143.

27. Iliya Harik, "The Origins of the Arab State System," in Salame, ed., *Arab State,* pp. 21–22, 35. Rashid Khalidi concurs that "the nation-state in the Arab world often has deeper roots than many of its critics are willing to grant. In the case of Morocco and Oman, these roots go back to true world empires with all the attributes of sovereignty, and with reinforcing religious and social factors which guaranteed their specifity . . . (T)hey have become nation-states with little apparent difficulty . . . In Tunisia and Egypt there was a sufficient historical sense of an independent identity for these entities to make an easy transition to the status of nation-states": "Prospects for Nation-State and Trans-National Arab Nationalism," in "Retreating States," p. 14.

28. Harik, "Origins of the Arab State System," pp. 20, 38–39.

29. Korany, "Alien and Besieged," pp. 72, 74.

30. Harik, "Origins of the Arab State System," p. 20.

31. Korany, "Alien and Besieged," p. 54.

32. Khalidi, "Prospects for Nation-State," p. 2. See also Ghassan Salame, " 'Strong' and 'Weak' States, a Qualified Return to the *Muqaddimah*," in Salame, ed., *Arab State*, pp. 226–227.

33. Vatikiotis, *Islam and the State*, pp. 10–11, 42–43, and ch. 2 *passim*. Khalidi similarly observes that for the Islamists, "Arab nationalism is a snare and a delusion, and indeed only communism draws more hostility from these movements" ("Prospects for Nation-State" p. 9). Interestingly, Mehmet Akif, a great Turkish poet and the author of the Turkish national anthem, wrote that "O, the community of Muslims, you are neither Arabs, nor Turks, nor Albanians, nor Kurds, nor Laz, nor Circassians. You are members of only one nation, and that is the great nation of Islam. You cannot pursue the cause of nationalism unless you give up Islam; and you cease to be Muslims, as long as you pursue the cause of nationalism," quoted by Tarik Z. Tunaya, *Islamcilik Cereyani* (Istanbul: Baka, 1962), p. 80, n. 1.

34. Bernard Lewis, "The Return of Islam," *Commentary* 61, no. 51 (January 1976), p. 40.

35. Bertrand Badie and Pierre Birnbaum, *The Sociology of the State* (Chicago: University of Chicago Press, 1983), p. 101.

36. Ergun Özbudun, "Antecedents of Kemalist Secularism: Some Thoughts on the Young Turk Period," in Ahmet Evin, ed., *Modern Turkey: Continuity and Change* (Opladen: Leske, 1984), pp. 25–44.

37. For the three types of relationship between state and religion, see Sadok Belaid, "Role of Religious Institutions in Support of the State," in Adeed Dawisha and I. William Zartman, eds., *Beyond Coercion: The Durability of the Arab State* (London: Croom Helm, 1988), pp. 147–63.

38. Harik, "Origins of the Arab State System," pp. 25–31. Hermassi argues that "attitudes to, and relations with, the state differ somewhat from the Maghreb to the Mashreg . . . Contrary to the Mashreg where the unionist ideology prevailed, the Maghreb saw the rise of the national state and of territorial nationalism . . . (N)ot a single liberation party in the Maghreb took up the motto of Arab Union": Elbaki Hermassi, "State-building and Regime Performance in the Greater Maghreb," in Salame, ed. *Arab State*, pp. 76–77.

39. Samuel P. Huntington, *Political Order in Changing Societies* (New Haven: Yale University Press, 1968), pp. 144–46.

40. Ergun Özbudun, "Turkey," in Myron Weiner and Ergun Özbudun, eds., *Competitive Elections in Developing Countries* (Washington, D.C.: American Enterprise Institute/Duke University Press, 1987), pp. 329–32.

41. Roderic H. Davison, "The Advent of the Principle of Representation in the Government of the Ottoman Empire," in William R. Polk and Richard L. Chambers, eds., *Beginning of Modernization in the Middle East: The Nineteenth Century* (Chicago: University of Chicago Press, 1986), p. 95 and passim.

42. Özbudun, "Turkey," pp. 332–34. Also Robert Devereux, *The First Ottoman Constitutional Period: A Study of the Midhat Constitution and Parliament* (Baltimore: Johns Hopkins University Press, 1963).

43. Afaf Lutfi al-Sayyid Marsot, *Egypt's Liberal Experiment, 1922–1936* (Berkeley/ Los Angeles: University of California Press, 1977).

44. Elie Kedourie, "The Genesis of the Egyptian Constitution of 1923," in *The Chatham House Version and Other Middle-Eastern Studies* (Hanover, N.H.: University Press of New England, 1984), pp. 168–69.

45. See Michael C. Hudson, *The Precarious Republic: Political Modernization in Lebanon* (New York: Random House, 1968), and the chapters by Ralph E. Crow, Iliya Harik, and Samir G. Khalaf in Jacob M. Landau, Ergun Özbudun, and Frank Tachau, eds., *Electoral Politics in the Middle East: Issues, Voters, and Elites* (London: Croom Helm, 1980).

46. Manfred Halpern, *The Politics of Social Change in the Middle East and North Africa* (Princeton: Princeton University Press, 1963), pp. 52, 59, 74.

47. For this debate, see especially Amos Perlmutter, "Egypt and the Myth of the New Middle Class: A Comparative Analysis," *Comparative Studies in Society and History*, 10 (October 1967), pp. 46–65, and Halpern's response, "Egypt and the New Middle Class: Reaffirmations and New Explorations," ibid., 11 (January 1969), pp. 97–108; see also James A. Bill and Carl Leiden, *The Middle East: Politics and Power* (Boston: Allyn and Bacon, 1974), pp. 84–88; Jean Leca, "Social Structure and Political Stability: Comparative Evidence from the Algerian, Syrian, and Iraqi Cases," in Dawisha and Zartman, *Beyond Coercion*, pp. 166–169.

48. See, among others, Fredrick W. Frey, *The Turkish Political Elite* (Cambridge: MIT Press, 1965); Frank Tachau, ed., *Political Elites and Political Development in the Middle East* (New York: Schenkman, 1975); George Lenczowski, ed., *Political Elites in the Middle East* (Washington, D.C.: American Enterprise Institute, 1975); Landau, Özbudun, Tachau, *Electoral Politics in the Middle East*, Part 3; R. Hrair Dekmejian, *Egypt Under Nasir: A Study in Political Dynamics* (Albany: State University of New York Press, 1971); also his *Patterns of Political Leadership: Egypt, Israel, Lebanon* (Albany: State University of New York Press, 1975); Hanna Batatu, *The Old Social Classes and Revolutionary Movements of Iraq* (Princeton: Princeton University Press, 1978).

49. Alan Richards and John Waterbury, *A Political Economy of the Middle East: State, Class, and Economic Development* (Boulder: Westview Pres, 1990), pp. 415–16.

50. Leonard Binder, *In a Moment of Enthusiasm: Political Power and the Second Stratum in Egypt* (Chicago: University of Chicago Press, 1978), pp. 26, 28–29, and passim.

51. John Waterbury, *The Egypt of Nasser and Sadat: The Political Economy of Two Regimes* (Princeton: Princeton University Press, 1983), pp. 303, 277, and ch. 12 passim. For a discussion of Binder's second stratum notion vis-a-vis the elite-mass (or state autonomy) model, see Hamid Ansari, "Limits of Ruling Elites: Autonomy in Comparative Perspective," in Dawisha and Zartman, eds., *Beyond Coercion*, pp. 220–38.

52. Ergun Özbudun, "Established Revolution versus Unfinished Revolution: Contrasting Patterns of Democratization in Mexico and Turkey," in Samuel P. Huntington and Clement H. Moore, eds., *Authoritarian Politics in Modern Society: The Dynamics of Established One-Party Systems* (New York: Basic Books, 1970), pp. 380–405. Richards and Waterbury argue that the Turkish and Tunisian examples may "tell us that commercial farmers who perform vital functions in agricultural production, who live in the countryside, and who often help organize the countryside politically for the regime, can better defend their interests than the older landlord class," *Political Economy of the Middle East* p. 402.

53. Skocpol, "Introduction," in Evans and Theda Skocpol, eds., *Bringing the State Back In*, p. 9.

54. Ellen Kay Trimberger, *Revolution from Above: Military Bureaucrats and Development in Japan, Turkey, Egypt, and Peru* (New Brunswick, N.J.: Transaction Books, 1978), pp. 3–4.

55. Richards and Waterbury, *Political Economy of the Middle East*, pp. 401–3.

56. Serif Mardin, "Turkey: The Transformation of an Economic Code," in Ergun Özbudun and Aydin Ulusan, eds., *The Political Economy of Income Distribution in Turkey* (New York: Holmes and Meier, 1980), pp. 25–53.

57. Richards and Waterbury, *Political Economy of the Middle East*, pp. 184–87.

58. Leca, "Social Structure and Political Stability," in Dawisha and Zartman, *Beyond Coercion*, p. 165.

59. For a thorough discussion of the rentier state, see Hazem Beblawi and Giacomo Luciani, eds., *The Rentier State* (London: Croom Helm, 1987).

60. Leca, "Social Structure and Political Stability," p. 184.

61. Dankwart A. Rustow, "The Military: Turkey," Ward and Rustow, eds., *Political Modernization in Japan and Turkey*, p. 388.

62. Nazih Ayubi, "Arab Bureaucracies: Expanding Size and Changing Roles," in Dawisha and Zartman, eds., *Beyond Coercion*, pp. 14–16; Richards and Waterbury, *Political Economy of the Middle East*, p. 197.

63. Ibid., p. 201. Joe Stork gives the 1977 government personnel figure as 580,132, and this does not

include the armed forces, an estimated 230,000 at that time, or nearly 200,000 pensioners directly dependent on the state for their livelihood. The number of government personnel in Iraq was only 9,740 in 1938, 20,031 in 1958, which means that in twenty years public bureaucracy grew some thirty times: "State Power and Economic Structure: Class Determination and State Formation in Contemporary Iraq," in Tim Niblock, ed., *Iraq: The Contemporary State* (London: Croom Helm, 1982), p. 39.

64. Rodney Wilson, "Western, Soviet and Egyptian Influences on Iraq's Development Planning," in Tim Niblock, ed., *Iraq: The Contemporary State*, p. 237.

65. Richards and Waterbury, *Political Economy of the Middle East*, p. 202.

66. Ayubi, "Arab Bureaucracies," pp. 16–18.

67. Ibid., pp. 26–27.

68. Michael C. Hudson, *Arab Politics: The Search for Legitimacy* (New Haven: Yale University Press, 1977), pp. 154–61.

69. Migdal, "The Transmission of the State to Society," Conference on "Retreating States," pp. 1–2.

70. Migdal, *Strong Societies and Weak States*, pp. 8–9, 37–40, and ch. 5.

71. Binder, *Islamic Liberalism*, pp. 13–14.

72. Richards and Waterbury, *Political Economy of the Middle East*, p. 50.

73. Ibid., ch. 9.

74. Leca, "Social Structure and Political Stability," pp. 197–198.

75. Binder, *Islamic Liberalism*, pp. 14–15.

76. Richards and Waterbury, *Political Economy of the Middle East*, p. 261.

77. See, for example, Robert Bianchi, *Unruly Corporatism: Associational Life in Twentieth-Century Egypt* (New York: Oxford University Press, 1989), pp. 178–204.

78. Emmanuel Sivan, "The Islamic Resurgence: Civil Society Strikes Back," "Retreating States," pp. 12–13, 15.

79. Binder, *Islamic Liberalism*, p. 12; Shaul Bakhash, "Islamic Liberalism," *Journal of Democracy* 1:2 (Spring 1990): 118.

80. Binder, *Islamic Liberalism*, pp. 337, 358; Bakhash, "Islamic Liberalism," p. 117.

81. Binder, *Islamic Liberalism*, pp. 10, 357–59; Bakhash, "Islamic Liberalism," pp. 119–20.

82. Ben-Dor, *State and Conflict*, pp. 253–54.

83. Michel Aflaq, *Fi Sabil al Ba'th* (Beirut: Dar al Tali'a, 1963), pp. 43, 46, quoted by Hudson, *Arab Politics*, p. 264. Albert Hourani notes that according to the Ba'th ideology, "Islam was the 'national culture' of the Arabs; it was a veritable image and a perfect eternal symbol of the nature of the Arab self.' Muhammad was 'all the Arabs', and it would be dangerous for Arabs to separate religion from nationality as the European had done," *Arab Thought in the Liberal Age, 1798–1939* (London: Oxford University Press, 1970), p. 357.

84. Dankwart A. Rustow, "Transitions to Democracy: Toward a Dynamic Model," *Comparative Politics* 2:3 (April 1970): 350–51.

85. Cited ibid., p. 351.

86. I. William Zartman, "Opposition as Support of the State," in Dawisha and Zartman, eds., *Beyond Coercion*, pp. 61–87.

87. Bianchi, *Unruly Corporatism*. For a review of Bianchi's book, see Daniel Brumberg, "An Arab Path to Democracy," *Journal of Democracy* 1, no. 4 (Fall 1990): 120–25. See also Mustapha K. El Sayed, "Professional Associations and National Integration in the Arab World, with Special Reference to Lawyers Associations," in Dawisha and Zartman, eds., *Beyond Coercion*, pp. 88–115. For Egyptian political parties, see Raymond A. Hinnebusch, *Egyptian Politics Under Sadat: The Post-Populist Development of an Authoritarian-Modernizing State* (Cambridge: New York: Cambridge University Press, 1985); Hinnebusch, "Political Parties in the Arab State: Libya, Syria, Egypt," in Dawisha and Zartman, eds., *Beyond Coercion*, pp. 35–60.

CHAPTER NINE

THE OTTOMAN ADMINISTRATIVE LEGACY
AND THE MODERN MIDDLE EAST

Carter Vaughn Findley

Is the Ottoman administrative legacy still alive in the modern Middle East? In a brief discussion, I can no more than identify key themes of the Ottoman administrative legacy and argue their saliency for the study of government and administration today. Surveying the history of politics and administration over the last two centuries, I find six themes of the Ottoman legacy that still seem important for the region.[1]

1. Centralization and the reassertion of state authority
2. Indigenous versus imported ideologies
3. Elite formation and inter-elite competition
4. Institutional expansion
5. Mass mobilization
6. The state's role in the economy.

A consideration of these themes can help to renew our sense of the historical integrity of the Islamic world's core region across the last two centuries, a time when regional coherence seems lost to many scholars' view.

Centralization and the Reassertion of State Authority

By ending the Ottoman monopoly over Black Sea navigation, causing the empire's first significant loss of Muslim-inhabited territory (the Crimea), and essentially ending Ottoman control of Egypt, the defeats of the late eighteenth century shocked the Ottomans into a new awareness of the infidel danger. The threat called for a new emphasis on military reform. No more than European rulers, however, could Ottoman statesmen achieve higher military effectiveness without making the state into a machine of greater power and efficiency overall.

A generalized effort to centralize and reassert state power ensued. Centralization quickly proved to have several aspects. Sultans Selim III (1789–1807) and Mahmud II (1808–39) began reconcentrating power at the center; later shifts between the Palace and the Sublime Porte illustrated the potential for high-level struggle over just where at the center power should be concentrated. Power also had to be projected outward to make the sultan's will felt in the provinces and, at times, beyond Ottoman frontiers.

Many aspects of centralization have been studied, but a key point does not always attract due note: Ottoman reformers did not doubt the desirability of maximizing state power. They found much to differ about, but the list includes little of the Anglo-American liberal idealization of little government or decentralization. The reason was partly a long tradition of belief in the state's power to regulate social and economic relations. In the reform era, Ottomans might argue behind the scenes over whether power should be concentrated in the hands of the sultan or his officials. In the first and second constitutional periods (1876–78, 1908–18) they talked about decentralization in the sense of "broadening the discretion" (*tevsi-i mezuniyet*) of provincial authorities. This is a kind of decentralization that became thinkable once the center disposed of elites and institutions that could be counted on to maintain its interests. The Young Turk period did include a movement for decentralization. It, too, aimed to save the state, by federalizing it, but did not carry the day.

In the Young Turk period, debate on the exercise of state power assumed a particular form, contrasting autocratic centralization, on one hand, with dispersion of authority under an idealized rule of law, on the other. Some dispersionists seemed to visualize a rule of law so complete that the boundaries within which each official would exercise his discretion would be legally defined. Ottomans discussed these alternatives in terms of *istizan* ("requesting permission," which one had to do for everything under Abdülhamid) and *salahiyet* (competence, discretion). Here, the alternative to despotism is not liberal democracy, with its idealized rule of laws rather than men, but rather a continental-style *Rechtsstaat*: an Ottoman Prussia.

The twentieth century has shown that despotism, when no longer decked in monarchial regalia, may reappear in bureaucratic necktie or military boots. Late Ottomans, with keen memories of the Hamidian despotism, perhaps cannot be blamed for not foreseeing this danger. Nor is it their fault that the continental universities they looked to classed the study of administration, not under political science, but under law. Among Ottomans, Ibrahim Hakki Pasha (1862–1918)—a pioneer expert on international and administrative law and briefly grand vezier—epitomizes this legalist mindset.

Through all the discussions about state power, the desirability of maximizing it was hardly questioned. Here we see the faith in the rightfulness of the powerful state that has led social scientists to compare Middle Eastern attitudes with corporatism in Latin America. Comparison, however, to a specific ideology rooted in Catholic thought and Iberian history may hinder, rather than facilitate, our understanding of an attitude whose counterparts have been legion in major centers of civilization all across Eurasia, from south and central Europe to the China Sea. Occasionally, in protected environments like ancient Greece, England, or Japan, high levels of decentralization might work. Elsewhere, submission to a powerful master usually seemed a worthwhile price to pay for justice and security. Authoritarian rule, the state's autonomy in relation to society, and demand for political "solidarism," rather than "pluralism," followed readily in these circumstances.[2]

In the post-colonial era, with its multiplication of sovereign states, many of which markedly lack organizational structures capable of taking a lead in development, demands on state institutions have only increased, as will be seen below in a discussion of the state's economic role.

Indigenous Versus Imported Ideologies

Reasserting state power soon proved to imply changing the nature of that power. For the Ottomans, enacting reforms required using the sultan's decree power and—as one moved from decrees to regulations and laws—reasserting the regulatory power traditionally identified with *kanun* (law promulgated by the state). Enactment of *kanun*, common in the sixteenth century, had later tapered off, so raising the relative prominence of the other types of law: custom and shari'ah. Reasserting state legislative power implied deemphasis on the shari'ah, which raised doubt about the state's Islamic commitment, especially when kanun was used to enact infidel innovations. Moreover, official minutes of high-level discussions during the late eighteenth-century crises show growing awareness that the state could no longer hew to old ideas of ghaza and jihad without risking disaster. Some intellectuals were ready to discuss universal peace almost as European international lawyers might.[3] Both external and internal affairs thus raised ideological issues.

What I have labeled "indigenous versus imported ideologies" consisted of a set of far-reaching cultural changes. In international relations, for example,

European artists' rendering of European diplomats being received by the grand vizier, above c. 1788 and below in the early 1790s, thus both before the Ottoman Empire had felt obliged to send resident ambassadors abroad. Thereafter, came "intensified efforts to use diplomacy . . . to protect the state."

SOURCES: (*above*) J. M. Jouannin and Jules Van Gaver, *Turquie*, Series *L'Univers; Historie at Description de Tous les Peuples* (Paris: Firmin Didot Freres, 1840); (*below*) Topkapi Palace Museum.

the change appears in intensified efforts to use diplomacy, not war, to protect the state. Perhaps the most notable milestone in this respect was the empire's formal admission to the concert of Europe by the Treaty of Paris (1856). Indeed, one can jump a century ahead in time and see the Turkish Republic with its membership in NATO and would-be membership in the European Community as continuing the Ottoman struggle to go from formal to real admission. In law, the consequences of reactivating kanun appeared in what legal experts call "legislative eclecticism"—the borrowing of laws from disparate sources. Historians still see this as bizarre. Troubling its consequences can well be for those who do it; but, in modern third world practice legal eclecticism is normal. In political thought, the clearest indicator of cultural change was the emergence of ideological controversy as a discrete, secular activity, as opposed to older, more inclusive ways of talking about state and Islam; here, as in many realms, the Ottomans led in changes that later spread to other Islamic lands.[4] Finally, the conflict of ideologies translated into cultural dualism, as seen in separate Islamic and secular schools and courts, in the coexistence of Islamic and westernizing modes of thought with almost nothing in common, and in the widespread cultural rootlessness that nineteenth-century Ottoman fiction obsessively depicts.[5]

In reaction to such cultural tensions, Ottoman and post-Ottoman ideological preferences have passed through three phases, characterized successively by liberalism, socialism, and reemphasis on Islam. Largely because the last two centuries, more than any other period in Islamic history, have been a time of encroachment by outside powers and ideas, the result has been an unstable ideological mix, in which both imported and indigenous ideas resurface from time to time, sometimes with explosive results.

Among imported ideologies, European liberal thought has been the most influential. The classical liberal program was enshrined in Ottoman imperial policy with the Anglo-Ottoman commercial treaty of 1838 and the Gulhane Decree of 1839.[6] The treaty committed the empire to free trade. The decree promised guarantees of life, honor, and property; equality between Muslim and non-Muslim; and the passing of additional laws to implement these promises. The decree has been more often praised than closely examined. The last of the decree's promises—the enacting of additional laws to implement the other promises—was surely the most significant. In a state that remained officially Islamic and presumably committed to the shari'ah, it was no understatement to say that new laws would be required to implement equality between Muslim and non-Muslim! One reason why Europeans complained that the decree was not observed was precisely that such a legal contradiction could not be resolved.

The adoption of free trade was no better thought out. Both reforms were adopted to get European support against Muhammad Ali, to whom free trade was expected to be especially injurious. But the Ottomans, too, had monopolies—state enterprises, we would call many of them—against which British free trade enthusiasts inveighed. Private enterprise as well would suffer from the loss of protection. Thus, 1838–39 brought the first "opening" (*infitah*) to the West, presenting policy choices similar to ones that have become familiar in recent years. The debt and bankruptcy crises that swept the Ottoman, Egyptian, and Tunisian governments in the 1870s and '80s underscore the similarities, while the foreign financial controls introduced then have their modernized form in the International Monetary Fund and its stabilization programs.[7]

While liberalism may have had the most lasting influence of any imported ideology, it was not the only one. In the twentieth century, socialism also had its day, mostly in hybrid, leftist-nationalist forms little restrained by Marxist thought. Significantly, Turkey influenced the wider region even here. Richards and Waterbury's recent *Political Economy of the Middle East* reveals anew how much Atatürk's example inspired other statesmen of the region, such as Bourguiba, Nasser, and Sadat.[8] Having combined liberalism with statism (*devletçilik*)—an idea derived partly from the Ottoman background and partly from foreign, especially Soviet, example[9]—Atatürk inspired Middle Eastern "socialists" as well as "liberals." As we shall see, Turkey's statist economic policy was a precursor for similar developmental ideologies in many other developing countries.

Since about 1970, with the reemphasis on Islamic ideas and values, focus has shifted, across the Middle East, from imported back to indigenous ideology. With this change, we move beyond the westernizing legacy of the Ottoman reform era. The Islamic reemphasis has, however, attracted attention to the Ottoman legacy in a different perspective. Whereas many Arab nationalists used to blame the Ottoman for the weaknesses of their own societies or even lump the Ottoman Empire together with the British and French colonial empires as examples of alien exploitation, many Islamic activists now again recognize the Ottoman Empire as the product of state-formation processes indigenous to the Islamic world and as one of the greatest empires of Islamic history. While this is some improvement over any view that lumped the Ottomans together with the British and French, this reinterpretation entails major risks that the Ottoman legacy will be misrepresented at the same time that it is rehabilitated, and that the Turkish Republic—especially the symbolic figure of Mustafa Kemal Atatürk—will be demonized in the process. Turkey itself is scarcely unaffected by these changing currents, although political movements of every hue still try to legitimize themselves by claiming loudly to be "Kemalist."

The Turkish republic has obviously gone further than other Ottoman successor states in opting for imported, Western ideology. Partly explained by the proto-secularist cast that its Turko-Mongol background gave the Ottoman state from the beginning,[10] this choice further reflects Turkey's unique, geographic potential to identify either with Europe or the Middle East. Asia Minor's reorientation under Atatürk is but one of several since ancient times. Halil Inalcik has spotlighted Ottoman proto-secularism; world historians have noted the chameleonlike cultural reorientations of what we now call Turkey.

Elite Formation and Inter-Elite Competition

As much as does the tradition of state-centrism, the Ottoman record in elite formation helps explain the ideological choices discussed above. By 1800, the Ottoman ruling class contained three important functional divisions: the military, the religious, and the scribal (later known as the civil) services. The reassertion of state power brought shifts in the relative standing of these groups. As these shifts occurred, episodic attempts were also made to upgrade the corporate forms of the various elites. Reference to the transformation in the collective fabric of the three elites will set the stage for examination of inter-elite competition and its ideological significance.

The elites' corporate transformation owed most to sultans Mahmud II (1808–1839) and Abdulhamid II (1876–1909). The process began even earlier with the founding of the military engineering schools (naval in 1773, army in 1795) and with Selim III's efforts to reform the military and create a diplomatic corps. Mahmud revived these efforts in the 1820s and 1830s, reforming conditions of appointment, service, and compensation for both the military and the civil officials (as it thenceforth becomes appropriate to call them: *mülkiye memurları*). In 1839, the Gulhane Decree terminated the worst disabilities of the slave status of the sultan's servants.

Abdulhamid later enacted European-style civil service regulations, setting up a personnel records system, appointment boards, and rules covering appointment, promotion, retirement, and administrative justice. He enacted analogous measures for other elites, as well. The Young Turks continued this process. The republic transferred this apparatus to Ankara; other successor states inherited at least some of the people who had worked in it.

Obviously, one cannot simply accept Abdulhamid's rules and regulations in such matters as found on paper. His behavior subverted the forms of rational, impersonal procedure. For the Middle East in general, massive evidence indicates the continuing significance of patronage networks to this day. Even so, the experiences of a particularly well-documented Ottoman official, in service from the 1840s to about 1900, indicate that the new systems did not remain only on paper but began to cut into the domain where favor and faction had once prevailed exclusively.[11] Similarly, while repression of initiative and procedural involution remain bureaucratic hallmarks to this day, a new kind of professionalism, characterized by professional associations, journals, and ongoing debate about what it meant to be a civil official, had clearly begun to develop by the Young Turk period. Recent research has shown the further development of analogous forms of associational life, outside government as well as inside, in various countries since then.[12]

In the competition that occurred among Ottoman elites as their corporate metamorphosis progressed, the religious scholars (ulama) were the first losers. A century ago, Ahmed Cevdet Pasha concluded from late-eighteenth-century debates on the Russian threat that the religious scholars had already lost the ability to advise effectively about such crises because the empire could no longer implement the traditional solutions they called for.

Thereafter, while Islamic activists were always present and influential with substantial segments of the public, the ulama became marginalized. The state chipped away at their foundation, not only through secular legislation, but also—in the Young Turk period—by taking control of the sharia courts, evkaf, and medreses away from the shaykh al-Islam and giving it, instead, to secular cabinet ministers.[13] Atatürk delivered the coup de grâce when he followed up the abolition of sultanate and caliphate by abolishing the office of shaykh al-Islam and the other institutional bastions that had made the official ulama a part of the Ottoman establishment. Ironically, Islamic activists who vilify Atatürk fail to notice that they usually agree with him about the uselessness of things like bureaucratized ulama. Indeed, one could go further and say that among the reasons why Iranian-style Islamic revolutions have not broken out elsewhere is the fact that Arab successor states, too, have essentially followed Ottoman example in limiting their ulama's autonomy—an achievement now challenged, to be sure, by the rise of militant activism outside of ulama ranks.[14]

Considering either the original impetus to reform or twentieth-century trends, one might have expected the military to benefit most from Ottoman reform. Things were not that simple. Much research remains to be done on military reform, and perspectives will surely change at points. Yet praetorians usually did not dominate in Istanbul during the reform era. One early motive for reform was, after all, the realization on the part of the ruling elite that the empire could no longer pursue its interests safely by jihad and ghaza. Increasingly, the men of the hour were diplomats, not soldiers.

Military reform required drastic institutional discontinuities. Abolishing the janissaries in 1826, and founding a new army in the midst of the Greek

Revolution, illustrate this point. Although efforts to create military academies and a school-trained officer corps went back at least to the 1770s, well before analogous efforts to train a civil elite, results came slowly for the military, perhaps because the costs and technical requirements were greater than those of modernizing the scribal officials' adab-culture. Tension between "school-trained" officers and "old troopers" (*mektepli* and *alaylı*) was another live issue, even in the late nineteenth century.

At times, too, large investments in military modernization appear to have been wasted. This was certainly true of Muhammad Ali's Egypt and Ahmad Bey's Tunisia. Ottoman sultan Abdulaziz, too, made his navy one of Europe's largest[15]—to what end? Under Abdulhamid there was the different problem that the sultan seems to have been highly suspicious of his military and concerned above all about keeping it from acting against him. By the 1890s, he had reason to fear.

The Young Turk movement did indeed bring the military into politics, a trend that culminated when Atatürk became president of the republic. One of many ways in which he outclassed some of his imitators, however, was to lend his overt support—as opposed, perhaps, to his body language—to the civilianization of executive authority. The long-lived İnönü used his prestige to keep this message alive. More recently, Turkey's military elites have still regarded themselves as custodians of the Atatürk legacy, but have faced an increasingly daunting task in attempting to control the republic's developmental course. The political dominance of military officers or former officers has remained more characteristic in Arab countries, but is coming to be viewed with increasing disillusionment of late.[16]

Returning to Ottoman times, we find that the last of the elites, the civil officials did emerge as the leading official elite of the reform era, at least until 1908. This was especially true of those who were prepared to learn French and meet the infidels on their own terms. The way the office of foreign minister became the springboard to the grand vizierate during the Tanzimat period represents the apogee of this trend. That was also the period when the westernizing vanguard of the civil intelligentsia began to differentiate into officials, on the one hand, and—with the rise of a publishing industry—professional litterateurs and political activists on the other.

Since 1908, civil official dominance has never again been so assured. However, a coalition of civil and military elites continued to dominate Turkey from 1908 to 1950.[17] The persistence of the infitah option—on through Hourani's liberal age,[18] the brief vogue of Arab socialism, and into the post-cold war era—has continued to give opportunities to the Tanzimat intelligentsia's heirs. They have diversified widely, from diplomats to managers and technocrats, in both public and private sectors.

Whichever elite has dominated at a given time, the whole phenomenon of elite formation is related to at least two other issues we must consider. One is the growth of the institutional structures the elites staffed. The other is the contrast between the Middle Eastern tradition of political and cultural elitism and the mass mobilization that has become typical of the modern world.

Institutional Expansion

Even as reform altered the elites' relative standing, it created what contemporaries saw as "big government." A look at the nineteenth century's institutional expansion reveals why civil officials made such a strong showing in that period. The nineteenth century's new governmental systems were usually staffed—apart from purely military functions—by civil officials, giving them a vast range of responsibilities and powers that their scribal predecessors had scarcely dreamt of.

In the empire's classic system, for example, the closest thing to a local administrator in a given locale was a cavalry officer (*sipahi*), who had been assigned to perform certain duties, and to compensate himself by collecting certain revenues in kind in that district. The judicial function, in all types of law, belonged to the qadi, a religious functionary. To collect revenues in coin, each province had a treasury agent, who was a scribal official. Land surveys, when they occurred, brought other scribal officials through with the survey party. By and large, however, the scribes did not administer the empire; they produced records, mostly in Istanbul, for others who did. In the provinces, the main "administrators" were military.

By the nineteenth century, the military establishment's old administrative role was mostly a memory, and civil officials were picking up one after another of the new governmental functions. Since the reasons for their rise have to do largely with their role as cultural mediators with Europeans, the institutions most associated with the civil officials' ascent included relatively small numbers of people: the diplomatic service initially had only five embassies. What created vast differences in numbers between the old scribes and the new civil officials was rather the functions that required creation of empire-wide infrastructure. Such functions included the new secular courts, the new schools, and especially the new system of local administration.

Americans familiar with a federal system need reminding that what was emerging in the Ottoman Empire was a centralized system, in which local government was primarily an administrative responsibility of the Interior Ministry, created in 1837. Local administration employed so many civil officials that the term *mülkiye* referred to both local administration, in particular, and civil officialdom, in general. Ottoman subjects who complained about "big government" were complaining about the way this administrative structure affected their lives—through its demands for censuses, passports, identity papers, quarantines, and taxes, and through its regulations on everything from headgear to street width to the press.

If centralization raised questions about the nature of the state, institutional expansion raised others about the quality of administration; and not without reason. Elsewhere, I have traced the downward spiral that led from free trade to paper money to foreign debt to bankruptcy and foreign financial control, permanently thwarting the effort at fiscal centralization, also decreed in 1838.[19] Under the circumstances, civil officials' compensation systems never functioned properly, and the resulting problems in behavioral standards undermined the whole reform effort. Unable to solve this problem, Abdulhamid manipulated it, for example, by timing the infrequent salary payments to achieve "mood control" over his hapless officials. The result was systemic corruption—a situation where even officials of spotless personal ethics faced irresistible economic pressure. By then, all the steps that had been taken toward rationalizing elite recruitment and promotion had been bent to make the bureaucracy into a huge patronage machine run by the sultan.

Again, the bizarre features of the late nineteenth century are not without twentieth-century parallels. The Ottomans expanded from some 2,000 scribal officials at the end of the eighteenth century to perhaps 35,000 civil officials by 1908, plus hangers-on who had been given appointments to make them beholden to the sultan. With motives rather like Abdulhamid's, Muhammad Reza Shah increased Iran's civil service to 304,000. In contrast, Nasser had populist motives and numbers to match: 1.3 million in his civil service. The Turkish civil service of the 1990s reportedly has between 1.5 and 2 million officials.[20]

The Ottomans may have experienced only an early phase in a growth process of longue durée, but they thought they suffered from "big government." They associated this especially with the civil officials who manned so many new agencies and rammed through so many westernizing reforms during the Tanzimat. The Young Ottoman Movement of the 1860s and 1870s illustrates the significance of these resentments for our fifth theme: mass mobilization.

Mass Mobilization

To say that our time is an age of mass mobilization is a truism validated daily by live television coverage of crowd scenes around the world. In the Middle East, this mobilization ultimately included efforts to shake off the region's millennial cultural and political elitism—efforts that climaxed in the midst of the twentieth century's unprecedented population explosion. Tradition dies hard, however. The Middle East is not the only region where age-old traditions of authoritarianism have found ways to survive, reclothed in populist garb. Everyday realities of the region, these problems date back to the shocks that propelled the Middle East into its modern era of accelerating change.

Opening an age when tried and true methods no longer worked, the late eighteenth-century crises expanded the scope and contentiousness of policy choices in a way that quickening change later intensified. The Tanzimat period opened when the liberal-inspired reforms of 1838–1839 dropped like depth charges into an Islamic society. To its critics this was a period of reckless, rapid westernization. The Tanzimat statesmen tried to counter the resulting malaise and the separatist nationalisms spreading in the empire with a mobilization strategy of their own: the redefinition of Ottomanism, no longer as the identity of the ruling class alone, but as a supranationalism that would win the loyalty of all the sultan's subjects. In time, the Tanzimat also provoked a reaction at the center: a new type of ideological movement, the Young Ottomans. Mostly of civil official background, the young Ottomans appropriated Ottomanism, infused it with real emotive fire, propounded an Islamic-modernist ideology for more guarded change, and strove to mobilize the public at least through their writings—primarily not, however, through political organization. The first constitutional period was partly their work.[21]

Legitimately empowered as neither Tanzimat statesmen nor most later Middle Eastern politicians have been, Sultan Abdulhamid also had the grit to squelch the Young Ottomans and other constitutionalists. Quantitative research on official living standards shows that economic depression favored him in this through the 1880s: prices fell, while incomes of the official intelligentsia, from whom the Young Ottomans rose, stayed level.[22] The Young Turks had begun to organize by the end of the 1880s, however. After bottoming in the 1890s, prices resumed the upward course that contributed to the revolution of 1908. Unconcerned about the Young Ottomans' Islamic modernism, the Young Turks otherwise revived and expanded their ideas. Significantly, Young Turk activism spread among the military as well as the civil official elite; and the Young Turks organized for action as the Young Ottomans had not. The significance of these differences showed in 1908.[23]

In the changed environment of the second constitutional period, political mobilization entered a new phase as multiple parties and political movements emerged.[24] The history of political parties has had its ups and downs since, but Turkey has probably come closer to developing a real network of national political parties than any other Islamic Middle Eastern country.

Of course, the political is only one aspect of mobilization in the broad sense. Other factors include demographic change as well as changes in transportation, communication, education, even military recruitment, especially the military form of mass mobilization. Of key importance was the spread of literacy and rise of print media popularizing new ideas in Ottoman, Arabic, and other languages.

Trying to save the empire, Ottoman elites strove to take advantage of all such processes and counteract separatist nationalism by promoting their paradoxical supranationalism. Extending our view from late eighteenth century to late twentieth, we see yet another paradox. For all their elitism, the Ottoman reformers stand at the opening of mobilizing processes that ultimately introduced a real measure of democratization into the region—socially, culturally, politically.[25]

Since these are trends of global scale, credit or blame cannot be assigned only to regional actors or forces. Still, the Ottoman elites, trying to preserve the state that conferred on them their privileged identity, played key roles in launching democratizing change.

The main problem about these changes only partly emerged before the empire fell. This is that the mobilizing processes occurred in a context where rapid demographic change steadily redefined needs. Under the empire, this problem appeared more in terms of population composition than absolute numbers. For example, the Ottomans' liberal-inspired commitment to equality evolved through three different versions. Over time, its beneficiaries shifted from non-Muslim minorities, to non-Turkish Muslims after 1878 (by which date territorial loss and the inflow of Muslim refugees had created a Muslim majority), and finally to Turks. Egalitarianism meant different things under the Tanzimat, Abdulhamid, and the Turkish republic. In Arab lands, the post-imperial reformulation of collective identity concepts continued even longer.

From the 1930s on, the unprecedented third world population explosion magnified mass mobilizers' problems—and successes, such as the achievement of majority literacy in most countries. Turkey's political vicissitudes in the 1970s and 1980s illustrate this point; Egypt's under Nasser and since do so even more vividly. Nasser's "neo-pharaonic" leadership style also illustrates how ambivalent even a charismatic Middle Eastern politician can be about the very mobilization he champions. Now that prevalent understandings of democracy extend beyond the old liberal concern with political rights to embrace social justice, overcoming such shortfalls would require curbing population growth and achieving socioeconomic development more significant than most of the region has yet seen. This leads to our final theme, that of state and economy.

State and Economy

In the Middle East, the current controversy over public sector versus private may look too much like a recent Western import to have precedents in the region. In fact, however, the Ottomans' traditional insistence on the state's primacy in relation to economy and society on the one hand and their official espousal of liberal economic principles as far back as 1838 on the other, demonstrate that the current controversy is not without local antecedents, some quite old.

To characterize the traditional Ottoman economy, we may begin by critiquing the old saw that the state existed only to wage war and collect taxes. The "circle of equity" (*adalet dairesi*), which political philosophers long used to portray relations between ruler and ruled, may have prettied the image of a polity that was no welfare state in today's terms. Yet the empire did have welfare policies. It used *waqf* to create public works and charitable institutions. It had limited pension systems. In economic policy, the concept of provisionism reflects concern for the general welfare. Applied in resupplying the capital, and generally in external and internal trade, provisionism reversed the now-usual concern for a positive balance of payments by emphasizing the inflow of goods, rather than money, so as to avoid scarcity.

The state also intervened in the economy in many ways that went beyond provisionism. The state fixed prices (*narh*) for staples. Through the state purchase (*mirî mubayaa*) system, it made producers sell it set quantities of needed goods below market prices. Finally, the empire founded state enterprises to produce goods it needed, like gunpowder. Here we have rudiments of a state sector.

The significance of Turkish practice for Middle Eastern approaches to economic development expanded with Atatürk's adoption of statism. Opening a new era, this was the first case where a developing country adopted a policy of economic planning and expanding the state sector in order to accelerate industrialization.[26] The regional significance of Atatürk's "Turkish paradigm"[27] appears clearly from its widespread imitation after 1945, until exhaustion of the "easy" import substitution phase forced the policy reorientation identified with Sadat's opening to the West, from which we get the term *infitah*, and Turkey's attempted transition to export-led growth.

With the abolition of the capitulations, decolonization, and the OPEC-era oil boom, economic conditions in the twentieth-century Middle East may appear to have changed beyond recognition. Yet the price-subsidy systems now basic to the third world version of the welfare state are not so different in intent from provisionism. Against the Ottoman backdrop, Atatürk's widely emulated expansion of the state's economic role was not as innovative as sometimes supposed. Nor were the Middle East's most advanced assertions of the state's economic role, as in Nasser's Egypt, totally divorced from Ottoman antecedent. Even the oil export phenomenon—far from an open sesame to diversification—recreates on grand scale the colonial economy's dependence on a single agro-mineral export. The distressing clarity with which continuities emerge in the economic history of the last two centuries—once changes in the terms for certain phenomena have been noted—spotlights how difficult it will be for most of the region to achieve high levels of economic development.

The Ottoman legacy remains relevant to the study of government and administration in the contemporary Middle East, despite changes as vast as the region's growth in number of both states and inhabitants. Important continuities can be encapsulated under six themes: assertion of state power, the clash of indigenous and imported ideologies, elite formation, institutional expansion, mass mobilization, and government's economic role. These continuities suggest that the history of administration and government in the Middle East has a coherence over the last two centuries comparable to that observed in the "old but dangerous" Eastern Question game.

NOTES

1. Except when otherwise noted, the discussion of the Ottoman legacy follows Carter Vaughn Findley, *Bureaucratic Reform in the Ottoman Empire: The Sublime Porte, 1789–1922* (Princeton: Princeton University Press, 1980); and Findley, *Ottoman Civil Officialdom: A Social History* (Princeton: Princeton University Press, 1989).

2. Making the comparison with Latin American corporatism and citing the seminal work on state autonomy by Alfred Stepan, *The State and Society: Peru in Comparative Perspective* (Princeton: Princeton University Press, 1978), Richards and Waterbury use "solidarism," borrowed from Durkheim via Ziya Gökalp, as their term for the Middle Eastern counterpart of corporatism. Alan Richards and John Waterbury, *A Political Economy of the Middle East: State, Class, and Economic Development* (Boulder: Westview Press, 1990), pp. 303, 330–52.

3. Virginia Harris Aksan, "Ahmed Resmi Efendi, 1700–1783: The Making of an Early Ottoman Reformer," Ph.D. dissertation, University of Toronto, 1990, pp. 312–15.

4. Cf. Carter Vaughn Findley, "The Advent of Ideology in the Islamic Middle East," Part 1, *Studia Islamica* 55 (1982): 143–69; Part 2, *Studia Islamica* 56 (1982): 147–80.

5. The classic work on cultural dualism is Niyazi Berkes, *The Development of Secularism in Turkey* (Montreal: McGill University Press, 1964).

6. J. C. Hurewitz, *The Middle East and North Africa in World Politics: A Documentary Record*, vol. 1: *European Expansion, 1535–1914* (New Haven: Yale University Press, 1975), pp. 265–66, 269–71.

7. Findley, art. "Mâliyye," EI2,VI, p. 288. Nineteenth- and twentieth-century debt crises form an excellent subject for comparative study. Cf. Alan Richards and John Waterbury, *Political Economy of the Middle East*, pp. 226–31 and passim; Emine Kiray, *Osmanlı' da Ekonomik Yapi re Diş Borçlar* (Istanbul 1993).

8. Richards and Waterbury, *Political Economy of the Middle East*, pp. 25–26, 50, 187–92, 302–4, 338, 435.

9. On Ottoman antecedents of the statist policy, see François Georgeon, "L'économie politique

selon Ahmed Midhat," in *Première rencontre internationale sur l'Empire ottoman et la Turquie moderne*, vol. 2: *La vie politique, économique, et socio-culturelle de l'Empire ottoman à l'époque jeune-turque*, ed. Edhem Eldem (Istanbul/Paris: Isis, 1991), pp. 461–79; Zafer Toprak, *Türkiye'de 'Milli Iktisat', 1908–1919* (Ankara: Yurt Yayinlari, 1982). For foreign antecedents, see Ilhan Tekel and Selim Ilkin, *Uygulamaya Geçerken Türkiyede Devletçiligin Oluşumu* (Ankara: 1982), passim; Bent Hansen, *Egypt and Turkey: The Political Economy of Poverty, Equity, and Growth* (Oxford: Oxford University Press, 1991), pp. 319–30.

10. Halil Inalcik, "On the Secularism in Turkey," *Orientalische Literaturzeitung*, 64 (1969), cols. 439–42.

11. Findley, *Ottoman Civil Officialdom*, pp. 281–92.

12. Findley, *Ottoman Civil Officialdom*, pp. 243–52; cf. Robert Bianchi, *Interest Groups and Political Development in Turkey* (Princeton: Princeton University Press, 1984); Bianchi, *Unruly Corporatism: Associational Life in Twentieth-Century Egypt* (New York: Oxford University Press, 1989); Donald M. Reid, *Lawyers and Politicians in the Arab World, 1880–1960* (Minneapolis and Chicago: Bibliotheca, 1981); Clement Henry Moore, *Images of Development: Egyptian Engineers in Search of Industry* (New York: Cambridge University Press, 1980).

13. Findley, *Ottoman Civil Officialdom* p. 132; Berkes, *Development of Secularism*, pp. 415–19.

14. Cf. Emmanuel Sivan, *Radical Islam: Medieval Theology and Modern Politics* (New Haven: Yale University Press, 1985), pp. 12–14.

15. Roderic H. Davison, *Reform in the Ottoman Empire, 1856–1876* (Princeton: Princeton University Press, 1963), pp. 264–66.

16. Richards and Waterbury, *Political Economy of the Middle East*, pp. 353–73.

17. Erik J. Zürcher, *Turkey: A Modern History* (London: I. B. Tauris, 1993), p. 4.

18. Albert Hourani, *Arabic Thought in the Liberal Age, 1798–1939* (Oxford: Oxford University Press, first published in 1962).

19. Findley, *Ottoman Civil Officialdom*, pp. 29–30.

20. Findley, *Ottoman Civil Officialdom*, pp. 22–23 and sources cited there. Latest official figures from colleagues in Department of Economics, Hacettepe University, Ankara, December 5, 1994.

21. Şerif Mardin, *The Genesis of Young Ottoman Thought* (Princeton: Princeton University Press, 1962).

22. Carter Vaughn Findley, "Economic Bases of Revolution and Repression in the Late Ottoman Empire," *Comparative Studies in Society and History* 28 (1986): 81–106; Findley, *Ottoman Civil Officialdom*, pp. 319–33.

23. M. Şükrü Hanioğlu, *Bir Siyasal Örgüt Olara Osmanlı Ittihad ve Terakkii: Cemiyeti Jön Türklük, 1889–1902* (Istanbul: 1986).

24. Tarik Zafer Tunaya, *Turkiye'de Siyasal Partiler, Cilt 1: Ikinci Meçrutiyet Dönemi, 1908–1918*, 2d ed. (Istanbul, 1984).

25. This is especially clear in education: Carter Vaughn Findley, "Knowledge and Education in the Modern Middle East: A Comparative View," in *The Modern Economic and Social History of the Middle East in Its World Context*, ed. Georges Sabagh (New York: Cambridge University Press, 1989), pp. 130–55; Findley, "Knowledge and Education," ch. 7 in *Modernization in the Middle East: The Ottoman Empire and Its Afro-Asian Successors*, ed. Cyril E. Black and L. Carl Brown (Princeton: Princeton University Press, 1992); Findley, "Problems of Democratizing Education in an Era of Explosive Population Growth," forthcoming with proceedings of the "Third Conference on the Transfer of Science and Technology Between Europe and Asia Since Vasco da Gama (1498–1998)," Istanbul, Research Center for Islamic History, Art, and Culture, October 1994.

26. Personal communication from Bent Hansen, 1985.

27. Richards and Waterbury, *Political Economy of the Middle East*, pp. 187–92.

CHAPTER TEN

OTTOMAN DIPLOMACY AND ITS LEGACY

Roderic H. Davison

Diplomacy has frequently had a bad name. In many works on diplomacy one meets the unfortunate pun of Sir Henry Wotton, a seventeenth-century English envoy, who wrote that "an ambassador is an honest man sent to lie abroad for the good of his country."[1] Similarly, diplomatic history has also been dismissed as "What one clerk wrote to another clerk." But these are caricatures of diplomats and of the history they make. In reality, diplomacy in a narrow sense is the art of communication and negotiation between the governments of sovereign states. Diplomats are the practitioners of this art. They make reasonable international relations possible.

In the wider sense, diplomacy is international relations. Diplomatic history is the history of international relations. It is replete with documents written by clerks, of course. But its essence is found in decisions made and actions taken (or not taken) by monarchs, presidents, prime ministers, grand viziers, foreign ministers, cabinets, ambassadors, military commanders, and others. The sum of the decisions and actions is diplomatic history, the history of how sovereign states got along with each other. It is the history of interacting foreign policies representing diverse interests.

Ottoman diplomacy, then, is Ottoman foreign relations, embodying policies, decisions, actions, and attitudes of sultans, grand viziers, foreign ministers, and ambassadors. The legacy of Ottoman diplomacy to the modern Near East comes principally from the later days of the empire's life, the nineteenth and early twentieth centuries, an age of territorial contraction. But some

Bridge over the Neretva River at Mostar in Herzegovina (1565). Destroyed by Croat artillery in November 1993.

Suleimaniya Mosque, Istanbul (1557). *Imperial Self-portrait: The Ottoman Empire as Revealed in the Sultan Abdul Hamid II's Photographic Albums.*

All picture not otherwise identified are from Türkiye Dişindaki Osmanli Mimari Yapıtları: Ottoman Architectural Works Outside Turkey, produced by the Turkish Ministry of Foreign Affairs.

Bachelor's Mosque, Berat, Albania
(eighteenth century).

Haram al-Sharif Mosque, Madina, Saudi
Arabia, reconstructed during the reign of
Sultan Abdulaziz (1849).

Açikbash House in Aleppo, Syria (eighteenth century).

Abdulrahmna Katkhuda Sabil-Kuttab.
Cairo, Egypt (1774).
Photo: André Raymond

Seyfullah Effendi Mosque, Sofia,
Bulgaria (1556).

Ghazala House, Aleppo, Syria (seventeenth century).

Minaret, Eger, Hungary
(seventeenth century).

Deli Husayn Pasha Mosque,
 Rethymnon, Crete
(midseventeenth century).

Ethem Bay Mosque, Tirana, Albania (late eighteenth—early nineteenth
centuries).

Madrasa Janina, Greece (seventeenth century).
Photo: S. Ćurčić

Hunkar Mosque Madrasa, Khania, Crete (seventeenth century).

Kumaracılar Khan, Nicosia, Cyprus (seventeenth century).

Baabda Palace, Beirut, Lebanon (1897, restored 1903).

Zaba Fortress, Jordan (sixteenth century, during reign of Sultan Selim I).

The New Mosque (al-Jami' al-Jadid, Mosquee de la Pecherie in French), Algiers, Algeris (1660).
Photo: Richard B. Parker

Karamanlı Ahmet Pasha Mosque, Tripoli, Libya (eighteenth century).

Barracks Mosque, San'a, Yemen (1990).

Suleymaniye Mosque, Damascus, Syria (1554—1555).

Bekir Mosque, San'a, Yemen (1579).

Attarin Barracks (now National Library), Tunis, Tunisia (1814).

Bayrak Mosque, Belgrade, Serbia (seventeenth century).

Ghazi Khusrev Bey Mosque, Sarajevo, Bosnia (1530—1531). This mosque is part of a much larger complex including a madrasa, bath, and market. IRCICA: Research Centre for Islamic History, Art and Culture, Istanbul.

Leaded Khan, Skopje, Macedonia (seventeenth century).

Idadi (preparatory school), Mosul, Iraq (nineteenth century).

The bridge on the Drina at Visegrad, Bosnia (sixteenth century). Its construction and history are celebrated in Ivo Andrić's novel of that name.

Hamza Bey Mosque, Thessaloniki, Greece (1467—1468). 9th Ephoreia of Byzantine and Post-Byzantine Antiquities, Thessaloniki, Greece.

Alaca Imaret, Thessaloniki, Greece (1464). Ephoreia of Byzantine and Post-Byzantine Antiquities, Thessaloniki, Greece.

Husam Pasha Mosque, Stip, Macedonia (seventeenth century).
Photo: S. Ćurčić

Muhammad Ali Mosque, Cairo, Egypt (early nineteenth century).
Photo: Richard B. Parker

Sharif Halil Pasha (Tombul) Mosque, Shumen, Bulgaria (1744/45).

Nurusmaniye Mosque, Istanbul, Turkey (1748—1755).
*Imperial Self-Portrait: The Ottoman Empire as Revealed in the Sultan
Abdul-Hamid II's Photographic Albums.*

Sinan Pasha Mosque, Bulaq, Cairo, Egypt (1571).
Photo André Raymond

Panorama of Jerusalem (nineteenth-century Bonfils photograph). The walls around the old city were restored during the reign of Sultan Suleyman Kanuni (the Magnificent) (sixteenth century).

important parts of the heritage stem from the earlier centuries of the Ottoman Empire, when it was expanding.

Diplomatic machinery formed no part of this heritage from earlier centuries. The Ottoman sultan, unlike other European monarchs of the sixteenth century and after, had no diplomatic establishment. He sent no permanent envoys abroad. He sent out ambassadors on specific missions, but they did not remain resident in foreign capitals. Other rulers sent envoys to the sultan— envoys who were resident in Istanbul. This lack of reciprocity fitted in well with the Ottoman assumption that the sultan was the preeminent ruler, to whom others should be deferential.

The sultans in these years of the empire's greatness did create one diplomatic link with other rulers, the capitulations, that had a profound effect on the foreign relations of the later empire and its successor states. The capitulations were willing grants by the sultan of certain privileges and extraterritorial rights, economic and legal, to other monarchs and their subjects. The object was to facilitate commerce. In later years the capitulations became enshrined in bilateral treaties with European nations who insisted on the privileges as their right and an Ottoman obligation. The extraterritorial privileges were expanded by the Europeans, liberally interpreted and often abused. Both the grant of privileges and the abuse of them had important consequences for the future.

Most of the heritage from the period of greatness that had a direct bearing on the diplomacy of the later empire came, however, not from specific institutions but from the very nature of the empire itself. Three aspects deserve special mention. The first is the Ottoman Empire's geographical extent. It was huge and anything but compact. The empire's tri-continental sprawl ran from the Moroccan frontier in northwest Africa to the Persian Gulf, from Hungary to the Caucasus, from the Crimea to Yemen. Central management of so much real estate presented problems.

Second, because of its expansion through the Balkans and up the Danube nearly to Vienna, the empire was a major European state. It was not, however, a member of the European state system, which was a collection of Christian monarchies. Nevertheless the Ottoman Empire was important to the European balance of power; Catherine the Great of Russia explicitly recognized this in the later eighteenth century.[2] An interesting early comment on the Ottoman Empire's importance to the functioning of the European state system is the dictum of Ottaviano Maggi, the sixteenth-century author of a well-known work on diplomacy, that a competent ambassador must know Turkish.[3]

Third, a vast diversity of peoples lived within the borders of the empire. Turks were the largest single language group, but constituted less than fifty percent of the population. The empire was in fact a collection of minority nationalities. This ethnic heterogeneity was not disastrous in the sixteenth century because individual identities derived not from nationality but from membership in a religious community—Muslim, Greek Orthodox, Armenian, Jewish, or other. But the languages did not disappear, and the ethnic groups remained to create problems in the future.

This said, the diplomacy of the later Ottoman Empire and its legacy to the future can best be considered under four headings, here expressed as questions: What was the situation of the Ottoman Empire in the nineteenth century? What principles and practices characterized the conduct of Ottoman foreign relations in that period? What has the Near East as a whole inherited from those principles and practices? What has the Turkish republic inherited from those principles and practices?

The Situation in the Nineteenth Century

Territorially, the Ottoman Empire remained large although by the start of the century it had lost Hungary, Transylvania, and the lands to the north of the Black Sea. With its many seas and islands, the empire possessed a coastline that was indefensible and borders that were amorphous in many parts of Africa and Asia. Militarily, the empire was weak. Three significant events demonstrated this weakness.

The first was Russia's victory of 1774 in the Black Sea and Balkan region, sealed by the treaty of Küchük Kaynarja and by a subsequent victory over the Ottomans in 1792. The second was Napoleon's conquest of Egypt in 1798, proving that the central portions of the empire, as well as its periphery, could successfully be invaded. The third was the naval probe of British Admiral Duckworth through the Straits and up to Istanbul itself in 1807. Although prudence dictated his withdrawal, the episode laid bare the vulnerability of the empire at its very center.

Military weakness was compounded by administrative weakness. The Istanbul government, by the start of the nineteenth century, had little or no control over many outlying provinces. Local strongmen in North Africa and some areas of the Balkans governed to suit themselves, and maintained their own armed forces. Tribal sheikhs in Syria and Iraq could sometimes do the same. Even in Anatolia the sultan's power to exert genuine control was often in doubt.

More dangerous, in the long run, even than local strongmen was the new spirit of nationalism that began to creep into the empire at the beginning of the nineteenth century. Ethnic minorities that had traditionally derived their identity from the religious community to which they belonged began instead

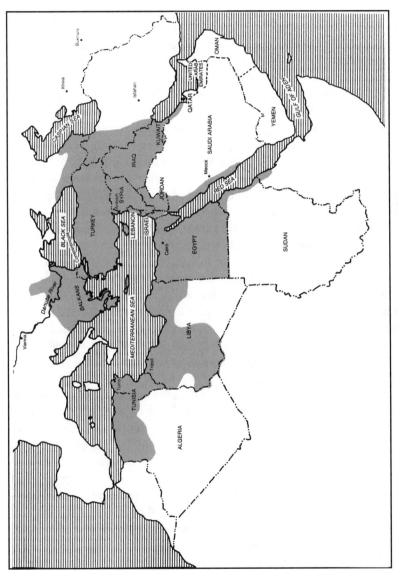

The Ottoman Empire at the beginning of the nineteenth century. Map by John T. Westlake, Princeton, N.J.

to look to a national identity. The nationalist virus spread from revolutionary France into the Balkans. Greeks first succumbed to it. They began to relearn their ancient glories; for some of the leading intellectuals and merchants the cultural revival led to a devotion to nation stronger than the devotion to Orthodoxy. In 1821 a Greek nationalist revolt against the Ottoman sultan broke out. By 1830 an independent Greece had been carved out of the Ottoman territory, less than half the size of present-day Greece, but a harbinger of things to come. The Greek revolt of 1821 takes its place with 1774, 1798, and 1807 as the fourth demonstration of Ottoman vulnerability—and this time to assault from within, as well as from without. Other Balkan nationalities later followed the Greek example, and still later the Armenians, Kurds, and Arabs of Asia.

Despite the territorial, military, administrative, and ethnic elements of weakness, the Ottoman Empire was still a strong state at the start of the nineteenth century compared to its neighbor, Iran. But this comparison was far less significant than comparison to the more compact and progressive Egypt of Muhammad Ali, effectively a state of its own although still part of the Ottoman Empire. And that comparison, in turn, was less significant than comparison to the great powers of Europe. France, Britain, Russia, Austria, and Prussia dominated Europe. All were centralized monarchies, more powerful than the Ottoman. All but Prussia were directly interested in the fate of the Ottoman Empire, and were active there diplomatically, commercially, and sometimes militarily. The Ottoman Empire had become "thoroughly ensnarled in great power politics."[4]

Further, in comparison to the European powers, the Ottoman Empire was also underdeveloped economically. This aspect of Ottoman weakness not only deprived the sultans of resources to stave off Europe, but invited European penetration. The penetration could be political as well as economic. It could be diplomatic. European ambassadors in Istanbul sometimes seemed to act like little sovereigns, and European consuls in the provinces like little lords. The Ottoman Empire was a "penetrated political system."[5]

The greatest danger to the Ottoman Empire's integrity lay in a nationalist movement or revolt within its lands combined with support from without by one or more of the great powers of Europe. The Greeks gained their independence only with military aid from Britain, France, and Russia, and diplomatic aid from all the great powers. The same story was repeated as other Balkan nationalities moved toward independence. Even when there was no drive for independence, minority peoples in the Ottoman Empire often solicited pressure on the Sublime Porte from one power or another.

From the viewpoint of the European powers, the weakness of the Ottoman Empire and the question of who would inherit its territories if it should break up or disappear constituted the Eastern Question. Would the powers partition the empire among themselves, and preserve the European balance of power in doing so? Would the nationalities who lived there divide up the empire? Or would they have to share it with outside powers? Above all, who would control the Straits—the Bosporus and the Dardanelles—and the great capital situated at the confluence of the Bosporus, the Golden Horn, and the Sea of Marmara?

The Eastern Question of the nineteenth century can perhaps be represented as a set of concentric circles. The most sensitive issue was at the center of all: who would control Istanbul and the Straits? Surrounding this central core was a circle of nationalities of the empire, representing their relations with the Sublime Porte and with each other. And circumambient around these two circles was the third, the world of European great power politics with its balance, its rivalries and divergent interests, and its penetrating influence in the Ottoman Empire.

For the Ottoman government, the Eastern Question was a Western Question: how to strengthen the empire in the face of the nationalities imbued with western-style nationalism, how to fend off intervention by the European powers, and in the end how to survive in a world dominated by the West. The Ottoman statesmen intended to avoid the fate that had overtaken Poland. When the term "Eastern Question" was first used in Europe in the later eigh-

teenth century, it meant "What will become of the Ottoman Empire and Poland?" In 1878 when Albert Sorel published his classic study of the Eastern Question, *La Question d'Orient au XVIIIe siècle*, he dealt with both the Ottoman Empire and Poland.[6] The territory involved was vast, a great belt reaching north to south across eastern Europe from the Baltic Sea to the Mediterranean. But Poland disappeared, partitioned three times by her great power neighbors. After 1795 Poland existed, as an independent state, only in the imagination of her poets. So the Eastern Question came to concern the Ottoman Empire alone, except for those occasions when Iran was also involved in great power machinations.

The aim of Ottoman foreign policy became, in effect, to avoid being another Poland. The Sublime Porte tried in the nineteenth century, then, so to act that the empire would not be simply an object of European great power policy—a cadaver for dissection, but an actor in its own right. How did the Porte try to do this? Three courses of action were followed.

The first was to rebuild the empire's military strength, a process that eventuated in the destruction of the janissary corps and the creation of a new western-trained army. The second was to regenerate the empire internally, involving efforts to reorganize many branches of government, to promote economic development, to draft more westernized and modernized codes of law, to establish secular state schools, and to inculcate a feeling of Ottomanism among all subjects as a counter to separatist nationalisms. These efforts met with varying success, sometimes minimal, occasionally considerable. The third course of action was to use diplomacy to defend the empire's independence and integrity and to fend off political or military intervention by European powers. The use of diplomacy requires more detailed analysis, and brings us to the second question.

Principles and Practices Characterizing the Conduct of Foreign Relations

THE CREATION OF A PERMANENT DIPLOMATIC ESTABLISHMENT

After an abortive start under Sultan Selim III, who sent resident ambassadors to four European capitals in the 1790s, the establishment came into continuous being under Mahmud II in the 1830s. Ottoman ambassadors resident in Paris, London, Vienna, and Berlin acted in the style of European ambassadors everywhere. Their functions were vigilance, advice, and negotiation in the diplomatic tradition: reporting of developments in their host countries, advice to the Sublime Porte, and negotiation on various matters with the host government in the interest of the sultan. During the ensuing century the number of Ottoman embassies and legations grew considerably, as did the personnel.

A concomitant development in Istanbul converted the traditional office of *re'is efendi*, which had been the usual contact for European ambassadors there, into an office of the foreign minister. Gradually a European-style foreign ministry evolved. In this ministry, as in the diplomatic posts abroad, an ever-increasing number of officials were at home in French, the language of nineteenth century international discourse. Greeks and Armenians who were fluent in French were employed in the ministry. Turks often learned it by working in the Translation Bureau of the ministry, or on the job in a European post; some were autodidacts. These developments in diplomatic practice made it much easier for the Porte to act effectively in the world of the European powers. The new establishment adopted many western-style techniques and procedures, both in the ministry and in the embassies, closely resembling those used by European governments.[7]

PRESERVING THE INDEPENDENCE AND INTEGRITY OF THE EMPIRE

Insistence on the preservation of the independence and integrity of the empire was repeated time and again to European diplomats. The integrity was written into the first constitution of the empire, promulgated in 1876. Article 1 proclaimed that the empire was a territorial unit that could never be divided for any reason. Although the preservation of its independence and integrity is basic to the foreign policy of every state, the principle was peculiarly important to the Ottoman Empire. Almost every question that foreign powers raised with the Sublime Porte concerned some portion of the Ottoman Empire itself. As one reads the files in the archives of the Ottoman foreign ministry, one finds that the major questions on which the Porte negotiated with other powers bore such names as Bosnia, Crete, Lebanon, Egypt, Cyprus, Bulgaria, Serbia, Moldavia, Wallachia, and Albania.[8] All were Ottoman territories.

In a sense, Ottoman foreign policy was domestic policy. For a great state this was humiliating. Ottoman diplomacy had to be almost entirely simply a defense of the empire's integrity. A parallel for the nineteenth century would exist if, for example, French foreign policy were centered on the desires and complaints of other powers concerning Normandy, Brittany, Poitou, Provence and Burgundy. One Alsace-Lorraine was enough for France. The Porte had many potential Alsace-Lorraines. Therefore, preservation of independence and integrity remained the basic principle.

SECURING A GUARANTY OF THE EMPIRE'S INTEGRITY
BY THE EUROPEAN POWERS

This corollary principle, or perhaps more correctly, corollary aim, had been suggested by Metternich at the Congress of Vienna in 1814, and by 1815 the

This cartoon, with caption in both French and Ottoman Turkish, has the Ottoman soldier guarding the cow labeled "the Ottoman countries" exclaiming to the myriad European milkers: "You've taken enough. Leave some for the proprietor."
source: from the Istanbul journal *Kalem* (July 1909).

Porte was willing to pursue it, but nothing came of the idea because Tsar Alexander would not cooperate unless changes in the Ottoman boundaries were made in Russia's favor.[9] During the Russian war of 1828–29 Pertev Pasha, the *re'is efendi*, proposed that a European congress agree on a guaranty; again nothing came of this.[10] Instead, in 1833, the Porte got the treaty of Hunkar Iskelesi, a mutual assistance pact signed with Russia after Russia had blocked Muhammad Ali's Egyptian forces from threatening Istanbul.[11] But this was not a real guaranty, even though it said that the tsar wished to maintain the "independence of the Sublime Porte." The Porte was always uncomfortable as junior partner in this unequal alliance with a traditional enemy; the treaty was allowed to expire during the crisis of 1839–41.

Other approaches to a possible guaranty of the empire were also unsuccessful until the conclusion of the Crimean War. Then, in the Treaty of Paris signed in 1856 by all of the European powers, article 7 affirmed that the pow-

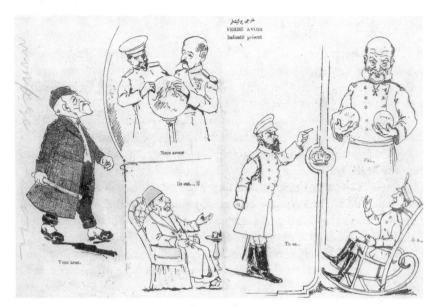

This Ottoman cartoon is captioned in French "The Verb 'To Have' Present Indicative" and reads clockwise from the left: "You have" (Britain?), "we have" (studying the globe, France and Germany?), "I have" (Austria, holding the two parcels labeled in Turkish "Bosnia" and "Herzzegovina"—annexed by the Austro-Hungarian Empire the previous year), "he has" (the Serb in his rocking chair), "you (familiar, with pointed finger) have" (Russia), and the seated Ottoman plaintively noting that "they (all the many European powers) have." Many Ottoman political cartoons of this era had captions in French, an indication of both the cosmopolitanism of the Ottoman political class and opinion molders as well as the heavy European presence.
SOURCE: from *Davul* (January 1909)

ers "respect the independence and territorial integrity of the Ottoman Empire" and "guarantee in common the strict observance of that engagement."[12] The Porte had won agreement to the principle. Whether the powers would keep their word remained to be seen.

ACHIEVING MEMBERSHIP IN THE EUROPEAN STATE SYSTEM

Related to the desire for a European guaranty, but also a separate aim of Ottoman policy, was the wish to become an accepted member of the European state system. Although a great state, the Ottoman Empire in the early nineteenth century was not part of the Concert of Europe, the pentarchy of powers who arrogated to themselves the leadership of the continent. In 1840 the Porte for the first time joined other powers (minus France, a maverick for the moment) as a signatory of a major diplomatic document, the Treaty of London, aimed at pushing Muhammad Ali of Egypt out of Syria.[13] The next year, France having returned to the fold that Britain, Austria, Prussia, and Russia had never left, all five powers signed the Convention of the Straits along with the Ottoman Empire.[14] Such was the first step toward becoming a member of the Concert.

During the Crimean War, in discussions about a possible peace, Âli Pasha, then foreign minister, drafted a treaty article that put the essence of the Porte's policy unequivocally: "The Contracting Powers, wishing to demonstrate the importance they attach to assuring that the Ottoman Empire participate in the advantages of the concert established by public law among the different European States, declare that they henceforth consider that empire as an integral part of the concert and engage themselves to respect its territorial integrity and its independence as an essential condition of the general balance of power."[15] Âli managed to include in this pithy statement four basic aspects of Ottoman policy: a) specification of the importance of Ottoman independence and integrity; b) an engagement (guaranty?) by the powers to respect those rights; c) acknowledgment that the empire was a member of the Concert of Europe; and d) acknowledgment that the empire was essential to the European balance of power. No peace eventuated at this point, and there was no treaty.

In article 7 of the Treaty of Paris in 1856, however, three of Âli's four desiderata were met. Only a reference to the balance of power was missing. Respect for Ottoman independence and territorial integrity was included, as noted above, and a guaranty by the powers of that stipulation. In addition, the Sublime Porte was admitted to the Concert—"to participate in the advantages of the public law and system of Europe."[16] The article became basic to all Ottoman foreign policy.

A declaration that the Ottoman Empire was essential to the European balance of power, had it been achieved, would have furnished the empire with still another sort of guaranty. In the nineteenth century the balance was conceived by European statesmen to be real, and to be operative. It was based on four rules: that the balance must be composed of three or more great powers; that no one power should be allowed to dominate; that no power should be too much weakened relative to the others; and that if one power made important territorial gains others should be allowed compensatory gains. The partition of Poland had exemplified the balance at work, as Poland's three neighbors each gained from her demise. Âli Pasha obviously wanted the Ottoman Empire to be a participant in the balance rather than its prey.

SUPPORTING LEGITIMATE GOVERNMENTS

Related again to the principle of territorial integrity was another principle of Ottoman foreign policy, that legitimate governments must be maintained and that revolution against them must not be supported. The Ottoman government was legitimate. Nationalist movements that fostered revolution were therefore illegitimate. The secession of provinces was not to be tolerated. National self-determination was unacceptable if it went against the interests of a legitimate government.

Obviously, the Ottoman Empire would go to pieces if self-determination were countenanced. Âli Pasha inveighed against any approach to that practice, such as allowing autonomy in a province, because "it would be impossible to prevent it from becoming rapidly and generally contagious."[17] Of course, during the nineteenth century a number of provinces largely inhabited by minority nationalities, did in fact become autonomous and later gained total independence. But whenever the Porte agreed to this, it was owing to the pressure of outside powers. The principle remained, even if honored more in the breach than in the observance.

SUPPORTING INTERNATIONAL LAW

Ottoman diplomats referred to law on many occasions, and to treaties forming part of that law. "No country is allowed to make its own laws superior to what is called the law of nations," wrote Foreign Minister Fuad Pasha, in condemnation of actions by Greece during a period of tension.[18] In the face of great power threats and interventions, weaker governments have characteristically sought refuge in law, and the Sublime Porte was no exception. The Porte was insistent to the European powers that treaties must be observed.

Usually, when taking this line the Porte was referring to the Treaty of Paris of 1856. Not only had the treaty fixed a relatively favorable territorial settlement, and not only had it brought the empire into the Concert of Europe, but it also laid down the principle of the nonintervention of other powers in the domestic affairs of the empire. Article 9 of the treaty stipulated that the sultan's communication to the powers of his reform decree, the Hatt-i Hümayun of 1856, "cannot, in any case, give to the said powers the right to interfere, either collectively or separately, in the relations of His Majesty the Sultan with his subjects, nor in the internal administration of his Empire."[19] Ottoman foreign ministers and diplomats in the ensuing years referred frequently to this principle of nonintervention, and sometimes emphasized at the same time the sanctity of treaties. Pacta sunt servanda. The observance of international law, the upholding of treaties, and nonintervention in the internal affairs of other states constitute the trinity of legal principles on which much of Ottoman diplomacy rested.

AVOIDING POSSIBLE LOSS AT THE CONFERENCE TABLE

Not so important as a basic principle, but still an Ottoman practice worth noting, was the tendency of the Porte to be skeptical of multilateral international conferences, and to avoid them when possible. Experience had taught the Porte that European statesmen, when gathered, would often like to solve problems at Ottoman expense, by favoring minority nationalities within the empire or by slicing off bits of Ottoman territory.

If the agenda of a conference was limited, and if the results were agreed to ahead of time, the Porte would be happy to attend. When attendance was unavoidable, and the results were likely to be unfavorable for the Ottoman Empire, its representatives tended to slow things down, to reserve the right to respond later, and to agree to something only provisionally while consulting the Porte for new instructions.

At the Congress of Berlin in 1878 the first Ottoman plenipotentiary, Aleksandr Karatodori (Carathéodory) Pasha, suffered humiliating treatment from Prince Bismarck, the congress president, because he adopted some of these tactics.[20] It was no wonder that the Porte preferred to avoid multinational conferences, especially if the other powers were likely to be in unfriendly unanimity on matters concerning the Ottoman Empire.

ENSURING THE SUPPORT OF ANOTHER POWER

The Porte sought in international relations always to have the support of one or more of the major European powers if there were any threat to Ottoman interests from others. All other powers did the same, of course, seeking support for their positions from others. But because the Ottoman Empire was weaker than the other five powers (six after the unification of Italy in 1861), its need of support was greater.

Threats to the empire were most likely to come from Russia. In two brief periods, 1798–1806 and 1833–1839, the empire was linked with Russia, enjoying Russian support against Napoleon and against Muhammad Ali. But these periods were exceptions, and in neither was the Ottoman-Russian relationship comfortable. The usual relationship was either correct, or antagonistic, and during the nineteenth century four Ottoman-Russian wars occurred. Only the Crimean War was not a defeat. The reason for Ottoman victory then was military support from Britain, France, and Sardinia-Piedmont. Nothing better illustrates the Ottoman need for great power support.

Because the Russian threat was the most frequent, because Prussia (Germany after 1871) was little interested in the Near East, and because Italy was relatively weak, support for the Ottoman Empire was most likely to come from Britain or Austria, and sometimes from France. In the nineteenth century the Porte found that Britain was its best hope, until 1882, when Britain occupied the province of Egypt and failed to evacuate. After 1890, in the days of Kaiser Wilhelm II, support was more likely to come from Germany.

It is often alleged that the Ottoman government was adept at playing one power off against another, as if Ottoman diplomacy were more deceitful than that of other powers. Certainly the Sublime Porte sought support from one or more powers against any other that threatened, primarily against Russia. But there is no evidence that the Porte played tricks on powers, or lied to one or another in order to provoke splits among them. The splits that existed among the powers were not of the Porte's creation. Austria and Russia were often at odds, most frequently over the clash of their extended interests in the Balkan area. The Porte could use this divergence to solicit Austrian help against Russia, but did not create the split.

Similarly, Britain and Russia were fairly constant rivals. Britain was always concerned to preserve the route to India through the Mediterranean against Russian or any other incursion, both before and after the Suez Canal was opened in 1869. It was said in the nineteenth century that British foreign policy had two bases: that God is an Englishman and that the route to India must be kept open. The Porte had nothing to do with creating this rivalry, but it could use it at times to seek British support, which the British in many cases willingly gave for their own reasons. Nor did the Porte create the Russian desire for free use or even control of the Black Sea Straits, which alarmed the British for most of the century. This desire was inbred in Russia. A deputy in the Russian Duma of 1915, just before the British were to attack the Dardanelles, became exercised about "the Straits, Tsargrad (the Slavic name for Istanbul), toward which the Russian people have striven, beginning with Oleg and Igor. . . . The Straits and Tsargrad must be ours and only ours."[21] Ottoman diplomacy was not, then, responsible for divergences among European powers, but sought to use those divergences.[22]

EMPLOYING STRATEGIC RETREAT

At times the Porte could not find a great power to give sufficiently vigorous support to counteract the pressure of others. In such cases, the practice of the Porte usually was strategic retreat: to back down as little as possible, and to preserve as much as possible.

In the years 1866–67, for example, the Porte was faced with uprising or pressure from Serbs, Romanians, Bulgarians, Greeks in Crete (backed by independent Greece), and the Egyptian governor, Ismail Pasha. Several great powers backed one or more of these movements. None was willing to support the Ottoman position completely.

The Porte then opted for strategic retreat in the questions concerning Serbia (evacuation of the last Ottoman garrison from Belgrade), and Romania (allowing a foreign prince to rule there), and the Egyptian governor (allowing succession by primogeniture and granting the title of khedive, in return for big payments). It could then have a freer hand in crushing open rebellions in

Bulgaria and in Crete.[23] Strategic retreat avoided the possibility of a greater loss in each case. And in each case the retreat was sealed by an agreed formula that preserved for the Porte as much as possible.

BORROWING, FINANCING

One Ottoman practice in its dealings with European powers seemed to be a necessity but brought unfortunate results. Beginning in 1854, the Sublime Porte borrowed money in Western European countries, through the sale of interest-bearing state bonds. Several series of bond issues were sold over the next two decades, mainly to European investors. Negotiating for the loans became one of the major tasks of the Porte's diplomacy. But by 1875 the Ottoman government, in financial crisis, had to default on interest payments.

The empire was not the only Near Eastern state in a financial quagmire; in the late nineteenth century Egypt, Tunis, and Greece also defaulted on interest payments of foreign loans.[24] In the Ottoman case, default led to the creation in 1881 of the Public Debt Administration, an Ottoman government organ but controlled by foreigners and operated in the interest of the European bondholders. This diminution of Ottoman sovereignty—the spectacle of foreigners controlling significant revenue collection in the empire, and its disbursement—was not soon forgotten.

AVOIDING FOREIGN SERVITUDES

Although its financial bankruptcy obliged the Porte to suffer this derogation of sovereignty, one of the principles of nineteenth-century Ottoman diplomacy was to avoid foreign servitudes. In practice, this meant trying to get rid of the capitulations that had become such a burden. After the Crimean War Âli Pasha made himself into the anticapitulation spokesman for the empire. He ended one memorandum to the powers about abuses under the capitulatory rights by saying that "the very existence of the capitulations hinders the regular functioning of the institutions, and the progressive advance of civilization, in the empire."[25]

The Porte was not strong enough to denounce the treaties in which the foreign privileges were enshrined, and in any case it often needed the support of powers who benefited from them. So there was no frontal attack. But occasionally laws and regulations issued by the Porte obliged foreigners to accept Ottoman jurisdiction and taxes, or curbed some of the abuses. Such were the land law of 1867 that allowed foreigners to own real property in the empire under certain conditions and the nationality law of 1869.[26] Denunciation of the capitulations had to wait until the Great War gave an opportunity.

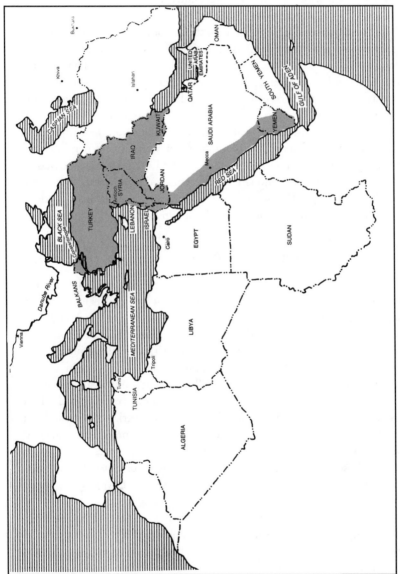

The Ottoman Empire in 1914. Map by John T. Westlake, Princeton, N.J.

EMPHASIZING ISLAM

Finally, one aspect of Ottoman diplomatic practice became important only at the end of the nineteenth century, and in the early twentieth. The Islamic character of the empire and the sultanate was emphasized somewhat by Sultan Abdulaziz (1861–1876), and much more by Sultan Abdulhamid II (1876–1909). The title of caliph was frequently used by the latter as a rallying point for Muslims not only within the empire but outside.

The Porte was never able to come to the aid of Muslims abroad who petitioned for help against the Russians in Central Asia, or against the Dutch in Indonesia. But contacts were maintained, and the British, French, and Russian governments were always a little wary of treating the sultan-caliph in such a way as to rouse massive protest among the millions of Muslims in their empires. Abdulhamid consciously promoted Pan-Islamic sentiment. One scholar has called pan-Islam a "hallucination."[27] It was not; the sentiment was real. The practical effects of Pan-Islam, however, were slim. When in 1914 the Ottoman government proclaimed a jihad against Entente powers, no mass risings against the Entente powers resulted. Britain did, however, take precautions in mobilizing Muslim troops. And millions of Muslims outside the Ottoman Empire continued to regard the sultan as caliph.

The Near East's Inheritance from Ottoman Principles and Practices

The inheritance is hard to define, because the Near East today is not a unit. The Ottoman Empire was a cocoon, out of which emerged as many as thirty independent states, depending on what one enumerates, and how, and when. Thirteen are European and, except for Turkey, may be left out of account here. But the states of Ottoman descent in Asia and Africa are also quite diverse.

Furthermore, each of them, except Saudi Arabia and the Yemen, emerged from the Ottoman cocoon not as a full-fledged state, but as a chrysalis in a colonial or mandatory or other relationship dependent on one of the European powers. Only after World War II did these countries become independent, by varying processes and in different years. The intermediate stage was another source from which to inherit principles and practices. Even so, can one identify some or all of the twelve characteristics of Ottoman diplomacy mentioned above in the foreign relations of states like Egypt, Syria, Algeria, and Saudi Arabia?

Without question, some of these characteristics are present. Each state has created a diplomatic establishment. Each emphasizes its independence and territorial integrity (and some, like Iraq or Libya, are expansionist rather than simply satisfied with integrity). Each government of each state in this coup-infected region has, so far as I know, claimed legitimacy and therefore claimed recognition and support from other powers. Probably most have at times appealed to the sanctity of international law, although I am unable to document this supposition. Certainly most, probably all, have been eager to borrow funds from abroad, whether through public bond sales (State of Israel bonds) or the more likely medium of loans from banks and governments of the leading industrial powers and from the great international financial organizations. Of course they have been even more eager for outright grants.

Any of the successor states who inherited some vestige of capitulations followed the Ottoman example of trying to get rid of them; the classic example is the success of Egypt in getting the powers to abolish her capitulations at the Montreux conference in 1937. Some of the successor states have at times employed a pan-Islamic outreach in their foreign relations. Many of these states have avoided international conferences if they feared the probable results; and at times, for other reasons, individual Arab states have not infrequently boycotted Arab League meetings, and several have avoided proposed conferences to settle the disputes between Israel, the Palestinians, and the neighboring states. Without question each successor state, when pressed by a great power or a coalition of superior strength, has, like the Sublime Porte, retreated slowly and yielded as little as possible.

But, are these similarities between Ottoman practice and contemporary Near Eastern state practice a legacy from the Ottoman example? Probably not. The practices are common to governments worldwide, except for the pan-Islamic activities, and could be learned from the nearby example of European powers in most cases. They could in fact be invented anew because of the perceived realities of any given state's situation.

Consider, for example, the emphasis on the independence and integrity of each state, along with the inevitable corollary that no foreign interference is to be allowed in a state's internal affairs. If Saddam Husayn maintains that a Kurdish enclave in Iraq's north imposed by outside powers, or a "no-fly" zone in the south similarly imposed, is a violation of Iraq's sovereign independence and integrity, does he do this because of the Ottoman Empire? If an Israeli government maintains that Jewish settlements in the West Bank are a domestic matter in which no outside power may interfere, is this owing to Ottoman precedent? Probably not. Parallels are there, but any direct legacy is obscure.

Parallels exist also in the larger relationships of the contemporary states to outside powers. As the Sublime Porte wanted to be a member of the European state system, so Near Eastern states today want to be, and have become, members of the newer world system, beginning with the admission of Iraq and Turkey to the League of Nations in 1932, and continuing on to the current membership of all the Near Eastern states in the United Nations.

Many of the modern states have become members of small regional pacts that have purported to offer some guaranty of mutual assistance in case of attack; most of these pacts have been quite transitory. No parallel exists between these and earlier Ottoman practices. But parallels do exist in the quest of Near Eastern states for support from outside great powers—support in financial aid, in the provision of arms, in promises of assistance of various kinds, and even in pacts promising military aid in the face of attack. The outstanding example of the latter is the Baghdad Pact of the 1950s, which was later metamorphosed into the CENTO. But few Near Eastern states have participated in such arrangements, and Egypt, at least, deliberately turned down such a guaranty/assistance arrangement with an outside power (Britain) in the Middle East Defense Organization (MEDO) proposal of 1953.

The most important parallel between Ottoman practice and the diplomacy of the modern Near Eastern states is probably the quest for support from a great power on the outside in the context of a split among the outside powers. Where formerly six dominant European powers existed with divergent interests, in the years since World War II the common pattern, down to 1991, was that of two blocs, West and East, each led by a so-called superpower. From the perspective of the Near East, the nineteenth-century split between Britain and Russia was replaced by the later twentieth-century split between the United States and the Soviet Union. As in the nineteenth century, the twentieth-century split was in no sense the creation of any Near Eastern state, but existed for outside reasons. As in the earlier century, so in the present one, the Near Eastern states could profit from the split. They could swing between the two blocs, or attach themselves for a time to one or the other. In 1955, for example, when the United States and the West failed Nasser in his quest for arms and financing, he looked to the USSR and the East. It is unlikely that Nasser learned how to do this by reading Ottoman diplomatic history.[28] The legacy from Ottoman diplomacy was faint, if indeed it existed at all. What did exist was a parallel in patterns.

For the Near East was still, as it had been, thoroughly ensnarled in great power politics. The focal point of the politics had, however, shifted south and east since pre-1914 days. After the treaties of St. Germain, Neuilly, and Trianon had settled the Balkan boundaries of the former Austro-Hungarian and Ottoman areas immediately after the Great War, and after the Lausanne treaty of 1923 had provided Turkey with relatively stable frontiers and afforded her the luxury of being nonrevisionist, the center of Near Eastern political instability shifted to the Arab lands south of Turkey. The mandated areas were a penetrated political system, as were the North African lands from Egypt to Morocco.

The most delicate issue in the Near East came to be the relationship of

Zionists to the people of Palestine. After 1948 the same most sensitive issue continued as the relationship of Israel to the people of the area, the Arabs of Palestine and the surrounding states. This inner circle, this center of discord, replaced the pre-1914 central circle of Istanbul and the Straits.

Surrounding the Arab-Israeli center was a large regional circle of conflicting interests. Until about 1945 the regional circle embodied principally the clash of the rising local nationalisms with the imperial powers (Britain, France, Italy). After World War II the regional circle became the contests among the increasingly numerous independent states of the region in addition to their continuing opposition to the vestiges of imperialism and colonialism.

Enveloping the regional circle was the largest circle of great power interests and conflicts, representing principally the tensions between the U.S./West and the USSR/East. In the pre-1914 days the outer circle of six great powers represented not only divergent national interests but also a balance of power. The outer circle of post-1945 did not. There was no balance, which requires three or more participants of roughly equal strength. The post-1945 outer circle represented a bipolar world, more unstable and therefore more dangerous, both for that world itself and for the Near East that it enveloped (p. 194).

The new context of the Eastern Question, parallel to but different from the pre-1914 context, is not a direct legacy from Ottoman diplomacy. In an indirect way, however, the modern Eastern Question is the heir of Ottoman diplomacy—but the heir of its failure rather than of its success. For Ottoman policy failed to save the empire. Both the foreign policy and the domestic polity of the Ottoman Empire collapsed in the holocaust of 1914–1918. The existence of European colonies and mandates in the Near East, and the subsequent emergence of many independent nation-states, derive from the failure of Ottoman foreign policy to keep the empire intact.

Furthermore, many of the international problems that affect the area were once Ottoman domestic problems. They form an important part of the legacy of failure. The relationship of Serbia and Bosnia, the relationship of Turkish Cypriots and Greek Cypriots, the nature of the administration of Lebanon, the political status of Jerusalem, the relationship of Baghdad and Basra to Kuwait, and many other problems, were once internal. Since the breakup of the empire they have become international, a negative inheritance from Ottoman times.[29]

One of the problems bequeathed by the Ottoman Empire to its successor states in the Near East deserves special mention. The title of caliph, flaunted by Abdulhamid II, continued to be accepted as belonging to the sultan by the Muslim populace within the empire, and by much of the Muslim world outside it, throughout World War I. When the sultanate was abolished by the Grand National Assembly in Ankara in 1922 and the last sultan-caliph was

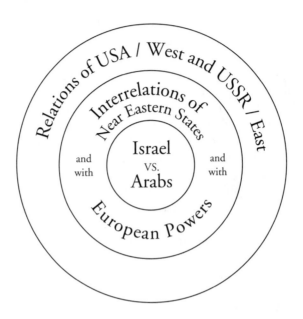

Relations of USA / West and USSR / East

Interrelations of Near Eastern States

and with

Israel
VS.
Arabs

and with

European Powers

declared deposed, he fled Istanbul on a British warship. A cousin was allowed by the Assembly to assume the title of caliph, but in 1924 the Assembly, under Mustafa Kemal's leadership, deposed the caliph too and declared that office abolished. The Ottoman legacy of a caliphate, therefore, was ephemeral.

After 1924 the real legacy of the Ottomans to the Muslim peoples of the Near East (and elsewhere) was not the caliphate as an institution, but as a series of questions: Is there in fact an office of the caliphate? Should there be a caliph? If so, who should it be? What is his authority? The problem has been agitating at times, and quiescent at times, but it continues to exist as part of the Ottoman legacy to the Near East.

Penultimate conclusion: the five P's—principles, practices, parallels, patterns, problems. If this brief survey of the legacy of Ottoman diplomacy has validity, the conclusion must be that the conduct of foreign relations by the states of the Near East today cannot be proven to derive directly from Ottoman principles and practices. It can be shown only that many parallels exist between Ottoman and present-day principle and practice. It can be shown, further, that patterns of relationships today are, in significant ways, similar to those that obtained in Ottoman times. Finally, it is clear that a number of international problems that affect the Near East today were once Ottoman domestic problems, internationalized only because Ottoman diplomacy failed to maintain the empire's independence and integrity. This said, one must consider a partial exception to these general conclusions: the Republic of Turkey.

The Ottoman Inheritance of the Turkish Republic

Modern Turkey has been the most direct and principal heir of Ottoman diplomacy. The republic of course inherited not only the central territory of the empire, including the old capital of Istanbul, but also a bureaucratic and military elite who helped establish a new state.[30] Furthermore, Turkey was independent from the start, rather than under control of a European colonial or mandatory power. Balkan states aside, only two other Ottoman successor states were independent immediately after the World War I—the Nejd that formed the core of what became Saudi Arabia and the Yemen. They were far from the Ottoman center and quite undeveloped. Turkey was a unique successor state.

A part of the republic's inheritance from the empire was negative—lessons of what not to do. The primary lesson was not to recreate the heterogeneous Ottoman state or to try to hold on to non-Turkish territory. The empire had been a burden; in the eyes of Mustafa Kemal Pasha the republic could not reassume it. "Do you know how many sons of Anatolia have perished in the scorching deserts of Yemen?" he asked one advocate of a big empire.[31] Furthermore, the heterogeneity of the empire weakened its foreign policy, in Kemal's view. "In a state which extends from the East to the West and which unites in its embrace contrary elements . . , it is natural that its internal organization should be defective. . . . In these circumstances its foreign policy, having no firm foundation, cannot be strenuously carried on."[32]

As a corollary, the republic under Kemal Atatürk's leadership firmly renounced also any pan-Islamic policy. He was willing to accept Muslim support in the struggle for independence, up to the treaty of Lausanne in 1923, but he called pan-Islam an impractical ideology and an illusion. He criticized Selim I, who was said to have taken the title of caliph after conquering Egypt, and declared that "there is nothing in history to show how the policy of pan-Islamism could have succeeded or how it could have found a basis for its realization on this earth."[33] Today the government of the Turkish republic has played an active role in cultural and economic cooperation among Muslim states, but it avoids political pan-Islam and the resurrection of the caliphate.

Another negative inheritance from the empire was the lesson not to borrow money abroad. The default on Ottoman bond interest payments, the bankruptcy that followed, and the foreign-dominated Public Debt Administration, were all examples of what should be avoided. For its first two decades the republic did avoid foreign borrowing. Since World War II it has accepted loans, mixed in with grant aid. But the caution learned from the empire's experience is still in evidence. Of other negative heritages, the most important is a lesson learned not from Ottoman diplomatic principles or practices, but from an Ottoman mistake: stay out of wars. Do not repeat the error of 1914 that led to the death of the empire. Thus in World War II Turkey, despite pressures, successfully walked a narrow path of neutrality.

On the positive side, some of the Turkish republic's inheritance from the empire has been fairly direct. An insistence on the independence and territorial integrity of Turkey has been basic to the republic's foreign policy. It started before the republic existed, when the national resistance movement led by Mustafa Kemal adopted in 1919 the National Pact emphasizing Turkish sovereignty within specified borders. It continued at the Lausanne peace conference in 1922–23, where the Turkish first plenipotentiary, Ismet Pasha, insisted on Turkish sovereignty so much that Lord Curzon, the conference chairman, exploded in anger against him.

Similarly, Ismet carried on at Lausanne the Ottoman struggle to get rid of the capitulations. The result in article 28 of the treaty signed on July 24, 1923, was the effective abolition of all capitulations, although Turkey agreed to employ foreign legal observers in its courts for five years.

Ismet's conduct of negotiations at the Lausanne conference, viewed as a whole, offers a splendid example of utilizing the splits among the great powers to gain advantage for Turkey. Ismet did not create these splits—between Britain and France, between Russia and the other powers—and was not deceitful, but was able to profit from making concessions to one or another, and seeking support from one or another, on particular issues. After the treaty was ratified in 1924, it became the international law basis to which Ankara governments often referred, as Istanbul governments had referred to earlier treaties.[34] The republican government believed that international law must be observed.

The Ottoman principle of seeking support from an outside power to counter the threat of another also found echoes in the republic's diplomacy. During the war of national independence, 1919–1922, when Britain was the most persistent opponent among the great powers, the fledgling Ankara government found diplomatic and financial support from the newly Communist Russia. In 1946–47, when Soviet Russia was the imminent threat with its claims to East Anatolian territory and to a dominant share in the control of the Straits, the Ankara government found diplomatic support from Britain and the United States. With the Truman doctrine this grew into continuing American economic and military support.

Turkey, more stable as a republic than was the old empire, did not actively seek an outright guaranty of its integrity and independence by the great powers. But it was eager to become a member of the North Atlantic Treaty Organization. With its admission to this defensive alliance in 1951 Turkey achieved a guaranty that operated if it were attacked; an armed attack on one NATO member was to be considered an attack against all. Turkey would therefore get help against any Soviet aggression.

Like the other successor states in the Near East, Turkey also wanted to be accepted as a member of the world state system. It was among the first such states to be accepted into the League of Nations. After the demise of the League, Turkey became one of the charter members of the United Nations at the end of World War II. But beyond this, Turkey has sought to establish herself as a member of the European state system. Already a member of several European organizations, including the Council of Europe, as well as the OEEC and the OECD, Turkey now seeks to become a full partner in the European Community. The EC is probably today the nearest equivalent to the Concert of Europe, which took in the Ottoman Empire in the nineteenth century. Like the empire, the republic insists that it is European.

In these several ways, modern Turkey is the heir of the Ottoman Empire's diplomatic principles and practices. It could be argued that, as in the case of the other Near Eastern successor states, direct inheritance cannot be proven. It could be that European example or even the sheer logic of Turkey's situation led it to adopt such practices. The link to the Ottoman Empire's practices seems, however, to be closer in the case of the Turkish republic than it is for the other Near Eastern states. And in one respect, the establishment that is the basis for all diplomacy, the link is incontrovertible. Modern Turkey is in many ways a new country, but it inherited the embassies and consulates, the archives, and some of the personnel of the Ottoman establishment. Individuals who began their careers under the sultans continued them and climaxed them under the republic.

One example will suffice. During the Great War, Numan Bey Menemenlizade, a young third secretary who had just taken a law degree at the University of Lausanne, began his diplomatic service at the Ottoman Embassy in Vienna. The empire he was serving collapsed, the empire to which he was accredited collapsed, but he continued in the service of the Turkish republic. In World War II, now known as Numan Menemencioğlu, he was foreign minister.[35] He represented the foreign ministry officials and envoys in posts abroad who were the direct heirs of the diplomatic establishment created by Sultan Mahmud II in the 1830s—the establishment that deals not in visionless officialized fatuity, as Siegfried Sassoon once called it, but in communication and negotiation between governments.

NOTES

1. Wotton's pun, which he wrote in Latin in a German friend's album, is explained at length in Ernest Satow, *A Guide to Diplomatic Practice*, 4th ed. (London: Longmans Green, 1957) with quotation from Izaak Walton, *Reliquiae Wottonianae*, 4th ed. (London, 1685), preface.

2. Letter of June 1772, in *Russkoe Istoricheskoe Obshchestvo Sbornik*, vol. 118 (St. Petersburg, 1904), p. 131.

3. Garrett Mattingly, *Renaissance Diplomacy* (Boston: Beacon Press, 1955), p. 217, quoting Maggi, *De Legato* (Hanover, 1596; 1st ed. Venice, 1566), ff. 55–7vo. The ambassador should also know Latin, Greek, Spanish, French, and German. English was not required.

4. L. Carl Brown, *International Politics and the Middle East* (Princeton: Princeton University Press, 1984), p. 3.

5. Ibid., pp. 4–5.

6. Its subtitle was *Le partage de la Pologne et le traité de Kainardji* (Paris, 1878).

7. Ercümend Kuran, *Avrupa'da Osmanlı ikamet elçiliklerinin kuruluşu ve ilk siyasi faaliyetleri, 1793–1821* (Ankara: Türk Kültürünü Araşirma Enstitüsü, 1968); Carter V. Findley, *Bureaucratic Reform in the Ottoman Empire: The Sublime Porte, 1789–1922* (Princeton: Princeton University Press, 1980), pp. 126–140; Findley, "The Foundation of the Ottoman Foreign Ministry," *IJMES* 3, no. 4 (October 1972): 388–416; Nezaret-i Hariciye, *Salname* (Kostantiniyye, 1302), pp. 178, 182–84, 186; Roderic H. Davison, "The Westernization of Ottoman Diplomacy in the Nineteenth Century," pp. 54–65, in Edward Ingram, ed., *National and International Politics in the Middle East* (London: F. Cass, 1986).

8. I am grateful to the Prime Minister's office and to the Ministry of Foreign Affairs of Turkey for permission to do research in the Başbakanlik Arşivi (Prime Ministry Archive) and the Diş-Işleri Bakanliği Hazine-i Evrak (Treasury of Documents of the Foreign Affairs Ministry) in Istanbul (cited hereafter as DBHE). Its records are now being recatalogued and integrated into the Başbakanlik Arşivi.

9. C. K. Webster, *The Foreign Policy of Castlereagh, 1812–1815* (London: Brill, 1931), pp. 429–30; Webster, ed., *British Diplomacy, 1813–1815*, (London: G. Bell, 1921), pp. 304–06.

10. Haus- Hof- und Staatsarchiv (Vienna), Politisches Archiv 34, Türkei 6, Berichte, Ottenfels (Istanbul) to Metternich #241B, November 10, 1828, and enclosures Huszar (Istanbul) to Ottenfels of November 4 and 8, 1828.

11. Text in J. C. Hurewitz, ed., *The Middle East and North Africa in World Politics*, 2 vols. (New Haven: Yale University Press, 1975, 1979), 1:252–53. Hereafter cited as MENAWP.

12. Text in Gabriel Noradounghian, ed., *Recueil d'actes internationaux de l'Empire ottoman* (Paris: Pichon, 1897–1903), 3:70–80; partial text in English in Hurewitz, *MENAWP*, 1:319–21.

13. Known as the "Convention for the Pacification of the Levant." Text in Hurewitz, *MENAWP*, 1:271–75.

14. Text, ibid., p. 279.

15. Ali Fuat Türkgeldi, *Mesail-i mühimme-i siyasiyye* (Ankara: Türk Tarih Kurumu, 1957–1966), 1:60–61; G. F. de Martens, ed., *Nouveau recueil général des traités* (Göttingen: Dieterich, 1843–1875), 15:670–71, protocol of session 11, April 19, 1855.

16. Text in Hurewitz, *MENAWP*, 1:320.

17. DBHE, Karton Siyasi 6, dosya 11, Âli to Musurus (London) telegram, January 16, 1867.

18. DBHE, Karton Siyasi 37, dosya 13, Fuad to Photiades (Athens) #18926/50, April 24, 1867.

19. Text in Hurewitz, *MENAWP*, 1:320.

20. See Roderic H. Davison, "The Ottoman Empire and the Congress of Berlin," in Ralph Melville and Hans-Jürgen Schröder, eds., *Der Berliner Kongress von 1878* (Wiesbaden: Steiner, 1982), esp. pp. 214–15.

21. C. Jay Smith, Jr., *The Russian Struggle for Power, 1914–1917* (New York: Philosophical Society, 1956), pp. 205–6, quoting a stenographic report of a February 9, 1915, debate.

22. All other powers acted in the same way. Some rejoiced in the splits, like the foreign minister of Austria-Hungary, Count Andrassy, in the War Scare of 1875. When he heard that the Russian chancellor had given diplomatic support to France in a manner to humiliate Bismarck, the German chancellor, Andrassy jumped on his desk, did handstands, and exclaimed, "Bismarck will never forgive it." A. J. P. Taylor, *The Struggle for Mastery in Europe, 1848–1918* (Oxford: Oxford University Press, 1954), p. 226, quoting from Eduard von Wertheimer, *Graf Julius Andrassy* (Stuttgart: Deutsche Verlag-Anstalt, 1910–1913), 2:243.

23. Roderic H. Davison, "Nationalism as an Ottoman Problem and the Ottoman Response," in William W. Haddad and William L. Ochsenwald, eds., *Nationalism in a Non-National State* (Columbus: Ohio State University Press, 1977), pp. 44–48.

24. Brown, *International Politics*, pp. 74–75; L. S. Stavrianos, *The Balkans Since 1453* (New York: Rinehart, 1958), pp. 472–473.

25. I. de Testa, *Recueil des traités de la Porte ottomane* (Paris: Amyot, 1864–1911), 7:548–54. This was in 1869.

26. Roderic H. Davison, *Reform in the Ottoman Empire, 1856–1876* (Princeton: Princeton University Press, 1963), pp. 260–64.

27. Niyazi Berkes, *The Development of Secularism in Turkey* (Montreal: McGill University Press, 1964), p. 270.

28. Ottoman diplomatic history is only now beginning to be studied, and written on the basis of the wealth of materials in the Istanbul archives. I am now engaged in writing a history of Ottoman foreign relations in the post-Crimean period, to about 1890.

29. The Ottoman Empire's breakup into national states has recently been a fashionable topic among Sovietologists, who talk about the "Ottomanization" of the former USSR. By this they mean its dissolution, once threatened and now largely achieved, although still proceeding in places, into states based on ethnic groupings. "Ottomanization" is not a useful term for this because the Ottoman breakup does not convey the essence of that empire. The most distinctive aspect of the Ottoman Empire was not its demise but its success in achieving and maintaining cohesiveness when it was composed of heterogeneous peoples of differing faiths, each religious community being allowed a certain degree of autonomy. The achievement of such cohesion is "Ottomanization." Whether the Russian empire ever achieved Ottomanization is debatable. If Sovietologists want a historic parallel for what has been happening in the former USSR, Austria-Hungary provides a better model; its dissolution took place in a very short time rather than over two and a half centuries, like that of the Ottoman Empire.

30. Dankwart Rustow, "The Army and the Founding of the Turkish Republic," *World Politics* 11, no. 4 (July 1959):513–52; Erik Jan Zürcher, *The Unionist Factor: The Role of the Committee of Union and Progress in the Turkish National Movement, 1905–1926* (Leiden: Brill, 1984).

31. Mustafa Kemal (Atatürk), *A Speech Delivered by Ghazi Mustapha Kemal, President of the Turkish Republic, October 1927* (Leipzig: Koehler, 1929), p. 592.

32. Ibid., p. 378.

33. Ibid., pp. 377–78; Herbert Melzig, ed., *Atatürk dedi ki* (Ankara: Sümer Matbaasi, 1942), p. 138.

34. Roderic H. Davison, "Turkish Diplomacy from Mudros to Lausanne," in Davison, *Essays in Ottoman and Turkish History, 1774–1923: The Impact of the West* (Austin: University of Texas Press, 1990), pp. 206–42. Treaty text in League of Nations, *Treaty Series* 28 (1924), pp. 11 ff.; partial text in Hurewitz, *MENAWP*, 2:325–37.

35. Ibrahim Alaettin Gövsa, *Türk Meşhurlari Ansiklopedisi* (Istanbul: Yedigün Neşriyati, 1946), p. 252.

→ PART FOUR ←

THE IMPERIAL ARABIC

Bernard Lewis documents the case that much modern Arab political vocabulary came via an Ottoman transmission belt. Although of Arabic origin, the present-day meaning of the Arabic words for, say, republic, citizen, or municipality can be traced to the Ottoman political class and intellectuals who in modern times wrestled with these new political concepts "made in Europe." The case Bernard Lewis presents as regards modern Arabic (and Turkish) political vocabulary is important in itself and also a useful corrective to the tendency to attribute major changes in the modern Middle East solely and directly to the impact of the West. As the etymology of Arabic political vocabulary reveals, much of what makes up the modern Middle East is better traced historically to the dialectic of the long-lived Ottoman-European confrontation.

In considering the Ottoman legacy in language Geoffrey Lewis offers a nostalgic account. The Ottoman language had a richness of vocabulary matched, he suggests, only by English. In both cases, vast borrowings from other languages (largely Arabic and Persian in the Ottoman Turkish case) produced this extensive, nuanced vocabulary. Yet, the surviving words that can be traced to Ottoman Turkish in the non-Turkish languages today are few. Interestingly, somewhat more culinary terms have survived, but does that add up to a significant cultural legacy?

Even modern Turkish represents a major abandonment of Ottoman vocabulary, spurred in this by Atatürk's nationalist goals which meant, Geoffrey Lewis notes, that "there was no longer to be one language for the rulers and another for the ruled." While deploring Turkish language reform that eliminated subtle shades of meaning Lewis sees the process as beyond the control of political authority (or cultural guardians, witness the unsuccessful efforts of French intellectuals to suppress "franglais"). Much of the legacy, he concludes, "has been lost simply through the passage of time, without the intervention of reformers. But it was great while it lasted."

CHAPTER ELEVEN

THE OTTOMAN LEGACY TO

CONTEMPORARY POLITICAL ARABIC

Bernard Lewis

On March 5, 1798, the day that General Bonaparte sent his campaign plans for the expedition to Egypt to the Directoire, he also sent a note to M. Gaspard Monge, his scientific adviser, in which he asked him to procure Arabic type and Arabic typesetters and interpreters, all of which he felt would be needed in the course of the expedition on which he was about to embark. The type and typesetters were procured from Rome, from the College of Propaganda at the Vatican, and he was able to collect four Middle Eastern Christians who were in Rome, with whose help he set up a French government printing office. The Orientalist Jean Joseph Marcel was in charge of the operation. The first documents were printed on board Napoleon's flagship, appropriately called *Orient.* The first document prepared, ready for distribution when they landed in Egypt, was a proclamation in the name of the French republic, "based on the principles of liberty and equality."

The translators' problem was not merely one of translating from one language to another, which would have been relatively simple. It was a problem of translating from one culture to another, from modern, late eighteenth-century western Europe, to an Islamic world still almost untouched by even the beginnings of westernization, and to find words, in a language—Arabic—that had not previously been called upon to express them, for a whole series of notions which, by the time of the French Revolution, were already commonplace in French and the other languages of western Europe.

The problem began in the first line of the first document—the proclamation issued in the name of the French republic. There was of course a word for "French," but what about "republic"? In 1798 there were several Arabic words which could be used to convey the sense of the word "republic" in one or another context, but there was no accepted term to translate the notion of "republic" as a form of government or as the name of a state.

But surely, it will be said, there must have been. After all, the medieval Muslims in Egypt, North Africa, the Levant had contact with republics in Italy: of Venice, of Genoa and other Italian states that traded extensively in the Muslim lands. True, but there was no technical term to describe their form of government. The late medieval Egyptian al-Qalqashandī, author of a bureaucratic encyclopedia, devotes many pages to foreign governments, their forms of organization, and the correct manner of addressing correspondence to them. Genoa, he says, was ruled by "a group of men of different ranks (*jamā'a mutafāwitū'l-marātib*)"; for Venice he refers only to the doge. The general practice, in the second or third person alike, was to address or allude to the ruler or group of rulers (e.g., *Signoria*) rather than to the state as such. No term was used—or apparently needed—for the existing republics in Europe with which the medieval Muslims later had dealings.

What about the classical Greek philosophic literature? Plato's *Republic* was well known to the Arabs, but they came across Plato in Greek, not in English or French, and the word which we normally translate "republic," from the Latin *res publica*, is the Greek *politeia*, which means the relation of the citizen (*polites*) to the city (*polis*), the nature, i.e., the rights and duties, of citizenship, and hence the polity, the political society.

Jumhūriyya at first sight is obviously and authentically Arabic. It comes from *jumhūr*, which means the mass, the multitude, and is an abstract noun. Lexically it is indeed Arabic; but historically, semantically, it is Ottoman Turkish. The word was used with the meaning of "republic" in Turkish centuries before it was so used in Arabic. In Turkish it was indeed used of the Venetian republic, not as *jumhuriyya* but simply as *jümhur*. Venedik Jümhuru was the Republic of Venice, and the same term was used a little later of the Dutch republic, of the American republic, of the French republic and others with which the Ottomans came in contact. *Jumhuriyya*, or, in Turkish, *Jümhuriyet*, was an abstract form, the original meaning of which, at its first occurrence, was not "republic" but "republicanism." *Jümhur* was republic, *Jümhuriyet* was republicanism, that is to say, the notion, the ideology of republican institutions. In time that distinction was blurred and, finally, *jümhuriyet* was generally accepted in Turkish and later in Arabic and other Islamic languages as the equivalent of the Western term "republic."

"Republic" means many different things. I remember many years ago reading in a magazine published by a group of Islamic Fundamentalists an article on the Caliph Umar, who was described as "the second President of the Islamic republic." My first reaction was one of shock at this misunderstanding of the nature of republican institutions. But when I reflected on republican institutions as generally practiced in many parts of the world, I thought that the writer of the article understood the term better than I did.

Many years ago George Antonius wrote a famous book in which he presented an interpretation of the process of modernization in the Arab world. This, he said, came principally through two routes: one through Egypt under the rulers of the line of Muhammad Ali and then during the British occupation, the other through the mission-educated Christians of Lebanon, those who went to American Protestant and to French Catholic schools and colleges. Certainly, both these channels were of major importance in the modernization of thought and, to a much greater extent, of language. But there was a third channel, no less important than either, which is missing from Antonius' account and from the many others that are based on it, namely, the Ottoman channel.

A very large part of the Arab world, the whole of the Fertile Crescent, was in this period under direct Ottoman administration. Even those parts not under direct Ottoman administration were at least under some form of Ottoman suzerainty that was often more than nominal. The Ottoman influence—not just political but also cultural and linguistic—was considerable. In Syria and Iraq a significant proportion of the educated population was bilingual in Turkish and Arabic and switched easily from one to the other. They naturally tended to use words common to the two languages with the same sense, sometimes carrying over a sense from one language to the other. And since Turkish was the language of the state and the administration, of most higher education and of the most modernized newspapers, magazines and books, it was from Turkish to Arabic that such transfers usuallly occurred.

Consider what Ottoman traces remain in modern Arabic political language and terminology. Obviously, there are purely Turkish words, principally, though not exclusively, in colloquial rather than literary Arabic: *dughri*, straight, from *dogru*; *kubri*, in Egyptian Arabic, a bridge, from *köprü*; *birinji*, literally "first," but in Egyptian and especially Syrian Arabic meaning "first class"; and some technical terms—like *chaush*, which in high Ottoman meant a herald or pursuivant, degenerated into meaning a noncommissioned officer and then a policeman and became Arabic in the form *shāwīsh*.

Often compound words are formed with Turkish prefixes or suffixes. Such for example are the many occupational terms ending with the Turkish *-ji* (in Egyptian colloquial -gi), or, of more directly political relevance, with the Turkish *bash*, head, either after the word—as *onbashi*, *yüzbashi*, *binbashi*, respectively one in command of ten, a hundred, or a thousand men; or before the word—as *bashmuhandis*, chief engineer, *bashkātib*, chief secretary, etc.

More important than these occasional Turkish terms are the many Arabic terms, to a lesser extent also Persian terms, which have been, so to speak, resemanticized as a result of Ottoman practice and influence. During the nineteenth and early twentieth centuries the Ottomans used Arabic and Persian, their two classical languages, in the same way that Westerners used Latin and Greek, our two classical languages, as a kind of quarry of lexical raw material from which to make new words. For example, "metaphysics" and "telegraph" are both English words of Greek etymology. There is however a very important difference between the two. We took "metaphysics" from the ancient Greeks, but the modern Greeks took "telegraph" from us. We just happened to use ancient Greek roots to designate something new. Telephone, telegraph, psychoanalysis, and such terms are new words made from Greek roots; they are not loan words from Greek. This kind of borrowing is totally different from the older Greek loan words, such as philosophy and sophistry, philanthropy and misanthropy, music and cacophony.

Exactly the same thing happened in nineteenth- and early twentieth-century Ottoman, where a whole series of new words were created, or old words given new meanings in Turkish, and then sometimes—not always—later passed from Turkish to Arabic, so that we may find a word which lexically is purely Arabic, but nevertheless is a loanword from Turkish into Arabic. One example, already cited, is *jumhuriyya*, which was adopted at a fairly early stage by the Arabs from Turkish. There have been many others.

From the area of government and state institutions two of the most remarkable are *dawla* and *ḥukūma*. Clearly Arabic terms, of great antiquity and widely used in classical Arabic literature, both in their modern usage are influenced or even transformed by Ottoman. *Hukuma* in classical Arabic means judgment, not government. It is an abstract noun from a verb meaning to adjudicate or to dispense justice. The famous tradition attributed to the Prophet, which is nowadays usually translated as "An hour of justice in government is worth sixty years of prayer," really means "An hour of justice in adjudication is worth sixty years of prayer." *Hukuma* went through an interesting development in the course of the centuries, but it is not until the nineteenth-century that we find *hukûmet* first being used in Turkish documents in the sense of government.

Dawla originally means a "turn" in the literal sense, a turn or vicissitude (*vicissim* in Latin means "in turn"), as when the first Abbasid Caliph announced that the Umayyads had had their turn, and "now it's our turn." His remark can be translated literally into colloquial English: Now it's our turn. From being "our turn," it came to be "our dynasty," and then, much later, "our state." *Dawla* in the sense of state is pre-Ottoman, and is well attested in classical Arabic. But the distinction between the state as an abstraction and the government as the group of people exercising the power of the state is a nineteenth-century development and was initially and for a long time exclusively Ottoman. The earliest example I have found is in a memorandum of Sadik Rifat Pasha, reporting a conversation with Metternich while he was visiting Vienna, in which he talks about the *düvel-i avrupanin hükûmetleri*, the governments of the states of Europe. The distinction is quite clear. He was obviously translating from a text in some other language, probably French.

Another word associated with the state is *qānūn*, a word of great antiquity and widely changing meanings which appears frequently in classical Arabic texts and especially in texts of the Mamluk period but acquires its modern meaning of an enacted law or code of laws in nineteenth-century Turkey when for the first time the state openly and explicitly enacted and promulgated laws. Previously this was done tacitly, almost surreptitiously, since in principle only God can legislate. Others did in fact produce new laws but never explicitly or openly. It was not until the nineteenth century that governments, and eventually even legislative assemblies, drafted and enacted codes of law. The term the Ottomans used was *kanun*, based on a long history of Ottoman usage going back at least to the time of Mehmed the Conqueror.

Another new term that came with a new institution is *baladiyya*, in Turkish *belediye*—municipality—a word unknown before the nineteenth century, as was the institution itself. The first *belediye* was established in a district in Istanbul about the time of the Crimean War, itself a major channel for Western influence. Looking for a term, they decided on *belediye—municipalité*, following the French fairly closely, the *iye* corresponding to *ité*. This innovation was followed by the establishment of other municipalities in other provinces of the empire, eventually reaching the Arabic-speaking provinces where *belediye* passed from Turkish into Arabic and is now the common word for municipality in, I believe, all parts of the Arab world.

These are the simple examples, where the change of meaning is clear, where the new term, like *belediye*, or the new sense of an old term, like *hukuma* or *qanun*, designates a new way of doing things, a new institution. There are other cases that are less obvious but no less important. Examples are two prominent figures in any Middle Eastern state: the *wazīr* (vizier) and the *muftī*. These surely are classical Arabic terms. There were viziers and muftis from earliest times.

The purely Arabic origin of the term *mufti* or of the related term *iftā'*, the mufti's ruling or responsum, is beyond doubt. There is some dispute about the etymology of the word *wazir*, some preferring an Arabic, some a Persian etymology. But the use of the term is well attested throughout the Abbasid period. Subsequently, it changed its meaning as the practice of the institution changed, but broadly it remained within the same limits.

In nineteenth-century Arabic, however—in Turkish, much earlier —these words acquired new meanings. In the Ottoman Empire, for the first time, the mufti is no longer what he was in classical Islam but becomes something much closer to a Christian bishop. The idea that the mufti has jurisdiction over a territorially defined area—a kind of see or diocese—and himself occupies a place in a hierarchy of lower and higher ranks, is Turkish. There are signs of such a development—one wouldn't put it more strongly than that—in the Seljuk period, but not until the Ottoman period do we find a whole elaborately articulated religious institution of muftis with territorial jurisdictions and a hierarchy with the Chief Mufti of the capital, known as the *shaykh al-Islam*, at its apex.

Many scholars have adduced a Christian inspiration for this and other Ottoman practices, "Christian" meaning not the religion but the Church. The institutions of Christendom were well known to the Ottomans. They conquered many Christian countries, they were familiar with the operation of Christian ecclesiastical institutions with which they had extensive dealings, and it seems fairly clear that the development of the Ottoman religious institution was in some measure influenced by the example of the Christian, especially the Orthodox, Church.

The title and function of the mufti are clearly classical Arabic and Islamic, but those of Chief Mufti, or Grand Mufti, are, with equal clarity, Ottoman. The idea of a mufti of a place, operating under the authority of the state, with a precisely defined jurisdiction, is not only alien but one might even say contrary to classical Islamic beliefs and norms. This usage has survived very vigorously in the modern period, where religious institutions in the successor states of the Ottoman Empire and in the successor religions of the Ottoman Establishment—Christian and Jewish as well as Muslim—seem to have retained much of Ottoman practice.

Wazir simply became the lexical equivalent of the French term "ministre" or in British usage minister, i.e., the political head of a department of government. The Ottomans used *nāzir* in this sense more often than *wazir*, but the latter became the common term in the Arab states. Not only the word for minister but the names of most of the ministries derive from Ottoman usage: external affairs—"Harijiye"; internal affairs—"Dahiliye"; military affairs— *Harbiye*; financial affairs—*Maliye*; judicial affairs or justice—*'Adliye*. Almost all of these came into modern Arabic usage from their Ottoman counterparts. The division into ministries, the names given to them, and one might go further and say the structure of these ministries, are very largely Ottoman.

In provincial administration, too, the Ottoman impact is enormous. The names of the various administrative divisions are almost all Arabic words, but were given their present meaning and usage in Ottoman times. The *vilâyet*, from the Arabic *wilāya*, is governed by a *vali*, from the Arabic *wālī*. But these words, *wali* and *wilaya*, did not have this sense of a provincial administrative unit and its governor which they have in modern Arabic. The *liwā'*, literally flag, a subdistrict of a *vilâyet*, is simply a literal translation from the Turkish *sanjak*. The ruler of a *sanjak* is called *miriliwa* and sanjak bey interchangeably in Turkish documents.

Kaymakam is an interesting example. Of ultimately French origin, it is of course the *lieu-tenant*, the one who occupies the place of another. Using Arabic lexical raw material to render a French term, the Ottomans translated it literally as *Kaymakam*, which then passed—or in a sense reverted—to Arabic in the form *Qā'im Maqām*. *Kaza*, the name of an Ottoman administrative district comes of course from the Arabic *qaḍā'*, denoting the jurisdiction of a qadi. But the Ottoman qadi was very different from the classical Islamic qadi. He was part of the administrative structure; he was himself an administrative officer with a territorially defined jurisdiction, and he was held in much higher regard than the classical qadi, who all too often had become a byword for corruption and inefficiency.

Ḍābiṭ, meaning officer, literally one who takes hold of or seizes something, is again Ottoman. This term was already in current use in seventeenth-century Ottoman Turkish. One finds it in the chronicles—when for example, in describing battles, they talk about the *zabitler*, clearly meaning the officers. The military ranks, as already noted, were designated by Turkish terms.

At one time, even in Egypt, where Turkish was very little used or even known, the words of command were given in Turkish, which neither the officers nor the NCOs and least of all the conscripts knew. But Turkish was the language of command, so Egyptian recruits being trained by British and Egyptian officers and NCOs were ordered to right turn or left turn or about turn or march or halt in Turkish. This is no longer true. Turkish words of command have been dropped, though some military titles still remain.

Turning from institutional and official language to the more elusive language of political ideology and action, one immediately thinks of *watan*, Turkish *vatan*. What could be more Arabic than *watan*—the fatherland, *la patrie*? Indeed, *watan* is an ancient term, occurring already in ancient Arabic poetry. The word, however, did not have the slightest political content. *Watan* means home, it means birthplace, it can even mean place of residence. There is a great deal of poetry about *watan*: about love of one's birthplace, the homesickness of travelers and exiles, admiring descriptions by a poet or a geographer of the place where he was born—a geographer, for example, describing the whole world, might begin with his birthplace, which he praises rather more extravagantly than the rest. One's *watan*, which is also used in the plural, *awṭān*, simply means home or country and is no more political than that. The political sense of the French *patrie* or English country, the unit of national identity, the focus of political allegiance, derives from European influence and can be dated with some precision from the first years of the French Revolution and the first Ottoman accounts of that Revolution, first in Turkish and later in Arabic. *Watan* became "patrie," and in the course of the nineteenth century very rapidly developed all the emotional as well as political overtones and undertones of the French *patrie* and its equivalents in other languages.

From *vatan* in Turkish comes *vatandash*, a person with whom one shares a *vatan*, in other words, compatriot. The Arabs used the term *muwāṭin* meaning one from the same *watan*—again, compatriot—and this acquired, both in Turkish and in Arabic, the sense of citizen, which it retains to the present day in both languages as well as in some others.

We have here an interesting divergence from the European patterns on which so many of these terms are modeled. *Watan* is a literal translation of *patrie*, and *wazir* could pass as a literal translation of "minister." But *muwāṭin* or *vatandash* is not a literal translation of "citizen"; there is a shift in terms and also in notions. The reason is not far to seek. The notion of citizenship in the Western sense, the right to participate in the formation and conduct of government, was quite alien. For Ottomans and Arabs alike in the nineteenth century, citizen meant compatriot. It had the connotation of identity and loyalty, but not of political rights.

There are other terms of a more explosive ideological content. One of the most powerful Arabic terms at the present time is *qawmiyya* from *qawm*, which one might translate approximately as "nationalism." It is used particularly of pan-Arab nationalism and it is very much a positive term, used to approve, not to condemn.

Strangely, *qawmiyya* is also of Ottoman origin. The earliest examples that I have been able to find, long before any in Arabic, are in Turkish texts of the late nineteenth century and occur in the form of *kavmiyet*. This is an unmistakably negative term used to decry those who set petty local loyalties against the greater loyalties of Islam or Ottomanism. Islam is good, Ottomanism is good—local nationalism is not good. In Ottoman Turkish the Arabic word *qawm*, Turkicized as *kavım*, is commonly used in the sense of tribe, and *kavmiyet* could be translated as tribalism, It is an interesting and surely significant development that *kavmiyet*, a Turkish term of condemnation for local, factional, sectional, tribalist loyalties, has become the main term used to designate Arabism in Arabic, that is to say, the larger pan-Arab loyalty as against the local loyalties of particular Arab countries, which are called *shu'ūbiyya*.

Qawmiyya has thus reversed its meaning, from a negative, belittling term to a positive, enlarging term.

Another word that passed from Turkish to Arabic and has since been dropped in Turkish is *ishtirākī*, meaning "socialist," from an Arabic word meaning "to share." This appears to have been first used in Turkish to describe the minute Ottoman Socialist party, and came to be the accepted Ottoman term. *Ishtiraki* in Ottoman meant socialistic. A socialist was of course *ishtirakji*. This has been dropped in modern Turkish as excessively Arabic and has been replaced by the international and therefore acceptable word *sosyalist*. *Ishtiraki* remains in Arabic as the normal word for socialist.

A very interesting case is the word *Inqilāb*, revolution. *Inqilāb* is of course classical, indeed Quranic Arabic. It meant revolution in the literal sense, i.e., rotation, but had no political meaning. The earliest example of *inqilāb* with the modern political meaning that I have been able to trace occurs in Turkish in 1870. An exile living in France talks about *inqilāb* in an Ottoman context, looking forward to an Ottoman revolution, the great Ottoman revolution to come. From that time onward the use of the word seems to have developed very rapidly, though there is an interesting bifurcation, for which I have not found a parallel in any other term, between Turkish followed by Persian on the one hand, and Arabic on the other.

In Turkish and also in Persian, *inqilāb* is seen as a good thing. It is a word that revolutionaries use of revolution. An *inqilabji* is of course a revolutionary. It was used by Atatürk to designate his revolution and later by the Islamic revolutionaries of Iran to designate their revolution. In Arabic, on the other hand, *inqilab* at some stage, perhaps in the mid-twentieth century, developed a negative meaning and came to be the Arabic equivalent of what in French is called "coup d'etat," in German "putsch," in Spanish "pronunciamento." English history happily provides no equivalent. The positive Arabic term for revolution is of course *thawra*.

The Ottoman material coming into Arabic is of two major kinds. The first is what one might call high Ottoman, classical, i.e., pre-Westernized Ottoman, such as *mufti* and *dabit* and *liwa*. The second, which is on the whole much more important, at least quantitatively, consists of the Ottoman versions of Western terms. This highlights the immense importance of the Ottoman channel of Western influence into the Arabic lands. A great number of these terms can be traced as nineteenth-century Ottoman neologisms created to represent or translate Western, mostly French, terms, using Arabic roots and then borrowed—or repossessed—subsequently from Turkish into Arabic.

The most important route by which these words came to Arabic is undoubtedly Ottoman education. From George Antonius one would think that the only education received in the Syrian lands in the Ottoman period was that given by the French and American missionaries, but they were by no means the only educators, nor the most important. In the nineteenth and early twentieth centuries an important network of schools—primary, secondary, collegiate—was established by successive reformist administrations in the Ottoman Empire, bringing modern education, as understood at that time, in the Ottoman Turkish language as developed and used at that time, to considerable numbers of native Arabic speakers in such cities as Aleppo and Damascus and Mosul and Baghdad and other, smaller places.

In addition, there were significant numbers of young men from these countries who went to Turkey for higher education. One of the major educational reforms of the Turkish reformers was the establishment in Istanbul of a series of schools closely modeled on the French *Grandes Écoles*—not universities, but professional schools of one sort or another. The two most important were the *Mülkiye* and the *Harbiye*—the *Mülkiye* trained civil servants, the *Harbiye* trained officers for the armed services—as well as a number of other schools teaching a variety of professions. These produced the educated governing and administering elite of the Ottoman Empire, and in all these schools, and notably the *Mülkiye* and the *Harbiye*, there were pupils from all the Arabic-speaking countries of the Fertile Crescent and some from even further away. One comes across the occasional Egyptian or North African, and a more than occasional Arabian from Yemen or other places.

The graduates of these schools were effectively bilingual, often more at home in Turkish than in Arabic, speaking Arabic with their families and their children and Turkish with their colleagues and friends, writing letters to each other in both languages, reading both currently. What could be more natural than that they should draw on the Arabic lexical vocabulary of Ottoman Turkish when speaking or writing in Arabic?

A second important channel through which this vocabulary entered Arabic is the law. One of the major changes of the Ottoman reforms was the establishment of a new system of law and judicial administration; new codes of law, mostly adapted from European models, and more important than that, a new system of judicature to administer these laws, so that for the first time that redoubtable figure of Western political history, the lawyer, makes his appearance in the lands of Islam—an awful event from which they have never fully recovered. Before that, there was only one recognized system of law, religious law, and only one group of certificated lawyers, the ulama. Now there was, not secular, that is a dangerous word, but non-Shari'ah law and a whole new profession of lawyers and judges to administer that law using, necessarily, a new vocabulary in order to draft laws and argue cases.

A third channel through which these new terms passed into common usage is the press, in many ways the most important of all. The very rapid development of the press all over the Middle East involved many significant changes. There were newspapers from the early nineteenth century, but they did not become really important until the Crimean War, when for the first time great numbers of Western correspondents were present, bringing with them that portentous new invention, the telegraph, and providing daily news to their newspapers at home. One English correspondent made an arrangement with a Turkish newspaper to provide daily reports, five days a week, from the battlefronts in the Crimea. This was the beginning of that fatal addiction to the daily fix of news from which all of us have suffered since.

The creation of the press required a whole new language, not only to discuss their own affairs, which was difficult enough, but also, as is necessary in a daily newspaper, to discuss the affairs of other countries too. The American Civil War, for example, was discussed at some length in Turkish newspapers, with interesting comments, as were many other events. The Arabic newspaper *Al-Jawā'ib*, founded in 1860 and continued for many years after that, was probably the most important single Arabic newspaper of the nineteenth century, surely the only Arabic newspaper with what one might call an international circulation all over the Arab world, all others being local. It was published in Istanbul under Turkish sponsorship, and the role of its founder and editor and contributors is surely very considerable in the development of the new political language.

With a daily press and a public, perhaps not large but nevertheless significant, interested in public affairs, it began to be more and more necessary to look outside. The Ottoman ambience still provided the immediate frame of reference, and much of the language of public discourse. After the Turkish Revolution, and the changes in the Turkish language from then onward, most of these words have disappeared from Turkish. They survive in Arabic. And the fact that they exist in Arabic and were banished from Turkish, in the mistaken belief that they were alien intruders who should be sent home whence they came, has served to confuse the picture and lead to a serious misunderstanding of the directions of influence.

Beyond the political language is the political culture represented by that language. To what extent has Ottoman political culture survived in the modern Middle East? One might argue that the classical Arab political culture has been eclipsed for too long for it to be effective and that the brief interval of Anglo-French rule was too brief for it to leave any lasting traces, and that insofar as there is any surviving political culture at all, it is that bequeathed, by the Ottoman Empire. This is surely an inquiry worthy of closer study.

CHAPTER TWELVE

THE OTTOMAN LEGACY IN LANGUAGE

Geoffrey Lewis

Of all the languages of the world, the only one that ever approached English in the richness of its vocabulary was Ottoman Turkish. English embodies countless elements taken long ago, or recently manufactured, from Latin and ancient Greek, as well as words from every country of the British Empire and other empires. The Ottoman Turks had at their disposal the entire learned vocabularies of the Persians and Arabs, together with words from the speech of their Byzantine predecessors in Anatolia and of the sultans' European subjects, which supplemented and enriched the ancestral vocabulary, though that by no means consisted exclusively of Turkish words, including as it did many Mongolian, Sogdian, and other borrowings amassed over the centuries. And how much of this vast wealth have the successor states of the Ottoman Empire inherited? First, the Arabs.

It is a commonplace that the Ottoman Empire never succeeded in endearing itself to its Arab subjects.[1] So it is not surprising that as soon as Ottoman rule came to an end, the Arabs set about ridding themselves of the Ottoman influence on, among other things, their language.[2] During the nearly four hundred years in which the Ottomans ruled their lands, a great many Arabs learned Turkish in the hope of advancement in government service, but the end of empire naturally put an end to that.

In the following discussion Turkish words, both Ottoman and modern, are in bold italics.

In Egypt, in the time of the Khedive Sa'īd (1854–63), Arabic became the only official language, as in Syria during Fayṣal's attempt to establish an Arab government there between 1918 and 1920, where a committee of departmental representatives, known as *Lajnat al-Dawāwīn*, was set up to decide on new Arabic terms that would replace the Turkish throughout the administration.[3] Nevertheless, the use of Turkish military terminology persisted in Syria for years after that, as it did in Iraq and Egypt. Although it is doubtful whether any Arab army nowadays uses the Ottoman names of military ranks, **onbaşı** (corporal), **yüzbaşı** (captain), and *binbaşı* (major)—there are new terms like *nā'ib 'arîf, ra'īs firqa, naqīb, rā'id, ra'īs awwal,* and *muqaddam*—the linguistic historian may hope that somewhere in the Arab world a naval captain is still *amīr alāy,* because *alāy* is a venerable Ottoman word, which came from the Byzantines, who in turn adopted it from the Romans.

There are, however, many other good Ottoman words still used in Arabic. The Syrians say *dogri* (**doğru**) for "straight ahead." In Egyptian houses, the room where the men sit is still the *selāmlik.* For "room" in general, the Egyptians still use *oda*; the dining-room is *odat il-akl* and the bedroom is *odat il-nawm.* The Turkish for "customhouse," **gümrük**, is still alive in Arabic,[4] as is *kubrī* "bridge," Turkish **köprü**, itself borrowed from the Greek *gephyra.* The use of the Arabic *ajzā'* "pieces" to mean "drugs," "chemicals," appears to have originated with the Turks. Its derivative *ajzākhāna* "pharmacy" certainly did; Persian though it looks, it was made in Turkey (**eczahane**). The Turkish agent suffix *-ci* is still alive for example in *ajzājī* "pharmacist," *qahwajī* "coffeemaker," *ṣufrajī* "waiter" (which is never used in Turkey), and *'arbajī* "driver of a *'araba*" (i.e., a wagon, coach, or cab). *'Araba* itself is probably part of the Turkish if not specifically the Ottoman legacy; Ibn Baṭṭūṭa, who first encountered the word when he visited the territory of the Golden Horde, seems not to have heard it before.[5]

The Balkan peoples, once they gained their independence, showed no less alacrity than the Arabs in abandoning the greater part of the vocabulary they had acquired from the Ottomans. More than a century ago, the Turkish element in Romanian was estimated at one-sixth of the total vocabulary, but nowadays it is restricted to such domestic terms as *cizmă* for "boot" (**çizme**); *masă* "table" (**masa**); *mintean* "short coat" (**mintan**); *chimir* "belt" (**kemer**); *hamal* "porter" (**hamal**); *han* "inn" (**han**).

So too in the other Balkan tongues. In Albanian an inn is *hani,* while in Serbo-Croat it is *mehana,* Turkish **meyhane**. In Serbo-Croat, "bag" is *torba*; in Bulgarian it is *čanta,* both of them Turkish. "Button" in Serbo-Croat is *dugme* (**düğme**), while box is *kutiya,* as in Bulgarian and Albanian. The immediate origin of this last word is probably the Turkish **kutu**, though the Turks got it from the Greeks. Greek still retains a number of Turkish words, such as *tembelis* for "lazy," Turkish **tembel**; *tzaki* for "hearth," **ocak**; *tsopanis* "shepherd," *çoban*; *tsabatsis* "scrounger," **cabacı**; *kafetsis* "coffeehouse proprietor," **kahve-ci**. It also has a large number of culinary terms, like *dolmadhes*, Turkish **dolma** "stuffed vine-leaves," and *tzatziki*, **cacık**, that splendid concoction of yogurt and garlic, cucumber and mint.

Indeed the culinary legacy of the Ottomans is as widespread as may be expected of one of the world's four seminal cuisines, both in the survival of a great many Ottoman culinary terms and of the foods they name, in places as far apart as Pakistan and North America: **yoğurt**, **baklava**, **kebab**, **rahat lokum**, **köfte**, **pilav**.

And what of the Turks, who might have been expected to hold on to the lion's share of the linguistic inheritance? When they dethroned the Ottoman dynasty and founded their republic, they were no less eager to purge their language of foreign elements than were the Arabs and the Balkan peoples, and the resulting purification has been the most comprehensive ever achieved by any nation.

Nor can Ottoman literature be considered a major part of present-day Turks' patrimony. With a few exceptions, if they read the classical authors at all, they read them in modern paraphrase, although this is not entirely the fault of the switch to the Latin alphabet. When the change was made, in 1928, many voices were raised to complain that it would cut the Turks off from their ancestral literature, ignoring the fact that the previous year's census had shown that only 1.1 million people out of a population of 13.6 million could read and write.

With a far more literate population now, one might suppose that anyone wishing to read the classical Ottoman authors would be prepared to devote the modest amount of time necessary to learning the old alphabet, but it is only the rare young Turk who does so. The reason, apart from the obvious one that tastes in reading have changed, is that now, after sixty years of ridding the language of Arabic and Persian borrowings, only dedicated professional scholars can fully understand the old literature.

The enormous resources of Ottoman Turkish were at the disposal of the modern Turks. They did not have to perpetuate the whole rich vocabulary; they were free to pick and choose, but many of their intellectual leaders deliberately elected to squander the legacy. The foreign as well as the native lover of the old language has to resist the impulse to regard this as a classic example of the *trahison des clercs*. Their concern was that all citizens of the new republic should speak, read, and write the same Turkish. There was no longer to be one language for the rulers and another for the ruled. That aim has to a great extent been achieved, though quite a number of words that the young have never known are still on the lips of those members of older generations who managed to escape the influence of the press and the schools, through which the *öztürkçe* ("pure Turkish") neologisms were introduced. The aim, however, has been achieved at a price.

Imagine a situation in which English has been subjected to a reform that eliminated the verbs "to state," "to communicate," "to affirm," "to declare," "to assert," "to express," "to narrate," "to impart," "to report," leaving us with only "to tell," as has happened to Turkish. In English, to express the concept of change, we have, besides "change" itself, "alteration," "mutation," "transformation," "variation," "permutation," "vicissitudes," "alternation," "modification," "metamorphosis." Many of these distinctions can be expressed in Ottoman: *istihale, tahavvül, tebeddül, tebeddülât, tagayyür, takallüp* and so on, whereas the modern Turk's choice is restricted to *degişmek* "to change" and *başkalaşmak* "to become different."

Consider too the various words that were available to the Ottomans for the concept of seeking knowledge. There was *istisfar*, "to ask someone to explain a text"; *istiknah*, "to seek to plumb the depths of a problem"; *istilâm*, "to make an official request for information"; *istizah* "to seek clarification"; *istimzaç*, "to make polite enquiries about someone's well-being" or "to enquire whether someone is *persona grata* to a foreign government." Only the last two find a place in *Türkçe Sözlük*, the dictionary most widely used in Turkey, and it marks both of them as antiquated; their meanings can be expressed only by reciting the dictionary definitions. Sometimes Turks who are aware of the impoverishment of their language try to express themselves by employing an Ottoman word, and sometimes they get it wrong.

The Turkish writer Orhan Okay makes a shrewd observation about the titles of the Turkish translations of four French philosophical works, the *Pensées* of Pascal, the *Méditations* of Lamartine, the *Réflexions* of la Rochefoucauld, and the *Idées* of Alain. He points out that the "Thoughts," the "Meditations," the "Reflections," and the "Ideas" all come out in the new Turkish as *Düşünceler* "thoughts," whereas in the older language they could have been distinguished as *Düşünceler, Murakabat, Tefekkürat*, and *Fikirler*. The same writer also remarks that *takdim etmek* "to offer humbly," *arzetmek* "to offer respectfully," *ihsan etmek* "to bestow," *bahşetmek* "to confer," *lûtfetmek* "to offer graciously," and *ita etmek* "to grant" have now all been replaced by *vermek* "to give" or *sunmak* "to present."[6]

Not all is lost, however. For example: *mümkün*, the Arabic *mumkin* "possible," is still current in speech, though in writing it is losing ground before the neologisms *olanaklı* and *olası*. In Anatolia it often replaces *imkân* in the sense of "possibility"; thus instead of *imkânsız* "impossible" one may hear *mümkünü yok* "it has no *mumkin*."

The Persian *nümune* "model" (*numūna*) and the Arabic *misal* (*mithāl*) "example" have not yet been totally edged out by the Turkish-looking but originally Armenian *örnek*. One solitary Arabic preposition, *ilâ* "to, toward" (*ilā*) survives, but only just; one still occasionally hears it used between numbers, *onbeş ilâ yirmi* "fifteen to twenty."

At this point the Arabist reader may well be thinking, "These words he calls Ottoman Turkish and whose passing he seems to regret are mostly Arabic. What have they to do with the Ottoman legacy?" Indeed, these words were originally Arabic or Persian, but centuries of use had made them Ottoman Turkish. Can one deny that those English words I have cited—"permutation," "vicissitudes," and so on—are English, just because of their Latin origin?

Moreover, there were many Ottoman words coined by the Turks from Arabic so successfully that they have become part of the Arabs' vocabulary, and these we may fairly call part of the Ottoman legacy. What could appear more Arabic than *madanīya* "civilization," whence obviously the Turkish *medeniyet*? But it was the other way round: *medeniyet* was a nineteenth-century Turkish invention, whence *madanīya*. The modern Arabic use of *waṭan*, originally "dwelling," for "native land" is also due to the Ottomans.[7] From the Arabic *assasa* "to establish" they created *müessese* "institution," borrowed back into Arabic as *mu'assasa*. *Ijtimā'ī*, now the regular Arabic for "social," was coined in 1860 by Şinasi, the first considerable prose writer of the Tanzimat period.

Ṣalāḥīya appears in the modern Arabic dictionaries with such senses as "competence, validity," but you will seek it in vain in older lexicons of the language; it is another Ottoman invention, still used by Turks in the form *salâhiyet* for "authority" in preference to the neologism *yetki*. The modern Arabic *i'dām* for "execution" is also due to the Ottomans; before them it meant only "annihilation." One of the most successful Turkish coinages was *tayyare* for "airplane." It was formed from the Arabic *ṭāra* "to fly" by an educationist and minor poet named Fazıl Ahmet Aykaç (1884–1967) and was speedily taken into Arabic, although some Arabs nowadays use *ṭā'ira* instead.

There were a great many Arabic-based words invented by the Ottoman Turks that the Arabs did not borrow, either because they felt no need for them or because they devised other ways of expressing the required meanings. Many of these Ottoman coinages, however, are still used in Turkish, for example the curious euphemism *idrar*, which in Arabic means "causing to flow abundantly" but in Turkish is a polite term for "urine." Among the many other quasi-Arabic words peculiar to Turkish are *muntazam* "regular," Arabic *muntazim*; *istihsal* "production," for which Arabic uses *intāj*; *istimlâk* "expropriation," "nationalization," Arabic *ta'mīm*.

For "coincidence," where the Arabs use *muṣādafa* or *ṣudfa*, the Turks use *tesadüf.* This too is a Turkish invention; *taṣādafa* in the sense of "to chance" is not classical Arabic, nor is *taṣāduf* used in Persian. Dare I say that the sixth form, with its implication of reciprocity, seems a better way of expressing "coincidence" than the real Arabic third form?

For "criticism," where Arabs use *naqd* or *intiqād,* Turks use *tenkid,* while for "critic," Arabic *naqqād,* the Turks use *münekkid,* or rather they used to use it before they turkicized it to *tenkitçi* and then replaced it with *eleştirici.*

An unnecessary but still current invention was *imha* (*imhā'*) "annihilation"; there was no need to make a fourth form verbal noun to express what in Arabic is expressed by *maḥw,* the verbal noun of the first form. It must be said, however, that there are very few such barbarisms in Ottoman Turkish; learned Ottomans knew their Arabic.

Ziya Gökalp was a poet and sociologist who lived from 1876 to 1924. Like many thinking Turks, then and now, he disliked the tendency to use a Western word instead of finding a word of their own. Unlike most of the would-be language reformers, he believed that the natural way to equip Turks with the vocabulary necessary for coping with the advances of science and technology was to follow the example of the Western nations. Just as they had recourse to Greek and Latin, the classical languages of their culture, so the Turks should use Arabic and Persian to form new Ottomanisms. He thought up *ruhiyat* for "psychology," *bedii* for "aesthetic," and *bediiyat* for "aesthetics."

His most successful coinage was a word for "ideal." Up to his time, the dictionary equivalent was *gaye-i emel* "goal of hope" or *gaye-i hayal* "goal of imagination," though probably most of the people who talked about ideals used the French *idéal.* Ziya Gökalp also invented *mefkûre,* based on the Arabic *fakara* "to think," which was enthusiastically adopted and remained in use for many years until it was replaced by the neologism *ülkü*; indeed, a dictionary published as recently as 1988 uses it to define *ülkü.* So it is entitled to be mentioned as a surviving part of the Ottoman legacy. It survives in another aspect too: in Turkish cities you will see apartment blocks named *Mefkûre,* as well as *Ülkü* and indeed *Ideal.*

Then there are genuine Arabic words used in Ottoman and modern Turkish in senses not their own; the obvious example is *şafak,* meaning not "dusk," as in Arabic (*šafaq*), but "dawn." In Arabic *fajī'a* means "calamity, disaster." So it does in Turkish, but it also has the specific sense of "tragedy," for which Arabic employs *trājīdīyā.* For "catastrophe," the Turks use *felâket,* as in the following dictionary definition (*Okyanus*) of *facia*: "Yüksek ruhlu insanların ağır felâketlerle karşılaşmalarını . . . anlatan tiyatro oyunu," "a drama telling how people of lofty soul are confronted by grave calamities." The Turks manufactured *felâket* from *maflūk*, which, although it appears in dictionaries of modern Arabic as well as of Persian, is not classical Arabic but a Persian invention, quasi-Arabic for "afflicted, miserable," made from the Arabic *falak* "celestial sphere," and so "destiny."

The adverbial use of the Arabic *tanwīn*, as in *resmen* "officially," *şeklen* "in form," has given rise to some solecisms: from Turkish *ayrı* "separate" came *ayrıyeten* "separately"; from Persian *pešīn* "in advance" *peşinen* as well as an Arabic feminine plural *peşinat* "down payment." From the Western *culture* and *normal* come *kültüren* "culturally" and *normalen* "normally," both more likely to be heard than read. Then there is *yakinen*, good Arabic and Ottoman for "certainly," which some Turks use to mean "closely," as if it were not from Arabic *yaqīn* "certain" but Turkish *yakın* "near."

Among the Arabic and Persian borrowings which the modern Turks have not discarded and probably never will, the greatest is *şey* "thing," which is of course the Arabic *šay'*. *Şey* comes automatically to the Turk's tongue when groping for a word or name or deciding what to say next. There is a story that one evening, when Atatürk was trying to find a native Turkish replacement for it, one of his guests said to him, "We can't do that! On Judgment Day, when all the Turks who have ever lived are raised from the dead, *şey* will be the first word they utter!" Equally sure to last is the word for "village," *köy*, in origin the Persian *kūy*.

Turkish has two words each for "white" and "black." "White" is the native *ak*, or *beyaz* from the Arabic, while "black" is the native *kara*, or *siyah* from the Persian. But the language reform has not succeeded in getting rid of *beyaz* and *siyah*, nor will it, because although their dictionary meanings are the same as those of *ak* and *kara* respectively, they are not synonymous with them. For the borrowed words are used literally, while the native words are used metaphorically: "black day," meaning a time of trouble, is *kara gün*, but "black hat" is *siyah şapka*. If you want to say "he is an honorable man," the Turkish idiom for which is "his forehead is white," "white" translates as *ak*— *alnı ak*; whereas if you want to say "his shirt is white," you use the Arabic— *gömleği beyaz*.

Vesika "document," the Arabic *wathīqa*, has generally been supplanted by *belge* but survives in *vesikalık fotograf* "ID or passport photograph."

Then there are a number of Ottoman words of Persian origin which the tongue of the people has contorted into more or less Turkish shape, so that they have escaped the eagle-eyes of the reformers. These include *çamaşır* "linen," from the Persian *jāmešūy*; *çerçeve* "frame," from *čārčūba*; *mintan* "short jacket," from *nīmtan*; and *merdiven* "staircase," from *nardubān*.

Islamic religious terms will naturally survive: *imam, müftı, müezzin,* and so on. So too will the names connected with religious structures, most of them borrowed from Arabic: *cami/jāmi'* "Friday mosque," *mescid/masjid* "local mosque," *mihrab/miḥrāb* "prayer niche," *minber/minbar* "pulpit." Apart from these and *kubbe/qubba* "dome" and *sütun* (Persian *sutūn*) "pillar," most architectural terms were and still are Turkish, because architects spend more time talking to masons and carpenters than to other architects. "Roof" is *çati*, "ceiling" is *tavan*, and "flying buttress" is *duvar dirseği* "wall-elbow."

One tiny part of the republic's legacy from the Ottomans is safely invested in Istanbul street names. If you walk down from Sıraselviler to Galata Saray, you will pass by or along *Turnacıbaşi Sokaği* "Street of the Chief Crane-Man"; *Ağa Hamami Sokaği* "Street of the Agha's Bath-house"; *Baltaci Çikmazi* "Dead-end Street of the Halberdier"; *Nöbetçi Sokaği* "Street of the Sentinel"; *Borazan Sokaği* "Street of the Trumpeter."

Where one might have expected Ottoman vocabulary to survive is in the conservative professions of medicine and law. In medicine the old terms now stand little chance against the twin forces of *öztürkçe* and the international terminology, the advantage lying with the latter, because many Turkish doctors receive at least part of their training abroad. In fact, French was the language of Turkish doctors in the first half of the nineteenth century. In 1838, when Sultan Mahmud opened the new Medical School in Istanbul, he told the students that they would be learning French, not for its own sake but in order to study scientific medicine.[8] A change came when the Ottoman Medical Society, founded in 1866, produced a dictionary of medical terms, for in preference to French the Society opted for Arabic, prescribing words like *zatürree* (*dhāt al-ri'a* "that of the lung") for "pneumonia" and *daüssaleb* (*dā' al-tha'lab* "fox disease") for "alopecia." Sometimes, presumably when no suitable term could be found in Arabic, they resorted to adapting or creating Arabic terms. Thus for "syphilis" they devised *daülefrenc* (*dā' al-Afranj* "the Frankish disease"). For "tuberculosis" they chose *verem*, the Arabic *waram* "swelling" or "tumor," still in use in Turkey alongside *tüberküloz*. Very few others of these terms long survived the Ottoman Empire, though it may be that some of them were taken up by Arab doctors and have lived on in the Arab lands.

The current situation in Turkey is that laymen call common illnesses by their popular, i.e., Turkish names. Among themselves, however, doctors generally use the French terms, such as *müsküler komplikasyonlar*, where, if one knows that *-ler/-lar* is the plural suffix, the meaning of the second word is evident, as is that of the first, once one realizes that its final syllable is not the plural suffix. In medical parlance, "alopecia," for example, is *alopesi*, whereas in common speech it is *saçsizlık* "hairlessness." "Caesarian," a doctor's word, is *sezaryen*, whereas "umbilical cord," a midwife's word, is ***göbekbağı*** "navel-tie." In medicine, in fact, the Ottoman legacy is negligible.

The situation in law is different. After the change to the Latin alphabet in 1928, the republic's legal codes, first promulgated in 1926, had to be rewritten. The new version of the Civil Code appeared in 1934, when the move to "purify" Turkish was just getting under way, and the drafters made a conscious effort to keep the language simple. But the passage of sixty years has made it virtually incomprehensible except to septuagenarians, since few young lawyers have the time to gain proficiency in Ottoman. For most of them the practice of their profession would be hard indeed were it not for the existence of what may fairly be termed a bilingual edition, in which the 1934 text is given on the left-hand page and a translation into the Turkish of the 1970s on the right.[9] Even though the sense of the right-hand pages may not always be crystal-clear now, in the 1990s, the lawyer can use them as a trot or crib, while quoting the original text from the left-hand page, if he is so minded, to impress his client or the court.

Words are born and words die,[10] and much of the legacy has been lost simply through the passage of time, without the intervention of reformers. But it was great while it lasted.

NOTES

1. There is a poignant acknowledgment of the evanescence of Ottoman power in some words of Falih Rıfkı Atay (1894–1971). On the outbreak of World War I he was posted to Jerusalem as private secretary to Cemâl Pasha, commanding the Fourth Army. In 1932 he published his wartime memoirs under the title of *Zeytindağı*, "Mount of Olives," for it was there that Cemâl Pasha had his headquarters. He revisited Jerusalem in 1956 and on his return home he wrote an introduction entitled "Ölberg" for a new edition of his book. It includes the following: "Ölberg is the German for Mount of Olives. The Arabic is Jabal al-Zaytun. And Zeytindağı? That's just the title I gave my book. There never was a Turkish Jerusalem."

2. A former student of mine who in 1988 performed the *'Umra*, the Lesser Pilgrimage, reported that the Saudis had demolished the Ottoman mosque on the traditional site in Medina of the Mosque of the Two Qiblas, with the intention of replacing it with a new mosque in Arab style.

3. Anwar G. Cheyne, *The Arabic Language: Its Role in History* (Minneapolis: University of Minnesota Press, 1969), p. 110.

4. Oddly, the Turks learned ***gümrük***, ultimately the Latin *commercium*, from Italian merchants, whereas the Italians now use the Ottoman, originally Persian, *divan*, in the form *dogana*. So too French *douane*, and Spanish *aduana*.

5. Gerhard Doerfer, *Türkische und Mongolische Elemente im Neupersischen* (Wiesbaden: Franz Steiner Verlag GMBH, 1963–75), 2:21.

6. Orhan Okay, "Kaybolan Nüanslar," *Yaşayan Türkçemiz* (Istanbul, 1981), 1:273–74.

7. Bernard Lewis, *The Emergence of Modern Turkey* (New York: Oxford: Oxford University Press, 1961), pp. 328–29.

8. Lewis, *Emergence of Modern Turkey*, pp. 83–84.

9. Hıfzı Veldet Velidedeoğlu, *Türkçeleştirilmiş metinleriyle birlikte Türk Medenî Kanunu ve Borçlar Kanunu* (Ankara, 1970, 3d impression 1979).

10. Occasionally words are resurrected. The last citation of the verb "to refurbish" in the *Oxford English Dictionary* is dated 1874. It was brought back from the dead in February 1969 by Mr. Walter H. Annenberg, when he came to London as U.S. Ambassador. The whole of Great Britain saw him on television, talking to the Queen and telling her that the Embassy residence was being refurbished. The quaintness of the word caught the public imagination and since then it has once again become current English. So there is still hope.

→ **PART FIVE** ←

EUROPE, ECONOMICS, AND WAR

Charles Issawi's review of the economic legacy is confined to a comparison between the Ottoman Empire and neighboring Europe. Left out of account are other world areas such as China and the Indian subcontinent. Left out as well are other major components of all civilizations such as religion or the arts broadly defined.

Within these limits Issawi offers a well-documented case that Europe outstripped the Ottoman lands in science and technology from early modern times onward. The limited Ottoman interest in economics and statistics as contrasted with Europe is also noted. Accordingly, the economic policies of Ottoman rulers over the centuries never really had a mercantilist or a capitalist phase. Instead, Ottoman economic doctrine may be defined as that of "the fiscal state" (here Issawi is citing Şerif Mardin) in which "major economic policy consisted in trying to maximize the tax yield from the rural economy."

Issawi's conclusion is bleak. The Ottoman world "did not enter the mainstream of progress in science and technology and it participated only marginally, and as a periphery, in Europe's economic activity and not at all in the development of its economic thought." His is a powerful argument within the confines of the problem posed. On the other hand, the Ottoman economic record compared with the rest of the world looks less dismal than when set alongside the West.

Even so, the case brought by Issawi provokes thought. Possessing a secure, centralized state well before most of the world, wasn't the Ottoman Empire better poised to embrace useful innovations than others in the third world? A more intensive look at the impact of Ottoman government upon the economic choices of its subjects is in order. Did the millet system, for example, foster or hamper economic initiative? While accepting that the Ottomans demonstrated a—to modern eyes—rather perverse use of tariffs and taxation, what can be said for the Ottoman accomplishment of providing a vast free trade area within its imperial borders?

Dankwart Rustow emphasizes the central role of warfare in both the Ottoman Empire's rise and its slow decline with a resulting political culture of "war on the frontiers, tolerance within." Not only was there no Ottoman equivalent to Europe's wars of religion, expulsions or forced conversations (as with Muslims and Jews of Spain) but the Ottomans welcomed such outsiders, several of whom came to play leading roles in Ottoman officialdom.

Those factors which earlier produced Ottoman might became, however, disadvantages when later facing a Europe whose dynamism and aggressiveness would change the world. European technological advances were matched by institutional changes such as conscription, begun in France in 1792, which revolutionized warfare. Henceforth, the once feared Ottomans had to play the difficult global game of catch-up. The Ottomans attempted Westernization especially in military matters, including conscription.

The Ottoman military legacy comes from that hectic period of hybridization of classical Ottoman and European ways that began with Sultan Selim III in the last years of the eighteenth century and continued in fits and starts until the end of empire. The legacy is seen most clearly in the Republic of Turkey, brought into existence by a military leader, Atatürk, who blended the Ottoman concept of centralized political leadership with the European notion of the nation-state. Turkey's "combination of established governmental structure and sense of national identity," Rustow concludes, is less evident in the post-Ottoman Arab world.

→ CHAPTER THIRTEEN ←

THE ECONOMIC LEGACY

Charles Issawi

Very little work has been done on the subject of the Ottoman legacy in the field of economics, and what I say must be regarded as highly tentative. Much of it will also be critical. Other contributors have drawn attention to the great Ottoman achievements. An empire that lasted six centuries and under which a host of nationalities and religious groups lived, most of the time, in reasonable harmony, is something to admire and praise. Unfortunately my assigned topic is economics, and economics never was the strong suit of the Ottomans.

My approach is, further, confined to a comparative approach of the Ottoman lands with neighboring Europe. I am not talking about China, of which I know little, or India, of which I know even less. Between them they have accounted for almost half of the world's population, and have represented, at various times, the peak of human achievement. What I am saying applies to the lands west of them, the Middle East (including North Africa) and Europe with its offshoots in the New World. And for this portion of humanity I return to the good old eoghteenth-century view, which claims that there is a continuous process that can best be represented by a rising line, with numerous breaks and setbacks.[1]

Of the generally agreed-upon constituent elements of a civilization—religion, art, literature, philosophy, natural science, learning, and technology—I will address only the last three. My reasons are twofold. First, because I believe these, and more particularly technology, constitute the main thrust that has pushed humanity from one stage of economic development to the next. Second, they are cumulative: the discoveries of one generation can be handed over to the next, which can then build upon them, though this often fails to occur. They have one thing in common: they represent the application of man's mind to fields in which, because it can work on large amounts of empirical data, human reason seems to operate most efficiently and to yield cumulative results. To a large extent statistics, and to a lesser extent economic theory, share this characteristic, with results I shall discuss later. If Kant had not preempted the term for a very different use, one could have called this activity "practical reason."

One can contrast these activities with religion, and perhaps with art, which in many ways are the finest flowers that humanity has produced. In those fields, the human mind, at an early date, reached dazzling heights and came up against barriers that have, so far, proved insurmountable. In particular, the higher religions reached peaks that have never been surpassed: Hinduism, Zoroastrianism, Buddhism, Judaism, Christianity, Islam. Each of them, in its way, glimpsed an important aspect of the ultimate reality we call God. All are, in their way, valid. And each has witnessed rises and declines in its carrier society and therefore presumably cannot be the major operating factor. Thus it is absurd to blame Islam for the decline of the Middle East since that region had reached a peak precisely under Islam, in the eighth to twelfth centuries.[2]

My main point is that in the early Middle Ages, the Middle East was *the* center of civilization (not to overlook the magnificent Tang and Sung dynasties but, as already stated, I am not discussing China). After that the center of civilization moved to Europe, and has remained there, and in Europe's American offshoots, ever since. In the fields of science, technology, and economic development, the main legacy of the Ottomans, and of their predecessors the Mamluks and others, was that they cut off the Middle East from the vivifying effects of close contacts with Europe. Hence the deplorable state of these lands, particularly the Asian parts, toward the end of the eighteenth century when their modern history begins. At that time, they were, by any acceptable economic, social, or cultural criteria, far behind not only Europe and North America but Latin America, Russia, Japan, and possibly China.[3]

In the nineteenth century, Europe, in the form of economic and political imperialism, did indeed impinge on the Middle East with a bang, pushing it forward but also injuring and distorting it, but that, too, is outside my present inquiry.[4]

The discussion that follows will briefly compare Ottoman science and technology with that of contemporary Europe and then treat economic theory, economic organization, and economic policy in both areas.

Science and Technology

The rise and high noon of the Ottoman Empire coincides with that of European science: the fifteenth-century precursors, Henry the Navigator and Leonardo; the sixteenth-century pioneers, Copernicus and Vesalius; the seventeenth-century giants, Galileo and Harvey, and so on to Newton and Leibnitz.

And what of the Ottoman Empire? Mehmet II reorganized the *madrasas*, greatly improving the teaching of mathematics, astronomy, and medicine. Under his successors, progress was made in geography and cartography and in 1579 an observatory, as good as those of Europe, was built in Istanbul. A good example of Ottoman science at its best was Taqi al-Din, an astronomer, clockmaker and inventor of various machines.[5] Around 1565 he wrote a treatise on mechanical clocks.[6] But in all these fields, except cartography, the traditional Muslim methods and books continued to be used and nothing was learned from contemporary Europe, except by a few Jews, Armenians, and Greeks who went to Italy for study. Moreover the various centers soon relapsed into mediocrity and the observatory was actually destroyed at the monarch's order, because of some unfortunate astrological predictions! It was not until the second half of the eighteenth and early nineteenth centuries that the Ottomans began to pick up the rudiments of Western science.[7]

The situation in the Arab provinces was even worse than in the capital.[8] The lingering effects of this unfortunate legacy is illustrated by the backward state of the natural sciences today, in spite of the vigorous efforts of the last sixty to seventy years, in the course of which tens of thousands of students have been sent abroad. According to UNESCO's *Statistical Yearbook*,[9] the most recent estimated number of potential scientists and engineers in Turkey was 14 per thousand of the population, in Lebanon 11, and in Egypt 10; in both Iraq and Syria it was under 3. These figures are of course far below those for Japan (58) as well as Europe and North America, though they compare well with some other third world countries, e.g., Ecuador 5 and Chile 6. But they are well below those for the Balkan countries: Greece 33, Bulgaria 26, and Yugoslavia 22.

Technology

We can now survey some of the leading aspects of technological activity, starting with agriculture which, in the Middle East as elsewhere, employed at least 80 percent of the population.

AGRICULTURE

The best single indicator of agricultural technology is the yield to seed ratio of wheat, since wheat was by far the predominant crop in both Europe and the

Middle East. Ashtor puts the ratio in medieval Egypt at 10 and contrasts it with 2–2.5 in Western Europe in Carolingian times; Bolshakov accepts these figures and believes that Syrian yields were 1.5 times those of Europe, or say 3–4.[10] The latter figure *may* also apply to medieval Anatolia. In the mid-nineteenth century, figures for Turkey and Syria were about 5–6; for Egypt yields were estimated at 14–15 by Napoleon's experts in 1800.[11] The Turkish and Syrian figures compare favorably with those for most European countries in the sixteenth to eighteenth centuries, but are distinctly lower than those for the nineteenth.

Considering that, except in Egypt, natural conditions are much less favorable in the Middle East, and that the agricultural revolution in Europe took place in the eighteenth century or later, one can say that, in this field, the Ottoman Empire did not suffer appreciably from its isolation until quite recently. It may be added that the American crops introduced into Europe—maize, potatoes, and tobacco—found their way to the Middle East quite early. An important Ottoman legacy in agriculture was the land tenure system and the Land Law of 1858 and other nineteenth-century legislation. It was not, however, conducive to economic development.[12]

MINING, METALLURGY, AND ARMAMENTS

The Ottomans, like other governments, were not terribly interested in agriculture, but they were very much so in mining, metallurgy, and armaments, which provided the sinews of war.

In all these fields, from the fifteenth century onward, Europe was technologically more advanced and innovative than the Ottoman Empire. Examples include the amalgamation process for silver, the use of blast furnaces for iron smelting, and the introduction and spread of water-driven machinery to crush ores and drain mines.[13]

The Ottomans tried hard to keep up with these developments by employing German and other experts to exploit their numerous mines. "They used the mining technique familiar to them in Germany, and even the laws regulating these Ottoman mines were the Saxon mining laws. These are extant in a Turkish version known as Kanuni-Sas, the Saxon Law."[14] Because of their isolation, however, the Ottomans tended to fall increasingly behind; in 1807 Thornton stated: "They call in no foreign assistance to work their mines,"[15] and by the early nineteenth century European observers were all reporting on the poor conditions of the Anatolian mines. A Hungarian expert working for the Ottoman government reported in 1836: "These mines are all in a deplorable state. They are run with great ignorance and therefore at considerable expense."[16]

When it came to firearms, the Ottomans made every effort to keep abreast of Europe, hiring experts (many of them converts to Islam), where necessary. Hence, "as late as 1683, some contemporary Austrian observers noted that the Turkish muskets were as good as those of the Austrians and, in some respects, in range for instance, better."[17] However, as early as 1592, "The Ottoman cannon, though often well cast, are described in Christian sources as ponderous and difficult to move, even with large teams of buffalo and oxen."[18] By 1794 the British ambassador rated the foundries as poor: "The Ottoman Empire never possessed more than two furnaces for casting cannons and mortars (of brass only) . . . and a third for iron shot and shells, all situated in Constantinople."[19] Even the overwhelming interest of the Ottomans in warfare did not allow them to keep up with European technology, which was the offspring of a different society and organization.

Shipbuilding techniques also failed to keep up with those of Europe and by the end of the eighteenth century the Ottomans were importing both warships and merchantships from the United States, Sweden, and elsewhere.[20]

One more point on this subject is relevant to the successor states. Minerals are very scarce in the Arab countries, but in one immensely important field Ottoman law had a great impact: oil. In Muslim law, as in Roman, and in contrast to Anglo-Saxon, subsoil resources belong to the state, not to the owner of the soil. Hence the Middle Eastern oil industry developed under the system of concessions granted by the state to a company, and not by bilateral contracts between the owner of the soil and the concessionaire, as, say, in Texas. This permitted the development of fields as a unit and, together with favorable geological conditions, explains the phenomenal productivity of the wells and very high profitability of the industry.

TEXTILES

The Middle East's preeminence in textiles is shown by such loan words as damask, gauze, taffeta, and many others. However, according to Ashtor, already by the fourteenth century "most Near Eastern industries were no longer able to compete with Western manufactured goods, imported by Italian and other merchants."[21] By the thirteenth century the virtual monopoly in silk fabrics enjoyed by the Muslims in Europe had been broken, and by the fifteenth Italian fabrics were selling in the Levant. So were woolen goods. Middle Eastern cotton cloth exports to Europe expanded rapidly in the seventeenth and eighteenth centuries, but were then hit by protective tariffs. By the nineteenth century machine-made textiles poured into the region, and many handicrafts were wiped out, though others managed to struggle on. Instead of being an exporter of manufactures, in the early modern period, and more particularly in the nineteenth century, the Middle East became an exporter of raw textile materials, particularly silk, cotton, and, for some time, flax. It was only at the end of the nineteenth century that modern textile factories were established in Turkey and Egypt.[22]

PAPER AND PRINTING

A paper mill was set up in Baghdad in 751, allegedly by Chinese prisoners captured at the battle of Talas. From there it spread to Byzantium and westward to Europe, and in the Middle Ages, Middle Eastern exports to Europe were very large. By the sixteenth century, however the bulk of Istanbul's consumption was met by European imports, though there was some local manufacture.[23]

The Arabs eagerly accepted Chinese paper, but not Chinese printing. In the 16th century Arabic books were printed in Italy and, in the following century, in other European countries. But in 1485 Sultan Bayazit II imposed a ban on the possession of printed matter in Arabic or Turkish, and this was confirmed by Selim I in 1515. It did not apply to Hebrew, Armenian, or Greek books, and presses in these languages were soon set up, as were others, also by Christians, in Syria and Lebanon. It was only in the eighteenth century that printing in Turkish began and, as Şerif Mardin points out, even then it encountered much opposition.[24]

MECHANICAL POWER

Before the invention of steam engines, mechanical power meant watermills and windmills. Both were invented in the Middle East, the watermill at the beginning of the Christian era and the windmill in the sixth century, but neither was much used in the region—the watermill because of the lack of suitable streams and the windmill for no obvious reason.

But both were greatly improved and widely used in Europe. In England in 1086, Doomsday Book shows that there was one watermill for every 195 inhabitants. This may be contrasted with the situation in the Middle East five centuries later. The corresponding figures were: 326 in Tokat, 460 in Malatya, and 1,424 in Safad, though the last figure may be due to an undercount of mills. In the rest of Syria, and in Iraq, Egypt, and Arabia, there were very few mills. Two more points may be noted: first, the power of the watermills represented a substantial addition to the labor force—in England at least one-third. Second, there were nearly two watermills for every English village, most of which were very small, which means that practically everyone was familiar with the machinery of the mill and with various attachments such as cams and cranks; watermills were used for a wide variety of industrial processes.[25]

The contrast was even more striking with windmills. In the flatter parts of Europe, where there was little waterpower, such as the Netherlands and eastern England, they played an enormously important role. In the Middle East, however, they went out of use in the Middle Ages. "A French traveler who visited Egypt in 1512 says explicitly that in this country there [were] neither water mills nor windmills" and al-Jabarti mentions those put up by the French in Cairo as an unfamiliar phenomenon. In Palestine, where windmills had been introduced by German crusaders, a few mills were set up in the eighteenth century.[26] Inadequate use of mechanical power was one of the main causes of the relative retardation of the Middle East, and the advent of steam, which began to be used for industrial purposes in England around 1700, greatly widened the gap.

Economics

This may be studied under three headings: economic practice, economic theory, and economic policy.[27]

ECONOMIC PRACTICE

To document adequately the difference in economic practices between Europe and the Ottoman Empire would require the writing of the economic history of the two areas over several centuries. Here only a few points may be noted.

First of all, Muslim law does not recognize the existence of corporate entities. This meant that joint-stock companies could not be formed to carry out large-scale enterprises, as they were in Europe. Of course Islam had many kinds of partnerships, including the *mudaraba*, under which different partners provided capital and enterprise, but these were very seldom of either large size or long duration.[28] The closest approximation to a corporation was the *waqf*, and although *waqfs* occasionally engaged in commercial activities,[29] they were a poor substitute since the vast majority were notoriously mismanaged.

Second, the prohibition of *riba*, though it never stopped lending or usury,[30] must have inhibited the development of banking and stock exchanges. In much of Europe, these institutions developed rapidly in the sixteenth and seventeenth centuries and managed to tap large savings. As a result, interest rates on government loans fell dramatically, to 6 percent in England after 1651, 4 percent in Holland in the 1660s, and 1.5 percent in Genoa after 1664.[31] For comparison, the U.S. government is now paying 7–8 percent and most European governments more—these high figures are, of course, largely due to inflation.

In the Ottoman Empire, on the other hand, the closest approximation to banks were the Galata *sarrafs* who exchanged currencies, granted loans, and discounted various receivables, but do not seem to have taken deposits. Interest rates were seldom below 25 to 30 percent, and often more. It was not until 1856 that the Ottoman Bank was founded, by foreign capital, and a stock exchange was established only in 1873 and led a rather anemic existence.[32] In Egypt modern banks and stock exchanges were established at about the same time, and proved more vigorous.

Insurance was another field in which Europe forged ahead. Marine insurance goes back to the fourteenth century and fire insurance was practiced a little later; life insurance goes back to at least the sixteenth century, but was not put on a sound basis until the establishment of life tables at the end of the seventeenth century.[33] But as late as 1851 the British ambassador complained about "the impossibility of insuring houses and property in Constantinople against the risk of fire." Foreign insurance companies then opened branches in the main Ottoman cities and Egypt but as late as 1900 only one was operating in Baghdad, a Swiss firm that undertook maritime insurance.[34]

Lastly, there is the question of accounting. After the introduction of double-entry bookkeeping, in the late thirteeenth or early fourteenth centuries, European methods of accounting became increasingly superior to those of the Middle East. The latter acquired modern accountancy only in the last hundred years or so, when it was introduced by foreign banks and other firms.

ECONOMIC THEORY AND STATISTICS

Europe's great achievement in theory was to conceive of the economy as a self-regulating mechanism obeying definite and understandable laws. This was first achieved in monetary theory, with Copernicus (1526), Jean Bodin and others formulating early versions of the Quantity Theory and Gresham's Law. The connection between money and the balance of trade was extensively debated by the mercantilists and by Locke, Cantillon, and others. Hume achieved a fine theoretical synthesis linking money and foreign trade and Adam Smith (1776), in addition to many other contributions, elaborated the notion of division of labor and free trade. Ricardo's *Principles* (1817) finally set economic theory on the path it was to pursue.[35]

A parallel development took place in the field of statistics: from the Middle Ages onward, Europe has always been interested in numbers, in counting men and things.[36] By the sixteenth century this activity had been systematized; "a large part of the work of the Spanish *politicos*, for example, consisted in the collection and interpretation of statistical figures—not to mention the English econometricians, who were called political arithmeticians, and their fellow workers in France, Germany, and Italy."[37]

Among the English, the foremost name is that of Sir William Petty, who has been called by Marx "the founder of political economy." In his *Political Arithmetic* (c. 1672) Petty writes: "Instead of using only comparative and superlative words and intellectual arguments, I have taken the course . . . to express myself in terms of *number, weight,* or *measure*" and he applied his method to various problems. His younger contemporary, Gregory King, made a careful estimate of the national income and produced an econometric study of the demand for wheat. Petty's friend and collaborator, John Graunt, worked on the London Bills of Mortality, starting the scientific study of demography and producing Life Tables. The Swiss Jacques Bernouilli developed the theory of probability in 1713. By 1786 the first economic graphs had made their appearance and in 1798 Evelyn had produced an index number for prices.[38]

Turning to the Middle East, in economic thought, as in the other social sciences, Ibn Khaldun towers above his contemporaries, whether Muslim or European.[39] His student, al-Maqrizi, also shows an understanding of economics and in his *ighathat al-umma bi-kashf al-ghumma* (The Succor of the Nation by Revealing the Misfortune) and his *shudhur al 'uqud fi dhikr al nuqud* (The Fragments of Necklace on the Subject of Coins) gives a very good analysis of the currency debasement and inflation that Egypt was undergoing. After that, however, there was very little progress. Cemal Kafadar's excellent thesis gives a thorough analysis of the economic thought of the leading Ottoman historians at the end of the sixteenth century.[40]

Faced with a sharp rise in prices, these authors could think of only one cause: the debasement of coinage that had been going on since the mid-fifteenth century, to which some added royal extravagance. This was correct, as far as it went, but took no account of the influx of silver from the New World which they, like European bullionists, welcomed. Their remedy was essentially price control. As Kafadar put it: "Our writers were frustrated by the uncontrollable rise of market forces . . . rather than coming to terms with these forces, they reasserted the primacy of politics which would not allow these forces to play an influential role."[41]

A further check is provided by the writings of the Ottoman bureaucrat Mustafa Ali (1541–1600), who has been described as "one of the most significant intellectual figures of the sixteenth century." And: "Ali was an important member of a group of relatively highly placed intellectuals who were gravely concerned over the course their society seemed to be taking in the late sixteenth century, when rapid changes struck economic, political and social structures all at once." And: "Mustafa Ali achieved posthumous fame largely by virtue of his tremendous historical output and his outspoken social and political critiques."[42]

I carefully read Mustafa Ali's *Counsel for Sultans* in translation,[43] and can affirm that it does not contain one economic thought worth noting or one that shows the kind of understanding to be found in Ibn Khaldun or sixteenth-century European writers.[44] Among the commonplace suggestions it contains are: provisions should be laid up against possible shortages; accurate figures should be kept on resources; the migration of lower class yokels ("Turks") to Istanbul should be discouraged by taxation; the public treasury should be protected against waste; the tyranny of the *beglerbeys* over fiscal agents should be curbed; the mixing of ranks should be stopped; provinces should not be subdivided; the currency should not be debased; bribes should be prohibited; standard prices should be set; arrears of taxes should be collected; salaries of soldiers guarding fortresses should be paid; and so on.[45]

I also read his description of Cairo.[46] It contains numerous observations on the manners and customs of Egyptian men and women, usually not flattering, including: "The despotical behavior of most of their governors is caused by their Pharaonization from drinking the water of the Nile" (p. 45). But only two significant economic observations are made. First "the absolute chaos of business life. In every shop several price rates prevail" (p. 44), a state of affairs to be remedied by regulation (p. 80). Second, in his Appendix he points out that Egyptians are gravely overtaxed, and the country is consequently declining (p. 80). Clearly, economics was not one of Mustafa Ali's main concerns.

In the seventeenth century, Koçu Bey, writing in 1630, and Katib Çelebi, around 1653, showed no greater understanding of economic matters, and the historian Naima took very little interest in them. Nor did the Egyptian historian al-Jabarti, until the Napoleonic invasion turned his world upside down.[47]

Passing on to statistics, one is struck by the low degree of numeracy of the Ottomans, as of their predecessors. It is not merely that their often good mathematicians took no interest in statistical theory or application but that their writers so seldom used numbers.[48] The wide range of figures which enabled Gregory King to estimate the national income, and which are so frequently used by Adam Smith to illustrate a point, were simply not available in the Middle East. As far as I am aware, no one bothered to look into the abundant data in the *defters*, add up the figures and use them. I should be surprised to learn that any Ottoman statesman knew the approximate population of the empire, much less its production of wheat or its shipping—though it is possible that a discovery in the archives will prove me completely wrong. Of course they knew the number of soldiers, and the tax and other revenues, and when necessary checked the available figures. Thus in 931 A.H (1524/25) "detailed lists were prepared . . . that compare the populations of each wage-receiving/[military] unit in 917 . . . in 926 . . . and in 931." This was prepared for the "Head Measurer who had been brought from Egypt by Selim I and appointed to work at the Treasury because of his mathematical skills."[49]

ECONOMIC POLICY

One should start with a significant fact: the Ottoman rulers lived within their means to a much greater degree than most of the European states, and bankruptcies—such as those of the Hapsburgs—were unknown. It is also possible that, in the sixteenth to eighteenth centuries, the Ottoman taxes were much lighter than European. If the figures given by Stratford Canning in 1809 are to be trusted, the amount reaching the government was only ḥ2,250,000 (much more must have been collected), compared to ḥ17 million in Great Britain and ḥ24 million in France.[50]

At this point a quotation from David MacPherson, writing in 1805, is apt: "No judicious commercial regulations could be drawn up by ecclesiastical or military men (the only classes who possessed any authority or influence) who despised trade and consequently could know nothing of it."[51] MacPherson had medieval European governments in mind, but his judgment applies even more to Middle Eastern governments.

In these, the dominant elements were bureaucrats and soldiers, whose interest in economic matters was limited to taxation and provisioning. Taxes supplied the revenues needed to defray the expenses of the court, the army, and the bureaucracy, and it is not surprising that almost the only statistics available in Arabic and Turkish writings are army lists and tax returns. Provisioning applied to the cities, whose inhabitants could be troublesome in times of shortage. Hence, elaborate measures were taken to ensure adequate supplies of grain and other necessities to the capital and large towns, and when goods were scarce maximum prices were often imposed.[52]

Of course, the rulers realized that a minimum of order and justice was necessary if the peasants were to produce the surplus on which they drew, and exhortations to apply both were frequent. But that seems to have been the sum total of interest in economic development. To quote Şerif Mardin:

> A shorthand notation for the Ottoman state may be "the fiscal state": by this is meant a state where major economic policy consisted in trying to maximize the tax yield from the rural economy. . . . But the attractiveness of grain culture [following the increased European demand for cereals] did not lead the Ottoman notables very far. The state had not engaged in the draining of marshes, the building of roads, the improvement of highways, the establishment of a postal system, and the dissemination of primary and secondary education as it had done in the West; it had not undergone a "mercantilist" phase of the Western European type; it did not have a "cameralist" phase with its economic engineering.[53]

Or, in Halil Inalcik's words: "The benefits of the state treasury and the needs of the internal market seem to be the only concerns of the Ottoman government."[54]

A few striking contrasts may be noted. Like Europe, but with a lag, the Ottoman Empire participated in the Price Revolution, and its currency suffered accordingly. But whereas the main European currencies were soon stabilized and experienced little or no depreciation thereafter, the Ottoman *akçe* showed a great, almost uninterrupted, decline beginning in the fifteenth century, well before the influx of American bullion, and continuing until the middle of the nineteenth century.[55] Stability was achieved in Europe not fortuitously but through the arduous efforts of the governments, as the history of Elizabeth's reign clearly shows, whereas in the Ottoman Empire (and Iran) the currency was continually debased. It should be added that, until the end of the seventeenth century, the power and resources of the Ottoman Empire were greater than those of any European country except perhaps Spain and France, which presumably implies that it had the means, but not the will or skill, to reform its currency.

We can also contrast attitudes to trade. Of course, the Middle Eastern rulers realized the importance of foreign trade, if only as a source of customs duties, and took some measures to stimulate it: for example, the building of caravanserais, upkeep of a few strategic roads and privileges granted to European merchants.[56] But whereas the Europeans thought of trade as a means of increasing national wealth and employment, as well as holdings of bullion, and took what they thought to be appropriate measures, the Ottomans were concerned only with revenues and supplies; duties on exports were as high as those on imports and the exporting of certain goods was prohibited. This is often attributed to the Capitulations, and was no doubt perpetuated by them until the very eve of the First World War, in spite of the Ottoman desire to change the tariff.[57] The original policies, however, were adopted by the Ottomans at the height of their power, of their own free will. Clearly, these policies must either have been regarded as favorable to the interests of the empire or, if not, the economic consequences must have weighed little against the political advantages sought. Besides, as Halil Inalcik pointed out, in the sixteenth century the Capitulations were "very beneficial for the Ottoman economy" since they attracted trade.[58]

Indeed, I have not come across a single reference to such general concepts as "exports," "imports" and "balance of trade" in either Arabic or Turkish sources before the nineteenth century. I have asked several scholars who have worked in the Ottoman archives, both central and provincial, whether they had ever seen such concepts used, and have not yet had a positive answer. However, the argument from silence should not be pressed too far. Inalcik quotes a passage from Naima, written early in the eithteenth century, which states: "People in this country must abstain from the use of luxury goods of the countries hostile to the Ottoman empire and thus keep currency and goods from flowing out. They must use as much as possible the products of native industry."[59] And Berkes states: "It was also recognized that the financial well-being of the country depended upon a favorable balance of trade, and, as the main source of commerce was seaborne, it was believed necessary to create a Turkish merchant marine."[60] In practice, however, the government made no attempt to protect shipping by the kind of Navigation Acts prevalent in Europe.

One last point may be noted: the difference in the attitude toward industrialization in the Ottoman Empire and Europe. In the latter, because of the relatively greater economic and political power of the traders and craftsmen, there was much consideration for the interests of producers, often at the expense of consumers. In the Italian, German, Flemish, and Dutch city-states, traders and craftsmen were in fact the predominant power, and shaped economic policy to suit their interests. Again to quote Cipolla:

> In the majority of cases there was a conscious effort to industrialize. At the beginning of the fourteenth century the conviction was widespread that industry spelled welfare. In a Tuscan statute of 1336, statements may be read which might have been written by the most modern upholders of industrialization in the twentieth century.[61]

But even such national monarchies as England and France also took commercial and industrial needs into account. By the fourteenth century both England and France were enforcing measures designed to secure a favorable balance of trade by curtailing the import of competitive goods and encouraging that of inputs into goods that could supply local needs or be exported; by expanding exports, especially those with a large "value added" component, for example, cloth rather than raw wool; and, more generally, by stimulating local production. By the seventeenth century a full-fledged mercantilist theory had developed and, in the 1660s, Sir William Petty was expressing a very "modern" concern with production and employment as the basis of national prosperity. Such views had a marked effect on government policy.

In the Ottoman Empire, however, I have not come across anything other than a few attempts in the 18th century, mentioned by Mehmed Genç.[62]

What was the Ottoman legacy in economic thought and policy to the Arabs? First of all, there was the profound lack of interest in economic matters. This can be seen by looking at any history of Arab (or Turkish) thought, e.g., the books by Albert Hourani, Raif Khuri, Niyazi Berkes, or Ahmet Sayar: the thinkers they studied were not interested in economics.

Starting in the 1830s, however, a certain concern with economic matters, and a realization of their importance, may be discerned in such Ottoman statesmen and thinkers as Sadik Rifaat, Sami, Cevdet, Mustafa Fazil (grandson of Mehmet Ali of Egypt), Khayr al-Din of Tunisia, and especially Namik Kemal, who during his stay in London imbibed Ricardian and Millsian principles. Their main emphasis was on the need for the state both to assure its subjects that they would enjoy the fruits of their labor and to remove various restrictions on their activity.

The translation of J. B. Say's *Catéchisme d'économie Politique* in 1852 and a book by Otto Hübner in 1869 constitute landmarks in modern Turkish thought. Say advocated Smithian liberalism and Hübner "national economy." Another landmark was the publication of Ahmed Midhat's *Ekonomi Politik* in 1286 (1869/70), which tried to take Ottoman conditions into account in expounding European principles of economics. Ohannes Effendi, who had studied in Paris and was to occupy many high posts, taught economics at the Mülkiye school and wrote a widely used textbook *Mebadi-i Ilm-i servet-i Millel* (1297–1879/80). Another source of economic knowledge was the *Journal des Economistes*, to which many Ottomans subscribed. In 1911 Parvus (Alexander Helphand) came to Turkey, diffusing Marxist and anti-imperialist ideas, and shortly after Tekin Alp (M. Cohen) wrote on economic matters in *Yeni Macmua*.[63]

Under the Young Turks, both before and during the First World War, many measures were taken to promote the economy and encourage the emergence of a national bourgeoisie, and many economic issues were debated. It was not, however, until the 1930s that the Turks had any adequately trained economists such as Ömer Celal Sarç. The same was true of the Arabs, with Muhammad Ali Rifat and Nazmy Abd al-Hamid in Egypt or Sa'id Himadeh in Lebanon, or statisticians such as Hamed al-Azmy and R. al-Shannawany. The situation has, of course, greatly improved since then.

Second, there was a profound distrust of spontaneous economic activity and of market forces. It was almost axiomatic that if a man is making a profit he must be exploiting his workers, or the public, or both. Hence the need for constant regulation of prices, wages, interest rates, and rent. This represents a Muslim tradition that goes back to the early Middle Ages.[64]

Third, was the ideas that the government should constantly be intervening in the economy, since it alone knows, and can implement, the public interest. Needless to say, this tendency has been greatly reinforced by European socialism and expressed itself in the wholesale, and on the whole disastrous, nationalizations of the 1960s in the Arab lands.

Last was a fiscalism that is only just being overcome—a preoccupation with government revenue, even at the cost of economic development.

In the fields of science, technology, and economics, the main Ottoman (and Mamluk) legacy in the Middle East was that, for over three centuries, the region was not prepared to learn from neighboring Europe. This meant that it did not enter the mainstream of progress in science and technology and it participated only marginally, and as a periphery, in Europe's economic activity and not at all in the development of its economic thought. In the last two hundred years the Middle East has made strenuous efforts to overcome the ensuing handicap, but it has done so under the unfavorable conditions resulting from European imperialism and the breakdown of the Ottoman Empire, and its success has been limited.

Three further observations are, however, necessary. First, it would be wrong to blame the Ottoman rulers for their indifference to science and economic activity, for that would be profoundly unhistorical. Like all peoples at all times, they had their priorities, which were not ours. Still, it would also be unreasonable to ignore the consequences of these priorities.

Second, if we accept the venerable (if historically inaccurate) European definition of the Ottomans as Turks and blend that in with the present-day (accurate) understanding of what is meant by Turk, then we can say that the Turks, rulers and subjects, did not exempt themselves from the burdens borne by the subject peoples. On the contrary, in addition to sharing in those ills they suffered disproportionately from another one, the burden of military service, which fell heavily on them.

Third, during the last hundred years or so, the Turks (as defined above) have played a leading progressive role in the region. As Bernard Lewis points out in his contribution, much of the modern political thought of the Middle East (including Iran) originated in Ottoman official circles, and the Ottoman Turkish language was the route through which political concepts came to the Arabs. In the eighteenth century they had acquired a much fuller understanding of Western science and technology than their Asian fellow subjects—though not than their Greek and other Balkan ones.

But with the advent of Muhammad Ali, Egypt became the bellwether of the Middle East, the first country to lay down railways, build modern ports and irrigation works, send students to Europe, open Western-type schools, establish financial institutions, and achieve rapid economic growth. By the turn of the century, however, leadership passed back to Istanbul, and has remained in the region that became Turkey. Many of the policies advocated by the Young Turks, especially the promotion of national as distinct from foreign enterprise and increasing state control over the economy, were emulated by the Arabs and Iranians, and most of Atatürk's reforms were imitated by both those peoples.

In many respects, the Arab countries and Iran followed, one generation behind, in the footsteps of Turkey. Thus the policies of the 1950s and '60s in the Arab lands recall those of Turkey in the 1920s and '30s. One can only hope that Turkey's new political and economic trend will prove sufficiently successful to exert a similar effect on her Asian neighbors.[65]

NOTES

1. For a fuller discussion, see Charles Issawi, "Reflections on the Study of Oriental Civilizations" in Wm. Theodore de Bary and Ainslie Embree, *Approaches to Asian Civilization* (New York: Columbia University Press, 1964), reprinted in Charles Issawi, *The Arab Legacy* (Princeton: Princeton University Press, 1981), pp. 147–56.

2. At the same time I am fully aware that religion is perhaps the most important single factor affecting the popular culture of a society, see Charles Issawi, "Empire Builders, Culture Makers, and Culture Imprinters," *Journal of Interdisciplinary History* 20, no. 2 (Autumn 1989):177–96.

3. See Charles Issawi, "The Middle East in the World Context," in Georges Sabagh, *The Modern Economic and Social History of the Middle East in Its World Context* (New York: Cambridge: Cambridge University Press, 1989), pp. 3–28.

4. See Charles Issawi, *An Economic History of the Middle East and North Africa* (New York: Columbia University Press, 1982).

5. See Ahmad Yusuf al-Hassan and Donald R. Hill, *Islamic Technology* (Cambridge: Cambridge University Press, 1986), pp. 16–17, 49, 59.

6. Edited and translated by Sevim Tekeli, *The Clocks in Ottoman Empire in 16th Century* (Ankara, 1966).

7. Abdulhak Adnan, *La Science chez les Turcs Ottomans* (Paris, 1939); Bernard Lewis, *The Muslim Discovery of Europe* (New York: Norton, 1982), pp. 227–28; Aydin Sayili, *The Observatory in Islam* (New York: Ayer, 1981).

8. I have been informed by Dr. Rushdi Rashed of the C.N.R.S. that certain 18th-century Egyptian manuscripts indicate an understanding of some aspects of European science, but to my knowledge no study has been made of these manuscripts.

9. UNESCO, *Statistical Yearbook 1989*, table 5.2.

10. E. Ashtor, *A Social and Economic History of the Near East in the Middle Ages* (Berkeley and Los Angeles: University of California Press, 1976), p. 50; O. G. Bolshakov, *Srednevekovyi Gorod Blizhnego Vostoka*, (Moscow, 1984), pp. 234–35.

11. B. H. Slicher van Bath, *Yield Ratios, 810–1820* (Wageningen, 1963) passim; Charles Issawi, *Economic History of Turkey* (Chicago: University of Chicago Press, 1980), pp. 214–25; Issawi, *The Fertile Crescent, 1800–1914* (New York: Oxford: Oxford University Press, 1988), p. 273; Issawi, *The Economic History of the Middle East* (Chicago: University of Chicago Press, 1966), p. 377.

12. For the effects of Ottoman land laws in the Arab countries, see Gabriel Baer, "The Evolution of Private Landownership in Egypt and the Fertile Crescent," and Doreen Warriner, "Land Tenure in the Fertile Crescent," in Issawi, *Economic History of the Middle East*, pp. 71–90; Caglar Keyder and Faruk Tabak, *Landholding and Commercial Agriculture in the Middle East* (Albany: State University of New York Press, 1991).

13. Domenico Sella, "European Industries," in Carlo Cipolla, ed, *Fontana Economic History of Europe*, 2:395; John U. Nef in *Cambridge Economic History of Europe* (Cambridge: Cambridge University Press, 1952), 2:458–69; H. Kellenbenz, *Cambridge Economic History*, 4:472–475.

14. B. Lewis, *Muslim Discovery of Europe*, p. 225.

15. Thomas Thornton, *The Present State of Turkey* (London, 1807), p. 24.

16. See Issawi, *Economic History of Turkey*, p. 284. For other equally unfavorable opinions, see pp. 281–88.

17. B. Lewis, *Muslim Discovery of Europe*, pp. 225–26.

18. V. Parry, "La Manière de combattre," in V. Parry and M. E. Yapp, *War, Technology, and Society in the Middle East* (New York: Oxford: Oxford University Press, 1975), p. 246.

19. See Charles Issawi, "Population and Resources," in Thomas Naff and Roger Owen, eds., *Studies in Eighteenth-Century Islamic History* (Carbondale: Southern Illinois University Press, 1977), pp. 160–161.

20. Dispatch from Carmarthen, March 155, 1789, PRO FO 78/10.

21. E. Ashtor, "L'apogée du commerce vénitien," *Venezia centro di Mediazione*, vol. 1 (Florence, 1977), pp. 318–21.

22. For details, see Issawi, *The Arab Legacy*, pp. 93–96; Issawi, *An Economic History of the Middle East and North Africa*, pp. 150–154, and sources cited.

23. See Issawi, *Economic History of Turkey*, pp. 314–15; Johannes Pederson, *The Arabic Book* (Princeton: Princeton University Press, 1984), pp. 60–67. For the Byzantines, see N. G. Wilson, *Scholars of Byzantium* (Baltimore: Johns Hopkins University Press, 1983), pp. 63–65.

24. Pederson, pp. 132–37; Şerif Mardin, "Some Notes on an Early Phase in the Modernization of Turkey," *Comparative Studies in Society and History* 3:3 (April 1961).

25. See Charles Issawi, "Technology, Energy, and Civilization," *IJMES* (August 1991) and Jean Gimpel, *The Medieval Machine* (New York: Penguin, 1976).

26. Ashtor, *Social and Economic History*, p. 308; Abd al-Rahman al-Jabarti, *'ajaib al athar*, vol 2 (Beirut, 1978), p. 231; S. Avitsur, "Wind Power in the Technological Development of Palestine," in David Kushner, ed., *Palestine in the Late Ottoman Period* (Jerusalem-Leiden: E. J. Brill, 1986), pp. 231–44; in the 10th century, al-Mas'udi discussed windmills, see Max Meyerhoff, "Science and Medicine" in Sir Thomas Arnold and Alfred Guillaume, eds., *The Legacy of Islam* (London, 1931), p. 333.

27. In this section I have drawn on my "Europe, the Middle East, and the Shift in Power," *Arab Legacy*, pp. 111–31.

28. See A. L. Udovitch, *Partnership and Profit in Medieval Islam*, (Princeton: Princeton University Press, 1970); Halil Inalcik, "Capital Formation in the Ottoman Empire," *Journal of Economic History* 29:1 (March 1969).

29. For examples, see Inalcik, "Capital Formation in the Ottoman Empire."

30. See sources cited in Issawi, *Economic History of the Middle East and North Africa*, p. 260n10 and Issawi, *Fertile Cresent*, pp. 443–45; also Inalcik, "Capital Formation in the Ottoman Empire."

31. Geoffrey Parker "The Emergence of Modern Finance," in Carlo Cipolla, *Fontana Economic History*, 2:443–45.

32. Issawi, *Economic History of Turkey*, pp. 339–41, 321.

33. R. De Roover, "The Organization of Trade"; M. M. Postan et al., *Cambridge Economic History of Europe*, 3:99–100 and *Encyclopaedia Britannica*, 11th ed. s.v. "Insurance."

34. Issawi, *Economic History of Turkey*, p. 326; Issawi, *Fertile Crescent*, p. 412; for the late Ottoman view of insurance see Niyazi Berkes, *The Development of Secularism in Turkey* (Montreal: McGill University Press, 1964), pp. 398–99.

35. For an excellent survey, see Joseph Schumpeter, *History of Economic Analysis* (New York: Oxford University Press, 1954).

36. For an illuminating example, see Issawi, *Arab Legacy*, pp. 119–20.

37. Schumpeter, *History of Economic Analysis*, p. 14.

38. Ibid., pp. 13–14, 526.

39. See M. A. Nashaat, "Ibn Khaldun, Pioneer Economist," *Egypte Contemporaine* 38 (1944); Charles Issawi, *An Arab Philosophy of History* (London, 1950), introduction, chs. 3 and 4.

40. Cemal Kafadar,"When Coins Turned Into Drops of Dew and Bankers Became Robbers of Shadows: The Boundaries of Ottoman Economic Imagination at the End of the Sixteenth Century," Ph.D. dissertation, McGill University, October 1986; see also Ahmed Sayar, *Osmanli Iktisat Düsüncesinin Cagdas Casmasi* (Istanbul, 1986).

41. Kafadar, pp. 108–9. All Ottoman statesmen and writers took for granted that economic forces and activities should be firmly under the control of the political authorities. In fairness to them, it should be pointed out that for a long time this system worked, i.e., the economy was able to produce the surplus revenue required for administration, war, and the luxury consumption of the rulers. Indeed in the 16th century, except for technological innovation, the Ottoman Empire did not compare unfavorably with Europe—see Charles Issawi's "The Ottoman-Hapsburg Bal-

ance of Forces" in Halil Inalcik and Cemal Kafadar, *Empire and Civilization in the Age of Suley-man* (Istanbul, 1991). It was only very slowly, with the sustained rise of Europe and decline of the Ottoman Empire, that the inadequacy of the economy became apparent, causing an eventual opening up in the 19th century. This presents a striking analogy with the Soviet Union, whose economy "worked" for a long time, producing a large surplus for investment and defense, but eventually was unable to keep up with the West.

42. Cornell H. Fleischer, *Bureaucrat and Intellectual in the Ottoman Empire: The Historian Mustafa Ali (1541–1600)* (Princeton: Princeton University Press, 1986), pp. 4, 8. 235.

43. Andreas Tietze, *Mustafa Ali's Counsel for Sultans Edition, Translation, Notes*, 2 vols. (Vienna: Ver-lag der Oesterreichen Akademie der Wissenchaften, 1979, 1982).

44. For the latter see Schumpeter, *History of Economic Analysis*, and Eric Roll, *A History of Economic Thought* (London, n.d.), ch. 2.

45. *Mustafa Ali's Counsel*, vol. 1, pp. 19, 39, 57, 59–62, 65, 66, 71, 82; vol. 2, pp. 11, 26, 30, 34.

46. Andreas Tietze, *Mustafa Ali's Description of Cairo of 1599* (Vienna: Verlag der Oesterreichischen Akademie der Wissenschaften, 1975).

47. See B. Lewis, "Ottoman Observers of Ottoman Decline," *Islam in History* (New York, 1973), pp. 199–213; Issawi, *Arab Legacy*, pp. 117–122.

48. An important exception, pointed out to me by Mr. Rabah Shahbandar, is the Nilometer of Egypt, which goes back to antiquity. The height of the Nile is often mentioned by historians. Presumably, knowing the exact height of the Nile on which crops—and therefore taxes—depended was too important a matter to be left to approximation.

49. Inalcik and Kafadar, *Empire and Civilization in the Age of Suleyman*, pp. 58–59.

50. See Issawi, "Population and Resources," *Economic History of Turkey*, pp. 389.

51. Quoted in the *Cambridge Economic History of Europe*, 3:281.

52. For 18th- and early 19th-century Istanbul, see Issawi, *Economic History of Turkey*, pp. 24–33, which includes a translation of an article by Lütfi Gücer on grain supply; see also the very infor-mative article by W. Hahn, "Die Verpflegung Konstantinopels durch staatliche Zwangswirtschaft," *Beihefte zur Vierteljahrschrift für Sozial und Wirtschaftsgeschichte* 7 (1926). For the 16th century, Rhoades Murphey, "Provisioning Istanbul: The State and Subsistence in the Early Middle East," *Food and Foodways*, vol 2 (London, 1988).

53. Şerif Mardin, "The Transformation of an Economic Code," in Ergun Ozbudun and Aydin Ulu-san, eds., *The Political Economy of Income Distribution in Turkey* (New York: Holmes and Meier, 1980), p. 29.

54. Halil Inalcik, "The Ottoman Economic Mind," in Michael Cook, ed., *Studies in the Economic History of the Middle East* (New York: Oxford: Oxford University Press, 1970), p. 212.

55. See graph in *Cambridge Economic History of Europe*, 4:458; O. L. Barkan, "The Price Revolution of the Sixteenth Century," *IJMES*, 1975; Issawi, *The Economic History of Turkey*, ch. 7. For an excellent and analytic account of the debasement of the Ottoman currency, see Inalcik and Kafadar, *Empire and Civilization in the Age of Suleyman*, ch. 1; it is worth noting that the late-16th-century historian Selaniki contrasted unfavorably Ottoman monetary policy with that of contemporary Europe (pp. 100–101).

56. Halil Inalcik, *The Ottoman Empire in the Classical Age* (London: Caratzas, 1973), pp. 121–66; Inalcik, "Capital Formation in the Ottoman Empire"; Carl M. Kortepeter, "Ottoman Imperial Policy and the Economy of the Black Sea Region in the Sixteenth Century," *Journal of the Amer-ican Oriental Society* 86, no. 2 (April–June 1966).

57. Issawi, *The Economic History of Turkey*, ch. 3.

58. Inalcik, "The Ottoman Economic Mind," pp. 214–15.

59. Ibid., p. 215.

60. Berkes, *Development of Secularism in Turkey*, p. 74.

61. *Cambridge Economic History of Europe*, 3:413 and, more generally, pp. 408–19.

62. *La Révolution industrielle dans le Sud-Est europeén* (Sofia, 1976).

63. See Şerif Mardin, *The Genesis of Young Ottoman Thought* (Princeton: Princeton University Press, 1962); Mardin, "Türkiyede Iktisadi Düsüncenin Gelismesi" (Ankara, 1962); and Ahmet Sayar, *Osmanli iktisat.* I am indebted to Nilüfer Hatimi, a graduate student at Princeton, for help in reading these books.

64. See Inalcik, "Capital Formation." The opinion of Jurji Zaydan may also be quoted: "Trade is the most important source of income in our country. Yet is part of the popular phantasies that wealth is not (to be) attained in a legitimate, *halal* manner," Thomas Philipp, *Gurgi Zaydan* (Beirut 1979), pp. 14–15.

65. Since this paper was written two important articles have appeared: Cemal Kafadar, "Les troubles monetaire de la fin du XVIe siecle et la prise de conscience ottomane du declin," *Annales, ESC* (March–April 1991), an excellent account of the Ottoman price inflation that develops further some of the points made in his thesis (see note 40); and Virginia H. Aksan, "Ottoman Political Writing, 1768–1808," *International Journal of Middle East Studies* 25:1 (February 1993):55–69, which has valuable informatin, particularly regarding the views of Ahmed Resmi and Koca Sekbanbasi on military reform. Neither article, however, requires modification of the general interpretation presented here.

CHAPTER FOURTEEN

THE MILITARY LEGACY

Dankwart A. Rustow

Warfare was central to both the Ottomans' rise (1290–1683) and decline (1768–1918). As the westernmost of the Turkish warrior principalities emerging from the collapse of the Seljuk realm in Anatolia, they soon found an inviting arena for expansion in the decaying Byzantine Empire. The political organization consolidated by Mehmed II (1451–1483) after his conquest of Istanbul (Constantinople) was first and foremost a military establishment designed to assure the continual outward expansion of Ottoman-Muslim rule and to support that effort by levying taxes and maintaining internal peace.

The empire's soldier-administrators were inducted into the sultan's service through wide recruitment, intense professional training, and merit promotion—a system far more effective than that of any of its European rivals at the time. Specifically, the Ottoman conscription system, known as *devşirme*, brought to the sultans' palace school in Istanbul a steady flow of young Balkan peasants who, by promotion within the elite janissary corps, could rise from subject to ruler status. Other recruits were Muslim migrants from the Caucasus or migrant-converts from Christian Europe.

The centrality of warfare in Ottoman history is confirmed by an important set of calculations in historical statistics. From 1450 to 1900, the sultan's realm was at war 61 percent of the time, a proportion exceeded, among European powers, only by Spain (66 percent); indeed for their expansionist period (1450–1700), the Ottomans hold the record with an average of eighty-five years of war per century.[1]

Top: Members of the Janissary Corps. J. M. Jouannin and Jules Van Gaver, *Turquie, Series L'Univers: Historie et Description de touss les Peuples* (Paris: Firmin Didot Freres, 1840). *Bottom:* 1st Infantry, Imperial Guards, late nineteenth century *Imperial Self-Portrait: The Ottoman Empire as Revealed in the Sultan Abdul Hamid II's Photographic Albums,* ed. Carney E. S. Gavin and the Harvard Semitic Museum, vol. 12 of *Journal of Turkish Studies* (1988).

Right: Troops of the Republic of Turkey on Parade. Photo by Joseph Szyliowicz.

Nonetheless, it is important not to take this military aspect of the Ottoman legacy out of context—particularly since Western historians all too often still rely on the memory of the Christian side in its warlike encounter with the Muslim Ottomans, and on distorted accounts of "the terrible Turk" and of "Armenian massacres" in the final, and often desperate, days of Ottoman decline.

Geography was a crucial feature in shaping the Ottoman military and political traditions. The "Middle East" is truly in the *middle.* Itself sparsely populated, it is at the very hub of the inhabited globe, linking three of the world's five continents and being intersected by branches of two of its three oceans. Throughout history, the Middle East has thus become the recurrent scene for rivalries among major outside powers or the arena for warfare among them. The region became crucial to the world-conquering ambitions of Alexander, Caesar, Hulagu, Tamerlane, and Napoleon; Russia's quest for warm-water ports, Germany's *Drang nach Osten* and the Italian claim to *mare nostro,* Britain's "imperial lifeline" to India and America's anti-Soviet strategy of containment.

Aside from some lush coastlines and river valleys (and with the notable exception of the twentieth-century discovery of petroleum), the Middle East has always been poor in agricultural and mineral resources. Nonetheless, its globally central location—and safe navigation through such waters as the Mediterranean (the sea "in the midst of lands") and the Red Sea—also have made the region a crossroads of long-distance trade since prehistoric times. That position, to be sure, declined as a result of the European circumnavigation of the Cape and discovery of the "new world"; yet it was partly restored by the opening of the Suez Canal in 1869, and more recently by the global rise of petroleum trade.

Given the region's importance for the worldly fortunes of commerce and the worldly misfortunes of war, it was perhaps natural that the Middle East should also come to embody mankind's otherworldly aspirations by giving birth to three great scriptural religions. Among these, Islam bestowed on the Middle East its longest period of regional peace and political unity, first under the Umayyad and Abbasid caliphs, and then under the Ottoman sultans.

The close links among commerce, warfare, and religion are strikingly personified in Muhammad himself, who became, by turns, a successful merchant, the recipient of God's "final" revelation, and "commander of the faithful" as they set out to expand the "House of Islam" at the expense of the "House of War."

Holy wars, crusades, and other religious enmities thus have been superimposed on geopolitical conflict and commercial rivalry in making the Middle East one of the most intense arenas of warfare throughout human history. The present essay will focus on the significance of war in the later, Ottoman phase of Middle Eastern history, and reflect on its historic legacy for the post-Ottoman Middle East.

The Ottoman Empire: War on the Frontiers, Tolerance Within

Warfare had been endemic throughout the Middle East and southeastern Europe well before the arrival of the Ottomans. Indeed, it had reached new levels of intensity with the Christian crusades from the West and successive Mongol and Tatar invasions from the East. Nomadic and other mercenary warriors were freely available to Seljuk, Byzantine, and Balkan rulers as well as to princes disputing dynastic succession. What the Ottomans brought was a more purposeful military organization that tended to draw to their ranks more of the available soldiery eager for pay or booty and a patient, long-term strategy that managed to benefit from the quarrels of others.

Before long, the more opportunistic of those quarreling princes found it useful to ally themselves with the sultans' victorious armies, and the commercial and agricultural classes among the subject populations came to prefer the stabler Ottoman form of government in an expanding and prosperous realm to the chaotic pattern of warfare of preceding generations.[2] The reason for this preference was simple. The Ottoman Empire, belligerent at its frontiers, was, by the standards of the times, remarkably peaceful within those widening borders. At its zenith in the seventeenth century, the empire stretched from Algiers in the west to the Caucasus in the east, and from Hungary in the north to Aden in the south—the largest, most durable, and most tolerant realm that the Mediterranean and Middle Eastern regions had seen since the fall of the Roman Empire.

Although it was known to Europeans as the "Turkish Empire," it is more properly designated as the *Ottoman* Empire. Indeed, its official name was *Devlet-i 'Aliye* or *Devlet-i 'Aliye-i 'Osmaniye*, or "High (Ottoman) State"— "Ottoman" being an Italian mispronunciation of 'Osman (or 'Uthman), the founder of the imperial dynasty. The Ottoman ruling class of Istanbul, of mixed Balkan, Caucasian, Turkish, and other descent, spoke a composite language, combining basic rules of Turkish grammar and syntax with a plethora of Arabic and Persian vocabulary—the phrase *Devlet-i 'Aliye-i 'Osmaniye*, for instance, consisting of three Arabic words linked by two Persian connectives.

The military-administrative establishment of the empire, headed by the grand vizier and the sultan-caliph himself, thus was centralized, comprehensive, and assimilationist. It was recruited from all parts of the imperial realm and beyond; but the higher its members rose on the social scale, the more they shed their ethnic antecedents to merge into the Islamic-Ottoman polyglot culture of Istanbul. There the viziers and pashas, the beys and effendis[3] prayed in Arabic (in mosques blending Middle Eastern and Byzantine architectural motifs), and enjoyed poetry modeled on the Persian classics from Firdawsi to Hafiz. They smoked tobacco and ate maize first imported from the Americas. They also eagerly adopted European fashions such as rococo architecture, a form of Italian headgear imported via Morocco and soon to be known as the "fez," and the planting of tulips imported from Holland—giving rise to an eighteenth-century Ottoman literary period known as the "Tulip Era."

In the parlance of this Ottoman upper class, the word "Turk" had long since become a condescending epithet for the illiterate peasantry of Anatolia. And those Turkish-speaking regions, of course, were only a small portion of the empire's total population, in which Arabs, Kurds, Armenians, Circassians, Greeks, Bulgarians, Albanians, Serbo-Croats, Hungarians, Romanians, and many other nationalities could live for centuries retaining their own traditional languages, customs, and religious practices.

The empire's judicial-religious establishments emphasized this diversity. Since the law of Islam, based on Quranic revelation and exegesis, applied, on its own terms, only to the Muslim believers, it was assumed that other "peoples of the book" (that is, Christians and Jews) would live by the law of their respective earlier revelations. The result was the so-called millet system of religious autonomy, the Muslim ulama (with their hierarchy of muftis and qadis culminating in the Grand Mufti or sheikh al-Islam in Istanbul) being drawn mainly from the Anatolian and Arab provinces; and Greek and Armenian Christians and Jews having their corresponding clerical establishments headed by a patriarch or grand rabbi also resident in Istanbul.

Considering that Christians or Jews could not serve in the Ottoman armed forces or the military government of the provinces, members of the non-Muslim millets were, in one sense, second-class subjects. Yet the overall socioeconomic structure of the Ottoman Empire was one of ethnic division of labor: Muslims furnished the military-administrative elite at one end of the social spectrum and most of the peasants and nomads in the empire's Asian and African portions at the other; and Christians (notably Greeks, Lebanese, Armenians, and Egyptian Copts), as well as Jews, dominated the Ottoman world of commerce, crafts, and industry—with the millet system guaranteeing the autonomy and imperial loyalty of each major group. Whereas each religious and nationality group was left to practice its own customs and beliefs, all of them benefited from the political stability and economic prosperity of an expanding realm. In addition, Christian and Jewish merchants in the Balkans were integrated into the system of frontier warfare as part of the advancing armies' supply lines.

This entire pattern of institutionalized linguistic and religious tolerance, ethnic division of labor, and denominational autonomy contrasted sharply with the organized persecution of non-Christians or Christians of other denominations throughout medieval and early-modern Europe—with its internecine Albigensian, Hussite, and Protestant-Catholic wars; and its expulsion or forced conversion of Spanish Jews and Muslims.

Indeed the Ottomans vastly benefited from this contrast. One specific instance was the voluntary conversion to Islam of the Bogomils. They had been a dissident Christian sect who, after the Ottomans' first withdrawal from the Balkans, had suffered a bitter persecution by both Roman Catholics and Greek Orthodox Christians. Thus the Bogomils welcomed the Ottoman reconquest of their region early in the fifteenth century, and provided the sultans with a solid Muslim population on their Balkan frontier in Bosnia. Another instance was the persecution of Jews in Spain after 1492, which prompted Sultan Beyazid II (1481–1512) to invite them to his empire, where they helped repopulate the newly conquered capital of Istanbul and transformed Salonika into a thriving center of trade.

The role of individual converts from Christian countries was equally notable. In 1727, a Hungarian Unitarian, who had become a refugee from the persecution of the Counterreformation, established the first Ottoman printing press. In the next decade a French adventurer, Comte de Bonneval, known after his conversion as "Humbaraci" (or Bombardier) Ahmed Pasha, thoroughly reformed the sultan's artillery corps.[4] The early Ottoman foreign service was based on the "Translation Office" at the Sublime Porte, staffed mainly with Orthodox Greeks. Following the suppression of the Polish and Hungarian revolutions in 1848, some of their surviving leaders rose to prominent positions in the sultan's service.

The contrast between Ottoman reality and European perception was strikingly illustrated at the Congress of Berlin in 1878, the first major meeting of European powers to which an Ottoman delegation was invited. Prince Otto von Bismarck, head of the German host government, had earlier shared the habit of his European contemporaries of thinking of the Ottomans as "Turks," Asiatic, Muslim, and backward. Now he was surprised to find the sultan's delegation headed by Karatodori Pasha, an Orthodox Greek from the Translation Bureau; and Mehmed Ali Pasha, Ottoman commander in the recent war against Russia—and a native of Magdeburg, not far from Bismarck's own family estate of Schönhausen.[5]

Europe, as it emerged from the Middle Ages, had quickly dissolved into a welter of kingdoms and principalities whose energies were largely absorbed in religious and dynastic wars. By contrast, the Ottomans consolidated their rule by unifying a thriving region around the Mediterranean and throughout the Middle East, and the wealth of the older provinces proved more than adequate to support Ottoman military expansion into the feuding European territories. Indeed, the Ottomans' military expansion soon became a cumulative and accelerating process: the richer the outlying provinces in a given round of conquest, the greater the disarray of their defeated Christian-European enemies, and the more plentiful the economic and manpower resources available to the Ottomans for the following round of military expansion.

Defensive Modernization and Imperial Defeat

Before long, however, the Ottomans' very successes generated a number of unexpected, dialectic side effects. The farther the Ottoman armies expanded the frontiers of the realm, the more they had to stretch their supply lines, and the more difficult the sultans and viziers found it to control the details of military campaigns from distant Istanbul. Their unprecedented control over the trade routes between Europe and Asia added to the Ottomans' revenues but also encouraged their European rivals to explore alternate routes around Africa—and, as it turned out, to the even richer "new world" of the Americas.

Soon, moreover, Europe's new commercial wealth and the intense rivalry among its commercial centers and princely states encouraged a spirit of technical innovation that crucially strengthened their military efforts. A striking illustration was the telescope. Galileo had been teaching at the university of Padua in the Republic of Venice when he first learned of the Dutch invention.

The year was 1608, and the gigantic naval battle of Lepanto (1571) in which the Venetians had destroyed the Ottoman fleet was still a vivid memory. No one could tell how soon the sultan might assemble a new fleet to reclaim his former supremacy. Therefore, even while applying himself to the dramatic confirmation of the Copernican, heliocentric theory, Galileo took care to present an early specimen of his new gadget to the Senate of Venice. He obtained a doubling of his academic salary by demonstrating to the city fathers how his new "spy glass" with its ninefold magnification would enable them to spot "sails and shipping that was so far off that it was two hours before they would be seen with the naked eye, steering full-sail into the harbor."[6]

Europe's intellectual ferment in the Renaissance and Reformation, moreover, was soon followed by a decisive political transformation. To the East, warfare against the Ottomans was carried forward by the expanding Hapsburg and tsarist realms based, much like the Ottoman Empire, on multiethnic coexistence. But in central and western Europe the ravages of the Thirty Years War (1618–48) forced emperor and pope to give up the pursuit of earlier claims to universal dominion; and instead induced the kings, princes, and republics henceforth to respect each other's choice of Catholic, Lutheran, or Calvinist Christianity—on the principle of *cuius regio, eius religio*. Before long, most of those countries were consolidated into nation-states with a centralized administration and higher education, a common language, and a collective consciousness.

One notable feature of the new nationalism was the innovation of military conscription (France 1792, Prussia 1809, etc.), which vastly increased the scale of military manpower, left the sultans' armies outnumbered, and thus further tipped the military balance against the Ottomans.

Much as the early Ottoman conquests had acquired a cumulative momentum, so did their defeats. Since the sultan's armies lived mainly from requisitioning in the areas behind the front, an even temporary military retreat tended to weaken the very regions that would have to be defended in the next round. In 1571, the Ottoman fleet had proved unequal to the Venetians' skill in shipbuilding and navigation. In 1683, improved European artillery broke the Ottomans' second siege of Vienna. By 1783, the Russian tsars completed their conquest of the Ukraine and the Crimea. In 1798 Napoleon Bonaparte led the conscript armies of the French Revolution to a landing in Egypt—in the very heartland of the Muslim-Ottoman realm. And by the nineteenth century, the sultans were faced with open rebellion by their Christian subjects in the Balkans and even their vassals in Egypt and other Muslim regions.

It is clear in retrospect that the crucial turning point in the Ottomans' military fortunes was the failure of the second siege of Vienna in 1683, followed in 1699 by the loss of Hungary, Transylvania, and even the Peleponese (what today is southern Greece). At the time it was only natural, however, that the rulers in Istanbul should see these as temporary setbacks, due to inept commanders, corrupt administrators, or other misfortunes; and soon to be remedied, perhaps, by a third siege of Vienna. And indeed some of the territories lost in 1683/99 were recaptured in 1718 (Peleponese) and 1739 (Western Wallachia—what today is the southwestern part of Romania).

But other setbacks followed that could no longer be so easily rationalized. Throughout the classical Ottoman period, warfare had been construed as a religious obligation: the aim of jihad was to spread the reign of the true religion to the corners of the earth. Yet in 1783 the tsar's formal annexation of the Muslim-populated Crimean peninsula inverted the previous pattern of Ottoman rule over Christians. Indeed it seemed to put into question the central Islamic tenet that earthly power belongs to God, the Prophet, and the True Believers.

Furthermore, the Peace of Kuchuk Kaynarja (1774) had forced the sultans to accept the claim of the Russian tsars to act as protectors of Christian minorities in the very capital of Istanbul—which presaged a long period of foreign interference in the empire's internal affairs. By contrast, the sultan's counterclaim that as caliph he remained the spiritual overlord of the Muslims in lost areas such as the Crimea had a hollow ring.

Those defeats of the eighteenth century at last prompted the sultans to act on the Roman adage *Fas est ab hoste doceri*:[7] "It is proper to learn from one's enemy." In the following century and a half of defensive warfare (1768–1918), the military became even more central to the empire's political and social structure; for, in addition to their soldierly role, they also became the spearhead of a far-reaching cultural transformation—a process aptly described as "defensive modernization."[8]

Eighteenth-century sultans had called on naval and artillery experts from Europe, some of whom converted to Islam and were absorbed into the traditional Ottoman hierarchy. By the 1840s, Ottoman cadets were sent for training in France, and later all of the Ottoman army's elite training was entrusted to Prussian officers. In World War I, almost every Ottoman army had a German officer either as its commander or chief of staff.

This process of European training initiated a far broader transformation: secularism instead of Islamic tradition as interpreted by the ulama; party politics, constitutionalism, and egalitarianism to challenge the sultan's autocracy; and even literary individualism and representation to replace the traditional esthetic maxims of divan poetry. All these trends are strikingly embodied in the career of Ibrahim Şinasi who, as a young Ottoman lieutenant, was sent to Paris to learn French, mathematics, and the latest arts of artillery; but became infatuated with the writings of Victor Hugo and Alphonse de Lamartine and the political ideas of the liberal revolution of 1848. Upon returning to Istanbul, he left the military to write romantic poetry and edit the first nongovernmental newspaper in Turkish. Indeed, the very title of Şinasi's newspaper, *Tasvir-i Efkâr*, or *Mirror of Thought*, implied a challenge of nascent elite opinion to established authority.

Throughout the nineteenth century, efforts at military reform thus created new difficulties. In 1807/8 provincial armies marched on the capital to depose the reformist Sultan Selim III. In 1826 Mahmud II killed off his janissary elite corps that had been resisting further reform. And in 1876 Şinasi's literary disciple Namik Kemal and others forced the deposition of two sultans and the adoption of the Ottoman Empire's first written parliamentary constitution—only to be arrested and exiled as the third of those sultans, Abdulhamid II, 1878–1908, suspended the new constitution.

The notions of civic equality and military conscription, embraced by mid-nineteenth century sultans to strengthen the empire's defenses and the loyalty of their subjects, turned out to be incompatible with the religious-political separation and symbiotic autonomy of the Ottoman millets. To resolve the dilemma, the European principle of universal military service for able-bodied males was applied only to Muslim subjects, with Christians and Jews given the option of paying a tax equivalent (*bedel*). Yet among the solidly settled Christian minorities, the increasing mobility of the early commercial and industrial revolution produced movements of national secession, encouraged by the victorious European powers, and leading to the independence of Greece (1830); Serbia, Romania (1878); and Bulgaria (1908). And soon that ideological virus came to spread to the Muslim majority itself. Thus, Namik Kemal's play *The Fatherland or Silistria* (1873), glorifying the heroic defense of a frontier fortress in the Ottoman-Russian war of 1856, was banned by authorities for catering to a subversive spirit of patriotism, and its author banished. In sum, the coexistence of a vast variety of nationalities, which had been the Ottomans' pride and strength in their days of glory, thus became an added liability in their days of decline.

The profound dilemma for the Ottoman Empire was that the reforms required to bring their armed forces up to European standards were bound to alienate those newly trained officers from the very traditions they had been expected to defend. Westernizing reforms, moreover, soon spread from the military outward throughout society, acquiring a momentum of their own. The heavy cost of military training and conscription required new taxes and a reformed administration to collect them, and soon new schools were required to train the tax collectors and other administrators—and yet more taxes and personnel to operate those schools. Still, the relentless pressure of defeat, notably in 1828, 1839, 1878, and 1911–13, left sultans and viziers with little effective choice but to accelerate the process of military, administrative, and educational transformation. The only part of the traditional establishment that proved immune to this pattern of Westernizing change remained the Muslim ulama, yet their influence was on a steady decline.

The official terminology for those Ottoman military-administrative reforms readily indicates their broadening scope. The program adopted under Selim III (1789–1807) was called Nizam-i Cedid, or "New Order," with a simple singular noun; that of Abdülmecid (1839–1861) was known as Tanzimat-i Hayriye or "Beneficent Orderings" in the causative plural; and the constitutional reforms of 1908 were forced upon the sultan by a group of rebellious officers calling itself *Ittihad ve Terakki Cem'iyeti* or "Society of Union and Progress."

The difficulties of expanding reforms amidst cumulative military defeats were succinctly summarized by Helmuth von Moltke (1800–1891), who had served in the Ottoman Empire before becoming Bismarck's chief of staff, in commenting on the dilemma facing Sultan Mahmud II (1808–1839): "For the accomplishment of his purpose it was indispensable . . . to raze to the ground any other authority within the compass of the Empire and to unite the whole plenitude of power in his own hand; to clear the site before setting up his own building. The first part of his great task the sultan carried through with perspicacity and resolution; in the second he failed."[9] And Fuad Pasha, an Ottoman mid-nineteenth century statesman, expressed a similar thought with bitter irony in a comment to a European colleague: "Our state is the strongest state. For you are trying to cause its collapse from without, and we from within, but still it does not collapse."[10]

The Legacy to Turkey and to Arab Countries

It was its final defeat in the World War of 1914–18 that permanently broke up the Ottoman Empire. Its Arab-speaking regions in northern Africa had been annexed by European colonial empires in the nineteenth century—Algeria (1830) and Tunisia (1881) by the French; Egypt (1882) and Sudan (1898) by the British; and Libya (1912) by the Italians. The Allied victory of 1918 resulted in an armistice line that detached the remaining Arab regions—also know as the "Fertile Crescent"—parts of which were subsequently assigned to Britain (Palestine, Transjordan, Iraq) and France (Syria, Lebanon). Further military incursions into the 1918 armistice lines by Allied (notably Greek) forces, were repelled by a military-populist resistance movement in what became known as the Turkish War of Independence (1919–22) under the dynamic and circumspect leadership of Mustafa Kemal Pasha (later known as Atatürk). By 1923, the newly proclaimed Republic of Turkey was internationally recognized—whereas the post-Ottoman Arab states attained their full independence only after World War II. While the military were to play a major role in the politics of all those twentieth-century post-Ottoman states, the contrast between Turkey and the Arab successor states is striking.

In the dissolution of the Ottoman Empire, Turkey inherited 93 percent of the empire's military and 85 percent of its administrative establishment,[11] and its War of Independence transformed centuries of imperial defeat into a new experience of nationalist victory. For its first quarter century, the Turkish Republic remained a benevolent one-party dictatorship, with Atatürk upon his death in 1938 succeeded as president by Ismet Inönü, who had been the field commander in the War of Independence, and later his prime minister. By the late 1940s, Inönü launched Turkey on its path toward democracy; and, after the first fully free election of 1950, he yielded the presidency to the victorious Democrat Party and himself assumed the new role of opposition leader.

Turkey's transition to democracy was interrupted by several military interventions, specifically in 1960–61, after the Democrat government with its heavy parliamentary majority had increasingly moved toward authoritarianism; the "coup by memorandum" of 1971; and the military regime of 1980–83, imposed after interminable deadlocks in a divided multiparty parliament and rampant right- and left-wing terrorism in the streets.[12]

Despite such setbacks, Turkey by the early 1990s seems to have moved toward full democracy, making military coups all but inconceivable in the future. Among the crucial landmarks are the victory of Turgut Özal's Motherland Party (1983) over the two parties artificially created by the 1980 junta; the 1987 referendum which readmitted to full political participation all the party leaders ousted and banned from politics by the 1980 junta; and the succession from Özal to Süleyman Demirel in 1993—the first occasion when one president of civilian background succeeded another.

It was not only the greater sense of responsibility of Turkey's politicians of military background that allowed Turkey to move toward democracy, but also its combination of established governmental structure and sense of national identity. The vast majority of Turkey's population are of Turkish national background, with the exception of small Greek, Armenian, and Jewish minorities and, above all, the substantial Kurdish minority in the southeast. Much of that Kurdish minority had joined in the rebellion against the newly proclaimed republic in 1924/25, and, after more than six decades of martial law rule, the region seemed to be moving toward full civic equality in the early 1990s.[13] Nonetheless, that trend was soon reversed when Kurdish nationalist guerrillas moved their headquarters from Lebanon to the autonomous Kurdish region of northern Iraq and intensified their campaign of violence—and the Turkish military forces escalated their repressive countermeasures.

Conversely, the vast majority of Turks live within the borders of Turkey, the one exception being the Turkish minority on Cyprus, where a "Turkish Republic of Northern Cyprus" was established after a Greek ultranationalist military coup and Turkish military invasion in 1974. The Turkic peoples of the former Soviet Union from Azerbaijan to Kirghizstan also speak languages closely related to Turkish—but the intense diplomatic and economic contacts since the fall of communism would seem to indicate that the common agenda will be one of close economic relations and perhaps regional organization rather than any "Panturkist" challenge to established national identities.[14]

In sharp contrast to Turkey, the post-Ottoman Arab states have faced a lack of governmental tradition, profound dilemmas of national identity, and a seemingly endless series of military defeats. In such a vacuum of effective national government, military coups soon become the standard technique for political change.

Among all the ex-Ottoman Arab countries, the only governmental continuity was found in hereditary rulers of regions such as Kuwait, Tunisia, and Egypt, where Muhammad Ali (1806–1849) had established de facto independence. The Arab Middle East also was the last of all outside regions to come under European imperial rule, at a time when that imperialism had grown self-conscious and apologetic—and when the European idea of nationalism had started to spread to the Middle East. Thus, the British in 1882 proclaimed a "temporary" occupation of Egypt that was to last until 1946 or, in the Suez Canal zone, until 1956. The Fertile Crescent in 1920/21 was made into "League of Nations Mandates," supposedly as a training for self-government. Yet (in contrast, e.g., to India) such foreign rule did not last long enough to establish any genuine governmental tradition. And the redrawing of Lebanon's boundaries by France, and the establishment of a Zionist entity under the British mandate over Palestine laid the ground for much future conflict. Algeria won its independence after an intense war of liberation (1954–1962). Everywhere else, postimperial independence was due as much to the exhaustion and withdrawal of European powers in the years after World War II, as to nationalist resistance.

Hereditary rulers such as the kings of Egypt and Iraq who had served, in effect, as vassals of European rule, enjoyed little respect; and Egypt's General Muhammad Naguib and Colonel Gamal Abdul Nasser in 1952 set an important precedent in deposing King Farouk by military coup, and actively playing Moscow against Washington. Other coups occurred in Syria in 1949 (three in one year), in Iraq in 1958, and in Libya in 1969.

Nonetheless, the postimperial vacuum was not the only factor encouraging military seizure of power. Equally important were the repeated military defeats at the hands of Israel (1949, 1956, 1967, 1973)—for, as Nasser indicates in his memoirs, it was natural for the military to blame their defeat not on themselves but on incompetent civilian rulers in the capital.[15] Above all, Arab populations have been torn by a threefold identity conflict between being Egyptian, Iraqi, Tunisian, etc., or Arab or Muslim.

Much like Italy and Germany in the nineteenth century, the Arab countries constitute a score of different political entities with a single language and cultural tradition. And the temptation, from Nasser of Egypt and Muammar al-Qadhdhafi of Libya to Saddam Husayn of Iraq has been to exploit the resulting frustrations by promising military unification on the model of Cavour's or Bismarck's wars of the 1860s. Also, in recent decades the militarization of politics within and among Arab countries was accentuated by arms imports due to cold war competition between Moscow and Washington and to the mounting oil revenues of the 1970s and 1980s.[16]

In sum, the major Ottoman military legacy to Turkey has been the disciplined and purposeful organization that made it possible for a leading Ottoman general such as Atatürk to reach out for popular support from every town and village in what became a victorious war for national independence within well-established and internationally recognized borders. By contrast, the Arab pattern has been one of defeat at the front and coups against unarmed civilians back home, with promises of pan-Arab liberation or revenge against Western imperialism. Still, it would seem that the long-term trend in Arab countries is toward national identity in existing boundaries on the nineteenth-century Latin American model, and that the evident failures of Nasser's United Arab Republic (1958–1961), of Qadhdhafi's attempts at expansion, and most recently of Saddam Husayn's aggression against Iran (1980–88) and Kuwait (1990–91) no longer make pan-Arab unification by war appear as a plausible option.

NOTES

1. Quincy Wright, *A Study of War* (2d ed.; Chicago: University of Chicago Press, 1965), p. 653, quoting Woods and Baltzly, *Is War Diminishing?* (Boston: Houghton Mifflin, 1915).
2. See Lord Kinross, *The Ottoman Centuries: The Rise and Fall of the Turkish Empire* (New York: Morrow, 1977), pp. 81–158.
3. Of the four titles, the first is Arabic, the next two are Turkish, and the last is derived from the Greek word *avthentos*.
4. Cf. Bernard Lewis, *The Emergence of Modern Turkey* (2d ed.; Oxford: Oxford University Press, 1968), pp. 45ff.
5. The problem that turned the later Mehmed Ali into a refugee was not political or religious but genealogical: he had been born as the illegitimate son of a German washerwoman and a French

soldier of Napoleon's army of occupation. Cf. my essay "Western Nationalism and the Ottoman Empire," in *The Mutual Effects of the Islamic and Judeo-Christian Worlds*, ed. Abraham Ascher et al. (Brooklyn, N.Y.: Brooklyn College Press, 1979), pp. 65f.

6. Arthur Koestler, *The Sleepwalkers* (paperback, New York: Grosset and Dunlap, 1963), p. 364, quoting from a boastful letter of Galileo's.

7. Ovid, *Metamorphoses* 4:428, paraphrasing Aristophanes, *The Birds*, v. 376.

8. For that term see Cyril E. Black, *The Dynamics of Modernization: A Study in Comparative Contemporary History* (New York: Harper and Row, 1966); and Robert E. Ward and Dankwart A. Rustow, eds., *Political Modernization in Japan and Turkey* (Princeton: Princeton University Press, 1964).

9. Quoted in Lewis, *Emergence of Modern Turkey*, p. 126.

10. Cited by Roderic H. Davison, "Environmental and Foreign Contributions: Turkey" in Ward and Rustow, *Political Modernization*, p. 103

11. Cf. Ward and Rustow, *Political Modernization*, p. 388.

12. For details see my *Turkey: America's Forgotten Ally* (New York: Council on Foreign Relations, 1987; updated paperback edition, 1989), ch. 4, and my article "Turkey," *Encyclopedia of Democracy* (Washington: Congressional Quarterly Books, forthcoming).

13. The use of Kurdish in public was legalized; some of the competing parties in the southeast openly appealed to Kurdish sentiment in the 1991 elections; and a new Human Rights Ministry in the government headed by Suleyman Demirel (1991–93) was headed by a person known to be of Kurdish background—as well as the Foreign Ministry. See D. A. Rustow, "A Democratic Turkey Face New Challenges," *Global Affairs* 8, no. 2 (Spring 1993): 58–70 at 61–63.

14. Cf. ibid., pp. 65–70.

15. Gamal Abdul Nasser, *Egypt's Liberation: Philosophy of the Revolution* (Washington, D.C.: Public Affairs Press, 1955).

16. On the role of the military in Arab countries after the Western withdrawal, see my essay "The Military in Middle Eastern Society and Politics," in Sydney N. Fisher, ed., *The Military in the Middle East* (Columbus: Ohio State University Press, 1963), pp. 3–20; on cold war competition in the region, cf. my essay "Safety in Numbers: Reflections on the Middle Eastern Balance of Power," in C. E. Bosworth et al., eds., *The Islamic World from Classical to Modern Times: Essays in Honor of Bernard Lewis* (Princeton N.J.: Darwin Press, 1989), pp. 781–800; and on the effect of oil revenues on arms imports, see my book *Oil and Turmoil: America Faces OPEC and the Middle East* (New York: Norton, 1982), pp. 278–84.

PART SIX

RELIGION AND CULTURE

In addressing the issue of Islam and the Ottoman legacy William Ochsenwald sees more change than continuity and more parallelism than direct influence of the Ottoman period on what followed. In religion as in politics the move from a multinational, multilingual, and multireligious empire governed by a distinctive small elite to nation states based on common language and culture challenged all manner of attitudes and institutions. For example, the status of ulama has sharply declined vis-à-vis the more secular and "modern" leadership. The centuries-old accommodation between Sufi mysticism and ulama legalism has also broken up in the post-Ottoman world. Nor have the Islamic fundamentalists now challenging the secular nationalists viewed the Ottoman period as a model. Moreover, the vast population increase has hampered the passing on of culture and tradition from one generation to the next.

On the other hand, the Ottoman Empire did bureaucratize the ulama and bring Muslim life under state control—religious education, law, the management of waqf endowments, the building and maintenance of mosques and other religious buildings, and the sufi brotherhoods—more effectively than any previous Muslim government. Much of this legacy continues. Indeed, the contrast between these post-Ottoman ulama living in the shadow of the state and their Shi'i peers in Iran is striking. That the radical Muslim fundamentalists throughout the Arab world and Turkey come overwhelmingly from outside the ranks of the traditional ulama whereas in neighboring Iran the mullahs seized power and still rule offers an important example of Ottoman influence.

In treating the Ottoman educational legacy Joseph Szyliowicz concentrates on Turkey, while suggesting that his findings apply to the Arab world as well, but to a lesser extent given the intervening Arab experience with Western colonial rule.

Even though the Ottomans had been engaged in educational reforms during the previous century the legacy left the new Turkey was meagre when measured against modern notions of mass education. The number of schools was limited and the disparity between the modern secular state system and the Muslim religious schooling continued.

Keyed to the attitude of a small governing elite ruling over the masses of the governed who were left to their own devices as regards education, the Ottoman educational philosophy was only slowly giving way to the new idea of a participatory citizenry. Reforms had tended to concentrate on the elite schooling at the apex of the educational pyramid (such as the Mulkiye and Harbiye, civil and military schools respectively). This elitist legacy continued into the Republican Turkish period. Carried over as well was the Ottoman assumption that learning was a matter of memorizing a corpus of information conveyed by authoritarian teachers. A highly centralized educational bureaucracy exercising state control over the entire system has been another legacy.

Also inherited from Ottoman times was the belief in higher education as an avenue of upward mobility. This is reflected in the achievement ethic that characterized the traditional Ottoman educational system and remains to this day.

Breaking with Ottoman tradition was the establishment of state control over (often absorption of) foreign private and missionary schools that had thrived during the last century of the Ottoman period. Since the 1960s, however, many private schools and even two private universities have been created, a development probably not linked to the Ottoman past.

Student activism, great advances in the education of women, a keen awareness of Western influence and concern about the relationship of Islam and modernity are other educational themes linking the Ottoman past and its Arab and Turkish successors.

CHAPTER FIFTEEN

ISLAM AND THE OTTOMAN LEGACY

IN THE MODERN MIDDLE EAST

William Ochsenwald

In considering the Ottoman religious legacy it is important to begin by analyzing the constructs of the Ottoman era and Islam. The Ottoman dynasty ruled for more than 600 years, from the late thirteenth Century until 1923, and its dominion extended during that time over a widely varying area, with fluctuating populations whose religious beliefs and practices differed. The ruling elite itself occasionally changed the nature of religious institutions and the relationship of religion to political practices. The expression of Islam in political life was directly influenced by these developments. To take just a few examples characteristic of differing time periods, the way ghazi customs and beliefs influenced the early Ottoman state in the fourteenth century was somewhat different from the role of religion in the sixteenth-century Ottoman Empire, influenced as the latter was by such factors as the new religious educational institutions of Istanbul and the problems posed by confronting the Shi'i Safavid dynasty in Iran. Both these situations differed from the nineteenth-century era of the Tanzimat reforms, when the public role of Islam in Ottoman life began to be limited by a secularizing trend in the education of the governing elite and yet was expanded by the ideology of the Pan-Islamic movement. Similarly, most Muslims living today have not been directly influenced by the Ottoman legacy because they were not alive in the Ottoman era. In the Middle East, Ottoman rule did not extend to Morocco, most of Iran, and some sections of the Arabian Peninsula. Some areas that were under the control of the Ottoman state were only superficially influenced by that experience, since Ottoman domination was either of relatively short duration, as in coastal eastern Arabia, or the Ottoman presence was often indirect, as in much of the Maghrib.

Islam during the Ottoman centuries involved several subgroups of Muslims as well as relationships between Muslims and persons of other faiths. Since most Ottoman Muslims, including the ruling dynasty, were Sunnis, the policies of the empire were concerned primarily with Sunni Islam. Examination of the complex relationships between Sunni Islam and Shi'i Islam, Christianity, and Judaism lies outside the scope of this chapter.

The most rewarding way of analyzing the Ottoman legacy for Islam in today's Middle East then is to consider primarily the last stage of the Ottoman experience, since it is closest chronologically to the present. Discussion is also limited to the lands that were part of the Ottoman Empire as of 1914, that are now inhabited by Sunni Muslims, either as a majority or as a significant minority, and that the Ottomans substantially influenced. In terms of contemporary political units, this involves Turkey; the Fertile Crescent countries of Syria, Jordan, Lebanon, Iraq, and, to some extent, Israel; Egypt; Libya; Yemen; and parts of Saudi Arabia, especially its western area of the Hijaz.

Another preliminary consideration involves the ways in which scholars have treated the subject recently. Both Middle Eastern and outside scholars writing in the early and middle parts of the twentieth century have tended to view the Ottoman Empire's general impact upon the Middle East as extremely negative. Nationalistic and secular-minded Turks, including scholars, chose either pre-Ottoman Turkish societies or Western European nations as models for the reconstruction of Anatolia following the devastation of World War I and the struggle for independence in 1919–1922. The role of Islam in the Ottoman Empire was consciously rejected. In the Arab lands the Ottoman experience was similarly opposed by nationalists, whether of the local or Pan-Arab variety, and also by those favoring some limited degree of secularization. Arab Muslims who wished to purify the faith from the accretions of the centuries since the period of the early caliphate also have viewed the Ottoman experience negatively.

Following World War II many Turkish and Arab intellectuals initially became even more attached to such views, but by the 1970s and 1980s a more nuanced and balanced interpretation of the Ottoman experience began to evolve. Several factors contributed to this change: more time had elapsed since the disastrous end of the empire, thereby creating a greater opportunity for objectivity; the value of the Ottoman Empire as a protector against external imperialism was clearer; Arab and Turkish nationalisms were found wanting by many; and researchers in the Ottoman archives made available vast quantitites of information on the functioning of the empire. While most religious fundamentalists in the Middle East continued to regard the former Ottoman state as having been detrimental to their cause some fundamentalists came to regard it as beneficial.

A gap continues to exist between most of those persons who studied Islam in the Ottoman Empire and those scholars who specialized in twentieth-century Islam. This gap reflects the feeling prevalent in the Middle East and elsewhere among both the general public and scholars that the Ottoman epoch had little positive relevance to the contemporary age. By the 1990s some favorable evaluations of the Ottoman experience and its legacy had emerged, but only among small groups. These included among others a few revisionist Saudi and Syrian historians;[1] Turkish social scientists oriented toward economic history, as well as the Foundation for Studies on Turkish-Arab Relations in Istanbul;[2] Abdeljelil Temimi and his associates in the Centre d'Etudes et de Recherches Ottomanes, Morisques, de Documentation et d'Information in Tunis; some Israeli historians who perhaps detected in the Ottoman experience reconciling experiences between Jews and Muslims; and some of the scholars associated with the British periodical *Middle Eastern Studies*. A majority of both secularizing modernizers and fundamentalist Muslims have still tended to deprecate the legacy of Sunni Islamic experience in the late Ottoman Empire for today's Middle East.

The Continuities of Islam and the Ottoman Experience

The basic set of beliefs that constituted the core of Islam were revealed in the Quran in the seventh century. The faith in the unity of God, the need to proclaim belief in Islam, the necessity of prayer, the obligations of fasting, the sanctity of pilgrimage, the expression of charity, the importance of struggling on behalf of the faith—all were stated definitively and were also expressed in the actions and example of the Prophet Muhammad. Subsequently, compilations of the sayings of the Prophet and, for Shi'is, the sayings of the Imams, along with various biographies of these figures established a larger corpus for interpreting the sacred text and created opportunities for nuanced readings of it. The working-out of extrapolations from the practice of the Prophet, as agreed by the consensus of the ulama, was in most cases in definitive form no later than a few centuries after that time.

Of course, a clearer understanding, a more finely tuned appreciation, and a more complete commentary on the implications of these basic beliefs became available as they were studied further in later centuries. Indeed, far-reaching developments in Islam took place after the collapse of the effective power of the Abbasid Empire around 950. Examples include the flowering of the Sufi mystical orders, the conversion of most of the population of the Middle East to Islam, development of an adherence to social customs that seemed to be integrated with religious values (as in the area of gender relations), and the evolution of more sophisticated concepts of the caliphate.[3] Thus the crucial elements in both Sunni and Shiʻi Islam were fully in place by the time the Ottoman dynasty began its expansion outward from Bursa in Anatolia in the fourteenth century.

The relationship between the Ottoman state and religion has captured the attention of historians, but for the Muslims of the Ottoman Empire the most important aspects of Islam were precisely those elements of personal faith and piety that were seldom discussed in written records. The comfort provided by belief in eternal life, the certainties established by codes of moral conduct, the group identity and occasional personal ecstacy made available through the Sufi organizations, the opportunity to supplicate and invoke God—all these and other similar matters helped Sunni Islam flourish during the Ottoman centuries.

For the most part behavior and belief paralleled the Sunni religious synthesis established in the Arab-Muslim lands in earlier times. Some modifications however were made in Islamic orthopraxy during Seljuk and Ottoman times, e.g., the adoption of preexisting saints and holy places as fit for Muslim veneration, or the use of tobacco and coffee.[4] Earlier marginalized approaches to Sunni Islam, especially among the Sufis, were now taken into the mainstream of acceptable behavior and belief.[5] This acceptance in turn caused revivalists, such as Birgivi Mehmed (1522–1573) and the Kadizadelis, and later the Wahhabi unitarians of Arabia (starting in the 1740s), to reject the religious tolerance often shown by the Ottoman state.

Perhaps the most significant change in the relationship of Islam and the state took place as the Ottomans organized the Sunni ulama. The state systematized the situation of the ulama in a number of ways. Clear hierarchical relations were created; the effectiveness of the ulama was expanded, even reaching into some of the villages; the Hanafi code of law was sponsored, but other Sunni codes were permitted and sultanic laws (kanuns) were decreed; and the institutional training and education of the ulama was advanced.[6] Ottoman supervision of the ulama, including even non-Hanafi dignitaries, usually resulted in the maintaining of high standards and credentials for teachers, judges, and interpreters of the faith. Sultans frequently sought ulama approval for their policies. Another consequence of this close supervision and clearer organization was that the ulama tended to become more subservient to the ruling elite in the state; however, in times when this elite was weak the ulama could then exert a substantial influence on it.

In many aspects of political life the role of Islam under the Ottomans was a continuation of examples and modes established under earlier Muslim states. Indeed, the Ottoman dynasty and governing elite saw many parallels with the Abbasid Empire.

The bases of legitimacy for the Ottoman state rested upon the twin pillars of Sunni Islam and Ottoman dynastic glory. The Ottomans expanded the realm of Islam through new and far-reaching conquests in Christian Europe starting in 1345. They later helped contain the expansion of the Shi'i Safavid and Christian Hapsburg states, thereby ensuring the victory of Sunnism in most parts of the Middle East and North Africa. The rulers actively promoted Sunni Islam through a wide variety of means, including maintaining the shari'ah, conserving the existing social order, and enforcing justice. They also helped Islam by establishing charitable foundations, building mosques, organizing advanced religious schools, supporting some Sufi orders, and partially codifying applications and procedures of the holy law. The state supported religious and scientific scholarship, as well as libraries, with an emphasis on legal studies and mathematics. After the conquest of the central Arab lands in the early sixteenth century, the Ottomans sponsored the pilgrimage to Mecca, and through subsidies to the Hijaz fostered Islam in its birthplace. The Ottoman rulers also venerated Jerusalem and gave its judges a high status.

Often pre-Ottoman practices and patterns of religious behavior were more thoroughly organized and regularized by the Ottomans, but in some cases relatively new applications of Islamic institutions or structures were created. Examples of the latter could be seen in Istanbul's Suleymaniye and Edirne's Selimiye mosque complexes, among the most beautiful in the world, constructed at the command of the sultans.[7]

Naturally, many aspects of public life did not involve religion to a significant degree, whether in the political or social arenas. And religious groups other than Sunni Muslims were also important for the Ottomans, though the relations between Sunni Muslims and others inside the empire were regulated for the most part according to standards acceptable to the ulama. The toleration usually shown by Ottoman elites toward minority religious groups and the more ecstatic Sufi organizations was remarkable, especially in comparison to the lack of religious toleration in many European countries at that time.

Paradigms based upon the supposed decline of the Ottoman Empire from about 1600 to 1800 have been abandoned or have undergone modification recently. It is now believed that in many facets of government and society the most important processes were those of readjustment rather than decay.[8] Still, the changing balance of power between Western Europe and the Ottoman realm in the eighteenth century made many elite Ottomans want military and technological change along European lines. During the nineteenth century the ever-increasing pressure of European imperialism—whether military, economic, or cultural in nature—plus indigenous drives toward reform and ren-

ovation resulted in substantial changes in Ottoman government and, to a lesser degree, in Ottoman society. A few illustrations drawn from the issues where
public life and Islam intersected illustrate the processes involved.

While its Sunni Muslim subjects continued to grant political legitimacy to
the Ottoman state on the basis of the twin pillars of dynastic and religious loyalty,[9] the religious identity of the empire underwent substantial modification.
In 1826 the Bektashi Sufi order was suppressed, while in 1866 the leadership
of the Sufi orders was consolidated under state control. The various religious-
ethnic minority communities at first sought equal status in treatment by government regardless of religious group (*millet*) membership, and by 1876 a written constitution derogated some powers from the ruler to the elected repre-

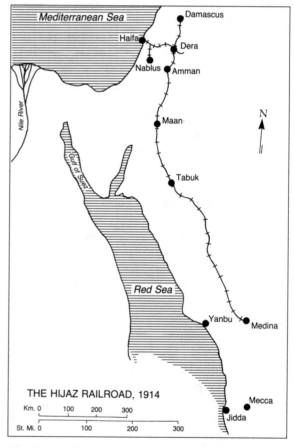

The Hijaz Railroad in 1914. Map by John T. Westlake, Princeton, N.J.

Ceremony marking the extension of the Hijaz Railroad spur to Haifa. *Sultan Abdul Hamid II's Photographic Collection.*

sentatives of the people. Representation in the Ottoman parliament partially corresponded to millet identity, and thus religious community continued to be a basis for political power within the Ottoman state framework. Anti-Ottoman revolutionary movements based on ethnic nationalism among the non-Muslim population often were reinforced by bonds of religious identity, and these in turn were frequently couched in anti-Muslim terms. The idea of nationalism serving as an alternative to Islam as a basis for state power reached the predominantly Muslim Arab, Albanian, Turkish, and possibly the Kurdish regions at a later time than it affected the Christian and Jewish minorities, but by World War I dynasty and faith were no longer the only viable intellectual alternatives for Ottoman Muslims.[10] Christian Arabs played a prominent role in the earliest formulations of Arab nationalism, which tended to be relatively secular in tone. As Muslim Arabs started to be interested in nationalism, the balance between ethnic, linguistic, and religious characteristics in national identity became more problematic.

Sultan Abdulhamid II promoted the concept of Pan-Islam as a counterbalance to nationalism, hoping to gain support among Muslims outside as well as inside the Ottoman Empire. Pan-Islam was a positive ideology in that it was intended to promote the welfare, common identity, and strength of the Muslim community; at the same time, Pan-Islam also gained support from the opposition to European and Christian imperialisms. To give this concept concrete expression Abdulhamid mandated in 1900 the building of the Hijaz Railroad, a holy railway designed to link the central Ottoman lands with the pilgrimage cities of Arabia, appealing for funds from Muslims around the world to help build the railway.[11]

The sultan also emphasized Ottoman claims to the caliphate. Even though earlier Ottoman sultans had included this title among many others they used, the weight given it in the context of a Pan-Islamic policy was new. The sultan's Pan-Islamic policy presaged the later use of Islamic religious symbolism and appeals to the community of believers for political and moral support in the twentieth century by such organizations and leaders as the Muslim Brotherhood and the Saudi monarchy. Yet in a rather contradictory fashion, Abdulhamid, like earlier Ottoman reformers, also promoted aspects of secularism. Two such cases were the growth in size and importance of government schools, which taught Islam but gave great weight to secular matters in the curricula, and the Mecelle law code completed in 1876, which though based on the holy law nevertheless represented a considerable departure from it in some ways.[12] Following the ouster of Abdulhamid, the Committee of Union and Progress promoted Turkism, while maintaining parts of the Pan-Islamic movement.

The emergence of various Christian communal ethnic-religious nationalisms, the spread of nationalism to several Ottoman Muslim ethnic groups, and the rise of Pan-Islamic ideology as sponsored by the state all contributed to a confused, inchoate, and occasionally contradictory political atmosphere in the Ottoman Empire during its last decades. This uncertainty about the identity and nature of the political community and its relationship to religion was matched later by similar problems that continued to bedevil many of the independent successor states following the end of the empire.

Outside the scope of Ottoman government other forces also promoted secularism. Arab and Turkish intellectuals became intimately involved with the prevailing currents of thought in Europe, e.g., the debate over evolution.[13] Elites who in earlier days would have studied Persian now learned French and necessarily began to adapt to the values present in European societies where they often went to study. Some of the ulama started to devote their energies to reconciling Islam and the new secular ideas; Muhammad Abduh of Egypt (d. 1905) was only one of many religious thinkers who participated in this process. Debates raged over the social implications of Islam in such aspects of life as gender relations, clothing, personal and group honor, artistic creation, and, more generally, the desirability of innovation.

As European countries gained direct control over various Muslim lands, millions of Sunni Muslims became refugees in an Ottoman Empire that while itself was shrinking nevertheless seemed to be the only Muslim state capable of resisting European imperialism. From the perspective of some Muslims, however, the Ottomans themselves with their Europeanizing reforms were losing credibility as the defenders of Sunni Islam. This view was especially held by Sunni revivalists including the Mahdists in the Sudan, the Sanusi brotherhood in Libya, and the Wahhabi-Saudi movement in Arabia. The ultimate cause of the disappearance of the empire came from multiple military defeats—in the war with Italy, the Balkan Wars, and most disastrous of all, World War I. The Ottoman call for jihad in 1914 was regarded by many Muslims as hypocritical in light of the Ottoman alliance with Christian Germany.[14] Other Middle Eastern Muslims concluded that an insufficient secularization and the resulting weakness of the Ottoman military as demonstrated during the war was the ultimate cause of the disappearance of the empire.

Sunni Islam in Formerly Ottoman Lands

During the twentieth century, a period noted for extraordinary changes and revolutionary upheavals throughout the world, the basic ritual and credal elements of Islam have proven to be extremely resilient and resistant to innovation. The important beliefs and rituals that constituted the core of Islam for personal faith, piety, and behavior have not changed greatly. Sources employed for arriving at the interpretation of the faith have also continued to be those accepted by earlier generations. These elements and beliefs were continuously present for the community of believers, and thus were conveyed to the contemporary period through the generations of Muslims living in the Ottoman era, but they were not uniquely Ottoman in any profound sense. In the context of major challenges experienced by Muslims, Islam provided a bedrock of spiritual stability and continuity.

The changes in Sunni Islam since 1918 were, in most parts of the Middle East outside the Turkish republic, neither direct effects of the Ottoman experience nor direct reactions against it. Many parallels can be seen, however, between the religious situation of the nineteenth-century Ottoman Empire and its twentieth-century successor states.

The greatest changes were in the social expression of what earlier Muslims had construed to be God's will on this earth. Among many such matters two of the most salient for the late twentieth century involved population increase and evolving concepts of gender relations.

An extraordinary increase in the population of the Middle East, most of which was Muslim, took place in the twentieth century—for instance Egypt's population grew from almost 13 million in 1917 to about 55 million in 1992. Fertility rates in Syria, Iraq, and Jordan after 1945 were among the highest in the world. The ability of Muslim religious institutions to reach their adherents was challenged by the increase in population and also by the considerable movement of people from the countryside to the cities.

Since spiritual guidance operating through traditional and government-approved means was often not available or was spread too thin to be effective, many Muslims sought alternatives, such as the Muslim Brotherhood (founded in 1928), a type of mass organization that had not existed in Ottoman days. As the number of Muslims grew, a strain was inevitably placed upon all sorts of religious institutions, including the pilgrimage to Mecca, as supervised by Saudi Arabia. While the rituals of the pilgrimage were practically unchanged for individuals, the regulation of the pilgrimage and the physical facilities needed to organize it on a mass basis were completely overhauled when compared to the pilgrimage system that had existed in the Hijaz in the last days of the Ottoman Empire.[15] Another consequence of the rapid population increase was a growing concern among theologians about family planning and related issues.

The relationship between men and women, particularly members of Western-oriented upperclass groups, changed in many parts of the Middle East.[16] Heated debates on such issues as veiling, the legal rights of women in regard to child custody, employment opportunities, and the value of secular education for women had started before 1914, but these debates grew increasingly important as the century progressed. In the new media of the cinema, radio, and television, as well as in literature and drama, women assumed a more prominent place in public life and became more independent of men. In most countries women gained the franchise, e.g., in Syria in 1947; eventually they held posts in governments. Probably in households personal relations between husbands and wives also changed to reflect new values and behaviors. These trends were most prominent in Turkey, and in the cities of the Fertile Crescent, Egypt, and North Africa, while only limited change took place in most parts of the Arabian Peninsula and in rural areas. The differential rate of change often seemed directly related to the degree of former Ottoman power, but the real cause was found in the openness of such areas as Damascus or Cairo to Europeanization.

Another twentieth-century change was in public life and participation in government. Until the 1979 creation of the Islamic Republic of Iran, and the subsequent 1980–1988 Iraq-Iran War, open quarrels between Sunnis and Shi'is tended to be relatively muted compared to certain earlier centuries. This tentative and partial rapprochement sometimes took place because of a new ideological framework provided by the nation-state, and on other occasions it resulted from a reaction against mutual enemies.[17] For instance, Sunnis and Shi'is in Iraq during the Mandate, the monarchy, and the early republic to a limited extent began to see each other first as Iraqis and only second as members of differing religious communities—although power was still held primarily by Arabic-speaking Sunnis, who excluded both Arabic-speaking Shi'is and Kurdish-speaking Sunnis from real influence. In Syria shared dislike of first France and later Israel tended to unite the Sunnis and various Shi'i groups.

In many parts of the formerly Ottoman Middle East, the basis of governmental legitimacy shifted from the Ottoman blend of dynasty and Sunni Islam to populist nationalism, but one should not exaggerate this change. National communities still often defined themselves on the basis of religion. Complex and shifting views on the interrelationships of language, ethnicity, and religion in national identity had initially formed in the last years of the Ottoman Empire;[18] now, in the period after World War I, these views were more fully articulated and put into practice in Turkey, the new Arab states, and Israel.

After the Armenian massacres and expulsions and the later population exchanges with Greece, Turkey became an almost completely Muslim country, in a way that Anatolia had not been in past centuries. Indeed, the only significant minority in the Turkish republic was the Kurdish population, but they, too, were Muslims. This overlap of religion and ethnic national identity existed despite the avowed secularism of the new Turkish nation-state.[19]

Greater Lebanon, as created by the French in 1920, was notably dependent upon the spirit and system of politics established in Ottoman Mount Lebanon after 1860. Many countries continued with the old mixture of dynasty and faith—most notably Saudi Arabia, down to the present day, but also for a time Yemen, independent Libya, and others. Even very secularly minded republics sometimes sought the support of Islam and the approval of the ulama for their policies in much the same way as the Ottomans had done, Nasser's relations with the official ulama and al-Azhar being a good example.

Still, the basic principle of government in the most heavily populated countries was populist nationalism, as had existed in the Ottoman Empire only in the few years when the 1876 constitution was actually in effect. Nationalists claimed greater priority should be given their ideology than religion, and the status of the professional men of religion declined. To the secular nationalists the specialized knowledge of the ulama and Sufis was useless or even detrimental, and the social benefits of religious training were few. Explicit anti-ulama sentiment was seldom expressed publicly, but the net effect of putting the nation-state first was to lessen the political importance of Islam.

Between 1920 and 1939, with major exceptions such as Turkey, Yemen, and Saudi Arabia, real political power in most parts of the former Ottoman Empire was held by external imperial powers, whose populations and governments were at least nominally Christian. This situation tended to exacerbate suspicions directed toward indigenous Christians held by some Middle Eastern Muslims, as in Iraq in the 1930s. These suspicions were similar to those present in Ottoman Damascus and Lebanon in 1860, but the unity demonstrated by most Christians with Muslims in nationalistic struggles after World War I, such as in Egypt in 1919, mitigated such feelings.

After World War II, as European direct power waned, political power in the more populated countries tended to gravitate toward leaders who in effect represented the viewpoints of the new middle class, often encapsulated partially within the military. In some cases the new rulers created a security state, using intelligence agencies and the secret police, as well as policy accomplishments, to maintain themselves in power. In societies like Ba'thist Iraq and Syria or Nasserist Egypt, government became far more interventionist in the economy, culture, and private life than had been the case even in the last days of the Ottoman Empire. Generally, such regimes tightly controlled religion and particularly the ulama, who tended to become mere servants of the state.[20]

Ironically, in the more conservative and rich oil monarchies the state also became far more powerful than the Ottoman regime had been locally, since these governments gained economic power from direct payment of petroleum royalties. Still, religion and society tended to be less rigorously controlled than in the security states. In Saudi Arabia, the ulama maintained a somewhat separate power base and could on occasion influence government decisions,[21] as in the long delay until 1991 in the issuance of guidelines for a consultative council. The concept of *shura* or consultation drawn from the Quran was often used in these countries as a basis for representative councils. Legitimacy in the conservative states rested in part on their sponsorship of Islam; Saudi Arabia in particular, as the supervisor of the pilgrimage, spent very large sums of money on improving transportation, housing, and access to the holy shrines in Mecca and Medina. In this regard, the Saudi government acted like the Ottomans, who had also sponsored and supervised the pilgrimage and subsidized the Hijazi holy cities.

Attention paid to the personal behavior of the leader or ruler also differed between the more secular, revolutionary regimes and the more religious, conservative ones. While the revolutionary leaders were not especially pious, most of them did nevertheless quietly follow the prescripts of Islam in their private lives. The personal behavior of the ruler and his family was more important in the conservative societies, as in the criticism launched against some of the Saudi princes for their profligate lifestyles.

Vast oil reserves and production gave the Middle East in the twentieth century an even greater importance for the rest of the world than it had possessed in the nineteenth century. Earlier, the chief significance of the Middle East was in its strategically and economically crucial location in the center of the Eastern Hemisphere, and in the spiritual attachment directed toward its religious sites and legacies by the world's major monotheistic faiths. The Ottoman Empire had played a role in the European balance of power system, and European and North American Christian and Jewish groups had sought to expand their religious and organizational influence into the Middle East. While these factors continued to play a role in the making of twentieth-century foreign policy, religion became somewhat less important as oil considerations grew in importance, particularly in the 1970s and afterward. The role of oil had only started to be felt in the last years of the Ottoman Empire, and even then Middle Eastern production was limited to Iran and Baku; its significance in the Middle East was a twentieth-century phenomenon.

Zionism also had begun in the last half century of the Ottoman Empire, but it came to world prominence with the Balfour Declaration of 1917 and the following struggle between Arabs and Jews. Zionism itself was largely created in Europe, outside the Ottoman lands. While competition between Arabs and Jews was heatedly debated in the Ottoman parliament after 1908,[22] the most important elements in what became the Arab-Israeli dispute were associated with events that took place after the disappearance of the Ottoman state from

Palestine. Arab Palestinian identity was usually expressed in terms of a secular nationalism, which both Christian and Muslim Palestinians supported. Even so, leadership of the Palestinian community in the 1930s was centered in the person of Hajj Amin al-Husaini, who held the post of Mufti of Jerusalem. Also, following the movement toward a compromise resolution of the Arab-Israeli dispute by the Palestine Liberation Organization (P.L.O.) in the late 1980s, some Palestinian Muslims rejected the P.L.O. and opted for a religiously based opposition to the existence of a Jewish state. The Palestinian Arab cause enjoyed support in other parts of the Middle East partially for nationalistic and moral reasons but many supported the P.L.O. because of Muslim religious solidarity. This question of Palestine preoccupied much of the Middle East for the second half of the twentieth century, contained serious ramifications for Muslim identity and group self-confidence, and led to repeated wars between the Jewish state of Israel and its predominantly Sunni Arab neighbors. The Arab-Israeli dispute after 1948 could be traced in part to factors that had first taken form in the last decades of the Ottoman Empire, although the dispute evolved far beyond that situation.

Other than in Palestine, where no independent Arab government held power, by the 1960s most of the Muslim Arabs of the former Ottoman lands usually lived under secularizing independent national governments. The victory of the secularizers in government was foreshadowed by the line of policy espoused earlier by some Ottoman reformers, as in the educational and legal changes enacted by the Committee of Union and Progress during World War I, but in many ways the Arab secularizers went a good deal farther in educational and legal reforms.[23]

Mass public education increased literacy, and many more Muslims were able to read and understand religious texts and tracts than had been the case earlier. The educational process in most parts of the Middle East was increasingly secular in content, even though religion was still taught in the public schools. Higher education in particular was influenced by European beliefs about the desirability of a division between religion and the state. The theoretical implications of Western science for widespread customary beliefs attached to Islam by the masses were usually not made clear in public discourse. Still, for the scientifically educated elite a distancing process often took place. This sometimes led to an ignoring of religion or a decline in the prestige associated with piety. One example was the apparent change in the social status of pilgrims to Mecca, who increasingly were drawn from lower socioeconomic groups.

Elements of the Ottoman legal code called the *Mecelle* remained in effect for many years in some parts of the former empire, including Jordan, Israel, Iraq, and, more generally, as an influence on the formulation of law in various areas.[24] The shari'ah was limited more and more often to the realm of personal status aspects of law, and even there modifications were made along secularizing lines. The authority of the government to create laws now came supposedly from the general will of the sovereign people, not from God's words as expressed in the Quran. Pious Muslims who opposed secularizing legal reforms favored the principle that Islam and not the people's will should be the basis of law.

A reaction against excessive state power and secularism variously labeled as Muslim renewal, Islamism, Islamic fundamentalism, or Islamic revivalism developed. Milder approaches, such as the early twentieth-century Salafiyyah movement, did not gain a large popular base of support. Similarly, the Pan-Islamic movement attracted attention during the 1920s and 1930s, but it accomplished little.[25] Following the abortive claim of Sharif Husayn, former Ottoman amir of Mecca and later King of the Hijaz, to the Caliphate in 1924, no other Muslim ruler gained recognition as caliph. The post-World War II expressions of Pan-Islam in the form of the Organization of the Islamic Conference or the World Muslim League also tended to be relatively ineffectual.[26] Then, after the loss of the 1967 Arab-Israeli War, and with the seeming failure of secular nationalisms, many Arab Sunni Muslims turned toward thinkers like Sayyid Qutb of Egypt. In 1979 the ascent of fundamentalists to power in Shi'i Iran also encouraged the emergence of Sunni fundamentalist groups in the Arab states and in Turkey. When some states moved toward democratic elections, as in Jordan in 1989, Sunni fundamentalists emerged as a major political force.

The fundamentalists often rejected the accretion of religious interpretation that had taken place during the Ottoman era in favor of an earlier, pre-Ottoman, and pristine Islam. They often opted for a rigid, puritanical scripturalism that rejected the premodern synthesis of ulama and Sufi views. Although Sultan Abdulhamid II's Pan-Islamic movement had parallels with late twentieth-century Pan-Islamic fundamentalism, for instance in a shared suspicion of the West, the differences were also substantial. One example of these differences was the Ottoman use of Sufi brotherhoods to spread Pan-Islamic concepts.[27] Post-World War II fundamentalists did not employ Sufi organizations in this way.

At the other end of the political spectrum from Pan-Islam and Islamic fundamentalism was Marxism, which had been espoused by a few small underground groups in the Middle East before the end of the Ottoman Empire, although its emergence as a substantial alternative to existing political systems came only after 1945. In Iraq after the 1958 revolution and in South Yemen after independence from Britain in 1967 Marxists became important players. In most parts of the Middle East they were usually suppressed by hostile governments or paralyzed by internal factionalism. One reason why Leninist-Stalinist Marxism had so little appeal in the Middle East was its avowed atheism. The challenge posed by Communism to Islam and the Muslim reaction against it in the twentieth century were somewhat parallel to the experiences of Marxists in the late Ottoman Empire, but differed in many ways because of the new international status of the Soviet Union and domestic changes taking place in formerly Ottoman countries.

Direct Ottoman Influences on Twentieth-Century Sunni Islam

If one turns from parallels with limited causal connections to more direct examples of the religious heritage of the Ottoman Empire for twentieth-century Sunnis, probably the most profound consequence has been the predominance of a relatively tolerant and well-organized Sunni Islam in the Middle East. The Ottomans stopped European Christians from conquering the Middle East for many centuries and thereby helped preserve the dominance of Islam there. At the same time the expansion of Shi'i Islam was vigorously opposed in the central Muslim lands. Ottoman tolerance of protected Christian and Jewish religious groups before nationalism was established set a precedent for the twentieth century that was often but not always followed. Ottoman systematization and bureaucratization of the Sunni ulama continued into post-Ottoman years in the former Arab provinces, with substantial consequences for the internal organization of the ulama and their relationship with the state and the Muslim community. While Sufi organizations were often derided and ignored in the twentieth century, their ability to persevere was related in part to the patronage that had been given them by the Ottomans in earlier times. The phenomenon of popular Sufism[28] side by side with an "official" Sufi hierarchy was another example of a parallel situation spanning Ottoman and post-Ottoman times.

Among the various individual countries of the Middle East, it was in the Turkish republic that the legacy of the Ottoman Empire for Sunni Islam was most influential, at least in a negative sense. The leaders of Republican Turkey reacted strongly against the Ottoman experience in religion, while their policies and views were largely formed in the context of the last decade of the empire, when the Committee of Union and Progress had already begun a movement toward secularization.

A major principle of the republic was secularism, and its implementation entailed serious changes from the Ottoman system of religion and government.[29] The caliphate claimed by the Ottoman sultans was abolished in 1924, after the sultanate had also been ended. (Despite various efforts in other Muslim states, the caliphate was not reestablished elsewhere and this venerable religious-political institution vanished.) Legal reforms completed the process of official secularization that had begun in the nineteenth century, as the shariʿah courts were dissolved. Sufi orders were outlawed and the call to prayer had to be in Turkish rather than Arabic. The 1925 uprising of Kurdish, tribal, and Naqshibandi groups opposed to the secular reforms was suppressed by the republican government. Turkey adopted the Gregorian calendar associated with Christian Europe, while the Muslim dating system was only used to determine religious holidays. Pious foundations came completely under the control of the state, and most of the ulama were dismissed from official employment.

All citizens were entitled to equality before the law, regardless of religion, according to the 1924 constitution. In the same document there was a statement that Islam was the religion of the state, but in 1928 this was removed. Religious schools were absorbed into the secular state system, which was rapidly expanded; eventually religious instruction in the schools was forbidden. Language and alphabet reform instituted by the regime had a profound impact upon religious culture.

The whole basis of the state was transformed from the Ottoman synthesis of dynasty and Islam toward a populist, secular nationalism that looked more toward the early history of Central Asian Turkic groups for inspiration than to the Abbasids, Seljuks, and Ottomans.

Social and symbolic changes were even more far reaching, since they often influenced Turkish Muslims more directly than political changes. Alcohol became legal for Muslims, the use of the veil by women was strongly discouraged, polygamy was outlawed, women were guaranteed by law equal rights with men in such areas as child custody, and many occupations that had formerly been reserved for men now had women working in them. Music, art, and architecture were oriented by the government away from earlier Islamic civilization and toward European models. A notable example was the erecting of public statues, especially of Mustafa Kemal Atatürk, the first president of the republic, and the leading figure in bringing about the secularizing changes.

Yet despite these and other reforms, in many respects the Turkish republic continued to follow certain patterns of Islam that had existed during the Ottoman Empire. Most importantly, the government made no attempt to change the basic elements of faith. While the Quran in Arabic was more difficult to read, and the government encouraged the use of a Turkish translation, the original was available, and theology could still be privately studied, using the same texts and methods as before. Private faith, pious behavior, and even newly illegal acts probably often continued as earlier, especially in the countryside where the government's power was less effective. The need for Islam as a guidance to ethical conduct and eschatological belief persisted. In at least one way the new government ironically enough increased the role of Islam in public life. Mustafa Kemal Atatürk was called the gazi or warrior for the faith because of his victories, while the War for Independence had some of the aspects of a holy war against the Greek Christians. Many early Ottoman rulers had been regarded as gazis, but military victories to support such a title had been few in the late nineteenth-century Ottoman Empire.

As the Republican Peoples Party relaxed its tight control over public life following World War II, and particularly with the advent of multiparty freely contested elections in 1950, a new approach to state-mosque relations came into play.[30] Those in Turkish society who opposed the extreme secularism of the early republic were now able to express publicly at least some of their views, and their votes were actively sought by political parties. Study of the old alphabet was permitted, a program to build mosques with state funds was fully funded, religious training schools were legalized, religious instruction in the schools was restored, and the call to prayer in Arabic was once again heard.

In the second half of the twentieth century a significant number of Turkish and foreign historians devoted their research to Ottoman history. New work was done on such topics as the processes of conversion from Byzantine Christianity to Islam, Ottoman-Safavid-Moghul relations, the functioning of pious foundations, career patterns among the ulama in the eighteenth century, the practical effects of the *Tanzimat* secularizing changes, and Abdulhamid II's Pan-Islam. As the results of these projects began to influence the Turkish public, the former complete disdain for the late Ottoman period was revised in some quarters to a more accepting attitude.

Some Islamic fundamentalists and Europeanizing secularists objected to this revisionist approach to Ottoman history. The National Salvation Party favored Islamic reforms in education, culture, and national governmental policy, but neither it nor its successors sought a return to Ottoman political or religious systems. Underground Sufi groups conducted their services more openly in the 1970s, and books and journals dealing with various aspects of Islam sold many copies.

Similarly, few leftists viewed the Ottoman experience favorably, and those Turks who wanted Turkey to join the European Economic Community, with the implication of eventual complete merger into a unified Europe, were basically content with the balance between religion and the state that had been struck under Atatürk, so they also opposed the Ottoman religious-state synthesis.

As military control of Turkish society following the coup of 1980 gradually relaxed, both fundamentalists and leftists emerged once more into the political system. New Sufi orders were founded. Yet, despite the growing popularity of the Sufi orders, the trend of Turkish society toward integration into

Europe was resumed. In architecture, painting, literature, cinema, and cultural life in general (though perhaps not in music), Turks had earlier moved away from Ottoman legacies of style, expression, and content. While Ottoman and Islamic motifs were adopted from time to time, as in urban architecture and painting, these seem to have been limited in appeal even though the 1980s brought a fashionable interest in Ottoman history and art, including Sufism.[31] Atatürk's changes have continued basically to the present. Thus, the Ottoman legacy has influenced Turkey chiefly in the way that the leaders of the interwar generation reacted against it.

In other ways the Ottoman Empire left a more substantial legacy for Sunni Islam in today's Middle East. In the first half of the century much of the adult population consisted of persons who had lived in the last decades of the empire, and their earlier experiences inevitably influenced their later behavior. Some former Ottoman officials and military officers became influential in the successor states, most notably in Turkey, but also in Iraq, Yemen, and Transjordan, among others. Very few of these influential persons, however, were drawn from the ranks of the ulama, Sufis, or other groups especially inclined toward religion.

The physical remnants of the empire included many religious structures, ranging from impressive imperial mosques to more humble but still enduring buildings in the provinces. Among such remnants was the Hijaz Railway, established as a pious foundation (*waqf*) to promote the pilgrimage. The fate of this pilgrimage railroad might stand as an examplar for the Islamic legacy of the empire. By 1926 control of the railway was divided between the British Mandate of Palestine, the French Mandate of Syria, the Hashimite Amirate of Transjordan, and the Saudis. Some sections of the railway continued to function, but the unity of the line was permanently disrupted, and the track in the Hijaz that had been destroyed during World War I was not rebuilt. Projects to restore the line after World War II faltered as the separate national interests of each country could not be reconciled. Other contributing reasons for the inability to revive this Ottoman legacy revolved around Israeli control of the Hijaz Railway branch to the Mediterranean, the legal ambiguity inherent in a railway whose ultimate owner was God, and the evolution of new transportation patterns and technologies that made the pilgrimage railway outmoded.[32]

While Turks were profoundly affected by the legacy of the Ottoman Empire, Muslim Arabs living in other former Ottoman lands were less influenced in religious matters by the Ottoman experience. Many parallels existed between nineteenth-century Ottoman experiences with Islam and those of twentieth-century Sunni Muslims in the Middle East, but often the similarities in these experiences were matched by equally striking differences. Secularism along lines initially experienced in European societies affected the nature of Islam substantially, particularly in the interaction between governments and individuals. These two strands of Islam—its basic structures coming from pre-Ottoman periods, and the impact of non-Muslim Europe—were more important causally than the legacy of late Ottoman Islam.

NOTES

I wish to thank Madeline Zilfi for her careful reading of an earlier draft of this paper and her many useful suggestions for improvement.

1. William Ochsenwald, "The Recent Historiography of Western Arabia: A Critical Examination," *Proceedings of the Seminar for Arabian Studies* 22 (1992):97–103.
2. See its *Studies on Turkish-Arab Relations Annual* (vol. 1, 1986-continuing).
3. Marshall G. S. Hodgson, *The Venture of Islam: Conscience and History in a World Civilization*, especially volume 2, *The Expansion of Islam in the Middle Periods* (Chicago: University of Chicago Press, 1974); Ira M. Lapidus, "Sufism and Ottoman Islamic Society," in Raymond Lifchez, ed., *The Dervish Lodge: Architecture, Art, and Sufism in Ottoman Turkey* (Berkeley and Los Angeles: University of California Press, 1992), pp. 15–32.
4. Ralph S. Hattox, *Coffee and Coffeehouses: The Origins of a Social Beverage in the Medieval Near East* (Seattle: University of Washington Press, 1985).
5. This adoption of some non-Sunni practices often accompanied strong hostility against such groups as the Druzes, as is pointed out in Abdul-Rahman Abu-Husayn, "Problems in the Ottoman Administration in Syria During the 16th and 17th Centuries: The Case of the Sanjak of Sidon-Beirut," *International Journal of Middle East Studies* 24 (1992):666–67. For a thorough discussion of Sufism in the Ottoman Empire, see the essays in Raymond Lifchez, ed., *The Dervish Lodge*.
6. Halil Inalcik, *The Ottoman Empire: The Classical Age 1300–1600* (London: Weidenfeld and Nicolson, 1973), see especially ch. 10 on law, and chs 16 through 20 on other aspects of Islam. Madeline Zilfi, *The Politics of Piety: The Ottoman Ulema in the Postclassical Age, 1600–1800* (Minneapolis: Bibliotheca Islamica, 1988) discusses the later period of changes in the career patterns of the ulama as well as such matters as Sufism.
7. Rafee Hakky, "The Ottoman Kulliye Between the 14th and 17th Centuries: Its Urban Setting and Spatial Composition," Ph.D. dissertation, Virginia Polytechnic Institute and State University, 1992.
8. Examples of this historiographical trend may be found in Rifaat Ali Abou-El-Haj, *The 1703 Rebellion and the Structure of Ottoman Politics* (Istanbul: Netherlands Historical-Archaeological Institute, 1984), and Thomas Naff and Roger Owen, eds., *Studies in Eighteenth-Century Islamic History* (Carbondale: Southern Illinois University Press, 1977).
9. A talk given in the Hijaz by an emissary from the Ottoman Sultan in 1892 showed the usefulness of these concepts; see Ottoman Archives (Istanbul), Yildiz 13.112/11/112/6, enclosure 2, draft of a speech for Ratib Pasha, no date (probably December 1891).
10. Bernard Lewis, "The Ottoman Empire and Its Aftermath," *Journal of Contemporary History* 15, no. 1 (January 1980):27.
11. William Ochsenwald, *The Hijaz Railroad* (Charlottesville: University Press of Virginia, 1980).
12. Carter Findley, "Medjelle," *Encyclopaedia of Islam*, New Edition.
13. Adel A. Ziadat, *Western Science in the Arab World: The Impact of Darwinism, 1860–1930* (New York: St. Martin's Press, 1986).

14. Jacob M. Landau, *The Politics of Pan-Islam: Ideology and Organization* (New York: Oxford: Oxford University Press, 1990), pp. 99–103.

15. One example of change was the considerable reduction in the transmission of disease; while improvement in this area had started under the Ottomans, it was sharply increased under Saudi control. See William Ochsenwald, *Religion, Society, and the State in Arabia: The Hijaz Under Ottoman Control, 1840–1908* (Columbus: Ohio State University Press, 1984), especially ch. 3; and David Long, *The Hajj Today: A Survey of the Contemporary Makkah Pilgrimage* (Albany: State University of New York Press, 1979).

16. Leila Ahmed, *Women and Gender in Islam: Historical Roots of a Modern Debate* (New Haven: Yale University Press, 1992), has a careful discussion of changes in the status of Muslim women, centered around Egypt for the modern period.

17. Hamid Enayat, *Modern Islamic Political Thought* (Austin: University of Texas Press, 1982).

18. William W. Haddad and William Ochsenwald, eds., *Nationalism in a Non-National State: The Dissolution of the Ottoman Empire* (Columbus: Ohio State University Press, 1977), especially ch. 1 by William Haddad, and ch. 2 by Roderic Davison; Rashid Khalidi et al., eds., *The Origins of Arab Nationalism* (New York: Columbia University Press, 1991).

19. Lewis, "The Ottoman Empire and Its Aftermath," contains a succinct account of the changes in political group identity from the later imperial period to the Turkish republic.

20. Roger Owen, *State, Power, and Politics in the Making of the Modern Middle East* (London and New York: Routledge, 1992), pp. 40–41.

21. Ayman al-Yassini, *Religion and State in the Kingdom of Saudi Arabia* (Boulder: Westview Press, 1985); William Ochsenwald, "The Islamic Revival in Saudi Arabia," in Shireen Hunter, ed., *The Politics of Islamic Revival* (Bloomington: Indiana University Press, 1988), pp. 103–15.

22. Neville J. Mandel, *The Arabs and Zionism Before World War I* (Berkeley and Los Angeles: University of California Press, 1976).

23. Owen, *State, Power, and Politics*, p. 40.

24. Findley, "Medjelle," *Encyclopaedia of Islam*, New Edition.

25. Martin Kramer, *Islam Assembled: The Advent of the Muslim Congresses* (New York: Columbia University Press, 1986).

26. Muslim solidarity and cooperation replaced total Pan-Islamic unity as a more realistic goal, particularly as sponsored by Saudi Arabia. For a thorough discussion of Pan-Islamic organizations and activities since 1945, see Landau, *The Politics of Pan-Islam*, especially ch. 6.

27. Landau, *The Politics of Pan-Islam*, pp. 51–54.

28. For a discussion of popular Sufism in recent times, see Valerie J. Hoffman-Ladd, "Devotion to the Prophet and His Family in Egyptian Sufism," *International Journal of Middle East Studies* 24 (1992), pp. 615–37.

29. Stanford J. Shaw and Ezel Kural Shaw, *History of the Ottoman Empire and Modern Turkey*, vol. 2 (New York: Cambridge: Cambridge University Press, 1977), pp. 384–88, has a concise discussion of secularism in the Turkish republic. Also see June Starr, *Law as Metaphor: From Islamic Courts to the Palace of Justice* (Albany: State University of New York Press, 1992).

30. The essays in Richard Tapper, ed., *Islam in Modern Turkey: Religion, Politics,, and Literature in a Secular State* (London: I. B. Tauris, 1991) illuminate many aspects of Islam in Turkey after 1950.

31. For a discussion of this trend that gives greater weight to the continued importance of Sufism and Islam in contemporary Turkey, see Cemal Kafadar, "The New Visibility of Sufism in Turkish Studies and Cultural Life," in Raymond Lifchez, ed., *The Dervish Lodge*.

32. William Ochsenwald, "A Modern Waqf," *Arabian Studies* 3 (1976), pp. 1–12.

CHAPTER SIXTEEN

THE OTTOMAN EDUCATIONAL LEGACY:

MYTH OR REALITY

Joseph S. Szyliowicz

In the case of Turkish education any attempt to identify linkages with the past is difficult because Atatürk deliberately challenged major Ottoman cultural values; his famous reforms were explicitly designed to destroy links with the past. The Arab states also present analytical difficulties, for there the Ottoman heritage was superseded by colonialism. Egypt and Tunisia, for example, came under direct European rule in the early 1880s (Algeria even earlier, beginning in 1830). These states were thereafter exposed to different educational systems and philosophies. Even the shorter period of the mandates in the Fertile Crescent managed to provide a different education model. That the Arab states of the former Ottoman Empire (excepting Saudi Arabia and Yemen) went from Ottoman rule to European rule and only thereafter to independence inevitably made for a different educational legacy than in Turkey, which moved in one step from its Ottoman matrix to being an independent state— and one whose leader was committed to dramatic modernization. Moreover, in Lebanon and Palestine foreign missionary schooling from at least the early nineteenth century played a role unmatched anywhere else in the empire.

Under these circumstances it is no easy matter to answer such questions as: Did Atatürk succeed in transforming Ottoman cultural values? Are there such discontinuities between the post-Atatürk era and the Ottoman tradition that the continuities are mythical rather than real? To what extent did colonial rule stamp Arab education with a unique imprint that differentiates it from the Turkish case?

Let us first consider the Turkish case beginning with the material inheritance that the Turkish republic received and then discuss features of the Ottoman educational system that are also characteristic of the contemporary educational scene. These I shall divide into two categories, those for which I find a strong link to the Ottoman past and those for which the linkage is, in my view, more indirect. Finally, I shall speculate about the possible influence of certain cultural traits such as the Ottoman worldview, definitions of knowledge, and attitudes toward the stranger. This is followed by a consideration of education in the Arab world, analyzing the degree to which educational practices there were similar to the Turkish case and were also be linked to the Ottoman past.

Inheritance Patterns

The Turkish republic was not heir to a rich patrimony. Although efforts had been made for over a century to create a modern system of schooling, only limited progress had been achieved by the end of World War I. And the years of fighting that followed severely damaged what had been so painfully built up. When the republic was finally established it possessed a small number of modern schools and a much larger number of Islamic schools that ranged from the primary level to sophisticated *medreses*. In the 1923/24 school year there were about 480 medreses with somewhere between 6,000 and 18,000 students. The secular system consisted of about 4,894 primary schools, 72 middle schools, and 22 lycées enrolling 342,000 (perhaps 20 percent of the cohort), 5,900 and 1,240 students respectively. Another 2,900 students were receiving a higher education.[1]

Another unfortunate legacy the republic inherited from the Ottoman Empire was a conservative orientation. Education is always Janus-faced looking to both past and future. It needs to socialize students into the existing society and culture, but since change is constant, students must be prepared to deal with the unknown, with the new. This requires that students learn to be creative and innovative, that they be able to manipulate knowledge.

The tension between these two roles characterizes every educational system, but if the schools are to contribute to national development they must socialize students into modes of thought that permit them to deal with problems of change in an effective manner. Such was the situation in classical Ottoman times when the goal of education was to graduate students who had not only memorized large bodies of information but who could also comprehend and analyze the issues involved. As a result, high standards of scholarship characterized the religious educational system and the Palace schools were producing elites of ability and vision.

Over time, however, the ulama became increasingly conservative and antagonistic to creative learning and to new ideas. The empire basked in self-satisfaction, contentment with its culture which it regarded as superior to that of Europe, of which it was largely ignorant. In short, the educational system became ossified, the society impervious to change and innovation.

The development of those Ottoman modern schools also came with various deficiencies. Those leaders first concerned about the survival of the empire realized the need to borrow Western methods of warfare, opening schools of naval and military engineering as early as 1776 and 1793 respectively. It soon became apparent that a modern army needed officers with many specializations, and one military school after another was opened. The reformers, however, did not define the problem in terms of overall educational transformation, in terms of introducing Western knowledge in all phases of Ottoman life.

Subsequently Ottoman rulers recognized that a modern bureaucracy was also essential if the state were to survive, and the famous Mulkiye Mektebi opened its doors in 1859. The recognition that an integrated system of modern schools was required, that a few specialized higher schools could not meet the empire's needs came later.

Two fundamental issues forced this change. First, students trained in the traditional schools were simply not prepared to deal with modern concepts and ideas. Second, new kinds of teachers were required. Accordingly two new kinds of schools were established, the Rushdiye, to prepare the graduates of the religious schools for a modern education and, second, teacher-training colleges (the Darül-muallim was opened in 1848). In time an integrated modern system ranging from the primary to the university was established, but it was never integrated with the religious system, which continued to function in the same manner as it had for generations.

These reformist educational developments created several tendencies that remain visible to the present. One might be called the "medrese mentality," which influenced the modern schools in the nineteenth century. All the modern schools, even the Darulfunun (the Ottoman University) were greatly influenced by the culture of the religious schools from which many of the teachers and most of the students came. Hence the traditional view that knowledge could best be acquired by memorizing specific texts and studying commentaries emerged as the dominant educational philosophy. Little attention was paid to the needs of the students and an authoritarian culture prevailed in all the schools.

These patterns prevail today with classroom formality and strict discipline. The teacher is the ruler, the students the ruled. Only the teacher possesses valid information, which is not be questioned by the students. They are not expected to be creative or innovative but to memorize their lecture notes.

Although there are a number of teachers who do not teach in this manner, who work with students individually, who encourage them to achieve their full potential, they remain a minority.

Over the years observers have criticized this phenomenon, which exists at all levels from the primary to the university. The famous report by Albert Malche (1932), which led to the replacement of the Darulfunun by Istanbul University, for example, noted the low quality of the teaching and the heavy emphasis upon memorization. Thirty-five years later a knowledgeable Turkish academic concluded that despite important changes "arrangements for the Ph.D. degree tend to perpetuate enfeebling, archaic practices derived from the past and thus contribute markedly to the continuation of formalized, repetitive, and impersonal teaching in universities."[2] Nor did the growing number of faculty trained abroad or the important changes in the structure and administration of Turkish universities after 1980 eliminate this medrese mentality. Students are still expected to take extensive notes during the professor's lectures, commit them to memory, and regurgitate them without question. An Ottoman *müderris* would feel quite at home in many contemporary university classrooms at all levels.

Curricula at all levels also retain many traditional aspects with too much information crammed into too many different courses. In the social studies course, taught in the fourth and fifth grades of the primary schools, which includes geography, history, and civics, for example, students are expected to learn many trivial details. A well-known columnist, Mim Kemal Oke, wrote about his son's homework in 1990:

> The number of districts in Turkey, the duties of the veterinary and financial administrations in the provinces. I cried out what are these? The child looks startled. The social studies unit of the 4th grade Social Studies textbook, he answers. I take the book, look through it and feel sick. It's not a book, it's garbage. . . . If, after 25 years of complaints we still have not changed this method of instruction and if we have left our children in the same plight, I ask how will we function in an age of knowledge?

Such an education does not prepare students to deal with complexity and change. Taught to view issues in absolutist terms, students are not adequately prepared to think logically, analytically, or comparatively.

As the number of modern schools proliferated so did the administrative functions. Ottoman bureaucracy was for decades efficient and effective but, in time, it lost these attributes and acquired numerous pathologies. The attempt to create a new administrative system staffed by the graduates of such schools as the Mulkiye was successful in some ways, but too many of the old practices were grafted onto it. Nor did the introduction of continental European patterns stressing centralization improve matters. Hence the new Ministry of Education, which was established to regulate and coordinate the modern state schools, exercised rigid control over all aspects of education—curricula, finance, textbooks, and the selection and appointment of teachers.

That tradition has continued to the present and the bureaucratic hand of the ministry lies heavily upon teachers and students throughout Turkey. Uniformity rather than creativity and innovation is favored. Rules and procedures are rigorously enforced. The visit of a supervisor to insure that the ministry's decrees are carried out is widely feared by teachers and principals alike. The defects of the Ministry of Education has been widely publicized over the years, but the organizational culture seems impervious to change.

The Ottoman reformers' decision to build a system of modern schools that paralleled the religious schools and essentially to ignore the latter led to a bifurcated system that served to divide rather than integrate the society. Each type of school went its separate way, with limited interaction between them, thus creating a major cultural cleavage within the empire. That gap was noted by many contemporary intellectuals, notably Ziya Gokalp who wrote: "One portion of our nation is living in an ancient, another in a medieval, and a third in a modern age. . . . How can we be a real nation without unifying this threefold education?"[3] Atatürk understood the threat that such a system posed to nation-building and he sought to destroy this legacy by abolishing the religious schools. Through these and his other well-known reforms Atatürk succeeded in establishing a secular state, but Islam remained a dynamic force that has influenced educational patterns and processes to the present.

It has done so in many ways, for Islam retains its cultural vitality. Although Atatürk virtually eliminated formal Islamic education (except for some Quranic courses at the elementary level and a research institute at Istanbul University), public pressures, after World War II, brought about the establishment of a Faculty of Theology at Ankara University and the introduction of Islamic content into various curricula. This trend was officially consecrated by the 1982 constitution, which provides that all students from the elementary through the lycée levels must take courses in Islamic religion and ethics. Altogether eight of the country's twenty-eight universities now have theology faculties.

Moreover there has been a marked increase in the number of schools designed to train religious leaders and teachers, the Imam Hatip Okullari. Beginning in the 1950s, their numbers began to grow and really exploded in the decade following 1975. In 1976 there were 73 religious training schools and 927 regular lycées, by 1989 the former had increased by 311 while the number of regular lycées had climbed by only 263.[4] Like the graduates of the regular lycées, many graduates of the religious training schools are eager to continue their education and a large percentage do well on the national university entrance examination. In 1985, for example, 40 percent of the entering fresh-men in Istanbul University's Political Science Department were products of these schools.

The emergence of these schools has been facilitated by another Ottoman legacy—the institution of the *waqf* (pious foundation), which played an important role in Ottoman history. Pious Muslims in all parts of the empire established waqfs to created and maintain schools, mosques, hospitals, fountains, and other public works. In recent decades, many such foundations have been established to support religious schools or students who wish to obtain a religious education.

Nor can one overlook the influence of Islam on the behavior and attitudes of the students. The 1960s and 1970s were characterized by overt violence between left-wing and right-wing groups, the latter including both extreme nationalists and religious elements.

Furthermore, recent years have witnessed a heated controversy over whether female university students should be permitted to wear the traditional Islamic head covering. In the eyes of many, including former President Kenan Evren, this form of dress violates the principles of Atatürk and undermines the secular character of the state. Accordingly YOK (the Higher Education Council established after the 1980 revolution to control and coordinate higher education) issued a regulation that called on students to dress "in a contemporary fashion." Protests by Islamic fundamentalist groups soon led to parliamentary action and legislation legalizing this headgear was passed in 1988. Secularists, including many academics, promptly questioned its legality and the Constitutional Court ruled against it in March 1989. Subsequently, in late 1990, the legislature passed a new law permitting women to wear the head covering at universities, but new challenges have been raised and the controversy continues. The Ankara University Medical Faculty, for example, has voted to boycott classes where women are dressed in this manner. Clearly, Islam, in one form or another, has reemerged as an important element in the Turkish educational system.

Elitism was another important characteristic of the Ottoman system that is evident today. In this case, however, fundamental social changes have profoundly influenced elitist expression.

In the Ottoman Empire, as in any society, educational patterns reflected the social system. Since there was a marked elite-mass gap, only a small minority of the populace received more than a rudimentary religious education and most of these were state officials of one kind or another.

The nineteenth century brought marked change. Educational opportunities expanded and the very role of the state in education was fundamentally redefined by 1869 legislation, which provided for compulsory free education at all levels. Although never fully implemented, this law should not be under-estimated. The Ottoman state no longer viewed education solely in terms of elite recruitment and training; it accepted responsibility for providing a modern education to all its citizens. The concern with democratization has been an important consideration in educational policy since the founding of the republic. Important efforts have been made (the Village Institute Movement, Literacy Campaigns, expansion of primary education) to provide educational opportunities to all segments of the population. Ironically, one consequence of the democratization of education may have been to reinforce the ongoing elitist tendencies for, the more the lower levels expanded, the greater the pressures for admission to the higher levels.

The nineteenth century also witnessed another change that relates to elitism. Until then a few select medreses produced the high-level ulama, the Palace schools the civil and military leaders. Henceforth the new modern schools were assigned that responsibility. The military colleges trained officers for the army, the civilian institutions like Galatasaray and the Mulkiye prepared the bureaucratic elite. At first, these schools served as important channels for social mobility since elite families were not interested in sending their offspring to such new institutions. They soon realized, however, that a higher secular education was the gateway to continued elite status and began to place their offspring in these schools. Thus, the competition for admission to those educational institutions that led to favored careers intensified.

This process continued in the Turkish republic and even accelerated as ever-larger segments of the population have sought to ensure that their offspring could enroll in a university. Governments of all political persuasions have tried to accommodate this demand but the growth in physical and human resources has not kept pace. As a result, quality deteriorated. The introduction of a national examination did little to improve matters. In 1989, for example, one million students competed for 165,000 places.

In this competition students of upper-class backgrounds have a distinct advantage, for the educational system continues to be marked by a sharp divide between the elite schools and the others. Such a cleavage exists, to a greater or lesser degree, in all countries but in Turkey it exists at all levels of the system and is related to the center-periphery division that has characterized society. The further one goes from the major urban centers, the poorer the quality of the education that is available. Moreoever, there is a marked difference in the achievement levels of students in the two clusters. In the national university entrance examination, for example, the majority of high performers are the graduates of various elite schools. And, graduates of certain universities find it much simpler to obtain desirable positions. For this reason, elite parents engage in various kinds of activities (seeking admission to particular primary schools, intensive tutoring, and the like) to secure their children's educational future.

The elitist legacy has yet another dimension: the new nineteenth-century schools were designed to prepare students for the bureaucracy and the military. These occupations (along with the religious) had always been preferred by Ottomans. Even though new professions emerged and acquired prestige as society modernized during the nineteenth century, and in this century private sector employment has become more attractive, the traditional occupations have retained their allure.

Conversely, other professions have remained low on the prestige scale. Two, of great significance for the country's future, fall into this category. The first is the teaching profession, which has always been accorded relatively low status and been poorly remunerated. As a result, it is difficult to find talented recruits and the quality seems to be dropping even further. And, though university faculty continue to enjoy relatively high prestige, the attraction of the academic profession has also decreased over time, though for reasons that are unconnected to the Ottoman experience.

Second, technical occupations had always been looked down upon in Ottoman society (the first vocational and technical schools in the Ottoman Empire were established to provide for orphans and other destitute children). That equation of inferiority with technical and vocational training became even stronger over time and only students with no other academic choices would enroll. In recent decades many have done so in the hope of eventually gaining access to a university. This situation continues to have a deleterious impact upon the country's needs for mid-level manpower. Recently, the World Bank has financed extensive programs to remedy this situation, but it remains to be seen to what degree they will be able to overcome this legacy.

Ottomanism or Republicanism?

There are other aspects of the Ottoman legacy for which continuity and influence cannot be specified so clearly, even though their roots lie in the Ottoman period.

The first is one of the most appealing features of the traditional Ottoman educational system, its dedication to merit and ability. For decades the medreses were centers of scholarship and the Palace schools graduated elites of distinction. Over time ascriptive criteria assumed dominance, but a concern with achievement always existed and continues to the present. Today, for example, the winners of the university entrance examination receive scholarships and are publicly recognized by the press. Still, although one can point to this and to other features of the contemporary scene that emphasize merit and ability, the thread that links the past with the present is not as strong and direct as those discussed earlier. Consistently, governments of all political persuasions have been willing to sacrifice quality for quantity at all educational levels.

The second is diversity, for the modern schools in Ottoman days included not only the state schools but missionary schools run by foreigners and private schools run by and for the ethnic minorities of the empire. Under the republic these schools were placed under strict state control and few such schools are to be found today. The distinguished Robert College, for example, has become Bosphorus University (Robert College does continue, however, as an elite private secondary school). With the growth in educational demand, however, many private schools were opened from the 1960s on. This trend aroused fierce opposition from those who felt that such schools were not democratic and would further entrench social distinctions. Still, many have been established, especially in recent years. There are even private universities now, graduating students of distinction. It does not appear, however, that this development can be attributed to an Ottoman legacy.

Third comes the education of women. Here one can find specific roots in the nineteenth and early twentieth century, for during those decades women were increasingly permitted access to modern knowledge, even at the university. Over time the number of women receiving an education increased steadily until today they account for a high percentage of students at all levels. Although this development does have an Ottoman past it is also surely part of the more generic modernization process taking place elsewhere as well.

Similar considerations apply to a fourth topic—student activism. Medrese students were apparently active as early as the sixteenth century. In the nineteenth century they demonstrated in 1853, 1859, and 1876/1877 when they caused the government to fall and were instrumental in bringing the great reformer, Midhat Pasha, to power. This episode marked a turning point. The activists were linked to outside actors and organized with their help. The precedent was not influential, however. The first formal student association was established at the Darulfunun during Atatürk's struggle for Turkish independence but no outsiders were involved.

The most important factor determining student political behavior was Atatürk's worldview. He specifically entrusted his revolution to students on two separate occasions, in a speech in Bursa and in the peroration to his "Nutuk," October 1927, declaring, "Turkish Youth! Your primary education is ever to preserve and defend the national independence, the Turkish republic. That is the only basis of your existence and your future."[5] Even so, students came into conflict with Atatürk's government on several occasions.

With the establishment of a multi party system students became extremely active politically, especially in the 1960s and 1970s when violence between student groups of different ideological persuasions was the norm. During this period, outside forces actively sought to use students for political purposes.

The military takeover of 1980 began a new era. The new regime was determined to destroy the terrorist organizations (in which relatively few students were involved) and to depoliticize the universities. The past few years have witnessed some student activism but on a relatively small scale, with demonstrations by small groups, especially Islamist students. Once again we are dealing with a phenomenon with an Ottoman heritage, but one whose character has been shaped by a variety of other factors.

The Cultural Heritage

Exploring how the Ottoman cultural heritage shaped the contemporary educational scene is more difficult to specify. Still, a few speculative observations can be suggested.

The first of these involves the degree to which the nineteenth-century Ottoman elites had looked to the West. In sharp contrast to earlier centuries they demonstrated their openness to new ideas, to the acceptance of new institutions. Hence part of the Ottoman legacy is a positive attitude toward the West, toward modernization.

In education one can point to several examples of an openness to the West that is not characteristic of many other Ottoman legatees, once they had achieved national independence. The modern schools were largely transplants and foreign curricula were adopted wholesale. This trend continued under Atatürk, who closed the Darulfunun and reopened it as Istanbul University, staffed with European (largely German) professors. His goal was to replicate a modern European institution as completely as possible. Many of his other reforms (e.g., the law reforms) are also of this type. One can also point to the construction of Atatürk University in Erzerum, which was modeled after the American land grant university.

The willingness to send students abroad for study is relevant. One should note that interesting experiment, the Ottoman School in Paris (1857–1874) and the general concern with foreign languages that dates back to the establishment of the famed Tercume Odasi (Translation Bureau). During the nineteenth century the preferred language was French, but German emerged rapidly and, especially following World War II, English. Several high schools and universities teaching courses in English have been established, and today a knowledge of a foreign language is practically a sine qua non for positions in the private sector and is rapidly becoming so in government as well. Practically every educated Turk knows at least one foreign language.

Reinforcing this orientation may have been another characteristic of the Ottoman culture—a strong tendency toward pragmatism. This was especially evident in the role played by the ulama elite in the nineteenth century. Despite the popular view that the ulama were opposed to change, there is much evidence suggesting that the higher ulama actively supported the efforts of reforming sultans to save the empire. Atatürk too was noted for his pragmatism, and he asked John Dewey to be a consultant. Although Dewey's influence upon educational developments may not have been great, it cannot be ignored.

Another aspect of the Ottoman past may have contributed to a willingness to accept Western ideas. Although the empire became the "sick man of Europe," it never lost its political independence. As a result it may have had a better capacity to deal with the challenge of the West than those states that were artificially created or fell under direct foreign rule. This is not to suggest that the contradictions existing between the traditional and the modern were easily resolved. On the contrary, they coexisted side by side in the educational and cultural realms and have continued to do so to this day. Still, the scope and intensity of the struggle is different from that which characterized most societies in the Arab world as is the willingness to import foreign institutions and practices wholesale. Not surprisingly, the Ottomans never resolved the paradox common to all reformers: how to save a traditional system by adopting new institutions.

Closely related is a disposition toward tolerance. The Ottomans were noted for their acceptance of different customs, beliefs, and values, for their openness to diversity. They welcomed refugees fleeing from political and religious persecution, and peoples of many different ethnic and religious backgrounds coexisted harmoniously within the empire for decades. Of course, like many other aspects of the legacy, this orientation waxed and waned over time. Nationalism created strong pressures in the nineteenth century and so did the ideological extremism that marked the 1960s and especially the 1970s. Violence remains a problem in some areas but there are indications that Turks of different ideological persuasions may be more willing to reach accommodations than heretofore.

This tendency is evident regarding Islam. The post-Atatürk era has witnessed a significant turn to Islam in many aspects of education. Still, it is not clear that the result has seriously undermined Atatürk's vision of a society where religion is a private matter. The graduates of the Imam Hatip Okullari, at least those who continue their education, for example, come to the universities with worldviews that can not be easily distinguished from those held by graduates of the regular lycées. Nor can one easily relate ideology to social background as was once the case. Many Islamist students come from upper-class backgrounds. And, unlike the situation in the 1970s when schools from elementary to university were polarized, students of different viewpoints are interested in communicating with their ideological opponents, and friendly discussions have taken place between the left and the right in many universities.[6]

Such interactions are facilitated by the emergence of a new group of "Muslim Intellectuals." They believe that Islam nurtures a spirit of scientific inquiry and that nothing in Islam contradicts the acquisition of knowledge. Accordingly religious intellectuals have sponsored conferences with Marxists and are seeking actively to appeal not only to engineers and scientists as heretofore but to social scientists as well. They believe that the solution to Turkey's problems can be generated only by Islamic thinkers educated in Western ways. They are active intellectually, writing for various journals, and using the modern Turkish vocabulary popularized by the Turkish Language Society.

Although one can find signs that the cleavages and polarizations of past decades are being eroded, relations between Islamists and secularists are still marked by significant tensions. Some members of each camp regard the new patterns of interaction with suspicion. In any case, elements of the Ottoman value system cited above—tolerance, pragmatism, independence—may all have influenced the apparent trend toward accommodation and reconciliation.

The intense debate concerning the relation between Islam and Western knowledge that took place during the nineteenth century may also have contributed to these developments. Several groups were involved. The Westernizers argued for the wholesale modernization of every aspect of Ottoman society and culture. Others maintained that only "technical" elements should be borrowed from the West. This was the position taken by many ulama who did not oppose the creation of new schools where this knowledge could be acquired as long as the traditional system continued to provide knowledge of Islamic culture and theology. A third position was advanced by a group that could be said to include Namik Kemal, Ziya Pasha, and Ziya Gokalp. Despite some differences, they generally advocated the development of a spirit of scientific inquiry within the Ottoman/Turkish cultural context.[7] That debate was settled temporarily by Atatürk, a devout modernizer, but like many other aspects of the Islamic legacy, debates over modern science and technology reappeared with the establishment of a multiparty system and have grown in intensity in recent decades.

The contemporary arguments resonate strongly with nineteenth-century antecedents and one can find strong, direct parallels in the positions advocated by various groups. Some still believe that it is possible to strip science and technology of its cultural context and utilize Western science and technology without importing its values. Most, however, have come to recognize the ways in which Western values are inextricably linked to its science and technology and argue for the development of an uniquely Islamic science and technology. Still, all Islamic groups accept the importance of learning Western science and technology as well as the importance of familiarizing themselves with the nineteenth-century debates.

Education in the Arab States

Although the impact of the Ottoman education legacy upon the Arab states was necessarily more attenuated because of the Western colonial rule that most later experienced, those characteristics of Turkish education rooted in the Ottoman past are also in evidence in Arab education.

This is especially the case in the culture that one finds in the schools since the colonial powers reinforced the traditional orientation toward discipline and formalism. As a result education throughout the Arab world is very authoritarian and discipline strictly enforced. Students are expected not to be participants in a learning experience but recipients of the teacher's knowledge. They concentrate upon memorizing their notes and textbooks. The good student does not raise new issues or ask questions but repeats, as accurately as possible, the assigned materials. The goal of education is to pass examinations that provide access to higher levels, not to achieve independent thought or to develop analytical capabilities.[8]

Also reinforced by colonialism was the strong Ottoman penchant for centralization. Everywhere ministries of education exercise practically dictatorial control over all aspects of schooling. Their primary concern is with uniformity and with conformity to the rules and regulations decreed by the center regardless of local needs and exigencies. Curricula, which seldom incorporate modern pedagogical theories, are expected to be taught in the same way everywhere.

Education is also believed to be an avenue of upward mobility. Every country has witnessed an irresistible flood of students seeking higher levels of education. Governments have acceded to this demand for political reasons, accepting the need to democratize educational opportunities at all levels. As a result, enrollments in secondary schools and in universities have climbed dramatically. Despite this increase, the gap between elite and mass remains evident since children of the elite gain access to the better schools and to preferred professional training. Although the need to prepare students for vocational and technical careers is widely recognized, efforts to do so have failed to overcome the traditional stigma. Students still prefer to enroll in programs that provide access to higher educational institutions. Teaching, too, remains a disadvantaged career.

In regards to Islam, however, one must note a dramatic difference between

Turkey and the Arab states. Arab leaders, with the exception of Tunisia's Bour-guiba, have been considerably more circumspect than was Atatürk in secular-ization policies. Thus, one would expect to find in the Arab world an unin-terrupted emphasis upon Islam in the educational system. This is indeed the case. Added to this has been the upsurge in Islamic feelings and activities in recent decades leading to religious studies being assigned an even greater role.

Parallels also exist when one considers those aspects of Arab education for which one cannot so easily identify a strong link to the Ottoman past. These can be summarized as follows. First, quality in every Arab state and at all lev-els leaves much to be desired; it is difficult to find institutions that are noted for their educational excellence. Second, diversity is quite limited; few private or foreign schools are to be found in the region. Third, women are being edu-cated in ever-growing numbers for reasons that stem from both an Ottoman past and present developmental requirements. It is, however, noteworthy that separate schools for women tend to be in those parts of the Arabian peninsu-la only lightly touched by Ottoman rule.

Another characteristic of Turkish education found as well in the Arab world has been student activism, with something like the same ebb and flow found in Turkey. Student politics, predominantly nationalist in the Western colonial period, Nasserist in the 1950s, and somewhat beyond and now seem-ingly increasingly Islamicist, are warily watched by existing governments while all outside forces seek to manipulate them.

Finally, one comes to the more nebulous question of what basic Ottoman values would seem to have left their mark on Arab education today. Certain-ly, the tendency to see the West as a model, to emphasize the study of West-ern languages, now increasingly English, to send student abroad for study may be seen, in part, as an Ottoman legacy. In some important cases the legacy, itself, was only secondarily Ottoman. The Egypt of Muhammad Ali and his successors and the Tunisia of Ahmad Bey and those who followed took steps that reflected (in Egypt's case often preceded) Ottoman practice.

The disposition toward tolerance and acceptance of diversity is clearly an Ottoman legacy. Moreover, the unfortunate erosion of that earlier tolerance can be traced more to exacerbated nationalisms and inflexible, politicized reli-gious movements both of which represent departures from traditional Ottoman approaches.

Generally speaking, it would seem fair to conclude that the different nine-teenth-century experience of major portions of the Arab world nominally under Ottoman rule (e.g. Egypt, Tunisia, and Lebanon) and the intervening period of Western imperial rule reduced the Ottoman educational legacy among the Arabs.

Myths and Realities

This attempt to trace the relationship between educational developments in modern Turkey and the Arab states to the Ottoman past suggests that we are dealing with both myth and reality. The Ottoman legacy has influenced many aspects of the region's educational system over the years and continues to do so today. On the other hand many aspects of the contemporary scene cannot be traced back to Ottoman times and have been shaped by other factors. One can identify some aspects where the linkage seems quite strong, others where it is more problematic.

The analysis also demonstrates the conceptual difficulties involved in efforts to identify the impact of the past upon the present. The most vexing issue is how to disentangle the Ottoman contribution from other influences, especially the extent to which one is dealing with an Ottoman as opposed to an Islamic heritage. The Ottoman Empire was an Islamic state but certain aspects of the legacy may have predated even the long-lived Ottoman Empire. For example, the emphasis upon memorization and the authority of teachers in the classroom can be traced to early Islamic schools. Adding still more complexity is the fact that such features were also commonplace in Europe in the nineteenth century and that colonial rule served to reinforce the existing tendency toward traditional pedanticism.

Whatever the roots, the legacy has not, in general, contributed in a positive way to the functioning of educational systems. Traditional values and practices hinder the creation of educational systems that contribute effectively to national development, and many of these elements will have to be replaced or abandoned if educational systems are to function in harmony with developmental requirements. Particularly significant in this regard are the continuing difficulties in achieving quality, overcoming the elites–masses gap, securing adequate teachers, improving educational administration, and developing adequate vocational and technical educational systems.

Such change is possible. Traditions need not be permanent. They can be and have been modified on many occasions. This may well be the case in Turkey today, for a major effort to restructure the country's educational system is underway. Whether these projects will be successful or whether they will suffer the fate of past attempts remains to be seen, but it is possible to point to a key determinant producing radical change in education—the political. As was the case in the Turkey of Atatürk, effective and wise leadership will be required. If such leadership is available and if the economic situation remains stable, then one may anticipate that Turkey will be able to build upon the positive aspects of its Ottoman legacy and to overcome the negative ones. The same opportunities are open to the Arab states. The challenge is to effec-

tively blend the positive aspects of the Ottoman heritage with the requirements of modernity, to create an educational system whose structure and
functioning permits the achievement of individual and societal aspirations.

NOTES

1. Ilhan Başgöz and Howard Wilson, *Educational Problems in Turkey: 1920–1940* (Bloomington:
    Indiana University Press, 1968), pp. 77–78, 233ff.
2. Osman Okyar, "Universities in Turkey," *Minerva* (Winter 1968):227.
3. Ziya Gökalp, *Turkish Nationalism and Western Civilization*, ed. and trs., Niyazi Berkes (New
    York: Columbia University Press, 1959), p. 278.
4. Z. Baloglu, *Türkiyede Eğitim* (Ankara: TUSIAD, 1990), pp. 136, 147.
5. Mustafa Kemal, *A Speech by Ghazi Mustafa Kemal* (Leipzig: E. F. Koehler, 1929), p. 723.
6. I have explored this topic in more detail in "Religious Education and the Future of the Turkish
    State" (Los Angeles: G. E. von Grunebaum Center for Near Eastern Studies, UCLA, Working
    Paper No. 21, 1992).
7. Fazlur Rahman, *Islam and Modernity* (Chicago: University of Chicago Press, 1982), pp. 46ff.
8. For a insightful evaluation of this and other characteristics of the contemporary educational situ-
    ation in the Arab world, see Byron G. Massialas and S. A. Jarrar, *Arab Education in Transition*
    (New York: Garland, 1991).

EPILOGUE

The contributions to this study have offered varied appraisals of the extent to which the Ottoman centuries are still shaping patterns of behavior or perception among the many peoples of Western Asia, Northern Africa and Southeastern Europe who share an Ottoman past. This was to be expected. Historians will always dispute the impact of the past upon the present. To cite an example from another time and place, several historians see the special characteristics of European feudalism as having contributed to the much later rise of modern democratic states in the West. Others, on the contrary, argue for a quite different set of formative factors arising much later in time.

There are no simple and no definitive answers to such questions. Yet, the ongoing scholarly dialectic does increase knowledge while also opening new, unanticipated lines of inquiry.

This book, in our view, is needed because the question of what remains of the Ottoman legacy in today's world has been largely ignored, and the reasons for this scholarly neglect have been adumbrated throughout. Ironically, whether it be a matter of Arab or Balkan or Turkish history this tendency to belittle or misrepresent the Ottoman past has prevailed—even if for different reasons.

ONE BUBBLE MORE!!

Examples of the complete mutual misperception dividing Europe and the Ottoman Empire, these juxtaposed political cartoons, now almost six generations old, also bespeak the deep historical roots of misrepresentations continuing to this day. *Above*: from *Punch*, January 6, 1877, suggesting that the impressive Ottoman reformist efforts are so many bubbles. *Right*: two matching political cartoons from the journal *Hayal* for the same time period, January and February 1877. *Top*: Dame Europe is warning the Ottoman not to think he has learned how to walk. *Bottom*: the Ottoman is making clear his being fed up with European-imposed training wheels.

As for the Western image of the Ottoman Empire (which all but specialists still usually and wrongly describe as "Turkey" ruled by "Turks") even the well-educated scarcely manage to transcend stereotypes based on adages and aphorisms gleaned from introductory Western Civilization courses. Let a few such citations illustrate the point (all are taken from mainstream Western sources):

"The Sick Man of Europe."
"The unspeakable Turk."
"The Turks, in their usual manner, tried to cheat both sides."
"En depit des apparences sumptueses et du ceremonial et de la representation, l'empire Ottoman ne fut que le fait d'une horde; il resta la horde."
" . . . and the Eastern Question can only be understood if we know how Orientals intrigue, how Western diplomats negotiate, and what Balkan peasants think about."
"It's over, and can't be helped, and that's one consolation, as they always says in Turkey, ven they cuts the wrong man's head off."[1]

This book is an effort to pose the question or, more exactly, the questions of the Ottoman legacy in today's world, for the questions and the possible answers are as varied as the countless rubrics by which one can analyze and interpret any society or civilization. Our goal has determined the method chosen which is that of addressing the larger issues by means of wide ranging, exploratory essays always with an eye to the comparative approach. Whatever the shortcomings we will see ourselves as having succeeded if we have been able to stimulate a needed scholarly debate.

We hope, accordingly, that this work will find its way not just to specialists in Arab or Balkan or Ottoman or Turkish studies but to scholars in general. Any historian interested in the subject of what remains when empires break up can profitably study the experience of the Ottoman Empire and its many successors. In a similar way, political scientists or sociologists seeking the roots (or the preconditions) of democracy or capitalism, to mention only these two, will find grist for their scholarly mill by looking at the Ottoman centuries.

Most important, in terms of immediate issues facing a troubled world, is the question of whether the ideology of nation states based on a presumed homogeneity of the "nation" (in culture or language or religion or some combination of all these) can provide the basis for world order, stability, and peace. The present troubles confronting yesterday's Yugoslavia or Soviet Union provide at the very least some hesitation concerning the Wilsonian ideal of self-determination of nations.

This is not to say that the distinctive Ottoman polity of imperial centralism while permitting considerable cultural, linguistic and religious autonomy can, or should, be restored. Nor it is to claim that the successor states, almost all of which have embraced one form or another of nationalist ideologies, compare poorly with the Ottoman matrix from which they have emerged. Such positions that nostalgically idealize or categorically condemn the Ottoman Empire are nothing more than ideology poorly disguised as history.

What can be said, however, is that the careful study of different sociopolitical arrangements, and the results they produce, are of use not just to the historian but to the statesman and the citizen. From this perspective, the characteristics of the Ottoman Empire and of its successors, with attention to what survived in the transition, offer important insights. History does not provide the controlled, replicable experimentation of the scientist's laboratory. The laboratory of past experience is the best we have.

Finally, an appeal to those of our colleagues who as Arabists, Balkanists, Ottomanists, or specialists in modern Turkey know well some part of the subject treated in this book: Just as the once vast Ottoman Empire has in this century been split into many smaller parts so do we today, with occasional exceptions, have high academic walls separating Arab, Balkan, and Turkish studies. Most of us cannot become expert in all the languages and all the complex history of that broad stretch of lands and peoples arranged clockwise around the Mediterranean from Albania to the Eastern border of Morocco. Moreover, a redrawing of scholarly specialization to embrace that entire area would dilute the very impressive move toward in-depth specialization that has characterized "area studies" in the decades since the Second World War.

Still, an occasional glance over the fence to see what is taking place in the neighboring scholarly field should prove useful. Patterns and practices that survived the division of the Ottoman commons are there to be discovered. One more solid reason, then, to study the Ottoman legacy.

NOTE

1. The quotations above are attributed respectively to the following: Tsar Nicholas I in 1853; Thomas Carlyle (1876); A. J. P. Taylor, *The Struggle for Mastery in Europe* (1954), p. 49; Edouard Driault, *La Question d'Orient* (1914, 8th ed. 1938), p. 11; Harold Temperley, *England and the Near East: The Crimea* (1936), p. vii; and Charles Dickens, *The Pickwick Papers* (Sam Weller), ch. 23.

THE OTTOMAN LEGACY:

BIBLIOGRAPHICAL SUGGESTIONS

Most discussion of what may have survived from Ottoman times is buried in the numerous books, monographs, and articles that treat the modern history of the many nations and peoples who once shared an Ottoman past. To mention all such works, spanning the broad fields of Arab, Balkan, Ottoman, and Turkish history, would take us too far afield.

Offered instead is a short list of writings that address somewhat more directly the issue of legacy. Some of these present only general, at times speculative, appraisals. Others are summary statements of a few pages in larger works on different subjects. Many treat only a single successor state (especially Turkey). This was to be expected. The possible Ottoman impact on any part of the post-Ottoman world has usually been ignored or misrepresented (if not both) or at best woven into "present-minded" history based on the nation-state premise of existing polities. Even so, it is to be hoped that the works listed below may complement a major goal of this book which is to stimulate the kind of in-depth research appraising the Ottoman legacy that remains to be achieved.

Rifaat Abou-El-Haj, "The Social Uses of the Past: Recent Arab Historiography of Ottoman Rule," *International Journal of Middle Eastern Studies* 14, no. 2 (May 1982). A severe critique of both Western and Arab scholars, the former for their "modernization" model and the latter for either a Pan-Arab or a local Arab country nationalism that ignores the centuries of Ottoman multinational pluralism. Abou-El-Haj, a historian of the Arab world in the Ottoman period, is especially concerned with historiograpy of the Arabs in Ottoman times.

Feroz Ahmad, *The Making of Modern Turkey* (London and New York: Routledge, 1993). The Introduction, "Turkey: A Military Society," gives a more nuanced interpretation of the Ottoman military legacy, emphasizing change over continuity. Chapter 2, "The Ottoman Legacy," offers an overview of several important themes including the tradition of the strong, centralized state.

Engin Akarli, *The Long Peace: Ottoman Lebanon, 1861–1920* (Berkeley and Los Angeles: University of California Press, 1993). A pioneering study of Lebanon during these years of the *Mutasarrifiyya* (*Reglement Organique*), based on an examination of Ottoman records as well as Arabic and European sources, with stimulating interpretations in the concluding chapter. Note, for example, the following: "(T)he Ottoman data, not to mention other evidence, suggest that an analytical distinction has to be made between confessionalism as a means of sociopolitical organization and integration, and confessionalism as a basis of nationalistic political identity and loyalty. In Mount Lebanon, the former helped generate a public sphere and integral polity, but the latter hampered the articulation of existing religious and cultural world-views into a broad political outlook that inculcated the individual members of different groups with a sense of common citizenship" (p. 190).

William L. Cleveland, *The Making of an Arab Nationalist: Ottomanism and Arabism in the Life and Thought of Sati' al-Husri* (Princeton: Princeton University Press, 1971). A useful way to trace the Ottoman legacy is through biographical studies of individual leaders whose lives spanned the Ottoman and post-Ottoman eras. Al-Husri offers an especially telling case study. The son of an Ottoman official and himself an Ottoman official and educator until almost the last days of empire, al-Husri in early life was so thoroughly Ottoman that this major ideologue of Arab nationalism always spoke Arabic with a heavy accent.

Roderic Davison, "Ataturk's Reforms: Back to the Roots," in his *Essays in Ottoman and Turkish History, 1774–1923* (Austin: University of Texas Press, 1990). Yes, Davison argues, Ataturk "decapitated" the Ottoman Empire, abolishing the sultanate and the caliphate. Still, his reformist program—such as set out in his celebrated 1927 Six Day speech—referred to "(c)onstitution, cabinet, parliament, elections, deputies, vilayet, vali, mutasarrif. These . . . heritages of political concept and institution from the Ottoman Empire, he accepted" (p. 243).

C. Ernest Dawn, "From Ottomanism to Arabism," in his *From Ottoman to Arabism: Essays on the Origins of Arab Nationalism* (Champaign: University of Illinois Press, 1973). The classic revisionist statement. Dawn also has a chapter in the Khalidi et al. book.

Selim Deringil, "Aspects of Continuity in Turkish Foreign Policy: Abdulhamid II and Ismet Inonu," *International Journal of Turkish Studies* 4, no. 1 (1987).

—"Ottoman Origins of Kemalist Nationalism: From Namik Kemal to Mustafa Kemal". *European History Quarterly* 23 (1993).

Deringil is especially concerned with tracing the transition from Ottoman to post-Ottoman Turkey. These two articles present a cogent case for continuity while offering a number of useful bibliographical references.

Robert J. Donia and John V. A. Fine Jr., *Bosnia and Herzegovina: A Tradition Betrayed* (New York: Columbia University Press, 1994). An argument that Bosnia had the historical roots to evolve into a multireligious state and society following the breakup of Yugoslavia, a much more benign prospect that was betrayed by those with other agendas aided by outsiders who implicitly accepted the "ancient hatreds" notion. The Ottoman legacy is given considerable attention, especially in chapter 3, "Religious Change and Bosnia's Distinct Situation Under the Ottomans."

Robert Haddad, "The Ottoman Empire in the Contemporary Middle East," *Aftermath of Empire: In Honor of Professor Max Salvadori* (Northampton, Mass.: Smith College Studies in History, vol. 47, 1975). A specialist on the modern history of the Arabic-speaking Orthodox Christian community, Haddad traces from that perspective the historical role of the "millet system" ending with a still starkly timely call for a "neo-millet system" as "an alternative to the essentially retrogressive pattern of the nation-state" (p. 59).

Albert H. Hourani, "The Ottoman Background of the Modern Middle East," in his *The Emergence of the Modern Middle East* (Berkeley and Los Angeles: University of California Press, 1981). First given as a public lecture as long ago as 1969, this piece by the leading scholar of modern Arab history, especially intellectual history, is filled with penetrating ideas. Citing the tendency of Arabs to ignore the Ottoman era Hourani writes: "Those who wish to replace the old political order of the Middle East, based on religious adherence, by a new one based on national loyalty, like other revolutionaries at other times, have used the image of some more distant past as a way of condemning the immediate past" (p. 1). He concludes by pointing out the many Ottoman links of those who gathered in Egypt in 1944–45 to create the Arab League: "They had been at school together in Istanbul, they had been in the same army or served the same government, that had a common way of looking at the world, behind the vision of Arab unity lay memories of a lost imperial grandeur" (p. 18).

Barbara Jelavich, *History of the Balkans,* 2 vols. (New York: Cambridge: Cambridge University Press, 1983). This general history of the Balkans provides a tantalizing few pages summing up the Ottoman legacy (vol. 1, pp. 165–68; vol. 2, pp. 104–5).

Kamal H. Karpat, "Millets and Nationality," in Benjamin Braude and Bernard Lewis, eds., *Christians and Jews in the Ottoman Empire,* vol. 1: *The Central Lands* (New York: Holmes and Meier, 1982). Concludes that Ottoman efforts to create a modern multireligous state to be successful would have needed to build on "the corporate traditions of organization, that is the *millet* system, under which the Ottoman peoples had lived for centuries." Instead, the Western nation-state model "was imposed on all the Ottoman peoples by their leaders regardless of their historical experience and political culture" (p. 166).

Kamal H. Karpat, ed., *The Ottoman Empire and Its Place in World History* (Leiden: Brill, 1974). A little book (129 pages) that includes articles by Arnold J. Toynbee, William H. McNeill, Halil Inalcik, Albert Hourani ("The Ottoman Background" listed above), Charles Issawi, Stanford Shaw, and Karpat. Although the matter of legacy is directly addressed only in the Hourani article, the book does provide a good discussion of the problem of prejudice, misperception, and neglect in the study of the long Ottoman era.

Elie Kedourie, " 'Minorities,' " in his *The Chatham House Version and Other Middle-Eastern Studies* (Hanover, N.H.: University Press of New England, 1984; first pub. 1970). A powerful polemic against the corrosive effects of nationalisms that broke up the Ottoman multinational synthesis. "The Ottoman system was far from perfect," Kedourie concludes. "It was narrow and hidebound. . . . But its conventions were well established and its modalities well understood. . . . If reforms were needed or were practicable, there is nothing clearer than that they could succeed only if they proceeded from native traditions and were accomplished with native means" (p. 316).

Rashid Khalidi, Lisa Anderson, Muhammad Muslih, and Reeva S. Simon eds., *The Origins of Arab Nationalism* (New York: Columbia University Press, 1991). The earlier notion of Arabs groaning under "alien" Ottoman rule has long been convincingly challenged by revisionist historians such as C. Ernest Dawn, Elie Kedourie, and Zeine Zeine. This book builds on that earlier work, providing in the process a much more nuanced picture of Arabism growing out of the Ottoman chrysalis. Reeva Simon, for example, in "The Education of an Iraqi Ottoman Army Office" offers a case study concluding: "(T)he legacy of this Ottoman military education transcended purely military matters. It led to a system of networking and politicization that would play a large role in Iraqi and Arab politics during the interwar years" (p. 161). See also Dawn and Muslih.

Bernard Lewis, "The Ottoman Empire and Its Aftermath," *Journal of Contemporary History* 15 (1980). An overview that raises many of the more interesting legacy aspects, especially as regards Turkey and the Turks. Lewis cites the Turkish journalist Falih Rıfkı Atay, who visited London in 1934 and later wrote a book that included the text of a speech he would have liked to give in England "if only I had known enough English." The speech read in part: "I too am the child of a great empire. We came to it in the last days of its decline, as to the leavings of a banquet. I don't know if you can imagine the geography of this Sultanate as it still was in the time of our grandfathers. Let me explain what happened to us taking your own geography as an example. We began to fight in Bombay. Fighting all the way across the continent we fell back upon London and made our last stand in Glascow. Now our borders are Dover. When the Ottoman Empire was already a hundred years old England without Scotland or Ireland was a little country of three million inhabitants and London a town of 40,000. . . . Because our empire was founded by conquerors its end was epic. Because yours was founded by merchants you are making a liquidation."

Bernard Lory, *Le Sort de l'Heritage Ottoman en Bulgarie: L'Example des villes Bulgares, 1878–1900* (Istanbul, 1985). Deals directly with the problem of the Ottoman legacy in Bulgaria in the latter decades of the nineteenth century, chiefly in the urban setting.

Şerif Mardin, "Power, Civil Society, and Culture in the Ottoman Empire," *Comparative Studies in Society and History* 11, no. 4 (January 1969). Mardin sees three aspects of Ottoman society: 1) Patrimonialism, 2) Absence of civil society, and 3) A sharp elite-mass cultural dichotomy as having continued right until the end of empire and then shaping (inhibiting?) developments in republican Turkey.

Muhammad Y. Muslih, *The Origins of Palestinian Nationalism* (New York: Columbia University Press, 1988). Chapters 1, "The Ottoman Background of Palestinian Politics," 2, "Arabism and Ottomanism: The Young Turk Period Before the War, 1908–1914," and 4 "Older Ottomanists and Younger Reformers in World War I" offer a stimulating case study of the move from

Ottomanism to Arabism/Palestinianism in one distinctive part of the Arab world.

Dankwart A. Rustow, "Turkey: The Modernity of Tradition," in Lucien W. Pye and Sidney Verba, eds., *Political Culture and Political Development* (Princeton: Princeton University Press, 1965). Concentrates on the transition from Ottoman to Turkish political culture. See also Rustow's "The Army and the Founding of the Turkish Republic," *World Politics* 13, no. 4 (July 1959) and "The Military: Turkey," in Robert E. Ward and Dankwart A. Rustow, eds., *Political Modernization in Japan and Turkey* (Princeton: Princeton University Press, 1964), two earlier statements of the military legacy that Rustow has treated in chapter 14 of this book.

Kamal Salibi, *A House of Many Mansions: The History of Lebanon Reconsidered* (Berkeley and Los Angeles: University of California Press, 1988). An excellent study of the "uses of the past" for ideological purposes. Chapters 8, "Ottoman Lebanon: How Unique?" 11, "The War Over Lebanese History," and the conclusion are especially relevant.

Peter Sugar, *Southeastern Europe Under Ottoman Rule, 1354–1804* (Seattle: University of Washington Press, 1977). The concluding chapter offers a broad treatment of the Ottoman impact on the Balkans.

Abdeljelil Temimi, "Problematiques de la recherche historique sur les provinces arabes a l'epoque Ottomane,' " *Arab Historical Review for Ottoman Studies* (AHROS) 3–4 (December 1991). Organizer of scholarly conferences and editor of AHROS, Temimi is a major force in fostering research and multinational scholarly exchanges. Several articles in AHROS are relevant, e.g., Temimi's "The Arab-Ottoman Historical Heritage and Its impact on the Arab-Turkish Relations" and Rachad Limam, "The Image of the Ottoman State and of the Turks in Tunisian School Manuals"—both in AHROS 7–8 (October 1993).

Nikolay Todorov, *The Balkan City, 1400–1900* (Seattle: University of Washington Press, 1983). A general assessment of the Ottoman legacy in the urban sphere.

Maria Todorova and Nikolay Todorov, "The Historical Demography of the Ottoman Empire: Problems and Tasks," in Richard B. Spence and Linda L. Nelson, eds., *Scholar, Patriot, Mentor: Historical Essays in Honor of Dimitrije Djordjevic* (Boulder: East European Monographs, No. 302, 1992). Introductory statement on the demographic developments in the Ottoman Empire and their legacy.

Wayne S. Vuchinich, "Some Aspects of the Ottoman Legacy," in Charles and Barbara Jelavich, eds., *The Balkans in Transition: Essays on the Development of Balkan Life and Politics Since the Eighteenth Century* (Berkeley and Los

Angeles: University of California Press, 1963). An early attempt at approaching the problem from an all-Balkan perspective. His *The Ottoman Empire: Its Record and Legacy* (Princeton: Princeton University Press, 1965), a general handbook, offers a limited summary of Ottoman history and institutions and a series of readings. "The Ottoman Legacy" (pp. 116–23) is typical of the generally negative Balkanist appraisals.

CONTRIBUTORS

Karl K. Barbir, Professor of History at Siena College, Loudonville, N.Y., received the Ph.D. in Near Eastern Studies from Princeton University. He is the author of *Ottoman Rule in Damascus, 1708–1758* (1980); of a forthcoming biography of Muhammad Khalil al-Muradi (1760–1791), historian and notable of Damascus; and of several articles and reviews.

L. Carl Brown is Garrett Professor in Foreign Affairs Emeritus at Princeton University. During most of his years as a Princeton faculty member from 1966 to 1993 he served as director of the interdisciplinary Program in Near Eastern Studies. His major research interest has been the political and diplomatic history of the modern Arab world, both Maghrib and Mashriq. His works include *The Tunisia of Ahmed Bey* (1974); *International Politics and the Middle East* (1984); and coeditor (with the late Cyril E. Black) of *Modernization in the Middle East: The Ottoman Empire and its Afro-Asian Successors* (1992).

Roderic H. Davison, A.B. Princeton, 1937, A.M. and Ph.D. Harvard, 1938 and 1942, is Professor Emeritus of History at George Washington University. He has also taught at Princeton, Harvard, and the Johns Hopkins School of Advanced International Studies. His teaching has been divided between European diplomatic history and Near Eastern history. He is a past president of the Middle East Studies Association, and of the Turkish Studies Association. Among his works are *The Near and Middle East: An Introduction to History and Bibliography* (1959); *Reform in the Ottoman Empire, 1856–1876* (1963); *Turkey: A Short History* (1988); and *Essays in Ottoman and Turkish History: The Impact of the West* (1990).

Carter Vaughn Findley is Professor of History at Ohio State University. He is the author of *Bureaucratic Reform in the Ottoman Empire: The Sublime Porte, 1789–1922* (1980); *Ottoman Officialdom: A Social History* (1989); and coauthor with John Rothney of *Twentieth-Century World* (2d ed., 1990).

Hal Inalcik received his Ph.D. from Ankara University where he then taught from 1943 to 1972. From 1972 to 1986 he was professor of history at the University of Chicago. He has also been a visiting professor at Columbia University and Princeton University. In 1993 he joined the faculty of Bilkent University. Among his publications are *The Ottoman Empire in the Classical Age: 1300–1600* (1973); *Studies in Ottoman Social and Economic History* (1985); *The Middle East and the Balkans under the Ottoman Empire* (1993) and *An Economic and Social History of the Ottoman Empire* (with Donald Quataert, 1994).

Charles Issawi, Bayard Dodge Professor of Near Eastern Studies Emeritus at Princeton University, has written extensively on the economics, economic history, and cultural history of the Middle East. His most recent books are: *An Economic History of the Middle East and North Africa* (1982); *The Fertile Crescent* (1988); and *Issawi's Laws of Social Motion* (enlarged edition, 1991).

Norman Itzkowitz is Professor of Near Eastern Studies at Princeton University. He is the author of *Ottoman Empire and Islamic Tradition* (1973); coauthor of *Mubadele: An Ottoman Russian Exchange of Ambassadors* (1970); and *The Immortal Atatürk: A Psychobiography* (1984).

Bernard Lewis is the Cleveland E. Dodge Professor Emeritus of Near Eastern Studies at Princeton University. He was a coeditor of *The Cambridge History of Islam* and the *Encyclopedia of Islam*. Among his works are *The Emergence of Modern Turkey* (1961); *Istanbul and the Civilization of the Ottoman Empire* (1963); *The Muslim Discovery of Europe* (1982), *The Political Language of Islam* (1988; *Islam and the West* (1993), *The Shaping of the Modern*

Middle East (1994); and *Cultures in Conflict: Christians, Muslims, and Jews in the Age of Discovery* (1995).

Geoffrey Lewis is a Fellow of the British Academy, Emeritus Professor of Turkish and Fellow of St. Antony's College in the University of Oxford. His principal publications on Turkish topics include *Teach Yourself Turkish* (1957); *Modern Turkey* (1955; 4th rev. ed. 1974); *Turkish Grammar* (1974; rev. ed. 1988). He has translated *Kâtib Çelebi's The Balance of Truth* (1953; rev. ed. 1988); *The Book of Dede Korkut* (1974); *The Atatürk I Knew* (Falih Rifki Atay's *Cankaya*, Istanbul 1981); *Haldun Taner's Thickhead and Other Stories* (1988); *The Life of Haci Ömer Sabanci* (Saffron Walden 1988); *Just a Diplomat* (Zeki Kuneralp's *Sadece Diplomat*, 1992).

William Ochsenwald, who received his Ph.D. in Middle Eastern History from the University of Chicago in 1971, is Professor of History at Virginia Polytechnic Institute and State University. He is the coeditor of *Nationalism in a Non-National State: The Dissolution of the Ottoman Empire* (1977); author of *The Hijaz Railroad* (1980), and *Religion, Society, and the State in Arabia: The Hijaz Under Ottoman Control, 1840–1908* (1984); and coauthor with Sydney N. Fisher of *The Middle East: A History* (4th ed. 1990). Professor Ochsendwald's articles have appeared in *The Middle East Journal, Die Welt des Islams, The Muslim World, International Journal of Middle East Studies, Arabian Studies, Middle Eastern Studies,* and the *Encyclopedia Britannica*.

Ergun Özbudun is professor in the Faculty of Economics, Administrative and Social Sciences at Bilkent University where he also chairs the Center for Studies in Society and Politics. He is President of the Turkish Political Science Association and Vice-President of the Turkish Democracy Foundation. He has been a visiting professor at numerous other institutions, including Columbia University and the Woodrow Wilson School at Princeton University. His writings on democratic politics both in Turkey and in comparative perspective include: *The Political Economy of Income Distribution in Turkey* (with Aydin Ulusan); *Atatürk: Founder of a Modern State*; and *Competitive Elections in Developing Countries* (with Myron Weiner).

André Raymond, D.Phil. Oxon (1954), docteur d'Etat de Paris-Sorbonne (1972), is Professor Emeritus at the Université de Provence (Aix-en-Provence). He served as director of the Institut Français d'études arabes in Damascus and of the first Institut de recherches et d'études sur la monde arabe et musulman at Aix-en-Provence. His works include: *Artisans et com-*

mercants au Caire au XVIIIème siècle (1974); *The Great Arab Cities in the 16th–18th Centuries: An Introduction* (1984); *Grandes villes arabes a l'epoque ottoman* (1985); *Le Caire* (1993); and *Le Caire des Janissaries* (1995).

Dennison I. Rusinow has been Research Professor in the University Center for International Studies and Adjunct Professor of History at the University of Pittsburgh since 1988. He holds a B.A. from Duke University and an M.A. and D.Phil from Oxford. From 1963 to 1988 he reported on current affairs in East Central and Balkan Europe for the American University Field Staff (AUFS). In addition to some 76 AUFS reports published between 1963 and 1991 he is the author of *The Yugoslav Experiment, Italy's Austrian Heritage,* and numerous contributions to collective works.

Dankwart A. Rustow is Distinguished Professor of Political Science and Sociology at the Graduate School of the City University of New York, where he is also editor of the quarterly *Comparative Politics* and chairman of *The Energy Forum,* a monthly discussion group for business experts. Earlier he served at Princeton and Columbia universities and at the Brookings Institution. His publications include *Comparative Political Dynamics* (with K. P. Erickson et al., 1991); *Turkey: America's Forgotten Ally* (1987); *Oil and Turmoil* (1982); and *A World of Nations* (1967).

Joseph S. Szyliowicz is Professor of Middle East Studies at the Graduate School of International Studies, University of Denver. He is the author of *Politics, Technology and Development* (1991); *Education and Modernization in the Middle East* (1973); *A Political Analysis of Student Activism: The Turkish Case* (1972); *Political Change in Rural Turkey* (1966); and coauthor and coeditor of *The Contemporary Middle East* (1965).

Maria Todorova holds a degree in history from the University of Sofia, where she was Professor of Balkan History. She has also taught or engaged in research elsewhere including, inter alia, Oxford, the Institutes for Balkan and Oriental Studies in Moscow and St. Petersburg, the Laboratory for Demographic History in Paris, and the Cambridge Group for the History of Population and Social History, the University of Maryland, the University of California at Irvine, and Rice University. She has been at the Department of History of the University of Florida since 1992. Her publications include *England, Russia, and the Tanzimat* (Sofia, 1980; Moscow 1983); *Balkan Family History and the European Pattern: Demographic Developments in Ottoman Bulgaria* (1993).

INDEX

Page numbers for illustrations and maps are in italics.